Ukraine

THE BRADT TRAVEL GUIDE

Andrew Evans

Bradt Travel Guides Ltd, UK
The Globe Pequot Press Inc, USA

First published 2004
Reprinted March 2004

Bradt Travel Guides Ltd
19 High Street, Chalfont St Peter, Bucks SL9 9QE, England
www.bradt-travelguides.com
Published in the USA by The Globe Pequot Press Inc, 246 Goose Lane,
PO Box 480, Guilford, Connecticut 06475-0480

ISBN 1 84162 084 X

British Library Cataloguing in Publication Data
A catalogue record for this book is available from the British Library

Photographs
Front cover Church of the Assumption, Kievo-Pechersky Lavra, Kiev (Andrew Evans)
Text Andrew Evans (AE), Mark Wadlow/Russia & Eastern Images (MW)

Illustrations CaroleVincer
Maps Steve Munns

Typeset from the author's disc by Wakewing
Printed and bound in Italy by Legoprint SpA, Trento

Author

Andrew Evans has lived, worked and wandered in Ukraine as a missionary, consultant, academic, NATO analyst, and travel writer. He completed his postgraduate work in Russian and East European studies at Oxford University, where he wrote and lectured on Ukrainian politics, history and culture. *Ukraine: The Bradt Travel Guide* is his first book.

PUBLISHER'S FOREWORD

The essence of a good guide is when the author has 'painted the picture' of his chosen destination, especially in a country that is little known to most travellers, and has injected his personal enthusiasm into the text so that even a brief riffle through the pages instils a desire to go there. But such enthusiasm needs to be balanced with accurate, practical information. Andrew Evans has achieved all this and more. It had never occurred to me to visit Ukraine – now I can't wait to go!

LIST OF MAPS

Contents

Acknowledgements

My greatest thanks goes to Brian Gratwicke, who has sustained me from the beginning; who braved the Ukrainian winter and acted as an invaluable consultant for this book. Also, a heartfelt gratitude to my wonderful family: to my father who inspired a love of history and places, my mother who taught me to write, and my brothers and sisters who always help me to look at things differently.

So many people helped me in Ukraine:

Many thanks to Andrei, Natasha and Ilyusha Tugai for their hospitality, enthusiasm, friendship and storage space; to the Chynoweths in Odessa and the LDS missionaries in Chernivtsi for special insights into both those cities. In Lviv, many thanks to Nazar Ivaskevych from MEEST-tour, Ihor Karabin and Lviv's PLAS scout troop for their help in the Carpathian Mountains. For useful information and double-checking facts, thanks to Andriy Miskiv, and much appreciation to Yuliya Misyuta for giving me such a great tour of Lviv. I am also very grateful for the willing support of the Lviv Tourist Board, Crimean Ministry of Tourism, Onyx Tour, the Rural Green Tourist association, the Carpathian Tourist Board in Ivano-Frankivsk, Lidiya Fedorivna and the staff of the Carpathian National Nature Park, Eugenia Travel of Odessa, Yalta Inturist, the staff of the Zaporizhian Cossack Museum, and Kharkiv's Gosprom tour agency. Thanks to the many kind Ukrainians who's generosity made my path light: especially Luda Koschuk and the Perozhak family in Yavoriv and Ivan and Nadya Vlasyuk in Kamyanets-Podilsky. I am also indebted to so many Ukrainians with whom I shared train compartments, for all-night conversations and plenty of good advice for this book.

Back in England, a sincere thanks to Hilary Bradt for giving me the chance to write about the country I love and deep gratitude to Tricia Hayne for making it all happen. Thanks to Sally Brock for dealing with three different languages in the typesetting. Much appreciation to Oxford University for research facilities, and a big thank you to Kirsti Samuels and Larissa Douglass for feedback on sections of the text.

Finally, thanks to all those whose names I never knew but whose excitement and love of Ukraine continues to inspire my own.

Introduction

When I first set foot in Ukraine, there was no such country in my world atlas, let alone anything like a travel guide. My first impressions were stringent and few: the streets were too dark and the cars didn't run. Public payphones were free (if they worked) and you could buy bread and milk with subway tokens. In winter there was no heat, and in summer, no water. One chose to eat cabbage, potatoes, bread and mustard, or nothing at all. I stayed two years and cried when I left.

Ten years later, hope has overcome despair and I have witnessed remarkable changes towards a secure society and better lifestyle for Ukrainians. Yet, it is the memory of the darker years that keeps me returning to this country again and again. Few countries boast a history so imminent as Ukraine's, and every little place bears such deep human meaning. The timeless exercise of daily survival allows little room for show, and that is why I love the bunches of dogs that roam the streets, the bundled-up grandmothers selling pails of bruised apples and the silent white blocks of apartments lined up in a row.

Ukraine is a land made from the simplest ingredients: wheat fields and wide skies, green mountains and rippling rivers. The resilient Ukrainian people complete the panorama, so that the child pulling weeds in a potato patch matches the splendour of the lofty gold domes of so many painted cathedrals. When I consider the famous sites people know and visit in Europe, I can only think what they are missing in Ukraine: hidden monasteries, picturesque mountain villages in the Carpathians, the rocky shores and sunshine of Crimea, the inland beauty of the Ukrainian steppe and the most undisturbed bits of old-world eastern Europe.

PLACE NAMES AND LANGUAGE

Ukraine is a land that has been inhabited by many people speaking many different languages. Most cities have a multitude of names that reflect past and present inhabitants. Furthermore, while Ukrainian transliteration has become a sign of patriotism and a show of separation from Russia, creative spellings have become politicised and a subject of contention. Not all present-day Ukrainian transliterations reflect common English names for Ukrainian cities (like Kiev versus Kijyiv, Odessa versus Odesa), and in this book, I refer to the standard English names. For other places, I have used Ukrainian names first and foremost (eg: Kharkiv, Lviv) except for those areas where Russian is the predominant language.

Otherwise, the transliteration of Cyrillic follows generally accepted English equivalents (as laid out in the language guide). There are certain exceptions, where transliterations have been adjusted to facilitate correct pronunciation. For the sake of simplicity, I have omitted all soft and hard signs in the transliterations.

While most of central Europe gets swept into the backpackers' circuit, and the avant-garde start to 'discover' Russia, Ukraine remains a sort of secret, in-between no man's land. There are still not enough beaten tracks near Ukraine to place it 'off the beaten track', but foreign tourists are scarce enough that you should feel special having made it this far. Ironically, Ukraine supports all the infrastructure needed for trouble-free travel: a stable hospitality industry has emerged and efficient trains, buses and planes allow travellers to go anywhere they choose with ease. In fact, the Ukrainian landscape engenders a mood for overland travel with its bustling stations and mesmerising views laid out between destinations. I have never experienced anything quite like that feeling of gazing out across the everlasting plain from a bus window, or staring at a white moon from a slow night train. Hopefully, many others will get to know the beauty and simplicity of this land that is 'on the edge'. May all your adventures be happy and unusual. *Schaslivoyi dorohy.*

FEEDBACK REQUEST

Ukraine is one of the fastest-changing places I know. Every time I return there's something new and different – this is part of the attraction. Keeping information fresh is a real challenge, and relying solely on one person's version of the country is impossible.

Meeting fellow travellers on the road has always been a useful occasion to swap stories and get good hard advice about the next place. So, once you've heard my travel stories, I want to hear yours. I would love to hear about your adventures in Ukraine, your impressions – your likes and dislikes. Not only do I love reading about the country, but I do want to know how the book was helpful or where you may have found it lacking. Please include any experience or information on hotels, restaurants, transportation, and the great spots you've discovered, and address them to me c/o Bradt Travel Guides, 19 High Street, Chalfont St Peter, Bucks SL9 9QE, England. Your contributions will help other travellers in the next edition.

Very best wishes,
Andrew Evans

Part One

General Information

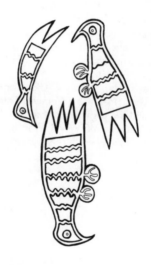

UKRAINE AT A GLANCE

Location Eastern Europe, 49° north and 32° east. Borders Russia, Belarus, Poland, Slovakia, Hungary, Romania and Moldova. Black Sea forms an extended coastline in south.

Size 603,700 km^2

Geography Steppe and flat plateaux, divided by Dnepr River

Climate Continental, with cold winters and hot summers. Ave temperature January –6°C, July 24°C. Southern coast of Crimea is Mediterranean in climate and vegetation.

Status Republic

Administrative divisions 24 *oblasts*, one autonomous republic, Crimea

Capital Kiev

Other major cities Kharkiv, Donetsk, Dnepropetrovsk, Lviv, Odessa

Population 49 million (estimate)

People Ethnic Ukrainian 78%, Russian 17%. Remaining 5% includes Poles, Belarusians, Hungarians, Romanians, Jews, Crimean Tatars, Armenians, Greeks, Romas.

Languages Ukrainian and Russian. Also Tatar and some Romanian, Hungarian, Polish

International dialling code +380

Time GMT + 2 hours (7 hours ahead of New York City)

Electricity AC is 200 volts, and the frequency is 50 hertz

Flag Two equally sized horizontal stripes of light blue and yellow gold

Public holidays

January 1 (New Year's Day), January 7 (Ukrainian Christmas), January 14 (Old New Year's Day), March 8 (Women's Day), May 1 (May Day – workers' solidarity and the pagan rites of spring), May 9 (Victory Day – a jubilant tribute to the end of World War II), August 24 (Ukrainian Independence Day), November 7 (Anniversary of the Great October Revolution)

The Country

GEOGRAPHY

Ukraine is situated in eastern Europe at 49° north and 32° east, and shares borders with Russia, Belarus, Poland, Slovakia, Hungary, Romania and Moldova. The Black Sea forms an extended coastline in the south. The country covers an area of 603,700 km² (232,000 square miles); in comparative terms, that's slightly larger than France but smaller than Texas. Ukraine is also the second largest country in Europe, if you want to count Russia as Europe. Ukrainians don't, stating with pride that Ukraine is the largest democracy in Europe.

Ukraine is mostly made up of vast steppe and flat plateaux. The Dnepr River runs south down the middle, dividing the country into traditional territories of right and left banks. Other major rivers include the Dnistr, Southern Buh, Pripyat and the Danube Delta south of Odessa. Roughly half of the Carpathian Mountain chain lies inside western Ukraine. Running diagonally southeast, the country's highest peak is Mt Hoverla at 2,061m (6,762ft). The Crimean Peninsula forms the southernmost point of the country that juts out into the Black Sea. Along the peninsula's southeast coast lie the Crimea Mountains, the highest being Roman Kosh at 1,543m (5,061ft). There are also some low rolling hills in Ukraine's far east and wide forests along the northern borders. Ukraine has almost no natural boundaries, a fact that explains a turbid past and the controversial political borders today. The country's very beginnings and continual existence can be attributed to its position as a free-moving crossroads of land, river, and sea routes between Europe, Asia, and the Middle East.

Climate

Ukraine has a continental climate, with cold white winters and hot summers; spring and autumn are short and mild but sunny. The further inland you go, the more extreme the temperature. The southern coast of Crimea is Mediterranean in climate and vegetation.

For the rest of the country, the average January temperature is –6°C, and the average July temperature is 24°C. The further east you move, the drier the climate.

Population

The total population of Ukraine is estimated to be 49 million, although a proper census has not been taken for more than a decade. Ethnic Ukrainians constitute the majority (78%) along with a significant Russian presence (17%). The remaining 5% include Poles, Belarusians, Hungarians, Romanians, Jews, Crimean Tatars, Armenians, Greeks and Romas.

Distribution is varied, but most Russians live in the eastern half of the country and in Crimea. Crimean Tatars obviously live in Crimea and Jews once made up at least a third of the population in Lviv, Odessa and Kiev.

3

ADMINISTRATION

Ukraine is divided into 24 *oblasts* and one autonomous republic, Crimea. Each oblast has a regional capital, and Kiev is the national capital. Kharkiv, Donetsk, Dnepropetrovsk, Lviv and Odessa are the largest cities.

Government

Ukraine regained independence in 1991 and now functions as a constitutional democracy, led by a president and ruled by a 450-seat parliament, the Verkhovna Rada. Leonid Kravchuk won the first elections in 1991 but his presidency was troubled by incredible inflation and so much public unrest that elections were brought forward, and Leonid Kuchma was voted in as the new president in 1994, then re-elected in 1999 for a second five-year term. Although his presidency has seen some improvement in the field of domestic economics, Kuchma's presidency has been fraught with serious corruption scandals and a shady legal process. Increased repression and a lack of freedom of speech led to major demonstrations in Kiev throughout the latter half of 2002. Kuchma's main opposition is his former Prime Minister Viktor Yuschenko, whose progressive 'Our Ukraine' block is the largest coalition in the Rada. A general lack of party consolidation means gaining majority support for legislation is tough (30 parties were registered for the last elections). The communists still make up the country's largest single party, but visitors are likely to witness the advocacy of nationalists, greens and various socialist parties. Ukrainians enjoy candid political discussion and will want to hear your impressions as a foreigner. Bear in mind that this is still an exciting time of change for Ukraine. You are likely to see politics out on the street.

Security

Ukraine occupies a difficult position in the world as the country is wedged between the superpower Russia, the expanding European Union and the Middle East. After independence from the Soviet Union, Ukraine sought distance from Russia through EU and NATO membership, but the process was delayed for obvious complications and lack of preparedness. While Ukriane recognises the need for some partnership with Russia, the two countries' troubled friendship continues. After putting to rest disputes about energy payments and control over the Black Sea fleet, Ukraine panicked in 2003 when Russia began construction of a long dam across the Kerch strait, with an aim to connect to Tuzla, a minute Ukrainian island. Protecting Ukraine's sovereignty from Russia will always be a prime national security interest.

Ukraine signed an agreement with the United States in 1994 to get rid of its nuclear arsenal in return for US$1 billion in aid. The NATO–Ukraine charter was signed in 1997 as a treaty of co-operation in conflict prevention, however relations turned sour when it was discovered that President Kuchma had illegally sold a nuclear radar system to Iraq. Ukraine still holds a sizeable arsenal of small arms which, with the country's poor economic situation, may give confidence to illegal arms dealers who fuel worldwide civil conflicts.

ECONOMY

Within the context of the much larger Soviet Union, Ukraine's a highly co-dependent economy. The Ukrainian SSR produced raw industrial material and grain in exchange for the consumer goods and energy of the other republics, namely Russia. After independence, the country was left to its own devices in the global marketplace, hoping that a swift liberalisation would affect only a temporary inconvenience. Unlike Poland, where a year of 'shock therapy' was followed by steady economic growth, Ukrainians often claim they got the shock without the therapy.

The early 1990s were harsh years for Ukraine. A lack of institutional reform meant the command government continued to command with little regard for the 'invisible hand' of the free market. Because so many people had worked for the Soviet military industry or for factories producing uncompetitive goods, output collapsed and unemployment soared. Those who continued to work would sometimes go eight months (or more) without getting paid. In order to deal with these debts, the government simply printed more money, so that between 1993 and 1994 inflation reached 10,000%. Of all the former Soviet republics at the time, Ukraine was the poorest, and for a while even Russian roubles were coveted currency.

Shuffling through pages of horrific statistics, international organisations bewailed Ukraine's impending doom, and yet people somehow survived year after year. Suddenly the experts began referring to Ukraine's pervasive shadow economy which encompassed elusive forms of black-market activity and the more innocent system of *blat*, a longstanding custom of exchanging favours for goods or services. Today, it is estimated that over half of Ukraine's money is kept outside the banking system.

Blatant corruption is also to blame for Ukraine's continuous economic setbacks. For a while, foreign investors completely stopped working in Ukraine due to the level of bureaucracy and criminal activity. There is some truth to stories about IMF and World Bank loans ending up in Swiss bank accounts since certain Ukrainian politicians have become billionaires overnight. At a lower level, some mafia-like groups rule large business networks in former industrial capitals. 'Privatisation' of Ukraine's economy constituted a few men divvying up Ukraine's natural resources and creating industrial monopolies. These oligarchs still control much of Ukraine's natural wealth and the country receives little benefit from sales of these exports.

The *hrivna* (abbreviation UAH) was introduced in September 1996 as the new currency, and in the last few years has remained stable. Less corruption and the streamlining of Soviet-like bureaucracies would help to improve the economy, but things are much better today than they were five years ago. In 2002 Ukraine ranked 80th (out of 173) in the UNDP's Human Development Index, up 20 places from the year previous. In 1998, Ukraine's GDP per capita was just US$750 a year and today the figure has risen to US$4,000; however, actual distribution of wealth is another matter as pensions and wages are still extremely low. In January 2003, President Kuchma successfully passed a bill to increase the minimum monthly wage from 185UAH (US$34) to 237UAH (US$45), but a decent, liveable salary in Kiev would be around US$300 a month. Pensioners and dependents on the state still suffer most, and many must supplement their incomes by doing physical labour.

The most positive change has been tax law reform, which has sparked a nationwide movement of entrepreneurs. For nearly a decade, small businesses were subject to random tax collections that favoured the corrupt and bankrupted start-ups. Now, the new laws require business owners to pay a base fee every month only, after which the s/he keeps all profits. It seems simple, but the change has been revolutionary for Ukraine and now you will see all types of private enterprises flourishing, most less than three years old. Ukrainians who emigrated to USA, Britain, or Portugal have also begun to return with hard currency in hand, ready to start businesses or invest, but despite any external show of prosperity, life is a day-to-day struggle for most. The adults you will meet have probably seen their life savings disappear and have gone hungry (or seen their children go hungry), but Ukrainians are survivors at heart and pulling through tough times is nothing new.

CONSERVATION AND NATURAL HISTORY

By tradition, Ukrainians live closely with the earth and esteem nature and wildlife as a vital part of their environment and culture; however, the push towards an effective preservation of Ukraine's natural spaces and wildlife is a contemporary struggle. A recent legacy of environmental degradation is the direct result of Soviet governance, but these days poverty entices continued misuse of the few remaining natural areas. International development schemes have tended to focus on Ukraine's economic woes and democratisation rather than the environmental concerns of the country, but you'll find most Ukrainians are very concerned about protecting that which was lost in the past.

In Ukraine, the percentage of cultivated land is higher than any other country in Europe and only 4% of the country is preserved in a series of very young, underdeveloped national parks.

A 'national park' in Ukraine rarely carries the attitude of protection that we often expect. Once land is designated, quotas are established to demarcate what percentage of the park should be 'protected', what may be used for agricultural purposes or for industrial development and where people may live. Travellers will find that some parks are filled with villages, roads and even factories. Then there are certain 'preserves' that exist beneath the veil of Soviet secrecy, where nobody is allowed in. Presently, Ukraine has 17 nature reserves, 12 national nature parks and four biosphere reserves (established by international bodies). The parks are concentrated in three areas: the Carpathians, the Crimea and Black Sea area, and the eastern steppe along the Russian border. The Ukrainian government has taken big steps towards more fully protecting these areas in the last five years, but a few can destroy it for everyone.

Serious water pollution and deforestation are the most serious threats to Ukraine's landscape. Rivers, wetlands and the coastline are still recovering from decades of Soviet industrial waste. An estimated 15% of Ukraine is still forested, and most of this territory lies in the north of the country (Polissya and Volhynia) and in the Carpathians. Oak and silver beech are prominent species in the north, and mixed deciduous and evergreen constitute the mountain forests. These are rare ecosystems and important wildlife habitats; however, visits to these protected 'virgin forests' often reveal areas where lumber poachers have entered and cut down thousands of trees.

Ukraine's flora and fauna was once a rare blend of European woodland species and the grasses and creatures of the Asian steppe. Today the scattered forests and grasslands still support small populations of deer, elk, wild boar, fox and hare. In the mountains of the Carpathians and Crimea there are still bear, wolves, lynx, and wild mountain sheep (moufflon). A very few European bison also remain in Ukraine and parks like Askania Nova have preserved animal populations that once thrived on the Ukrainian steppe such as the Saiga antelope and Przewalski's horse. The *Red Book of Ukraine* is a reference publication that keeps track of Ukraine's endangered species (both plant and animal); however, it is used more frequently as a field guide, which reveals the state of Ukrainian wildlife. Most national parks and natural history museums will have an illustrated copy; it is only printed in Ukrainian but always lists Latin names. With the dire state of animal life, travellers are strongly discouraged from participating in 'hunting tours' offered by many local tour operators. Remember that it is a lack of regulation rather than an abundance of wildlife that caters to foreign hunters.

Ecotourism has already helped to influence positive conservation measures in the most immediate areas of concern, and your visit to any natural area only encourages increased protection. Ukraine's bird species are a plentiful and unique resource in this respect, and bird lovers will be pleased and surprised by the odd species they can see here. For serious birders, the Black Sea wetlands and the Dnistr and Dnepr river deltas are a must-see, as these are an important migration stop and the nesting grounds for literally hundreds of species. Other unique areas to see birdlife are in the Carpathian Mountains and the parks of Volhynia and Polissya.

History

A visit to Ukraine is pointless without some knowledge of all that has transpired in this land – few countries boast a landscape so closely tied to their history. I should tell you to sit back and relax – it is a long story, and it's not over. The fact that people are reading a guidebook on Ukraine is a historical feat in itself.

Very little history is written in English about Ukraine as a land and people. Theirs tends to be treated as a peripheral history – historically it has been a peripheral land. Reading the history of Russia, of Poland, Lithuania, the Jews, Turkey, Greece and Austria will give you fair glimpses of what happened in Ukraine. Only since independence has the country been treated as a whole in the context of its current borders.

Most aspects of Ukrainian history seem to breed controversy and so a summary of the country's tumultuous past should be treated with sensitivity. The uncertainty of what things mean today makes the past a field of landmines. Does history show the Ukraine a land of inherently independent people, market-oriented and civilised, or are they really just the descendants of barbarians and serfs? The intertwining of Russian and Ukrainian history makes the task more difficult. Even the way words are spelt and pronounced can express a particular political view and shrink the truth.

Neither the greatest written tragedies nor the most adventurous Hollywood films could compete with Ukraine's history. There are no good guys or bad guys, only heroes and victims. The awe that visitors feel will be inspired by the story of the land as much as the land itself.

ANCIENT HISTORY

Soviet propagandists liked to focus on the USSR's prehistoric beginnings in order to show a continued line of development from crouched-over bipeds clutching spears to the glory of Space Age socialist industry and organised communist society. The humble beginnings of man were elevated to such dizzying heights because they lived in this particular homeland that held [inside it] an individual destiny. To a certain extent the propagandists were right. Beneath the melting glaciers of the ice age lay very rich soil that allowed Neolithic people to cultivate grain and raise livestock. Much earlier prehistoric sites have been found along the shores of the Black Sea, the Dniepr River, and the Dniestr, showing that Palaeolithic man was also resident in Ukraine. These inhabitants ventured further from the riverbank as the land ice cleared, and permanent settlements were known from 5000BC onwards. One of the first groups of people given a name is the Trypillians. They lived in what is now southwest Ukraine and later expanded eastwards. Since the first millennium BC numerous 'civilisations' have been identified all over the region through archaeological digs that show distinct agricultural societies living in the Ukrainian steppe, mixed with the effects of nomadic tribes from the east.

EARLY CIVILISATIONS

The Scythians provided a colourful ancestry for those who call themselves Ukrainians today. A nomadic civilisation of Iranian origin, they lived in thick felt tents and wandered the southern Russian Plains and Central Asian steppe in wagons pulled by horses. Around 750BC, those passing into the western steppe of modern-day Ukraine settled and began cultivating grain and raising animals, most likely assimilating with the local population. Most of what is known about the Scythians comes from the Greek historian Herodotus, who painted a picture of fierce and barbaric warriors with intriguing beliefs and rituals that focused on war and death. Scalps were taken in conquest and used as personal napkins by each warrior, and the skulls of enemies were padded with gold and leather and used as drinking chalices. They wore elaborate tattoos, developed an ornate art-form of animal symbols and were some of the first humans to ever ride horses. The Scythians left their mark in the form of large burial mounds, known as *kurhany*, which can be seen in south-central Ukraine and Crimea today. Throughout modern Ukrainian history the legacy of the Scythians has been either highlighted by militaristic regimes, or else downplayed by those who wish to disassociate Ukraine from an uncivilised Asian context.

Weakened by attacks from Persia and Macedonia, the Scythians were finally overshadowed by the Sarmatians who predominated the region from 250BC. The Sarmatians were Iranian in origin but more Slavic in appearance. They had blond hair and wore trousers and leather boots. Most noted were their women, who were skilled in horseback riding and warfare. Their 'reign' lasted until AD250 when their infighting prevented them from defending themselves.

From the 6th and 7th centuries BC, the Greek empire had also been expanding. Trading outposts were established around the Black Sea coast where the raw materials of nomadic tribes were exchanged for the luxuries of civilisation. Crimean ports like Chernoseus and Theodosia soon became the bustling crossroads of a declining Greece with the dawn of Rus. Other semi-nomadic tribes crossed into Ukraine for certain periods, attracted by raw materials and river trade routes. The Ostrogoths came from Sweden and would either protect or attack the local trading posts, depending on their mood. In AD600, the Khazars established their own empire touching the eastern half of the region. Their presence brought some discipline to the area and protection of the trade routes, allowing for two centuries of relative peace and prosperity. It was during this time that the first Hellenic Jews arrived in Ukraine. Many believe this marks the entrance of the Jews in Eastern Europe.

Kiev and the Eastern Slavs

From whence come the Slavs? Controversy surrounds the debate, fuelled by changing notions of national image today. By the 6th century AD, a definitive cultural and linguistic group was living in eastern Europe and it is accepted that this was an indigenous population mixed with the various nomadic overlords. From this emerged three groups of tribes. The South Slavs moved into the Balkans, the Western Slavs moved into modern-day Poland and Central Europe, and the Eastern Slavs moved into what is now Ukraine, Belarus, and Russia.

Nature was the predominant force in the life of the Eastern Slavic tribes. Their beliefs and everyday tasks centred on their relationship with the natural world. In the woods of northern Ukraine lived the Derevlianians (from the Slavic *derevo*, 'tree'). On the rolling plain of central Ukraine lived the Polianians (from the Slavic *pol'*, for 'field', or 'plain'). These people were known for being skilled in agriculture and cattle-raising. They produced grain in the fields and caught fish in rivers and streams. In the forest they hunted game and collected honey and wax from beehives. Every natural element had its own spiritual manifestations. Perun was the more popular god of thunder and lightning. Svaroh was the sky, and he had two sons: Dazhboh, the sun, and Svarozhych, fire. Before war, sacrifices and prayers were offered to Volos, god of animals. Lesser spirits inhabited the forests, marshes, fields and bodies of water.

In a land that was relatively flat, the Eastern Slavs used the available hilltops to build protective fortresses. These fort cities were called *horodyshcha*, from whence comes the modern Ukrainian word for city: *horod*. Legend tells us that Kiev started as just such a town in AD560, and that its founding was a family affair. Kii, Shchek and Koriv were three brothers of the Polianian tribe. Their sister, Lybed, is often shown standing at the helm of a Viking longboat with her three brothers rowing her gently onwards. She pointed out the spot that felt right, and each sibling settled a separate hillside. A city emerged in between which they named after their eldest brother Kii. Three hills in Kiev still bear their names today.

The Varangians

While the Eastern Slavs were beginning to secure their land with strongholds, another civilisation was busy tearing down fortresses in other parts of the world. The Vikings had ravaged most of Western Europe by the 9th century AD and were now ruling over several scattered kingdoms, diversifying their traditional pillaging with some trading. They were especially keen to access the more extravagant goods of the Byzantine Empire and sought an alternate route to Constantinople. Cutting through the lands of the Eastern Slavs seemed to be the best solution, and several of the local tribes were already paying tributes to the Varangians (the Slavic term for the Norse tribes). At first the Varangians made a route from the Baltic, down the Volga, and into the Caspian Sea, but this area of the Khazar Kaganate was under more frequent attack and the route eventually proved unstable. The established route from the Varangians to the Greeks went from the Baltic Sea over to Lake Ladoga, to Novgorod, down the Lovat River, down the Dnepr, and across the Black Sea to Constantinople. Kiev swiftly became an important trading centre because of its midway point on the route to Byzantium, as well as its axis point on the east–west caravan routes that connected Europe to the Silk Road. The journey from Kiev to Constantinople took six weeks and was the most dangerous part of the voyage. Raids were common, especially during the passing of rapids on the Dnepr, some of which had to be portaged. Usually, two or three sailors would strip naked and ride the boat through the white water, while the remaining crew would line both sides of the banks and keep watch for attack.

Controversy surrounds the exact relationship between the Varangians and the Slavs. Based on the chronicles that have been kept, there was no general law applicable to the tribes collectively, which led to frequent warfare amongst the Eastern Slavs. In an attempt at peace, the Slavs sought an overlord and went to the Varangians with the ever-famous line: 'Our land is great and rich, but there is no order in it. Come rule over us.' Politicians and academics do not like the idea of importing Germanic tribes to establish law and discipline, but this is the history that the average Ukrainian likes to remember.

KIEVAN RUS

Rus civilisation officially began with the reign of the Varangian princes over the regions' trading posts in the latter half of the 9th century. Kiev was 'discovered' by Askold and Dir, two close associates of Rurik, lord of Novgorod. They ruled the city and took tribute from the local Polianians. In AD860, they raided Constantinople and came back with enough booty to make Novgorod jealous. When Oleh (Helgi), a fellow Varangian prince, heard the news, he relocated to Kiev, killed Askold and Dir and became the first prince over all of Rus. He made Kiev his capital, and spent the majority of his reign bringing the other Eastern Slavic tribes under his rule. The empire of Kievan Rus was expanded, eventually extending from the Black Sea in the south to the Gulf of Finland in the north. Oleh also had his turn with Constantinople, dramatically nailing his shield to the city gates before his massive looting. A treaty was finally signed with Byzantium, exempting Kievan Rus from paying tributes or duties, which encouraged trade between the two societies. Byzantine traded their gold, silk, exotic fruit and spices for the furs, wax, honey and slaves of Kievan Rus. The raw materials were taken as tribute from the various Slavic tribes and slaves were taken in war with outsiders and from recalcitrant tribes.

Ihor (Ingvar) succeeded Oleh and lived out a highly unglamorous reign. He spent most of it trying to get unruly tribes to pay their taxes. The Pechenegs, a Turkic people of the Volga region, disrupted trade and stability with their frequent raids between 915 and 920. Ihor launched one failed strike on Constantinople leading to the loss of favoured-trading status with the Byzantine Empire. He was finally killed by the Derevlianians who were annoyed by the irregularity of his tribute collections. His wife Olha (Helga) stepped into his place and sought vengeance for her husband's death in a series of bloody massacres on the Derevlianians. Legend holds that she held a funeral feast for her dead husband, letting the Derevlianians drink themselves into a coma before having her retinue chop them to pieces. She then instated a new system for collecting tribute throughout the empire, localising the process and making it more practical and regular. Rather than attack Constantinople, she went on a diplomatic mission to the Byzantine capital seeking to reinstate favourable terms of trade. Here she converted to Christianity, was baptised and given the Christian name of Helena. The emperor Constantine was her godfather.

Helena's son, Svyatoslav (Sveinald), took after his father when it came to diplomacy, but fortunately found more success as a warrior. He came to power in 962 and soon after brought the Vitchian tribe into the empire. When the Khazar Kaganate asked for his protection against the Pechenegs, he attacked the eastern empire instead, razing their capital to the ground. He conquered the Volga Bulgars and then took over the Bulgarian kingdom with the help of the Byzantine emperor. He eventually lost Bulgaria to Byzantium and was killed by a Pecheneg ambush on his boat near some of the Dnepr rapids. In Scythian fashion, the Pecheneg khan made a drinking cup from his skull.

While Svyatoslav had spent most of his life outside Kievan Rus, his sons had been ruling the empire in his place. In 972, his oldest son Yaropolk became the grand prince in Kiev, Oleh ruled over the Derevlianians, and Volodymyr/Vladimir reigned in Novgorod. A feud between the two older brothers led to blows and Yaropolk murdered Oleh. Fearing the same fate, Volodymyr went into hiding in Scandinavia. He returned to Novgorod with a Viking army and launched an attack on Kiev. He took the city easily and had Iaropolk executed as a murderer.

Volodymyr's reign is characterised by his will to civilise Kievan Rus and make it a secure and stable empire. He wrote out the first code of law which he called the *Russkaya Pravda*, and was probably the first ruler ever to grant paganism the status of a state religion. He also established a system for the transfer of power based on a collection of joint principalities under Kiev. During his reign, Rus reached its greatest territorial expanse, but Volodymyr did not dedicate himself to expanding his borders or launching raids in other lands. Instead, he established an order that would carry Slavic civilisation through the centuries.

As the story goes, the Byzantine emperor was indebted to Volodymyr for his swift response to quell a rebellion in the Byzantine Empire. For a reward, the emperor offered him his daughter, the imperial princess, with just one catch: the marriage would take place as soon as Volodymyr converted to Christianity. He might have done it for the girl, but he had probably been thinking about a new religion for a while. He was keen to strengthen his own empire and to integrate Kievan Rus with other surrounding empires and Volodymyr had noticed how the organised religions of the Jews, Christians and Muslims had furthered their own empires and served as an effective diplomacy. According to legend, Islam was rejected because of the Koran's restriction on drink, and Judaism was rejected for all of its restrictions. Christianity already had a small presence in Kievan Rus, and during Justinian's reign in Constantinople, much of the Crimea was Christian.

In AD988, Volodymyr returned to Kiev with his new bride and a new state religion. All the people of Kiev were marched into the Dnepr, and the river's waters were blessed by Byzantine priests while Volodymyr watched from the bank. In this way all of Kievan Rus was baptised and the Slavic nation made Christian. The statues of Perun and other pagan gods were torn down and beaten with sticks. Churches were built in Kiev and throughout all of Rus. Volodymyr dedicated one tenth of the state revenue to the Church and its clergy. Despite his 800 concubines and known executions of Christians prior to his conversion, Volodymyr was canonised a saint after his death. He is remembered as a wise ruler who brought enlightenment and security to Kievan Rus. Today, his statue stands on the left bank of the Dnepr, holding a tall cross in his hands.

Volodymyr's plan of an organised succession to power was quickly forgotten in a bloody and drawn-out sibling rivalry. Two younger brothers, Boris and Hlib, accepted death rather than break their Christian vow of peace, and were made saints. The fighting weakened the capital and made it vulnerable to repeated nomadic raids. Yaroslav of Novgorod rushed to Kiev and succeeded in fending off the Pecheneg invasion in 1024. In remembrance and gratitude to God, he built St Sophia's Cathedral. Now the established grand prince of Kievan Rus, Yaroslav 'the Wise' continued the more dignified traditions of his father. His reign is marked by cultural growth, legal development and rapprochement with Byzantium. Through a series of seven strategic marriages – of his children and himself – he became relative to the rulers of Sweden, Hungary, Norway, France, Poland, Byzantium and Germany. This was European integration at its best.

These same methods of 'international relations' were copied by Volodymyr Monomakh, who married the last Saxon princess of England. He was popularly known as a defender of the poor: the crowds in Kiev rioted for him to take the throne even though it was not his to take. His reign (1113–25) marks the last great ruler of Kievan Rus before separate principalities broke away and became self-governing. Kiev was still the largest city in the region (12th-century Kiev had twice the population of London at the time) but local principalities became more independent and competitive, destabilising the city through constant battle and changes of power. In 1169 Monomakh's grandson ransacked Kiev and left the city reeling.

THE GOLDEN HORDE

Nomadic invasion was no news for the citizens of Kiev so they paid little attention when the Mongols first attacked on the Kalka River in 1223. Instead of moving on to Kiev however, the Mongols retreated and returned from the north years later. At the onset of the winter of 1240, the grandson of Genghis Khan – Batu Khan – came and decimated Kiev, bringing the last of Rus into the Mongol's military confederation, the Golden Horde. The Mongols never colonised the region fully and respected the local culture and religion, even exempting the church from tribute. They put locals in places of power and had them do the dirty work of extracting each city's payment. It was a despotic realm and discipline was cruel. Unlike the Russians, the Mongols stayed in Ukrainian land for less than a century.

LITHUANIA AND POLAND

If Rus had become the Asiatic East, then Lithuania was its Wild West. For centuries, the pagan tribes of the Baltic forests had been a divided society of mutual raiding. This changed when the warrior Mindaugas brought together a combined tribal force in order to fend off the armed proselytising of the Teutonic knights. They held them back in Prussia, and the Grand Duchy of Lithuania expanded eastward. By the latter half of the 14th century, the Golden Horde had begun to lose power in the region and from 1344 the Lithuanians already ruled the far western principalities of Galicia and Volhynia. Algirdas, grandson to Mindaugas, defeated the Mongols at the Battle of Blue Waters on the Dnepr in 1362 and took Kiev with the charge that 'all Rus simply must belong to the Lithuanians.' The Lithuanians returned some of the order from the days of Kievan Rus and were a welcome change from the Mongols. The local nobility was incorporated into a ruling class and the land became a collection of ordered principalities. Many Lithuanians adopted Orthodoxy and learned to speak the local language that was now being called Ruthenian.

Polish expansion began in Galicia when the Polish-born leader Boleslaw was murdered on suspicions that he was still too Catholic. Having previously signed a treaty of spoils with the king of Hungary, the Poles moved into these western principalities with the ideological support of a Roman church that opposed Orthodoxy. The following century marked a severe cultural shift for Galicia. Catholicism was introduced, Latin became the official language, and Czech, Polish and Hungarian nobles were given land grants.

The Grand Principality of Lithuania was by far the largest in the area, yet they faced threats from all their neighbouring nations: the Teutons were crowding the Baltic Coast in the north, Muscovy looked nostalgically towards the lands of Rus and Mongol raids were still a force to reckon with in the far east. Fearing they would lose the Ruthenian lands to the Russians, or worse, the Tatars, they sought a union with Poland that would enable combined forces of defence. The joining of the two countries was solemnised in the form of a marriage between Grand Prince of Lithuania Jogailo and the Hungarian Queen of Poland Jadwiga (the Polish king, Casimir the Great, left no male heir). The prince converted to Catholicism and in less than two years, Jadwiga had annexed Galicia to Poland. The rest of the Lithuanian principality was not so easily absorbed.

Jogailo stayed in his seat as king, but his cousin Vytautas began to rule Lithuania as a separate state. This lessened the Polish influence on the country, but it did not last long. Laws were passed that gave Lithuanian boyars the same rights as the Polish nobles, if they were Catholic. As the ruling élite of Poland and Lithuania became closer, the Ruthenians became more disenfranchised. In 1430 Prince Svidrigaillo led a campaign to sever ties with Poland completely, but the Poles responded with their own puppet candidate who proved more popular with the Lithuanian élite. Sigismund of Starodub became the effective ruler of Lithuania and the Poles began to control more Ruthenian territory.

Lithuania was forced to co-operate with the Poles, as the threat of Muscovy and the Tatars increased. In 1522, the traditional principality of Chernihiv was lost to Moscow, a city that was now on a mission to gather Orthodox lands. Tatar invasions continued and then a full-fledged war began with Muscovy. Lithuania was financially drained and sought help from Poland. In 1569, a meeting was held at Liublin to decide the terms of the agreements. Realising that the Poles sought only to annex their lands to Poland, the Lithuanian and Ruthenian delegates walked out. The meeting continued nonetheless and the union was sealed; when the delegates returned, they had to settle. The Polish *Rzeczpospolita* was formed which would have an elected king, a parliament, common currency, and a joint foreign policy. The land of the Ruthenians became attached to the Polish crown and the Ruthenian élite were quickly assimilated into a joint ruling culture. These nobles now spoke Polish, worshipped as Catholics, and enjoyed the favoured status of the Polish royalty. The lower class Ruthenians were pushed to the fringes of their own society. Complicated laws based on religious discrimination and language kept Ruthenians out of the cities and out of positions or power. 'Ruthenian' came to mean peasant, and the Ruthenian language became the tongue of the countryside. These divisions were favourable to the Poles, who were tapping into the growing wealth of western Europe by trading food, in particular grain. Lands were combined into larger estates, and Ruthenian peasants were now forced to offer free labour to the nobles in exchange for the use of their own plots. Inside the Polish Commonwealth, cultural and economic disparity grew with the exploitation of the Ruthenians by the nobility.

THE COSSACKS

By the 16th century, western Europe had had a long tradition of feudalism, but the Polish landowners had only just introduced the system, enjoying the cashflow from the grain trade. Uninspired by their new lot in life, many peasants simply fled to the Central Dnepr basin, the lands stretching across the plains north of the Black Sea. Here was a no man's land of sorts, a shifting frontier, unregulated by any foreign nobility. Other peasants were sent to cultivate the area, sanctioned by the Polish nobles themselves. Hoping to increase grain production, the Commonwealth offered massive tracts of land rent free for up to 20 years in the unsettled steppe of the east.

This system brought two benefits to the Commonwealth. More grain could be produced and bought at low prices and then sold to western Europe. Secondly, an effective buffer zone was in place, protecting the kingdom from outside invasion. This borderland kept separate the civilised worlds of Poland, Lithuania and Muscovy from the barbaric Muslims of the Crimean Khanate and Ottoman Empire. This land was 'on the edge' of civilisation, or in the local language, 'U-krayi-na.'

A series of fortresses had been built to create a safety line for the Polish Commonwealth, stretching from Kiev out toward the western lands of Volhynia and Galicia. The land outside this line was called the *dike polye*, or 'wild field'. Constant raids from the south made the *dike polye* a precarious place to settle. The Tatars of Crimea had been left behind in the rescinding tide of the Golden Horde and continued to launch attacks to the north. By the 1500s they controlled most of the Black Sea coast and its Greek and Genoese trading posts. Crimean Tatars and Ottoman Turks came at least yearly on slave-collecting sprees, robbing the settlers, wrecking farms, and severely depopulating the frontier.

Without the protection of overlords, the locals began to take matters into their own hands. A new brand of fighter emerged, dedicated to protecting his crops, family and land from continuous invasion. They became talented horse riders and disciplined warriors, earning their place as the genuine heroes of Ukrainian folklore. They gave the country its national costume and many of its folk songs and dances. It is impossible to compare the Cossacks with warriors like knights, the samurai, or the cowboys of the Wild West. It was a unique time in a very wild frontier. Trained and prepared, they still spent most of their time on the farm, gathering only when it was necessary to fend off invaders or else attack enemy cities. It was these enemies that christened them 'Cossack', the Turkic word for 'freeman'. They were outsiders, excluded from any of the surrounding civilisations, and who in turn had established their own loose-fitting system of rule of law and sword.

The Zaporizhian Cossacks

The popularity of the Cossacks spread across Eastern Europe and young men who tired of the plough and the master's whip dreamt of running away and joining one of the bands of rebels. The Zaporizhian Sich became the unofficial headquarters of the Cossacks, based in a fortress town built on an island in the middle of the lower Dnepr. Here the Zaporizhian Cossacks emerged as a vaguely democratic military regime. Any Christian male of any nationality and social class was free to join, or leave. Every member had equal rights and all voices were heard in the open air *Rada* that became the forum for decision-making. Women and children were forbidden from entering the Sich. Leaders were elected to be the *'hetmans'* but had no power during peacetime. Only during a campaign could they enforce strict discipline.

The attacks on the Turks began as basic counter-offensives but soon turned into lucrative shopping trips to supplement their own wealth. Over one 20-year segment, the Cossacks raided all the Turkish ports along the Black Sea and set the city of Constantinople on fire twice. The oversupply of booty had the price of slaves falling. The neighbouring nations were grateful for this 'Christian force' against the infidel Turks, and would offer them commissions to protect against raids. Yet the Cossacks were really only loyal to themselves, and soon they were making their first forays into Polish Galicia. For the first half of the 17th century, organised Cossack raids in Poland were the norm. King Stefan tried to stop the invasions by offering hefty stipends to some Cossacks if they would join his army against Muscovy as well as fight the 'rebel' Cossacks. This divided the Cossacks and made the Zaporizhian Sich more determined against Poland.

Of all the Cossack warriors, the most revered is Bohdan Khmelnytsky. Born of Ruthenian nobility, he had served in the Polish army and had spent two years as a prisoner of the Turks. He later moved to the 'wild field' and spent most of his life quietly farming in what is now central Ukraine. He was a Cossack in that he helped keep the peace of the countryside from time to time. In 1646, however, a Polish neighbour beat to death his young son and then kidnapped his betrothed. As a Ruthenian outsider, his story had little pull in the Polish courts. He turned to the Zaporizhian Sich and incited enough enthusiasm for a campaign against Poland. He then made an alliance with the Tatar Khan who gave him 4,000 cavalry to help in his attack.

Khmelnytsky's army smashed the Polish force that same year at Zhovti Vody ('Yellow waters'). He continued his march towards Warsaw with a mission to destroy the Commonwealth of Poland. Cossacks allied to the Polish king soon deserted and joined with the Sich, while the Ruthenian peasants used the state of anarchy to revolt against the nobility, government officials and Jewish financiers. It was a murderous campaign all around. Catholic churches were burned and the priests brutally tortured. Massive pogroms were carried out on Jewish towns, many of them led by Khmelnytsky himself. Within a few months, the Cossack *hetman* had driven out the Poles, and for three years he controlled the territory between Lviv and Poltava.

By this time, the Tatar support had gone home and the *hetman* found that his jurisdiction was no longer secure. He began to consider a new overlord that would offer protection from the Poles while giving a chance for autonomy. Khmelnytsky turned to the Orthodox tsar of Muscovy as the less evil option. In 1654 the *hetman* met the tsar's emissaries in a church in Pereyaslav, a town below Kiev on the Dnepr. After swearing loyalty to the tsar, the Cossack stormed out when the delegation explained the tsar's power was absolute and that they would never make a reciprocal oath to his subjects. Hours later he wearily returned and agreed to the deal. Muscovite officials were sent into all the towns, and the tsar became the 'autocrat of all Great and Little Russia.'

Ruin

The next 30 years were less than glorious and are referred to as the 'Ruin'. Russian, Polish, Cossack and Tatar armies marched back and forth fighting for control of their own piece of Ukraine. Khmelnytsky's successors were unpopular and the countryside fell into disunity. In the west, the *haidamaky*, a band of runaway serfs and peasants, lived in the woods and raided the nobles' estates. The Cossacks' ranks became bureaucratic and ineffective. Only in 1686 did Poland and Russia sign an accord of 'Eternal Peace' which split the land right down the centre. Kiev and all lands east of the Dnepr fell into the hands of Muscovy, while Poland ruled the west.

The Russian leaders had little interest in autonomy within their empire. Peter I and Catherine II were both determined to centralise their empire, and used the English subjugation of Ireland as their model. The countryside was strictly ruled and all economic activity regulated by Russia. Trade was restricted to Russia at fixed prices. Some Cossacks were employed by the tsar as a useful protective force, but he did not appreciate their loyalties to other Cossack bands. The Zaporizhians were soon dubbed enemies of the tsar and a warrant went out for their execution. The Sich fortress was destroyed by the Russian army in 1775.

LITTLE RUSSIA AND THE RUSSIAN EMPIRE

The Russian Empire was now the largest in the world, and Catherine II was intent on settling the southern portions of Little Russia. In her own words, she had 'recovered that which was torn away'. She presented tracts of land to Russian nobles and her German compatriots to win co-operation and pay for favours. Special labour concessions enticed local and foreign peasants to come and work on these new estates. The colony of New Russia welcomed a million people to the area in less than 50 years. Orthodox Serbs persecuted under the Catholic Hapsburgs were given former Cossack lands and renamed it New Serbia. The Crimean peninsula was won from the Turks and quickly colonised by Russians, Greeks, Armenians and Jews. All of Little Russia became a land of grain production to feed the Russian Empire and to provide them with the raw materials to trade with Europe.

Malorossiya (Little Russia) was drawn into nine provinces and each ruled by a tsar-appointed governor. It was a harsh regime, in which the tsar had unlimited power over all his subjects, and a cruel police force to impose it. The military held a strong presence and mandatory conscription for 25 years of service increased their size. Press-gangs collected the masses of unwilling. Life was a dim prospect for the millions of serfs who were owned, purchased and sold by their landowners.

Tsar Alexander I had a slightly more liberal regime, but was prone to indecisiveness. Discontent grew and talk of reform was the banter in St Petersburg salons. Hidden societies flourished. Following Alexander's death in 1825, the infamous Decembrist Revolt erupted in a failed attempt to oust the incoming tsar. Nikolai I responded with the trappings of later Soviet standard: a secret police

UKRAINIAN NATIONALISM

The romanticism of western Europe made its way to the Russian Empire and into the hearts of a new class of educated élite. In Ukraine, a university had been founded in Kharkiv in 1805 where the gentry and clergy could send their children for higher education. Members of the rising intelligentsia focused their efforts on the intellectual questions of the empire and its masses. With romanticism came a heightened interest in the natural realm, and viewing people in their natural habitat. They idealised the peasant lifestyle and its characteristics became symbols of a growing national consciousness. In Ukraine, the intelligentsia sought out an individual history and folklore that made it unique from Russia.

Recognising Ukraine's separate language was key to the birth of Ukrainian nationalism. For centuries, Ruthenian had been a language of uneducated peasants, and in the Russian Empire, 'Little Russian' was merely an underdeveloped dialect of Russian itself. For the first time, the spoken vernacular was used in books and for intellectual debate. In the far east, the Kharkiv Romantics sought to produce a literature written in the unadulterated language of the countryside. Their books of folktales, songs and poems were well received and helped fuel the empire's curious fascination for Little Russia.

In 1840, Taras Shevchenko published his most famous collection of Ukrainian poems, titled *Kobzar* after the wandering bards that once roamed the Ukrainian countryside. The book was an honest picture of everyday Ukrainian life yet written in exquisite golden prose that was not Russian. Shevchenko became instrumental in the nationalist movement, although much more so after his early death. The book is still treated as the standard of Ukrainian literary achievement and the benchmark for the modern Ukrainian language.

Under the Austro-Hungarian Empire in the west, Ukrainian nationalism was stifled by the Polish, Romanian, and Hungarian nobility who maintained their own nationalist aspirations against the Hapsburgs. The Spring of Nations Revolt in 1848 led to the abolition of feudalism after which the *Rusyny* (Ruthenian) population petitioned the emperor for cultural allowances. It was granted and a Ruthenian council established that allowed separate schools to function in the Ruthenian (Ukrainian) language. Modern Ukraine's cultural divisions of east and west can be traced to the imperial age of Austria and Russia when allowances were permitted in the one and forbidden in the other.

force, paid informers and strict censorship over printed material. He introduced brash cultural reforms that aimed at making everyone more Russian. The local élite was quickly acculturated into the greater 'Russian tribe' and the class divide widened along cultural lines.

The changing empire

The Crimean War (1854–56) highlighted the inefficiencies of the Russian Empire. Hundreds of thousands of peasants rushed to Kiev to join the fighting in the hope they would now be considered freemen. In battle, the Russian army came intimately close to Western foreigners and was made to witness its own backwardness. The empire could not compete with the leadership and industry of the Western nations, as seen in their ultimate defeat at Sevastopol.

Serfdom was the issue at hand, and Tsar Alexander took the throne in 1855 with the statement that it was better to 'abolish serfdom from above than to wait until the serfs abolish it from below'. Ukrainian peasants in the mid-19th century lived a life not dissimilar to the peasant farmers of feudal England. Their lives and their work were owned by their masters and living conditions were appalling. Life expectancy was never above 40 and alcoholism was rampant. Change was inevitable, but the delay was prolonged by the unresolved issues of land ownership. Russian nobles tended to understand the need to give some land away to the peasants, whereas the gentry in Ukraine were very reluctant to lose control of such a lucrative asset.

Serfdom was abolished in 1861 but the change did not ease the peasants' life. They were still not free to leave their village without specially issued passports. Land was distributed for their use, but they had to buy it from the government, which forced peasants into a tremendous debt that could last a lifetime. In addition, 20% of their payment was to be paid in labour obligations to the landowner. Serfdom remained de facto. The land they did receive as their own tended to be less fertile and much smaller in size than their former plots. The common land of forests and pastures went to the nobility and left the freed peasants with no access to wood or fodder.

New reforms eased the tension but did not resolve the ultimate issues of class and exploitation. Trials began to be held openly and military service decreased to six years. Education improved and local governments called *Zemstvo* were set up as committees to decide on tax spending for the region. A head tax was issued which hit the peasants hardest, and most goods like sugar and tea were heavily taxed. Class differences were more noticeable between the peasants. The wealthiest group had somehow made their farm profitable and were known as *Kulaks*, while the middle (*Seredniaky*) and the poorest peasants (*Biadnaky*) worked for them, or hired themselves out to the gentry landowners. The nobility itself was in decline since few knew how to run an estate without free labour but Ukraine remained the granary of Europe. At the turn of the century, Ukraine was producing 90% of the Russian Empire's wheat exports, while annually the Ukrainian peasant consumed one-third the amount of bread of a peasant in western Europe. Emigration became an increasingly attractive option, and Ukrainian national dress was a recognisable sight on the boats to Canada and America.

Industrialisation came late to Ukraine. Not until a railroad was built did a major industrial pull begin in the 1890s. In the valley of the Don River, or *Donbas*, a furious coal extraction was carried out and mines soon covered the whole region. Such industry was often the work of foreign investors who sought to make a profit from cheap raw materials in a country that lagged severely behind western Europe. The Welshman, John Hughes, came to the Donbas to impart his knowledge of Welsh coal mining and gave his last name to the regional capital: Yuzovka. Iron became the purpose of Krivy Rih and Russia used the raw materials from both places to provide the steel needed to build a new industrial society. Workers were imported from Russia, the urban population grew and the proletariat was born.

Revolutionary unrest

The ideas of Marxism spread quickly among the intelligentsia after the philosopher's books made headway in the 1870s. Within 20 years, the Russian Group of Social Democrats had been founded in Kiev, while other groups sprung up in Ukraine's industrial cities. These early Marxists were usually Russian and Jews – an honest reflection of the urban population that was interested in a predominantly Russian labour force. Agrarian socialism was its greatest contender for the revolutionary limelight. Earlier movements focused on the plight of the peasants, and used the peasant commune as a common symbol of Ukraine's inherent socialism. Sincere attempts were made to rally the peasants' support for a leftist political struggle against the tsar. The *khlopomany* movement (*narodnyky* in Russian, or 'people for the people') involved campaigns of students and intellectuals who would dress up like peasants and proselytise the revolution in the rural areas. The peasants rejected them as impostors.

Revolutionary enthusiasm was everywhere, but its ideas and representatives were split into odd-paired camps of ideologies and disparate brands of socialism. In 1881, the terrorist group, Narodnaya Volya (People's Will), believing that only violent means would bring about needed change, assassinated Tsar Alexander II. In 1901, the populist Socialist Revolutionary Party was founded in Ukraine and also advocated political murder. Kiev was soon targeted for the new tsar's anti-revolutionary activity. The peasant uprising in Poltava of 1902 sent a strong nationalist message to Moscow and an individual brand of revolution was bred in the south. The Revolutionary Ukrainian Party was founded and became the vanguard for the Ukrainian nationalist political movement. Many of the leftist parties joined forces in the Union of Liberation of 1904, but those who were looking towards liberating Ukraine found the Marxist pull for centralisation discouraging. The parties did find common ground in their push for an end to autocracy and a parliament elected by universal suffrage. Tsar Nikolas II grew alarmed by this new coalition and sponsored a collection of violent ultra-rightist groups to put down the revolutionaries. Known as the Black Hundreds, they indiscriminately beat and killed anyone that was not tsarist, Orthodox or Russian. Blamed for the rise of revolutionary activity, the Jews suffered the bloodiest of pogroms in Ukraine, particularly in Odessa.

THE REVOLUTION IN UKRAINE

The Bloody Sunday massacre of 1905 occurred thousands of miles away in Petrograd (St Petersburg), but it set the revolution alight in Ukraine. A peaceful protest of factory workers ended when hundreds were gunned down by the tsar's troops. All the latent anger of revolutionary talk and party politicking turned to massive protests. In Ukraine, the proletariat led strikes that shut down the major cities. The peasants became more brazen and launched an expropriation of the Ukrainian countryside. Individually, they began to openly steal the gentry's crops, wood, tools and livestock. Collectively, the peasants would meet in front of the church and head towards a chosen estate with crude weapons in hand. The landowner would be forced to sign his estate away to the village council and the adult males would then redistribute the newly acquired property amongst the villagers. The rising fury led to the tsar reluctantly issuing his 1905 October Manifesto, which granted the vote to all Russian men and called for the establishment of an elected State Duma, to be led by the reformer Stolypin.

The new parliament found its powers were severely limited by the autocrat. Strikes and protests continued across the empire, and maintaining the peace became a violent task. Stolypin sought a soft revolution and supported a vision of conservative loyalists gradually implementing social change. The Duma was dissolved repeatedly and Stolypin's reforms were too little too late. He was shot during an intermission at the Kiev Opera House, while in the midst of conversation with Tsar Nikolas II.

Within days of the news of the February Revolution of 1917 reaching Kiev, the nationalist movement had mobilised. The Rada was established in March, modelled after the Cossacks' self-governing assembly. It assumed the most representative body, and soon the Ukrainian Socialist Revolutionary Party joined, as well as the Peasant Congress. By May they had issued a list of requests to the provisional government who were now attempting to hold the empire together. The Rada demanded recognition of Ukraine's autonomy, separate Ukrainian army units, and Ukrainians to take up the civil posts in Ukraine. The provisional government ignored the document, embroiled in its own confusing struggle for authority. The Rada then published its First Universal Declaration that called for a *Sejm* – Ukraine's own national assembly with a sovereign general secretariat. When it was granted them, Ukraine's ethnic Russians were outraged. Kiev's provisional government eventually collapsed, unable to deal with the conflicting aspirations of Ukrainians and Russians.

World War I and Ukrainian independence

The internal mayhem of the revolution was made worse by the external war on the empire's borders. On the eastern front of World War I, Russia once again witnessed its own backwardness against the powers of the West in the most tragic manner. The faltering government stranded the army, millions were killed, and industry came to a standstill. Ukrainians found themselves fighting each other as soldiers in the ranks of the Austro-Hungarian and Russian imperial armies and by 1917, Ukraine was being suffocated. The Bolsheviks had come to power in Russia and were now fighting for a universal 'dictatorship of the proletariat'. In Ukraine, this proletariat lived mostly in the industrial eastern regions of the country. Like Lenin, they viewed nationalism and the independence movement as bourgeois and old-fashioned. The Bolsheviks had originally joined the Rada, but broke away after many disagreements and relocated to Kharkiv. Here they declared the creation of a Soviet Ukrainian Republic.

The Rada backdated its Fourth Universal Declaration for January 22nd 1918, in which they declared Ukraine's independence. It was a frantic move in the shadow of an imminent Bolshevik takeover and the Rada looked for outside help. Not trusting Lenin to represent Ukraine's best interest, the Rada sent its own delegation to the talks at Brest-Litovsk. German occupation of the country, in exchange for food, seemed the best option. Even as the agreement was made, the Bolsheviks invaded Kiev. Miniature militias stood up against the army, albeit symbolically. One defiant group of 300 youths was surrounded and shot in Kiev. Yet within three weeks, the German/Austrian advance arrived and forced the Bolsheviks back to Kharkiv. However, the Germans found the country disorderly and were displeased with the inefficiency of the promised food deliveries. The authority of the Rada was uncertain and they could not satisfy their protectors' demands. Out of pure frustration, the German army disbanded the Rada at the end of April 1918.

A conservative government was put in its place that mimicked the monarchic Cossack *hetmanate*. The leader, Skoropadsky, was generally disliked, but was a welcome answer for the terrified nobles fleeing Russia. For a brief time, Kiev became a safe haven of hedonist escapism for the dispossessed gentry. Ukraine became the new theatre where the central powers fought for a Bolshevik downfall. However, when the armistice was signed, the Germans quickly retreated from Ukraine, leaving the vast territory at the mercy of its subterranean tension.

CIVIL WAR

The inconsistencies and contradictions of the Russian Revolution were gruesomely played out on Ukrainian soil during three years of civil war. The Bolshevik's Red Army invaded Ukraine from the north hoping to expand the revolution and secure its power over the former empire. The gentry and monarchists of Russia's imperial age backed the White Army. Keen to stop the ideological threat of communism and to quickly re-establish the old regime, the allies of the Entente – namely Britain and France – also gave military support to the White Army. The two armies competed in cruelty, which earned them a loss of support from both the peasantry and the proletariat. Food and horses were requisitioned by the passing forces, and the local men were forcibly conscripted. Both invading armies engaged in free-for-all violence: women were raped, homes looted, and towns destroyed. In the cities, factory workers were shot if they failed to meet the impossibly high industry quotas set to supply the ruling army.

The Ukrainian nationalists gathered in the west in hopes to rebuff the foreign influence on their land and start an independent state. A new nationalist government, the Directory, was founded in December 1918, but lasted only three months. A former leader of the Rada, Petlyura now led the largest nationalist band. Another independent Ukrainian state was proclaimed in Lviv after the fall of the Hapsburg monarchy, but was soon rejected by the Poles. The Galician rebels joined with Petlyura to fight in the civil war, but were betrayed when Petlyura made an agreement with the Poles to give up claims for Galicia in exchange for their assistance against the Bolsheviks. But after a quick defeat in Kiev, the Poles retreated.

The millions of peasants felt little allegiance beyond their village and carried out indiscriminate attacks on the nationalists, imperialists, Bolsheviks and Jews. These 'Green' peasant bands and 'Black' armies contributed to the pandemonium and sapped the energy of the greater armies. The most prominent of these fighters was Nestor Makhno. He was a homegrown Ukrainian hero with an intellectual bent for anarchy. Like many in his day, he had spent time in prison but also published academic essays on his political views. His competent army gained the respect of the local peasants who often collaborated in his terrorist forays.

The year of 1919 was one of bloodshed and chaos in Ukraine. Six separate armies ravaged the country, each with confused notions about its ultimate aim. Kiev changed hands five times in one year. The historian, Orest Subtleny, explained it best when he said: 'Ukraine was a land easy to conquer but almost impossible to rule.' Control of Ukraine's raw materials were a desired advantage for the greater war effort throughout the former empire. The Donbas was targeted, and the Red Army tried to implement some pre-emptive collectivisation on the peasantry. Neither the Red nor the White Army could feed or clothe its soldiers. Desertion was the norm and in 1919 one million soldiers fled from the Red Army. Villages suspected of hiding deserters were decimated and soldiers fleeing combat were shot by their generals. Soldiers' uprisings were commonplace on both sides, and officers were cruelly tortured before being killed.

The Bolsheviks launched a successful invasion at the end of 1919 and took all of Ukraine in the following year. The Ukrainian Soviet Republic was reinstated. The Whites departed from Crimea, and the Ukrainian nationalist government retreated to Poland. Makhno went into hiding in Romania. The Bolsheviks had won the war, but at a tremendous price: 1.5 million of Ukraine's civilian population died in the scramble for power. The Jewish population suffered especially. Nationalists and anarchists carried out vicious pogroms that killed over 50,000 Jews. The Whites viewed the Jews as the chosen people of the Bolsheviks and killed over 100,000 of them. The Red Army simply killed Jews as bourgeois anti-revolutionaries, in spite of the Jewish leaders within the Bolshevik party.

SOVIET UKRAINE

Bolshevik severity was justified as 'war communism' and meant Ukrainians were expected to release all belongings and food to the Red Army. Everything was nationalised, and grain was requisitioned from the peasantry. Out of protest, many peasants stopped planting. An accompanying drought led to a devastating famine, where hundreds of thousands died in Ukraine.

After moving Ukraine's capital to the eastern city of Kharkiv, the Ukrainian SSR joined the Soviet Union in a December 30, 1922 referendum of Bolsheviks in Ukraine. Lenin said Russia and Ukraine would be joined in a 'Union of Equals.' The new socialist republic included most of the territory of the present day, with the exception of Galicia and Volhynia and certain borderlands. Kharkiv remained the republic's capital until 1934.

Lenin was sensitive to national sentiments and realised that, when presented in the colours of the local Ukrainian culture, the Bolshevik pill was more readily swallowed. A policy of *korenizatsiya* (making roots) was established to bring non-Russians into the communist party and earn co-operation from all Ukrainians. Ukrainian culture and language were preached like a new religion. Russian party officials had to study Ukrainian and speak it to their Ukrainian counterparts. Education turned Ukrainian and the plague of illiteracy disappeared. More people learned to read than ever in the history of the country, but the only Ukrainian books at hand somehow always featured the communist party and pictures of smiling Red Army soldiers.

Ukraine did not convert easily to communism. The years of war, the deadly famine and the present economic woes did not seem the shining end to the revolution they envisioned. The Bolsheviks were still very unpopular throughout the whole Soviet Union and peasant uprising continued in Ukraine. The Kronstadt Mutiny against the Red Army in St Petersburg alarmed the Bolshevik leaders and moves were taken to ease the tension between ruler and ruled. Before he died in 1924, Lenin introduced the New Economic Policy (NEP) which aimed largely at appeasing the peasantry, albeit temporarily. Taxes were lowered, and peasants were permitted to sell grain at market prices. Collectivisation was halted and foreign investment encouraged. It was capitalism actually, and it gave immediate results. With new incentives, agricultural production increased, and industry flourished. The cities witnessed a new class of trade and businessmen that wore imported suits and sold foreign luxury goods.

The tragedy of Stalinism

Stalin had wangled the seat of party general secretary through sheer treachery and was now eager to push forth his concept of a centralised industrial union. Most of all, he hated the wealthy NEP men and the Kulak peasants who had prospered during the mid-1920s. In 1928 Stalin introduced his 'revolution from above' with a five-year plan. This was a series of gargantuan industrial goals for the cities and major collectivisation of the countryside which was repeated in a second five-year plan. Sceptics to such massive change in so short a time were answered with Stalin's famous quote: 'You can't make an omelette without breaking eggs.'

Ukraine already had a large industrial base and hundreds of new factories were added. Ukrainians poured into the cities and dramatically changed the ethnic make-up of the workforce. Zaporozhia became a city of steel mills and Kharkiv started building tractors. The Dnepr hydro-electric plant made it all run. Living conditions were terrible and discipline severe. Everyone was pushed to the limits. On a summer day in 1935 a young coal miner in eastern Ukraine named Aleksei Stakhanov cut 102 tons of coal in just six hours. This was over ten times his mine's personal production goal. Stalin made him a national hero overnight, and a new cult of Stakhanovism had every worker sweating his way towards superhuman industrial achievements. Underneath the show of rapid industrialisation was the reality of waste, inefficiency and poor quality.

Soviet figures for industrial growth were based on parallel growth of the food supply. The state believed it would buy grain cheaply from the peasants, feed the cities and sell the surplus abroad for profit. When they offered to buy the grain at a minute fraction of market price, the peasants refused to sell. Hoarding grain drove up the market price even higher. Stalin called for the liquidation of the Kulaks as a class. Any peasant who owned something was suspect. During 1929–30, hundreds of thousands of Ukrainian peasants were packed on freight trains, shipped to the frozen tundra of Siberia and ordered to settle the land. Most died of cold and starvation.

Collectivisation itself was a disaster. The remaining peasants revolted while the secret police and army used brutal force to take farms and move people. Resisters were shot on sight or else arrested and sent to Siberia. Out of protest, the peasants often killed their animals rather than let the government have them. Ukraine lost 50% of its livestock this way. The new collective farms were highly unsuccessful and directed by unskilled Russian party activists. Grain production fell drastically.

The famine

Stalin called for even higher grain quotas and sent in military generals to supervise the seizure. Hired gangs went from farm to farm, tearing up floorboards and torturing peasants in search of hidden grain. Drought in 1931 killed the remainder of the flailing crop yields. After two years of grain requisitioning, most of Ukraine's food supply had been confiscated and the countryside was left to starve. Peasants ate rats, bark, leaves, dirt, and one another. Skeletal bodies were a common sight in city streets and whole villages died together. The famine of 1932–33 was the ultimate tragedy for the Ukrainian nation. Figures vary widely, but it is generally believed that 3 to 6 million Ukrainians starved to death. The tragedy went unnoticed in the West and in much of the Soviet Union.

The Great Terror

The thirties also brought an end to *korenizatsiya* and any remaining idea of a union of equals. Stalin had no tolerance for opposition and targeted the intelligentsia. A new regime of terror rid the country of non-compliance. Scientists, church leaders, writers, editors, historians, and musicians disappeared. The traditional Ukrainian *kobzari* (bards) were invited to a conference and shot on sight. Purges cleansed the party of infidels who were charged with all manner of '-isms' and lack of vigilance. The accused were shot or sent to the gulag prison camps of Siberia. In 1934, the Ukrainian Communist party lost over 100,000 members in one year. New purges in 1937–38 eliminated the entire leadership of the Ukrainian Soviet government and the Ukrainian Communist Party. Soon, even the most random accusations would end in disappearances and executions. The Stalinist terror introduced a paranoia that kept people circumspect for the remainder of the Soviet Union.

World War II

The Soviet army 'liberated' Galicia and Volhynia after Poland fell to the Germans in 1939. The policies of the Soviet regime were not well received in these western provinces and about half a million people were deported to Siberia. The Nazi attack on the USSR in June 1941 took Stalin by surprise. Resistance in Ukraine was futile. In western Ukraine, fascism sounded better than Stalinism. The

German soldiers were perceived as liberators and given a hero's welcome in some towns.

Kiev was captured in September 1941 and soon after the whole country was occupied by Nazi forces. Knowing the advantage of raw materials in Ukraine, Stalin called for a scorched earth policy in the Red Army's retreat. All political prisoners were shot, electricity plants destroyed, factories blown up and mines flooded.

The three-year Nazi occupation of Ukraine was brutal and exploitative. The collective farms of Ukraine were now feeding the Third Reich, and the Germans had a particular interest in such a fertile land. A common anecdote tells of train-loads of rich Ukrainian topsoil being shipped to Germany. Two million Ukrainians were also exported to Germany as forced labour. These *Ostarbeiter* (Eastern Workers) lived as slaves during the war, but were met with suspicion or imprisoned upon returning for their 'collaboration' in capitalist Germany.

There were approximately one and a half million Jews in Ukraine prior to the war. Days after the Nazi invasion, the calculated killing of Jews commenced. The majority of Ukraine's Jews were not sent to concentration camps, but rather were collected, shot and buried in mass graves. The 'final solution' was the annihilation of Ukraine's thousand-year-old Jewish community. Controversy surrounds the level of Ukrainian collaboration in the Holocaust and with the Nazis in general. Anti-Semitism has a long history in Ukraine, and many of the massacres on Jews were in fact carried out by the Ukrainians. Like the civil war, there was someone fighting for everything – Jews, Poles, Germans and Russians were all targets. Sizeable partisan armies fought against both Germans and the Soviet Army in attempts to liberate Ukraine.

By 1943 the Soviet Army returned to Ukraine. Kharkiv was lost and re-conquered twice in a series of notorious tank battles on the Eastern Front. Within six months, only the environs of Galicia remained in German hands. At the Yalta Conference of 1945, held in Crimea, Galicia and Volhynia were designated to the USSR from Poland. One million Poles moved to the new Poland, while half a million Ukrainians relocated to the Ukrainian SSR. The borderlands of Transcarpathia and Bukovyna were also incorporated. At the war's end, it was figured that one out of every six citizens of the Ukrainian SSR was killed in World War II.

Khrushchev

United in anger towards the German fascists, Stalin was able to direct the people's emotions towards rebuilding a wrecked country. Hundreds of war memorials still stand as symbols of overcoming one form of oppression in Ukraine. The mood was one of frenzy and inevitability. What had been destroyed had to be rebuilt quickly. Millions of Russians moved south to Ukraine, mostly to work in the factories. Cities exploded with growth.

Stalin died in 1953 and Nikita Khrushchev took his place at the helm of the communist party. Khrushchev was Russian by birth, but had climbed the political ladder in Ukraine, playing an instrumental role in the Kiev purges and overseeing the economic reconstruction in that republic. He had a folksy appreciation of the land and wore embroidered Ukrainian shirts and liked to hear Ukrainian songs on his visits. Khrushchev also liked to wax lyrical about the Slavic brotherhood of Ukraine and Russia. The year 1954 marked the 300th anniversary of the Pereyaslav Agreement between Khmelnytsky and the tsar. Big celebrations were planned and the communist party issued '13 theses' that spelled out the everlasting union of the Ukrainians and the Russians. As a commemoration gift, Khrushchev annexed

Crimea to Ukraine. Most Russians say that he was drunk at the time. In fact, the Crimea proved to be a loaded present.

Khrushchev gained in popularity when he denounced Stalin and introduced the 'thaw' – a period of relaxed censorship and general freedom. The standard of living improved, and many families were given their own flats after decades of living in communal housing. The cookie-cutter concrete slab apartment buildings seen from Lviv to Vladivostok are Khrushchev's doing. In Russian, they were nicknamed '*khrushchoby*' – the general secretary's name crossed with the word for slum. They may be ugly, but the Soviet Union successfully housed its entire population in a very short time. Khrushchev moved between relaxing his grip then tightening the reins on Soviet society. The intelligentsia were periodically targeted, as were the churches.

The last decade of Soviet rule in Ukraine was one of decline and stagnation. The weaknesses of the centralised government only made the autonomy of Ukraine and the other republics more evident. Brezhnev was old and ill during his time as general secretary and both Chernenko and Andropov died soon after coming to power. These leaders were the old political élite who still glorified Stalin and ignored the telltale signs of internal degradation.

PERESTROIKA AND INDEPENDENCE

The young reformer, Mikhail Gorbachev, then claimed the highest seat in the communist party in 1985. He held a firm belief in the superiority of socialism, but also had a distinct resolve to transform the clumsiness and rigidity of the Soviet Union. *Glasnost* (Openness) allowed more freedom of expression than previously seen in the USSR. The reforms of *Perestroika* (Reconstruction) liberalised the economy and decentralised the political structure like never before.

On April 26 1986, the Chernobyl nuclear plant exploded 100km north of Kiev. The initial disaster was expounded by the reluctance of the government to confess the accident. Only after nearly a week did knowledge of the event reach the very people that were in the greatest danger. Hundreds died from the first heavy doses of radiation, but the real tragedy lay in the countless living with chronic ailments and the thousands of deformed children born in the following months. While the power plant was a Soviet plant, it was located in Ukraine and the Ukrainians found that they would suffer most for it. The Soviet government proved ineffectual in remedying the situation, and Chernobyl is still Ukraine's festering sore. The ecological damage is permanent, but the long-term effects on the people are still unknown.

Nationalist sentiment grew more vocal as people tested their boldness with Glasnost. In the summer of 1988, thousands gathered on several occasions in Lviv and Kiev with a variety of protests, but mostly for autonomy. This was probably the last time the KGB arrested anyone for being pro-Ukrainian.

All over the Soviet Union, people from every republic were speaking their mind and their message was freedom, but not necessarily independence. Gorbachev had never intended things to go this far and he tried frantically to keep some order to the union. In September 1989, the Ukrainian nationalist party, Rukh, was founded as an opposition to the communist party in Ukraine. Gorbachev fired Ukraine's leading communist, Shcherbytsky, realising that repression of Ukrainian self-determination only hurt his position with the other republics. In 1990, democratic elections were permitted for the first time at the republican level. The Supreme Soviet, or Verkhovna Rada in Ukrainian, would be open to non-communist parties.

In 1990, students from Lviv and Kiev camped out on the newly christened Maidan Nazelezhnosti (Place of Independence) and began a hunger strike calling for swift and major changes, including a stop to military service outside Ukraine and nationalisation of communist party property. Joined by politicians from Rukh, the demonstration was successful and the changes announced in the Rada.

Meanwhile in Moscow, communist hardliners were conspiring against the liberal reforms. In August of 1991, Gorbachev was vacationing with his family in Foros, Crimea, when he was put under house arrest and a state of emergency declared for the whole Soviet Union. The ringleaders of the coup sought to put the communist party back on track and prove Gorbachev a traitor. The Ukrainian communists could either comply and fall under a supposed new dictatorship, or support the 'democrats' in the party and split the Soviet Union. The Chairman of the Rada, Leonid Kravchuk, finally denounced the coup right before it failed. The collapse of the central government in Moscow left Ukrainian communists to rush for a decision on total independence and keep some aspect of authority in their own territory. The voting was almost unanimous, and on August 24 1991, Ukraine was declared independent. Gorbachev made a final effort to keep some sort of union alive, but, in a hunting lodge outside Minsk, Yeltsin made a secret agreement with Kravchuk and Belarussian Chairman Shushkevich that put the ineffectual CIS into place. The Soviet Union ceased to exist.

THE LAST DECADE

Kravchuk was elected president at the end of 1991 and it seemed the same communist administration was in place as before, only under a different name. Privatisation of the country's wealth was a monument to shady deals, and a stark few turned astronomically wealthy overnight. Organised crime unashamedly ran business enterprises but seemed to be the only kind of organisation in the country. Mafia shootings were no longer shocking and corruption was the norm at all levels of government.

The following years were painful. Inflation rocketed to over ten thousand percent. Cut-out paper coupons were printed as a temporary currency and made invalid before they'd come into wide use. People continued to go to work but received no salaries. The shops were either empty or closed, and food or clothing could be bought only on the streets. Winters were the hardest with heat and electricity rationed. Russia threatened to shut off the gas supply to Ukraine when the country could not pay its bills.

Kuchma was elected in July 1994 as a progressive alternative to the communist party. He was reported to dedicate hours to learning Ukrainian during his campaign in order to appeal to the hard-core nationalists of the west, but his support came mostly from his home town, the very industrial and Russian-speaking city of Dnepropetrovsk.

For a very short while, there were some fears Ukraine would split down the middle. Ukrainians in the west were speaking Ukrainian and feeling European. In the east, Russian speakers longed nostalgically for the convenience of the Soviet Union. The propaganda of Ukrainian culture began to dominate. Street names were changed and children nationwide started reciting Shevchenko at school. The new constitution appeared in newspapers everywhere in 1996 declaring Ukrainian as the only official state language – but most people couldn't read it.

Kuchma was re-elected in 1999, but his presidency was soon tangled in scandal when it was suspected he was behind the brutal killing of Ukrainian journalist, Georgy Gongadze. The crime has yet to be solved. The murders of other journalists were thought to be connected to the presidency and then it was revealed the president was also connected to a private weapons deal with Saddam Hussein's Iraq, in breach of international sanctions. In October 2002, the communist party led days of protest in Kiev against Kuchma's corruption and abuse of power. NATO 'uninvited' the Ukrainian president to its Prague summit that year, but Kuchma attended anyway, inspiring a last-minute switch from English to French seating cards so that the United Kingdom and United States would not be seated next to Ukraine. Since then, Kuchma's reign has become decisively less democratic.

Overall, independent Ukraine has made big changes in a very short time. The economic situation has stabilised, democracy is steadily finding its way and Ukrainians seem more hopeful about the future. But ten years is too short a time to be making generalisations and today the story of Ukraine still continues as it has for centuries. On one level, everything has begun to match the 'Developed' world, but scratch the surface and the timelessness of earlier struggles is revealed. This turbulent past has cultivated a superhuman patience in Ukrainians so that the nation's deep resolve seems tied only to those things with proven regularity: the seasons, their families, and the ability to survive.

For the first time in their history, Ukrainians are allowed to know all of their history, so that a current sense of national rediscovery inspires both those who live here and travellers from abroad. It is difficult to go anywhere in Ukraine and not feel overcome by all that has transpired in this place.

The Ukrainians

PEOPLE

Anyone who has been to Ukraine knows that getting to know people is far more important than visiting any prescribed sights. Long after you've forgotten the name of some church in Kiev, you will recall individuals and their stories, even if your conversations were carried on by made-up sign language. The title 'Ukrainians' is meant to include everyone and anyone that lives in Ukraine – a truly diverse gathering of 49 million people. Ethnic Ukrainians make up the majority, but even that majority is made up of various shades of 'Ukrainian-ness'. The classic caricature of the Zaporizhian Cossack is still perceived as the ultimate Ukrainian personage, but travellers will find Ukrainians to be lots of things: a Poltava cabbage farmer, a Kiev professor, a Crimean Tatar, an Odessa Jew, a Galician student, or a Russian coal miner.

Only a few, very broad, generalisations are worthy of describing Ukraine's people:

Ukrainians live closely to the earth. Every season has meaning, as does the blossoming of each plant. Urban Ukrainians will leave the city during the summer to live in their small cottages (*dacha*) and to work their individual plots. Most Ukrainians survive the winter by eating food they have produced themselves.

As with most societies, families play a key role in Ukrainian life. Members of an extended family depend on one another, a strong support network that goes far beyond the limitations of the West's independence and rugged individualism. Grandparents may raise children, young people look after the elderly and food and cash are shared all around.

Ukrainians like to have a good time by eating and drinking, singing songs, and telling stories and jokes. They like to talk a lot and most have a natural intellectual bent manifest in their conversational musings. By custom, Ukrainians are very hospitable and will gladly open their home to a stranger they have just met and trusted. Guests are always offered some sort of refreshment – at least tea, if not a meal.

Language

Ukrainian is the official language, except in Donbas where Russian is officially recognised and in Crimea, where both Russian and Tatar are recognised (and spoken). The Russian language is still used throughout much of the country, but Ukrainian is coming into wider use with the growth of national consciousness. In the Carpathians, there are areas where Romanian, Hungarian and Polish are spoken.

Ukrainian is an Indo-European language of the Eastern Slavic family of languages. The original root language is now referred to as Old Church Slavonic, as it is still used in the Orthodox liturgy. Discernible versions of Russian, Ukrainian and Belarusian had emerged from Slavonic by the mid-12th century. Two Byzantine missionaries, St Cyril and St Methodius travelled to Ukraine in the

THE UKRAINIAN CALENDAR

Names for the months in Ukrainian bear no relevance to the Roman calendar, although Russian has adapted the Latin names. The Ukrainian year follows nature's tempo as a simple but poetic remark to earth's changes.

English	Ukrainian	Root and meaning
January	Sichen	*cut*; a cutting wind
February	Lyuti	*fierce*; cold and biting
March	Berezen	*birch*; the birch forests begin to bud
April	Kviten	*flowers* blossom
May	Traven	the *grass* grows
June	Cherven	*worms* crawl from the earth
July	Lypen	the *lime tree* blossoms; flowers are collected for tea
August	Serpen	*sickle*; the harvest begins
September	Veresen	the *heather* blossoms
October	Zhovten	*yellow*; wheat fields and forest leaves turn yellow
November	Lystopad	literally, *falling leaves*
December	Hruden	*balls* of snow fall

late 9th century and established a written language for the land, hence the Cyrillic alphabet, which combines Greek and Latin letters to fit Slavic sounds.

After centuries of linguistic repression, it has become very important for Ukrainians to speak Ukrainian in a show of independence and solidarity. Everything is written in Ukrainian and in most of western Ukraine people will only speak Ukrainian. However, Russian is also an important language in Ukraine, and visitors often wonder how similar/different the two languages actually are. The closest comparison to the relationship between Russian and Ukrainian might be Spanish and Portuguese. Ukrainians tend to have no problem understanding Russians, while the opposite is rarely true. Ukrainian sounds much softer and is much more poetic in some respects, while Russian has benefited from centuries of high culture and literature during which time Ukrainian was spoken mainly by the rural peasant population. Ukraine's politics of language is all very controversial right now, so its best to learn a little of each. You'll find many people speak a fairly common mixture of the two, called *surzhyk*.

UKRAINIAN CULTURE

Ukrainian culture is evident everywhere you travel in the country, but most of what tourists will want to see is present only during country festivals, holidays or in more traditional areas. Allowing for exceptions, older Ukrainian traditions and customs are followed with more gusto in western Ukraine (Podillya, Galicia, Volhynia and the Carpathians), central Ukraine (Poltava and Cherkasy region) and throughout most rural areas.

Symbols

Ukraine's official coat of arms is a gold **trident** (*tryzub*) on a blue field, probably linked to the Greek god of the sea, Poseidon. Prince Rurik of Kievan Rus was said to use the same symbol and old coins and bricks from the period of Prince

Vladimir are also decorated with the trident. In the small bursts of independence in 1918 and in the Carpathians during 1939, the trident was re-adopted to show separatism from ruling powers. During the late Soviet period, nationalist demonstrators would flash 'trident' hand symbols with their three middle fingers held apart. The national emblem was made official in 1992. You will see it everywhere and on everything.

Plants, animals and trees are also important symbols for Ukrainians. The **sunflower** has always been used to represent Ukraine, and if you visit in summer you will see why. The *lipa* (lime tree or linden) is considered the most important and symbolic of Ukrainian trees, and Ukrainians use the flowers and leaves for all kinds of herbal remedies. The **sickle** of the Soviet flag actually comes from Ukraine where it has always been an important symbol of the country's traditional agricultural lifestyle. Ukraine's own **flag** does look a lot like the Ukrainian landscape: a light blue sky over a golden field of wheat or sunflowers. The origins however date back to the Hapsburg monarchy in 1848 when the Supreme Ruthenian Council adopted the flag of a golden lion on a blue background. The lion eventually disappeared but the colours stayed. Cossack flags were generally red and white, and various nationalist peasant and anarchist bands have used banners of red, green and black.

National dress

The Ukrainian national costume typically is worn only for festivals and ceremonies (like weddings) but is the most prominent display of culture for most people. Traditionally, women wear a white embroidered tunic over which a scarlet woven *platya* (skirt) is wrapped and secured with a colourful belt. The ensemble is completed with leather boots, a flowered head wreath with long coloured ribbons and several red clay, beaded necklaces. Men wear baggy Cossack-style trousers tucked into low boots, a long silk sash belt and the traditional *rubakha,* an open cotton shirt with intricate embroidery around the neck. A recent fad has Ukrainian businessmen substituting the sober shirt and tie of the West with the more colourful *rubakha*.

Arts

Classic romantic painting did not feature as strongly in Ukraine as it did among the European élite of Paris and St Petersburg, but there are a few important exceptions. Repin and Aivozovsky are the most renowned Ukrainian painters, and you'll find most art museums have at least one of their pieces, along with well-intentioned collections of other Ukrainian-themed paintings. Soviet Ukrainian propaganda is only now being widely considered an art-form, with its colourful posters and sober messages. A few permanent exhibits of Soviet artwork exist in Kiev and some souvenir shops sell prints.

The most traditional form of Ukrainian painting is that of the floral motif, usually painted on black lacquered platters or, in some areas, around the doorways and windows of homes. Colours are always bright, and the designs symmetrical and full.

Although religious in theme, icon-painting is very much the ultimate Ukrainian form of rendering human images. Figures or faces of Christ, Mary, the apostles and saints are painted on wood and sometimes decorated with gold. Important Orthodox icon-painting schools existed in Kiev and Chernihiv, which have set the standard for most Slavic icon imagery today. In homes, icons are placed in the corner of a room, usually opposite the door, and a small sheaf of wheat is placed underneath to ensure peace and prosperity for that home. Traditionally, this sheaf

UKRAINE VERSUS RUSSIA

Ukraine is NOT Russia. Just like Canada is not America, and Scotland is not England, Ukraine is too often defined by the shadow of its powerful neighbour. The last decade exhibits Ukraine's longest recognised independence, attributed by many to keeping Russia at bay in the post-Soviet era. In Ukraine, attitudes towards Russia range from friendly association to deep animosity, although most families embody the microcosm of a bi-national relationship: one parent might be Russian, the other Ukrainian, and relatives can be found on both sides of the border. In general, the two countries are neither too distantly related for total cultural separation, nor different enough to get along.

For now, Ukraine's recognised independence from Russia is the most important fact in the relationship and many Ukrainians now embrace everything that sets Ukraine apart from Russia. People will be quick to tell you that Russian civilisation was actually founded in Kiev, that Ukrainian is the older and more sophisticated Slavic language, and that famous Russian writers, or great Soviet leaders, were born and bred in Ukraine. Ukrainians like to consider their homeland inhabited by the more spirited and unconventional of the Slavs.

The current government-sanctioned cultural renaissance promotes all things Ukrainian, while Russian is somewhat politically incorrect. At school, children make cut-out paper sunflowers and learn Ukrainian folk dances. All official government business is conducted in the Ukrainian language and most place names have been changed, if only by one letter. This separate national consciousness has energised society somewhat, but has also led to feelings of self-alienation for those who's culture is more closely linked to Russia. The slang term Russians use for a Ukrainian is *Khokhol*, from the Tatar words for blue and yellow. In return, the Ukrainians will refer (rudely) to Russians as *Kotsap*, meaning 'Little Goat', but having the same effect as 'jackass' in English. Hopefully, a more comfortable cultural balance will emerge, but travellers should be sensitive to the past struggle of Ukrainian cultural survival as they witness the present show of nationalism. Keep in mind that, whatever Ukraine may be, it is not Russia, but it is the intertwining of the two histories and cultures that makes Ukraine such a fascinating place to explore.

was cut from the last sheaf of good grain and tied with a ribbon during *Obzhynky*, the Harvest Festival.

Handicraft

Ukraine's greatest artistic expression comes alive in the everyday experience of work and survival. For example, the large tile stoves of traditional Ukrainian homes were always the warmest part of the house. In winter, a family would spend most of the day (and night) on top of the warmed tiles. For a few centuries, painted stove tiles were revered as a high art from.

Eggs hold all kinds of symbolic meanings for Ukrainians, and eggs are often used in fortune-telling or folk cures. The quintessential Ukrainian craft is the decoration of *pysanky*, or Easter eggs. After blowing out the yolk and white from a small hole in the shell, melted wax and different coloured dyes are used in a batik-like process to produce a layered pattern of intricate designs. Traditional patterns are usually geometric or show basic representations of flowers or animals. Like all Ukrainian art, *pysanky* vary from region to region, and the craft has been kept alive largely by the diaspora.

Rushniki are the most basic art-form in Ukraine but the most widespread in tradition. Calling them 'hand towels' doesn't do them justice, although technically that's what they are. The long white clothes are embroidered with bands at either end in simple geometric patterns. Traditional designs and colours differ by region. Mothers are supposed to embroider *rushniki* for their sons before they leave home, and a young bride will be sure to embroider enough for her trousseau. In Ukrainian homes, the clothes are used for special occasions: holiday meals, for holding newborn children or for a christening, for weddings, for welcoming guests with bread and salt, and for shrouds at funerals. In many Ukrainian churches, *rushniki* are draped over the icons and altars.

Rather than cover the whole piece of material, Ukrainian embroidery decorates only the edges of simple white cloth with colourful geometric designs cross-stiched around the wrists, hems and neckline. Designs vary, but besides triangular and diagonal shapes, crosses, flowers and leaves are traditional. In the Carpathians, animal shapes hold special meaning.

Ukrainian woodcarving is either intentionally crude and rough, or else incredibly refined and inlaid with beads or shells. Small shaped boxes and lids are customary, along with bowls, plates, spoons, combs and pipes.

Literature

Taras Shevchenko is Ukraine's national hero and eternal poet laureate who wrote *Kobzar*, esteemed as the greatest written work in the Ukrainian language. His statue and portrait are ubiquitous and, as a rule, children memorise his poetry at school. Nikolai Gogol, author of *Dead Souls* and *An Inspector Calls* is probably better known in the West. His short stories take place in Ukraine's countryside and describe well the superstitious world of Ukrainians. Lesya Ukrayinka, whose pen name means 'Ukrainian forest' started the writer's circle called the 'Pleiades' and wrote lyrical poetry in Ukrainian while there was a ban on the language. Most cities have streets named after her, if not a memorial. Writers like Kotlyarevsky and Kotsyubinsky also wrote during a time of linguistic repression and their homes now stand as national shrines. Ukraine's literary canon also includes Russian writers like Pushkin and Chekhov who wrote and lived in Ukraine for part of their lives. Ukrainians hold writers in high esteem and every town will boast about the famous men and women who might have stayed there. Few people know that the English/Polish writer Joseph Conrad was also born in Ukraine, and Balzac spent a good deal of time in the country.

Ukraine enjoys a 98% literacy rate and the people enjoy reading. Writing and reciting poetry is also a national hobby. Owning books is a status symbol and most individuals harbour vast libraries in the smallest of apartments with Ukrainian, Russian and international literature. Soviet culture also permitted the reading of approved Western writers, namely Ernest Hemingway, John Steinbeck, Jack London and Sir Conan Doyle, so you will hear them mentioned often.

Folk dancing

At weddings, holidays, festivals or indeed any day, dancing is a very important part of celebrating. Folk dances are normally conducted by large groups of paired couples, but different dances have evolved from specific regional terrains. The wide open spaces of the Ukrainian steppe influenced the unique style of folk dancing that involves running, leaping and people forming extensive circles.

IMMIGRATION

There are millions and millions of Ukrainians who do not live in Ukraine, following a number of emigrations throughout Ukraine's bumpy history. The largest and most well-known Ukrainian community is in Canada, concentrated in the western province of Alberta. This prominent Canadian-Ukrainian population has been instrumental in supporting Ukraine's present cultural rebirth. Several Ukrainian communities also thrive in the United States in cities like Baltimore, Cleveland and, most recently, in Brighton Beach, New York. Both Argentina and Australia have significant Ukrainian settlements as well. Among these communities you will always find a number of Ukrainian Orthodox churches, *banya* (baths), folk dance troupes, Ukrainian markets and schools. Needless to say, cultural preservation at any cost has kept these communities alive for more than a century.

Dances from the mountainous Carpathians are performed in small circles and involve more fancy footwork and jumping up and down. Ukraine's national dance is the *hopak*, a very energetic ensemble where women spin and encircle the men, who perform a number of difficult acrobatic stunts in the front, including the well-known squat kicks and split jumps of the Cossacks. Traditional Cossack dances excluded women and the *hopak* was originally a stage for physical competition between the warriors. Now, nearly every folk dance performance will include at least part of the *hopak* in a charged mood of dancing, clapping and very fast music. Larger folk dance troupes tend to be based in Kiev, western Ukraine and around Poltava, where so many Ukrainian dances originated.

Music

Ukrainians sing when they are very happy and when they are very sad. It seems as though the centuries of upheaval favoured the preservation of songs to any other kind of material culture, and if there is anything that brings Ukrainians together, it is their music. Today, most Ukrainians sing at large gatherings: birthday parties, weddings and holidays. Once started, they can sing for hours and everyone in the room (of all ages) will know all the lyrics and the accompanying harmony.

The traditional Ukrainian instrument is the large tear-shaped *bandura*, normally with 60 strings. Strummed like a harp and tuned like a guitar, the *bandura's* music has an enchanting sound. Once played by the Cossacks, today you see buskers playing them in the streets and subway stations. Traditionally, blind children were taught to play and sing historical and religious songs in order that they might have an occupation. Named *kobzari* for the lute-like *kobzar* they played, these bards walked from village to village playing on request in exchange for food and alms. Many of the songs you hear date back to the era of the *kobzari* with a series of short stanzas that tell a staggered story, sometimes through dialogue. It is not uncommon for a set tune to have over a dozen verses, with repeated choruses in between. The music is always in a minor key, which adds a melancholy tone.

Ukrainian folks songs are normally about love, vodka, or love and vodka. Some are ironic and humorous, but most are wistful or solemn. 'Kozak Viyizhdzhaye' is the dialogue of a weeping girl and her Cossack, who is about to ride off into the unprotected 'wild field' of Ukraine. She begs to go with him, and in each verse he asks her what she will eat, where she will sleep, what she will do in far off Ukraine? In 'Oi Verbo, Verbo!' a young maiden sings to a weeping willow tree, telling of her betrothal to the town drunkard and her plans to run away on a horse. Today, most people sing with a classic Russian guitar, accordion or without any accompaniment. Soviet folk songs also add to the national repertoire, and almost every adult male can sing you a song about being homesick and lonely out on the front.

If you want to buy some good folk music, check the tables on the Maidan Nezalezhnosti in Kiev. Most of these sellers are from western Ukraine and are showing their patriotism by acquainting tourists with Ukrainian culture. Mariya Burmaka is one of the greatest Ukrainian folk singers, and her earlier cassettes add a fitting soundtrack to the landscape. Nina Matviyenko is known best for her haunting voice and pre-Christian folk songs, and most music dealers will have her recordings, as well as those of folk singer, Mariya Mykolaychyk.

Traditional religious music is integral to Ukrainian culture and there are few sounds more celestial than an Orthodox choir singing. The singers normally stand in a small balcony in the back of the church by the entrance and respond to the priest throughout the service. Most churches and monasteries will have recordings of Orthodox chants and singing for sale.

Ukraine's national anthem is entitled 'She Ne Vmerla Ukrayina' ('Ukraine is yet alive') and is meant to reinforce the country's perseverance through suffering. The anthem is played morning and night on the national radio station in the same fashion of the old Soviet anthem.

Ukrainian pop music is going full force in its artistic licence, sometimes mixing folk elements into modern beats (I recommend Iryna Bilyk). The Russian techno music you hear in taxis, marketplaces and long bus rides has a giveaway polka bass line that will stay in your head long after you've left the country.

BELIEFS AND RELIGION
Orthodoxy
For most Ukrainians, Orthodoxy and nationality are one and the same. Ukrainian Orthodoxy asserts that theirs is the original church of ancient Kievan Rus, brought to them by the Apostle Andrew and that the union of Slavic culture and Christianity was destined to occur in Ukraine. By nature, Ukrainian Orthodoxy is also highly mystical and meditative, and Ukrainians employ the outer rituals of prayer, fast and iconography as methods towards a deeper spiritual process. The religion's philosophy is based largely on the writings of the early Christians and Gnostics of the wider Middle East, as well as a millennium of Slavic monastic work.

Orthodox **saints** (svyaty) are the holiest of religious symbols and most churches will hold at least one body of a saint, a physical remnant or an icon. Different saints perform different functions, for instance, Nikolai the Miracle Worker is popular in times of need or emergency. People will visit his icon in the church, pray to it and post a candle near it. Posting candles is both a sign of faith and an offering, and every church will sell different sizes of long beeswax candles for different degrees of prayer.

Icons are central to Orthodox worship and are much more than a picture of a favourite saint. Painted on wood or covered with gold and silver-plating, blessed icons carry holy powers of protection, healing and fortune. Believers visit and pray to icons in churches and monasteries and most taxi or bus drivers will keep an icon on their rear-view mirror to protect their vehicle. In homes, icons are placed in the top of the farthest corner opposite the door of a room to bless and protect the family's space.

Traditional Orthodox church buildings are built in the shape of a Greek cross. Those from the Byzantine era were made of stone with the typical rounded domes of the period. Traditional churches from the 15th to the 17th century are usually built from wooden beams criss-crossed in log-cabin style and fitted only with joints and pegs (no nails). Younger cathedrals are larger and made of stone, brick and mosaic with the onion-shaped domes normally associated with Orthodoxy. On the inside, most churches have a highly decorated *iconostas*, covered with images of the saints and closing off the back apse of the church. Only priests are allowed behind this sacred wall.

A normal Orthodox Sunday mass lasts about two and a half hours. Prayers are chanted and a small choir sings out chilling responses while aromatic *ladan* (incense) smoke fills the church. You'll notice there are no chairs inside, because it is considered a sin to pray or worship sitting down. Instead, believers will stand or periodically prostrate themselves on the ground. All night vigils and extra-long church services are not unusual, and the faithful will continue to stand for up to seven hours. Shorter services during morning and evening weekdays are easier times to visit. Taking part in an Orthodox church service is an amazing experience and travellers should make it a priority during their stay in Ukraine. The problem is that most churches do not appreciate having tourists running around untethered. Only visit churches with a spirit of reverence: men should remove their hats and women are supposed to cover their heads. Even if the church's interior is beautiful, taking photographs indoors (especially during a service) is very offensive. You can avoid conspicuousness by buying a candle and lighting it in front of your favourite icon as you are walking around the church.

The Soviet era was a time of severe religious repression, but now Orthodoxy has become the most important sign of patriotism and independence. Society now divides itself among *verushy* and *neverushy* (believers and non-believers) and nearly every town will have at least one new church under construction. So much of the religious architecture that tourists see today was only renovated in the last five years, but historically Ukraine has always been considered the more spiritual country (compared to Russian Orthodoxy). In the USSR, Ukraine had more churches than all the other republics put together and a majority of Orthodox clergymen were Ukrainian. Two of the most holy sites in Slavic Orthodoxy are located in Ukraine: Kiev's Pechersky Lavra (Caves Monastery) and the Pochayiv Monastery near Ternopil. Today, in terms of numbers of physical churches, Ukrainian Orthodoxy is the largest Orthodox Church in the world; however, three separate Ukrainian churches consider themselves the Ukrainian Orthodox Church, and the government recognises four:

Ukrainian Orthodox Church (Moscow Patriarchate)

Throughout the Russian Empire and the Soviet Union, the church and Christianity fell under the jurisdiction of Moscow. After independence, the Ukrainian Orthodox Church that still recognised Moscow's ecclesiastical authority was named as such, and it is still the largest Church in the country. Followers exist all over Ukraine, but its presence is largest in Russian-speaking areas of the east and Crimea, though it still owns churches all over. In order to appeal to some Ukrainians, a few parishes are Ukrainian-speaking, but traditionally, all services are read in Old Church Slavonic. The Caves Monastery in Kiev is the headquarters of this church in Ukraine.

Ukrainain Orthodox Church (Kiev Patriarchate)

In an attempt to break away from Russian influence after independence, the Ukrainian metropolitan (with the government's help) formed an independent Orthodox Church in 1992 with the intent to offer a centrist version of Ukrainian culture that coincided with the political movement towards Ukrainian unity. The Moscow Patriarch excommunicated the Kiev Patriarch for his rebellion and both churches still bicker about property and territory. St Mikhayil's Monastery of the Golden Domes and St Vladimir's Cathedral in Kiev are the Church's most prominent sights.

Greek Catholics (Uniate)

During the centuries of Polish rule in western Ukraine, the Orthodox believers made a symbolic compromise in order to appease the government and preserve their culture. The Ruthenians agreed to pay allegiance to the pope in Rome, but they would keep their Ukrainian Orthodox doctrine and service. The church was made illegal in 1946 but officially reinstated when Gorbachev met with the pope in 1989. Greek Catholic beliefs are a mixture of old Byzantium and Galician folk culture. Concentrated in western Ukraine and the Carpathians, Greek Catholics tend to promote a strong nationalist culture. St George's Cathedral in Lviv is their ecclesiastical centre. To identify a Greek Catholic church, look for any tapestry or picture of the pope and the absence of the habitual Orthodox iconostas. In western Ukraine, Roman Catholics are called 'Polish Catholics'.

Ukrainian Autocephalous Orthodox Church

During the window of Ukrainian independence at the time of the Russian civil war, nationally conscious Ukrainian believers sought autocephaly (self-rule) from the Russian Church, believing they should be able to worship in their own language. The Church was formed in 1919, but later fell victim to Stalin's early repression of nationalities and the Church was declared illegal in 1930. The Autocephalous Church survived in exile, mainly through the Ukrainian diaspora in North America, although the Church was said to meet frequently in Ukraine in the forest. The state gave official recognition to the Church in 1993. Like the Greek Catholic, the Autocephalous is concentrated in western Ukraine and is the most nationalist of Ukraine's churches. UAO churches are most easily recognised for their exquisite embroidered *rushniki* used as simple but powerful decorations (although some Greek Catholic churches also have *rushniki*).

Other beliefs

Many scholars believe that **Judaism** came to Europe from the Middle East via Ukraine. In the 19th century there were over 3 million Jews in Ukraine; today there remain about 250,000. Synagogues can be found in the cities of west and east Ukraine, many of which have just recently been returned to the local Jewish communities. **Baptists** constitute Ukraine's traditional form of evangelical Christianity, brought by missionaries over a hundred years ago. The Crimean Tatars are Sunni Muslims by faith so that **Islam** holds a visible presence in Crimea. As much of southwestern Ukraine was the frontier of prolonged war with the Turks, many of the castles and even some former churches in the region were once mosques. Since independence, Ukraine has seen a flood of missionary activity and a significant rise in religious pluralism. Slavic **paganism** has come back into open practice in recent years among small non-conformist groups, but with all due respect, most Ukrainian spirituality is already deeply rooted in early paganism.

The supernatural

Despite a national pride of all things scientific and factual, a world of superstition rules the lives of many Ukrainians. Be prepared to pick up a few of your own during your travels.

SANCTIONED SUPERSTITIONS

- Never shake hands through a doorway. Doing so is a sign of insincerity, misfortune and ill will to the other person.
- Never cross paths with or move ahead of a funeral procession (even buses will wait until they pass). Doing so means you are searching for death.
- Whistling indoors means all your money will fly out the window.
- When you see a baby, do not faun over the child, look the baby directly in the eye or tell the parent how cute and precious the baby is. It is bad luck – the child may get sick and you may inadvertently pass on the evil eye.
- Never give an even number of flowers – it symbolises death.
- To avoid jinxing yourself when tempting providence, spit over your left shoulder.
- Sit down before leaving on a long journey. Rushing off brings bad luck on the road.

Orthodoxy and the trappings of organised religion have done little to hide the Ukrainian cultural connection between the natural and supernatural spheres, and between the pagan and Christian. According to Ukrainian tradition, all forms of nature have a spiritual personality: there are spirits in the fields and in the trees and evil water nymphs in the rivers called *rusalky*. The spiritual world can either help or harm, but most people just notice the harm.

The *nechysta sila* ('unclean power') is the cause of all wickedness, evil and human woes and can be avoided only through spiritual *zaschyta* ('protection') that stems from a combination of Christian and pagan customs. During Christmas, for example, an axe is placed outside the door to ward off evil spirits. The headache of supernatural ailments is the evil eye, which can affect you in a number of ways: depression, fatigue, toothache, quarrelling with your spouse, bad luck or spoiled food. Wicked people can pass on the evil eye just by looking at you, as can nice people who simply look at you in the wrong way (with jealousy or condescension). The best prevention against the evil eye is by wearing small mirrors under your clothing (front and back) that reflects 'the eye' back to the sender.

Ekstrasensa is the Ukrainian/Russian version of spiritual foresight or ESP. The gifted (usually older women and *babushki*) can look into the future and work things for or against someone's favour through black or white magic. Rituals are based on physical manifestations of metaphysical ideas and usually involve Orthodox icons, bibles and crosses. The use of herbal medicine is also normally combined with some sort of supernatural healing or with the help of 'bio-energy'.

HOLIDAYS

Most traditional Ukrainian holidays fit into a meticulous Orthodox calendar which changes from year to year. **Easter** is the most important of these holidays, and in Ukrainian Orthodoxy, believers will fast for the Lenten period by abstaining from meat and dairy products. All-night church services (standing!) and ritual parades around the church at midnight mark the beginning of the *Velyky Dehn* ('Great Day') and the festivities begin. Tall, yeasty sweet cakes called *paskhy* are baked at home and then brought into the priest for blessing, along with other food and decorated Easter eggs. The traditional greeting is *Yisus Voskres!* ('Christ is Risen!'), to which you are expected to reply *Va Istynno Voskres!* ('Truly, He is Risen!').

Ukrainian **Christmas** is a colourful and mystical holiday, celebrated quite differently from most Christian cultures. On Christmas Eve, single youths will travel from house to house singing *kolyadki,* cheerful Ukrainian carols to wish a good evening and good health to neighbours and friends. Singers will stand beneath the main window of the house, brandishing large sacks and continue singing loudly until the window is opened and the homeowner drops Christmas treats into the bags. The practice goes on well into the night. In the home, a meal of 12 dishes is often served to symbolise the 12 apostles. A single candle is set inside a special braided bread loaf called *kolach* and the family eats *kutya,* a semi-sweet mixture of cooked wheat, honey and poppy seeds eaten only on Christmas Eve.

New Year became the most important holiday of the year during the Soviet era, where emphasis on the first of January detracted from any national or religious recognition of Orthodox Christmas on the seventh. Christmas trees (*yolka* in Russian, *yalynka* in Ukrainian) are put up for New Year and children receive gifts from *Dyed Moroz* (Father Frost) who wears dark blue robes and is accompanied by his helper, the princess *Snigorichka* (Little Snowflake). The evening is marked by a gigantic meal that is meant to last all night long with heavy drinking, singing and dancing (in that order).

The most important summer holiday takes place on midsummer's eve from July 6 until the morning of July 7. **Ivana Kupala** began as a pagan festival in honour of the deity of the summer, *Kupalo,* but the holiday's connotation was shifted towards Christianity's John the Baptist, hence *Ivana* (St John's) *Kupala* (Bathing) and the festival's common translation St John's Eve. Ritual cleansing through fire and water are the main objectives of the evening. In the early evening, medicinal herbs are gathered and couples search in the woods for a special fern that is meant to promise them happiness. Unmarried women are supposed to weave a head wreath of leaves and flowers (*vynok*), place a candle in its centre, and set it into a flowing river. If the wreath floats, she will be married within the next year, if it sinks she will not (*vynok* symbolise love and protection, from whence comes the Ukrainian word for marriage, *vynchaniya*). During the night of Ivana Kupala, participants immerse themselves completely in a lake or stream, and then, later, a roaring bonfire is lit and men and women hold hands and leap over the flames. The fire is meant to heal all ailments, and the couple who keeps their clasp held through the flames will stay together. Ukrainians celebrate Ivana Kupala more than any other pre-Christian holiday.

The Soviet holidays of May 1 (Labour Day) and May 9 (Victory Day) are still widely celebrated with big military parades and fireworks. November 7 (October Revolution) is recognised but most businesses stay open. May 8 (International Women's Day) is celebrated much like Mother's Day in the West. Flowers and cards are presented to women of all ages, and men are supposed to cook for their wives/mothers/girlfriends/sisters.

Births, deaths and weddings

The oak is one of many holy trees in Ukraine, and in the olden days, when a boy was born, a small oak branch was thrown into the water where he was bathed for the first time, so that he would grow up to be strong and solid, like an oak tree. When a girl was born, a clump of red *kalina* berries would be thrown into the water so that she would grow up to be beautiful. Nowadays, the most important event is a baby's baptism performed by an Orthodox priest. Until a baby is baptised, the child is highly susceptible to the evil eye and is more likely to fall ill. Infant baptisms are by immersion and a cross of silver or gold is placed around the child's neck to be worn for life.

GRANNIES

Ukraine's human landscape features an abundance of old ladies who seem to be everywhere and are always very busy sweeping streets, carrying Atlas-sized bundles, or selling things. Why so many? In World War II, the Soviet Union lost over 20 million citizens, the majority of whom were male soldiers. Their sisters, widows and mothers survived, and now make up the majority of the elderly population. No other demographic group in Ukraine has endured as much as these women. After the devastation of the war, they spent their 20s and 30s rebuilding the country, and the rest of their working years keeping the USSR going. They retired just in time for Ukrainian independence and then watched their entire pension repeatedly devalue. Today, most female pensioners receive around US$30 a month and are left with no other choice but to go back to work. Enterprising grannies in their 70s and 80s have had to find ways to supplement their income, usually through very hard work. Many will sell roasted sunflower seeds, flowers, herbs and anything else out on the street. Others undertake hard-labour jobs that pay little but at least pay, and it is not uncommon to see old women carrying pick axes, shovels, or large buckets to a construction site or through the market. *Bábushka* ('grandmother') is the respectful term used to address all elderly women (*babulya* or *babusya* in Ukrainian, or simply *baba*). *Babushki* hold a vital role in Ukrainian culture and society, since most young mothers are expected to work, and traditionally, young married couples live with the bride's parents. In consequence, nearly all Ukrainian children are raised by their grandmothers. Ukrainians think fondly of their grandmothers, and will constantly quote them as a source of wisdom. Grandmothers are responsible for telling grandchildren stories, teaching them folk songs, religion and how to dance. Perhaps detrimental to their own image, grandmothers warn recalcitrant grandchildren of *baba yaga*, an evil grandmother witch who eats children and lives in a house with chicken legs deep in the Ukrainian forest (it works to keep children in their beds).

Grannies also feel compelled to feed others: their families and their guests. Nothing compares to the privilege of eating a meal prepared by a real live *babushka*. For visitors to Ukraine, grannies also present a rare access to living history. Most have lived under the Stalinist regime, some have fought as partisans, and others have built tanks in factories or conducted scientific research in Siberia. They *all* know how to survive. Buying their sunflower seeds or flowers is a nice way to keep the grandmothers in business and if you ever want to give a gift, just think of what your own grandmother would like.

When someone dies, the body will be set in an open coffin so neighbours, friends and family can pay their respects. Funeral processions make long slow parades that follow the deceased (usually on the back of a truck) towards the cemetery. It is bad luck to cross paths with a funeral procession and you will see traffic redirect itself for miles or completely stop. After the burial, families and friends will return at nine days, 40 days and a year after the person's death date, as the spirit of the departed is said to be near the grave during this time. Flowers, candles and food are brought to the graveside and a meal is eaten on site. A small glass of vodka will be placed on the gravestone, from which the spirit will take 'sips' until the glass is empty.

In western Ukraine, a bride-to-be will travel from house to house with her friends all in national dress, inviting people to the wedding, singing folk songs and requesting blessings and good wishes from everyone in the village. Traditional Ukrainian weddings take place in October or November, after the harvest is over. Marriages in churches have come back into practice only during the last decade. During the Soviet period, weddings took place in front of a bust or painting of Lenin in special 'marriage palaces'. After the ceremony, couples would lay a bouquet of flowers near a war memorial or Lenin's statue. These days, the tradition continues, but the flowers are brought to Shevchenko's statue instead. After a vodka toast at a wedding dinner, guests will frequently shout *Gorko!* ('It's sour!'); the bride and groom must kiss one another to sweeten the other's lips. Shouts of *Gorko!* followed by kissing continue throughout the day, even without the vodka toasts. Wedding parties last for days, even after the bride and groom have left on their honeymoon.

FACE TO FACE WITH UKRAINIAN CULTURE
Manners and mannerisms

Ukrainians are incredibly hospitable and generally understand that foreigners are not always privy to their cultural idiosyncrasies. These are a lot more fun to figure out on your own, but here are a few tips:

- Greet each other and introduce yourself as you would anywhere else. If you are a man, do not shake a woman's hand unless it is offered to you. Ukrainians love business cards and will pull them out at any time. Bring some if you have them. When entering someone's home, take off your shoes near the entrance. Normally you will be offered slippers to wear. If you have been invited as a guest, bringing a small gift or flowers is customary.
- Turning down a drink is considered a very rude gesture and for some carries the same weight as refusing to shake hands. If you are a non-drinker or just want to hold back, a determined *nyet* will hardly do the trick. Stating religious or health reasons is met with more understanding and causes less offence. No matter how hardcore one's habits, don't ever expect to keep up with a Ukrainian drink for drink. I have yet to meet a non-Ukrainian who can.
- At birthday parties, weddings, anniversaries, holidays, and generally most gatherings Ukrainians will make poetic toasts to one another and particularly those who are to be honoured. As a foreign guest, toasts will be made to you, and you are expected to toast in return. A mere 'thank you' or 'cheers' just won't do. Be vociferous and flowery, ending with very specific wishes of good will (eg: 'that our most wise and beautiful host discovers secret happiness and fortune throughout the next year').
- Before you eat, say '*Smachnoho!*' (like '*bon appétit*') to the others at the table. As a guest, you will be fed and fed and fed. If you completely empty your plate or bowl, it will be refilled. If you leave too much on your plate, your host will say you don't like his/her cooking and they will be offended. Either way, you can't win.
- The Soviet era created a society that was anything but service-oriented. Dealing with certain concierges, waiters, hotel clerks or ticket sellers can be a taxing experience, especially if you are used to a culture of Western customer service. Being ignored or shouted at can get frustrating. Sometimes it takes making a small fuss to get the attention of the person on the other side of the glass. Being polite but persistent is the best policy.

- Standing in a queue (line) also gets little respect in Ukraine. You may find that after waiting 20 minutes, someone will cut in front of you. Be assertive and try to come across as confident. Always be prepared with your request. If you get to a window and are still fumbling for money or a ticket, then someone else has the right to push you aside and take your place, and they will. When a bus, tram or subway appears, queues disappear and everyone pushes and shoves to get in. If you try to be your version of polite, you may never get on. Learn to throw your body into it and say *izvinitye* ('excuse me') or *probachteh* in Ukrainian.

POVERTY

The people of Ukraine suffered tremendously during the economic crash and social ills of the early post-Perestroika years. In less than ten years after independence, Ukraine's population declined by six million through massive emigration, a swift rise in the death rate and a dramatic drop in the birth rate. Begging is looked down upon culturally, but people still do it, although much less than in most countries. On the other hand, a small percentage of Ukrainian society has become extremely wealthy, especially the *byznesmeny* who got rich quick from privatisation 'deals'. These 'New Russians' are the subject of countless jokes that mock their lack of taste and value. A real middle class is emerging in Ukraine but, overall, people are still quite poor and spend most of their time acquiring the basic needs of life. Coming to terms with dire poverty is something travellers must do all over the world, but in Ukraine the real problem stems from witnessing poverty among such an educated and technologically advanced people. Know that your presence in the country is already a sign of progress. Spend your money wisely, but make sure you spend it. Encouraging small private enterprise through patronage is one of the best ways to 'give something back' during your trip in Ukraine.

Gifts

There is no need to lug an extra suitcase of provisions to hand out to Ukraine's poverty-stricken. You can buy all the basics in the country and a lot more. Gift-giving in Ukraine is sentimental and highly symbolic so don't feel compelled to make an overtly significant contribution. Plus, a lot of Ukrainians believe all foreigners are millionaires, so any irregular display of your financial prowess may bring you uncomfortable demands for sizeable loans or secret explanations of far-fetched business proposals. Token gifts showing appreciation are fine. If you are invited over for dinner, bring a box of chocolates, flowers (odd number) or a bottle of something. Creative and personal gifts will please even more: English books, nifty kitchen gadgets, and any luxury items that hold some merit when from another country (perfume, sports team paraphernalia, tourist knick-knacks).

Preparations 4

WHEN TO VISIT

Despite common misconceptions that Ukraine borders on Siberia and is normally freezing, summer is not the only time to visit. Really, Ukraine has four distinct seasons, and each provides different scenery. Travelling from June to September does promise warmth, sunshine, long days, green fields, leaves on the trees and lots of fresh fruit in the markets. Tourist facilities will also be in full swing and the more colourful cultural festivals take place towards the end of the summer season. Keep in mind that Ukraine gets hotter than you'd expect and air conditioning is still a rare luxury. Spring and fall are generally warm and mild, and the October harvest is the most picturesque moment for Ukraine's countryside. Snow covers the ground from late November until April and the prettiest snowfall occurs in late December. January and February are the coldest months and you must plan your time to correspond with just seven hours of daylight. Travelling in the dead of winter requires a lot more patience but the season is a fact of life in Ukraine, so why not?

You should also consider holidays and festivals you may want to observe during your visit. Orthodox Easter (the weekend following Catholic Easter) is the biggest religious holiday of the year with lots of public display and ritual. May celebrations (May 1 and May 9) involve massive parades that still demonstrate the military fervour of Soviet holidays. For the most Ukrainian of Ukrainian events, Ivana Kupala falls at the end of the first week of July and is celebrated more passionately in western Ukraine. August visitors to eastern Ukraine will witness the sunflower fields in full bloom. The Christmas/New Year holiday is the very worst time to get around since the whole country shuts down for nearly two weeks, everything is booked up and everyone is inebriated. If you are in the country, stay in one place and join the party. Crimea sees its biggest tourist rush during July and August. If you want to avoid crowds on the peninsula but still catch the heat, go in June or September. The best time to hike the Carpathians is in late spring or fall when there is little rain and the animals are most active.

Public holidays

Modern Ukrainian holidays are a blend of traditional religious holidays, old and new Ukrainian national festivals, and Soviet anniversaries. Most business are closed on the following:

January 1	New Year's Day
January 7	Ukrainian Christmas
January 14	Old New Year's Day (By the pre-revolutionary calendar. Why end the party?)
March 8	Women's Day
May 1	May Day (celebrating workers' solidarity and the pagan rites of spring)

May 9   Victory Day (A jubilant tribute to the end of World War II)
August 24   Ukrainian Independence Day
November 7   Anniversary of the Great October Revolution

In addition, there is at least one Orthodox holiday for each day of the year, including name days. This fact does not correspond well with the belief that it is a sin to work on any Orthodox holiday.

TOUR OPERATORS
UK

Biosphere Expeditions Sprat's Water, Near Carlton Colville, The Broads National Park, Suffolk NR33 8BP; tel: 01502 583085; email: info@biosphere-expeditions.org; web: www.biosphere-expeditions.org. A non-profit-making organisation that arranges hands-on wildlife conservation projects. Expeditions involve collecting data on wolves and migratory birds on the Black Sea coast just north of the Crimea.
Interchange Interchange House, 27 Stafford Rd, Croydon, Surrey CR0 4NG; tel: 020 8681 3612; fax: 020 8760 0031; email: gordon@interchange.uk.com; web: www.interchange.uk.com
Intourist 7 Wellington Terrace, Notting Hill, London W2 4LW; tel: 0870 112 1232; email: info@intourist.co.uk; web: www.intourist.co.uk. Also offices in Manchester and Glasgow.
Regent Holidays 15 John St, Bristol BS1 2HR; tel: 0117 921 1711; fax: 0117 925 4866; email: www.regent-holidays.co.uk
Russia House Gospel Court, Borough High St, London SE1 1HH; tel: 020 7403 9922; fax: 020 7403 9933; email: russiahouse@btinternet.com; web: www.the-russiahouse.net
Ukraine Travel Falcon House, Victoria St, Chadderton OL9 0HB; tel: 0161 652 5050; fax: 0161 633 0825; email: info@ukraine.co.uk; web: www.ukraine.co.uk. Custom-made trips for Ukraine, specialist travel and visa support.

US

Scope Travel 1605 Springfield Av, Maplewood NJ 07040; tel: 973 378 8998 or 1 800 242 7267; fax: 973 378 7903; email: info@scopetravel.com; web: www.scopetravel.com

Canada

Chumak Travel Agency 52 Mabelle Av, Suite 1215, Toronto, Ontario M9A 4X9; tel/fax: 416 234 56 04; email: ukrainetour@ukrainetour.com; web: www.ukrainetour.com. Open since Ukrainian independence, specialising in professional, private and student travel, tours and visas.
RJ's Tours 11708 135A St, Edmonton, Alberta T5M 1L5; tel: 780 415 5633; fax: 780 415 5633; email: rjstours@tourukraine.com; web: www.rjstours.shawbiz.ca. Cruises and large, escorted, group tours.

In Ukraine

Regional chapters give additional particulars about local tour agencies. Be wary of companies that advertise themselves as 'travel agencies' which are often covers for shady operations that help Ukrainians get out of the country. Instead, search for operators specialising in *priyom* ('incoming') tourism. The following are the largest and most secure of Ukraine's larger tour operators with a reputation for professionalism:

Albion Kiev, Chervonoarmiyska 26; tel: 044 461 9746; email: info@albion.com.ua; web: www.albion.com.ua. Bus tours to Crimea combined with Lviv and Kiev.
Eugenia Travel Odessa, Rishelyevskaya 23; tel/fax: 0482 220 554; email: janna@eugen.intes.odessa.ua; web: www.eugeniatravel.com. Black Sea cruises, Odessa and Crimea, as well as the rest of the country.

Krymtour Simferopol, Schmidta 9; tel: 0652 250 350; email: info@krymtur.com; web: www.krymtur.com. Specialists for Crimea.

Mandrivnyk Kiev, Poshtova Ploscha 3; tel: 044 463 7604; email: mandrivnyk@adam.kiev.ua; web: www.mandrivnyk.com.ua. Cruises and basic city visits.

Meest-Tour Lviv, Shevchenka 23; tel: 0322 728 710; email: office@meest-tour.com; web: www.meest-tour.com. Trekking in the Carpathians and Crimea; adventure tourism

New Logic Kiev, Mikhayilivska 6A; tel: 044 462 0462; email: incoming@newlogic.kiev.ua; web: www.newlogic.com.ua. Best for young independent travellers.

Olymp Travel 24 Shovkovychna St, Kyiv, 01024 Ukraine; tel: 044 253 7108; fax: 044 253 8329; email: welcome@olymp-travel.kiev.ua; web: www.olymp-travel.kiev.ua. A nationwide company offering comprehensive 'theme' tours.

SAM Kiev, Ivana Franka 40B; tel/fax: 044 238 6959; email: raskin@samcomp.kiev.ua; web: www.sam.com. The largest and most-established in the country.

Sputnik Kiev Pushkinskaya 9; #21; tel: 044 228 09 38; fax: 044 464 1358; email: income@sputnik.kiev.ua; web: www.sputnik.kiev.ua. Longer excursions and diverse tours combined with Russia trips.

Ukrzovnishintour Kiev, Khmelnytskovo 26; tel: 044 229 8464; email: uit@uit.kiev.ua; web: www.uit.com.ua. Travel for business and leisure.

UNA Travel Agency Kiev, Dovzhenko 1, #16A; tel: 044 241 7502; fax: 044 490 9178; email: una@una.kiev.ua; web: www.una.kiev.ua. Ecotourism and adventure tours.

RED TAPE

Ukraine has turned bureaucracy into an art-form that never fails to amaze Ukrainians and foreigners alike. Suspicion, indifference and micro-management are holdovers from the Soviet age and ticket-taker attitudes still prevail. Regulations and procedures habitually change as well. As long as you don't think like a consumer, and come with a lot of patience, you'll get by just fine.

All Ukrainians are issued identification passports at the age of 16 and this is the document police want to see when they ask for *bumahy* (papers). Your passport is your 'papers' so never go anywhere without it on your person, as you will be asked to show it. Obviously, you should keep a photocopy of your passport's front page and Ukrainian visa separate from your passport, as well as any other valuable forms or information: it makes getting a new passport much easier. Because independent travel is such a new concept, lone foreigners will appear suspect to various authority figures: police, ticket sellers, guards or soldiers. Only police have the authority to see your passport and they are under international obligation to return it immediately. As long as you have a valid visa, there is no problem. If you find that you do get called into a police station or they want to search your bags, nonchalant cooperation is the best policy, but don't be afraid to put up a reasonable fuss (for instance, there is no need for anyone to open your camera). These days, people would rather chat with a foreign traveller than arrest them, so a frank and friendly demeanour will help any situation.

Visas

Besides the Cyrillic alphabet, a pesky visa is the number one deterrent that keeps travellers from venturing into Ukraine. Visitors rightfully comment that a country so lovely should be more accessible, yet fail to acknowledge that Ukraine is presently more accessible than it ever has been. Hopefully, the situation will continue to improve for tourists.

Citizens of Poland, Russia and the countries of the former Soviet Union (except Turkmenistan) are exempt; everybody else needs a visa, obtained in advance from a Ukrainian embassy or consulate. Exceptions to the visa rule include Black Sea cruise passengers who do not need a visa if they are stopping for a day in ports like Yalta and Sevastopol, or cities like Odessa and Simferopol, where special visas can be issued on site.

Overall, few visa applications are ever rejected, but the process can be lengthy, tedious and expensive. Travellers must submit the visa application form with a passport still valid for six months *after your return* from Ukraine, two passport size photographs and the initial fee, payable by money order only: £50 (US $90) for the normal ten-day processing, double that for 'speedy' three-day processing. Visas are based on purpose of visit – Tourist, Business, Private or Transit – and each requires different forms and/or additional fees.

Tourist visas are the most obvious choice and require an additional letter of invitation from a Ukrainian or foreign tourist agency, or a confirmation from a hotel. If they are licensed, they can issue an invitation letter (for which you will be charged). Usual procedure has the Ukrainian party faxing the official invite to your country's embassy and presenting you with a confirmation number to be matched with your visa application. Organised tours often take care of all this for you.

A convenient sidestep to the tourist rigmarole is the **private visa**. Designed for foreigners visiting friends or family in Ukraine, you simply state the name and address of the person you are going to visit and where you might travel. If you don't know anybody in Ukraine, make some friends beforehand. Citizens of the EU, Canada, USA, Japan, Switzerland, Slovakia and Turkey *do not* require an invitation letter when applying for a private or business visa, cutting out the biggest headache of the application process. A private visa is also the best option for independent travellers, since you are not committed to a specific itinerary and the process is the easiest when applying on your own.

Visas are generally issued for three months, and for six months if you are from a favoured nation (above). It used to be that foreigners were required to register at the OVIR (Ministry of Interior's Office of Visas and Registration) within three days of entering any city, but this is only an issue if you are planning on staying in one area for longer than six months. If you seek to extend your visa, you must apply well in advance at the local OVIR office.

Travellers passing overland between Russia to Europe require the quicker and cheaper **transit visas**, which usually give you four days in the country. Applications require proof (another visa or one-way ticket) that you will be moving on. If you are planning on leaving and re-entering, make sure to apply for a double- or multiple-entry visa, which adds significant cost but offers a safety measure for chronic wanderers. Visas are issued in person at the embassy or by mail and consist of a full-page sticker in your passport. You'll find that your visa becomes a constant reference during your travels as all hotel registrations and ticket purchases must take down your visa number (someone out there is tracking your movements!), and many need to see the page in order to know how to spell your name in Cyrillic.

Immigration and customs

Both processes can be long and unfriendly, although, as with everything, it's getting better. Slow queues and a lot of questioning are just part of the drill but, as long as you have your visa and don't look too suspicious, you will be allowed in. Present yourself in the simplest manner and declare a specific goal or itinerary, even if you do plan on taking to the open road.

Customs can be a more demanding process. Upon entering the country you will be issued a customs declaration form that you will need to fill in with details. You *must* have the form when you leave, so keep it somewhere safe throughout your trip. The declaration is mainly to assess how much cash you are bringing into the country and what you end up taking out (see *Money*, page 62). Everyone has their own way of dealing with border guards and there is no single word of advice applicable to the Ukrainian *tamozhniki* although, in general, it helps to be honest and open, but not too honest and open. After losing a valuable amount to souvenir hunters, the Ukrainian government now prohibits the export of any national art treasures without special permission. These include antique icons, rugs and dishes, some Soviet medals, and coins. Most Ukrainian dealers are aware of the law and sell only goods that can be exported, and there tends to be one official at customs who knows what is legal and what's not.

Embassies and consultates

Australia Consulate of Ukraine, Level 3 Edgecliff Centre, 203–233 New South Head Rd, Edgecliff NSW 2027; tel/fax: +61 293 285429

Belarus Starovilenska 51, 220002 Minsk; tel: +375 17 283 1990; fax: +375 283 19980

Belgium 30 Av Albert Lancaster, 1180 Bruxelles; tel: +322 379 21 00; fax: +322 379 2179

Canada Embassy of Ukraine, Consular Section, 331 Metcalfe St, Ottawa, Ontario K2P 1S3; tel: +613 230 8015; fax: +613 230 2655 web: www.infoukes.com/ukremb; Consulate General of Toronto, 2120 Bloor St West, Toronto, Ontario M6S 1M8; tel: +416 763 3114; fax: +416 763 2323; web: www.ukrconsulate.com

Czech Republic De Gaulla 29, Prague 6; tel: +42 02 33 342000; fax: +42 02 33 344 366

France 21 Av de Saxe, 75007, Paris; tel: +33 1 43 06 07 37; fax: +33 1 43 06 02 94

Germany Albrechtsrasse 26, 10117 Berlin; tel: +49 30 288 87 116; fax: +49 30 288 87 163; web: www.botschaft-ukraine.de

Hungary Stefania 77, Budapest H-1143; tel: +36 1 422 41 20; fax: +36 1 220 98 73

Israel 50 Yirmiyahu, 62594 Tel Aviv; tel: +97 23 602 1952; fax: +97 23 604 2512; web:

Japan 3-15-6 Nishi Azabu, Minato-ku, Tokyo 106-0046; tel: +813 5474 9770; fax: +813 5474 9772; web: ukremb-japan.gov.ua

Moldova Sfatul Taril 55, 277004 Chisinau; tel: +3732 582 151; fax: +3732 585 108

Poland Aleja Szucha 7, 00580 Warsaw; tel: +48 22 625 0127; fax: +48 22 629 8103; web: www.ukraine-poland.com

Romania Calea Dorobantilor 16, Sector 1 Bucharest; tel: +40 1211 6986; fax: +40 1211 6949

Russia Leontievsky 18, Moscow, 103009; tel: +095 229 1079; fax: +095 924 8469

Slovakia Radvanska 35, 811 Bratislava 01; tel: +42 12 5920 28 11; fax: +42 12 5441 26 51; web: www.ukraine-embassy.co.il

Turkey Sancak Mahalessi 206 Solak N 17, Yildiz Cankaya, Ankara 06550; tel: +90 312 441 5499; fax: +90 312 440 6815

UK Embassy of Ukraine, Consular Department, 78 Kensington Park Rd, London W11 2PL; tel: +44 20 7243 8923; fax: +44 20 7727 3567; Consulate in Edinburgh, 8 Windsor St, Edinburgh EH7 5JR; tel: +44 131 556 0023, fax: +44 131 557 3460

USA Embassy of Ukraine, 3350 M St NW, Washington DC 20007; tel: +1 202 333 0606; fax: +1 202 333 0817; web: www.ukremb.com; Consulate General of Ukraine in New York, 240 East 49th St, New York, NY 10017; tel: +1 212 371 5690; Consulate General of Ukraine in Chicago, 10 East Huron St, Chicago, IL 60611; tel: +1 312 642 4388; fax: +1 312 642 4385

GETTING TO UKRAINE
By air

Even though it's part of Europe, Ukraine was traditionally perceived as a long-haul destination by the airline industry, although a gradual increase in direct flights shows a change in attitudes. Today, most major European carriers fly to Kiev at least once a week. Aerosvit is Ukraine's largest international airline and offers the best connections between international flights and domestic destinations, but they do not fly to many western European cities. Ukraine International Airlines flies to most European capitals and code shares with several western European airlines.

From Europe

Austrian Airlines has been flying to Ukraine the longest of any European carrier, and now offers regular services to Kiev, Kharkiv, Odessa and Dnepropetrovsk (all via Vienna). British Airways flies five days a week direct from London Heathrow to Kiev Borispol, as does Air France from Paris de Gaulle, Lufthansa from Frankfurt and Munich, and KLM from Schipol. Prices vary, but expect to pay at least £250 (US$400) for any round-trip ticket from London to Kiev (three hours). Cheaper tickets can sometimes be found on East European carriers. Czech Airlines flies every day to Kiev Zhulyany with an optional stopover in Prague, and Lithuanian Airlines offers similar deals via Vilnius. Besides Kiev, LOT Polish Airlines also flies to Lviv, and Malev Hungarian Airlines flies to Odessa. Ukraine International Airlines has direct flights from all major European capitals to Kiev, with numerous connections inside Ukraine. Another alternative is flying with Turkish Airlines, with connections every other day from Istanbul to Kiev (two hours).

From North America

The only direct flights from North America to Ukraine are on Aerosvit, which offers regular flights from Toronto and New York to Kiev. Prices range from £320 to £400 (US$500 to US$600). Otherwise, Austrian Airlines, British Airways, KLM, and Lufthansa offer the most competitive and comfortable transatlantic connections to Ukraine via their respective hubs. Travellers tend to leave Canada or the US the night before and arrive in Ukraine the following afternoon.

Other routes

Various Ukrainian airlines and charter flights service all the recent hotspots for Ukrainian travellers: Bangkok, Malta, Egypt and Cyprus. Singapore Airlines advertises itself as the best connection from Ukraine to Australia, New Zealand or Southeast Asia on the Star Alliance via Frankfurt. From Russia, Transaero and Aeroflot fly to all major Ukrainian cities, but this is not a convenient way to travel from western Europe since it requires a screwy airport change in Moscow and a long layover. However, Aeroflot still keeps the former communist world together and their stopover in Moscow is the cheapest way to get to Ukraine from India and Africa.

Overland

Ukraine is much closer than people realise, so that travelling across Europe to get there sounds more daunting that it actually is. From an American perspective, the trip from Paris to Kiev is the same as driving from New York to Denver. The route across Germany and Poland is the quickest, but many would argue that crossing the Czech Republic and Slovakia or Hungary is much more beautiful. Either way, going overland can be a romantic endeavour and fairly cheap.

By bus

Numerous bus companies travel from western Europe directly to Ukraine, most of which are Ukrainian companies offering direct service from Germany, Belgium, France and the UK to Kiev and Lviv (with Lviv Inturtrans; web: www.lviv-inturtrans.com.ua; email: info@lviv-inturtrans.com.ua). Eurolines shares tickets on its one Antwerp–Kiev bus that can be joined from London, although this costs more than going to a Polish destination and then continuing on Ukrainian transport (web: www.eurolines.com). The bus journey to Kiev from London takes two days and two nights, so you must consider whether the money you're saving is worth sitting upright for 48 hours and being forced to watch the latest Hollywood blockbusters dubbed into Polish. From the UK, the very cheapest way to get to Ukraine is on a two-day Eurolines bus from London Victoria to Rzeszow, Poland, usually costing £80 return (US$120). From Rzeszow there are frequent buses that cross the border to Lviv (three hours). Other options are quicker buses that travel to Warsaw or Krakow, and then continue on to Lviv or Kiev on an overnight train.

By car

Everyone should drive across Europe at least once in their lifetime, and the trip from England to Kiev by car does not risk becoming too clichéd an adventure. For many, all is well until they get inside the country. If you have the luxury of bringing an old car that you don't mind losing, then do. There's also the option of driving to Ukraine, then switching to planes and trains to get around inside the country. The most direct route is from Brussels: follow the E-40 east and just keep driving across Germany via Cologne and Leipzig to the Polish border at Görlitz; in Poland drive via Wrocław, Krakow and Przemyśl to the border at Shehini. The E-40 continues in Ukraine through Rivne and on to Kiev, then through Kharkiv and Luhansk. Stay on the road and you'll end up in Kazakhstan. Slovakia and Hungary are also 'easy' border posts that are accustomed to lots of European traffic. The following chapter advises on driving inside Ukraine (see pages 70–1).

By rail

Ukrainian trains still travel from all of the former 'Eastern bloc' capitals, and this can be a fun way to make your entrance into the country. Direct overnight trains from Berlin, Belgrade, Budapest, Bucharest, Warsaw, Krakow, Bratislava, Prague and Sofia all go to Kiev, often via Lviv. With central European travel pretty standardised these days, budget-conscious travellers can save cash by combining a cheap flight or bus to Berlin or Prague followed by an overnight train. The fast train from Berlin Zoo Station to Warsaw Central takes only five hours and costs around US$20, and from Warsaw there are daily trains to Lviv (11 hours) or Kiev (20 hours). There's also the daily direct train from Berlin to Kiev (24 hours) which effectively instils a historical mood.

There are so many trains between Russia and Ukraine it's not worth listing them all, but this is the most convenient way of getting into Ukraine from the north. The dozen or so Moscow trains usually pass through Kharkiv (12 hours) and Kiev (14 hours) on their way to Crimea and the Black Sea coast. A dozen more trains travel in from Russia's east and the Caucasus. Some might consider beginning or finishing their Trans-Siberian excursion in Ukraine, as there are regular trains between Vladivostok, Kharkiv and Kiev. There are also plenty of trains from the Baltic States; however, most travel through Belarus which requires a tricky transit visa and a lot of bureaucracy and it's worth doing only if you intend to spend some time visiting Belarus. Otherwise, go through Russia or Poland. Remember that a US$5 surcharge is added when buying international rail tickets in Ukraine.

Crossing borders

The Ukrainian border is no exception to general stereotypes about border guards, but things have improved so much over the past decade that the former peculiarities are hardly worth mentioning. As long as you have your visa sorted out beforehand, no border should pose any problems. If a situation does arise at the border, meekness is always the best policy.

If you are on a train, border checks are usually made in the middle of the night, which can be slightly annoying. The train will make its last stop in one country (say, in Russia) and all the Russian immigration officers will come through and stamp your exit visa, followed by the customs officials who also look like soldiers. After the all-clear, you'll drift back to sleep while the train rattles on for 20 minutes or so, then a whole new set of immigration officers, this time Ukrainian, will come on, followed by their customs officials. Normally, the train conductor is expected to alert the guards when they have a foreigner among the passengers (ie: those with EU or US passports), which is why they seem to come straight to your compartment. The whole process can take up to an hour, with a lot of door slamming and hall conversation and flipping and re-flipping through your passport.

Crossing on a bus used to make for unpleasant experiences since most passengers were smuggling consumer goods to sell in Ukraine. Black-market activity is back to a minimum and buses are no longer targeted by greedy, underpaid customs officials. Buses and cars may face very long queues at the border, with the heaviest traffic in the summer. Most border posts are open 24 hours now, but on the smaller roads the gates will close at midnight and open the following morning. If you are driving into Ukraine, make sure you have your vehicle registration, proof of auto insurance and a lot of patience. Foreigners entering by car are still somewhat of an anomaly and the guards will need time to come to grips with your situation.

Russia and the Caucasus
Ukraine shares a love/hate relationship with Russia that seems to intensify at the border, where things are either remarkably easy or else inexplicably complicated. The two countries seem an obvious travel combination, but keep in mind that it is more difficult to get a Russian visa than a Ukrainian one and in my experience I've found there is less hassle in travelling from Russia into Ukraine than the reverse. The most clear-cut route is on the train from Moscow to Kharkiv via Kursk and Belgorod, but there are just as many Russian trains travelling to Kiev via Bryansk. Still, most Ukrainian trains follow the old Soviet plan, meaning they lead to Russia. Southern routes cross eastern Ukraine and head to the north Caucasus (Krasnodar) and the Russian Black Sea resorts (Sochi, Adler). It is no longer possible to take any direct trains to Georgia and Armenia since all the railroad tracks in Abkhazia have been blown up. Most other routes are closed due to the war in Chechnya, so the alternative is taking a ship from Crimea to Turkey and then travelling overland to the Caucasus.

Belarus
In a few short years, Belarus has gone from being the most progressive country in the region to the most repressive, so that the most attractive tourist feature may be its status as the only rogue state left in Europe. The anti-foreigner stance is a tragedy, for the country is truly beautiful. Frequent trains travel from Minsk to Kiev via Gomel, and most of the trains from the Baltic states and Kaliningrad pass through Belarus (Ukrainians report that the current train to Minsk is like a time machine that carries you back to the Soviet era). Foreigners are also required to buy medical insurance at the border.

Receiving any kind of Belarusian visa is a daunting task, and if you get so far as to be allowed into the country, be prepared to deal with being followed and watched. Anyone you interact with will also be interrogated once you've left. If you are simply passing through, you must have a transit visa, a document that forbids an overnight stay in the country. Countless reports tell of Belarusian guards using 'invalid' transit visas as a means of extortion, but even if they threaten you with jail, there is no reason to hand over foreign cash to a guard (you have the right to contact your embassy). Sadly, for the time being, the best policy is to completely avoid Belarus.

Romania and Moldova
Odessa and Chernivtsi are the main entry points from either country depending on where you are travelling from. The north of Romania is quite rural but there is plenty of cross border traffic from Suceava into Chernivtsi and regular overnight trains from Bucharest. As Romania becomes more EU-oriented, visa restrictions have been loosened; however, many train and bus routes between Romania and Ukraine pass through Moldova and therefore require a transit visa. Moldova is slightly behind Ukraine in terms of ease of travel and bureaucracy. Also note that trains to and from Chisinau (Kishinev) have a reputation for theft.

Poland
Entering Ukraine from the west is the easiest and most obvious choice when travelling from Europe. Since Polish transportation is frequent and reliable, it is easy to get right up to the border and then take any number of buses across. The two basic routes are Przemyśl–Lviv or Lublin–Lutsk. There are also more Ukrainian trains to and from Poland than any other country (besides Russia) so your options are varied. All trains must stop at the Polish-Ukrainian border and the wheels changed to fit a different gauge while the cars are suspended (with you still inside them).

Hungary and Slovakia
Uzhogorod is the main entry point from both countries with frequent trains and buses to Budapest and Bratislava. From Slovakia, you can simply hike into Uzhgorod from Sobrance or take any number of buses, while the Hungarian border post and international train junction is at Chop, 20 minutes south of Uzhgorod. Both posts are known to be fairly relaxed as they deal with a majority of cargo traffic from Europe.

By sea
Passenger ships sail regularly to Ukraine from Turkey (Istanbul and Samsun) and Israel (Haifa) – an unconventional Eurasian link that is only now being discovered. Black Sea cruises seem to be slowly regaining their former popularity, although for the present none originate in Ukraine, and they tend to spend no more than one day each in ports like Odessa, Sevastopol and Yalta. If you want to permanently disembark you will have to make prior arrangements and pre-arrange a visa. There is also the ferry from Russia to Kerch, although this is not so much a sea passage as it is an overland route from Russia's north Caucasus region. Private yachts docking on Ukraine's Black Sea coast are still considered a novelty, so be prepared for a lot of bureaucracy, especially in Sevastopol. For more information on travel by sea, check the regional chapters for Crimea and the Black Sea.

HEALTH
with Dr Felicity Nicholson
Despite US State Department warnings, Ukraine is not the dreaded third-world country it is often made out to be. Every country has its bugs to which travellers will always be more susceptible.

Immunisations

Although there are no specific vaccinations required for the Ukraine, it is recommended that visitors should be up to date with **tetanus** and **diphtheria** (every ten years), **typhoid** and **hepatitis A**. A single dose of hepatitis A vaccine (eg: Havrix Monodose, Avaxim) lasts for one year. It can be boosted after this time to provide cover for at least ten years. The vaccine is best taken at least two weeks before travel but can be taken even the day before, as the incubation period of hepatitis A is at least two weeks. The vaccine has replaced immunoglobulin, which should no longer be used.

The newer typhoid vaccines (eg: Typhim Vi) are about 80% effective and last for three years. It is worth taking, unless time is short and your trip is one week or less.

For trips of four weeks or more you should also consider **polio** (ten yearly), **hepatitis B** and **rabies**. Hepatitis B is especially relevant if you are working in a hospital or with children and rabies is recommended if you are either handling animals or are likely to be more than 24 hours from medical facilities. Ideally three doses of each are needed and should be taken at least three weeks before travel. However, if time is short then two doses, or even one of either, are better than nothing at all. For hepatitis B, only Engerix B is currently licensed for the rapid course.

Tuberculosis (TB) has reached epidemic proportions in Ukraine during the last decade, and it is known to be a highly persistent strain of the disease. The BCG vaccination for tuberculosis is routinely given in the UK between the ages of 11 and 13, whereas in the USA only high-risk individuals are vaccinated as a matter of course. If you have not been vaccinated, and are over 35, it is probably not worth having, as there is some doubt as to its efficacy. But don't worry, tuberculosis needs prolonged close contact with an infected individual and is still treatable. Symptoms of active TB include a permanent, crackling or dry persistent cough, fever (most often at night), fatigue and weight loss. Avoid long contact with anyone who coughs all the time, and if you think you may have been infected, or else you've just spent a long time in Ukraine, get a TB test as a precaution. Treatment includes a long-term daily medication ritual, so the sooner you begin the better.

Tick-borne encephalitis is common in the Ukrainian forest. Travellers at risk include anyone visiting the Ukrainian countryside from April to August, but you should only consider being vaccinated if you are going into the country for more than three weeks or if you intend to spend most of your time in the woods. In the UK, vaccine is available only on a named-patient basis, so has to be pre-ordered. A new, faster schedule allows the three doses needed to be given over a four-week period. Whether or not you are vaccinated you should always take general precautions against ticks: wear loose, long-sleeved shirts, long trousers that cover your limbs and are tucked into your socks or boots, and a hat. You should also use a tick repellent with DEET. At the end of the day, check for ticks on your body and hair. This is easier to do with another person as the ticks are small and hard to see. It is especially important to check the heads of children, who are more likely to get ticks from overhead branches. Hikers in the Carpathians tend to be prone to tick bites, since mountain paths can fade into scrubby woods where you must push through low pine branches.

Travel clinics and health information

A full list of current travel clinic websites worldwide is available on www.istm.org/. For other journey preparation information, consult www.tripprep.com. Information about various medications may be found on www.emedicine.com/wild/topiclisthtm.

UK

Berkeley Travel Clinic 32 Berkeley St, London W1J 8EL (near Green Park tube station); tel: 020 7629 6233

British Airways Travel Clinic and Immunisation Service There are two BA clinics in London, both on tel: 0845 600 2236; web: www.britishairways.com/travelclinics. Appointments only at 111 Cheapside; or walk-in service Mon – Sat at 156 Regent St Apart from providing inoculations and malaria prevention, they sell a variety of health-related goods.

Fleet Street Travel Clinic 29 Fleet St, London EC4Y 1AA; tel: 020 7353 5678; web: www.fleetstreet.com. Injections, travel products and latest advice.

Hospital for Tropical Diseases Travel Clinic Mortimer Market Centre, 2nd Floor, Capper St (off Tottenham Ct Rd), London WC1E 6AU; tel: 020 7388 9600; web: www.thhtd.org. Offers consultations and advice, and is able to provide all necessary drugs and vaccines for travellers. Runs a healthline (09061 337733) for country-specific information and health hazards. Also stocks nets, water purification equipment and personal protection measures.

MASTA (Medical Advisory Service for Travellers Abroad), at the London School of Hygiene and Tropical Medicine, Keppel St, London WC1 7HT; tel: 09068 224100. This is a premium-line number, charged at 60p per minute. For a fee, they will provide an individually tailored health brief, with up-to-date information on how to stay healthy, inoculations and what to bring.

MASTA pre-travel clinics Tel: 01276 685040. Call for the nearest; there are currently 30 in Britain. Also sell malaria prophylaxis memory cards, treatment kits, bednets, net treatment kits.

NHS travel website, www.fitfortravel.scot.nhs.uk, provides country-by-country advice on immunisation and malaria, plus details of recent developments, and a list of relevant health organisations.

Nomad Travel Store 3 – 4 Wellington Terrace, Turnpike Lane, London N8 0PX; tel: 020 8889 7014; fax: 020 8889 9528; email: sales@nomadtravel.co.uk; web: www.nomadtravel.co.uk. Also at 40 Bernard St, London WC1N 1LJ; tel: 020 7833 4114; fax: 020 7833 4470 and 43 Queens Rd, Bristol BS8 1QH; tel: 0117 922 6567; fax: 0117 922 7789. As well as dispensing health advice, Nomad stocks mosquito nets and other anti-bug devices, and an excellent range of adventure travel gear.

Thames Medical 157 Waterloo Rd, London SE1 8US; tel: 020 7902 9000. Competitively priced, one-stop travel health service. All profits go to their affiliated company, InterHealth, which provides health care for overseas workers on Christian projects.

Trailfinders Immunisation Centre 194 Kensington High St, London W8 7RG; tel: 020 7938 3999.

Travelpharm The Travelpharm website, www.travelpharm.com, offers up-to-date guidance on travel-related health and has a range of medications available through their online mini-pharmacy.

Irish Republic

Tropical Medical Bureau Grafton Street Medical Centre, Grafton Buildings, 34 Grafton St, Dublin 2; tel: 1 671 9200. Has a useful website specific to tropical destinations: www.tmb.ie.

USA

Centers for Disease Control 1600 Clifton Rd, Atlanta, GA 30333; tel: 877 FYI TRIP; 800 311 3435; web: www.cdc.gov/travel. The central source of travel information in the USA. Each summer they publish the invaluable *Health Information for International Travel*, available from the Division of Quarantine at the above address.

Connaught Laboratories PO Box 187, Swiftwater, PA 18370; tel: 800 822 2463. They will send a free list of specialist tropical-medicine physicians in your state.

IAMAT (International Association for Medical Assistance to Travelers) 417 Center St, Lewiston, NY 14092; tel: 716 754 4883; email: info@iamat.org; web: www.iamat.org. A non-profit organisation that provides lists of English-speaking doctors abroad.

Canada
IAMAT (International Association for Medical Assistance to Travellers) Suite 1, 1287 St Clair Av W, Toronto, Ontario M6E 1B8; tel: 416 652 0137; web: www.iamat.org
TMVC (Travel Doctors Group) Sulphur Springs Rd, Ancaster, Ontario; tel: 905 648 1112; web: www.tmvc.com.au

Australia, Thailand
TMVC Tel: 1300 65 88 44; web: www.tmvc.com.au. Twenty-two clinics in Australia, New Zealand and Thailand, including:
Auckland Canterbury Arcade, 170 Queen St, Auckland City; tel: 9 373 3531
Brisbane Dr Deborah Mills, Qantas Domestic Building, 6th floor, 247 Adelaide St, Brisbane, QLD 4000; tel: 7 3221 9066; fax: 7 3321 7076
Melbourne Dr Sonny Lau, 393 Little Bourke St, 2nd floor, Melbourne, VIC 3000; tel: 3 9602 5788; fax: 3 9670 8394
Sydney Dr Mandy Hu, Dymocks Building, 7th Floor, 428 George St, Sydney, NSW2000; tel: 2 221 7133; fax: 2 221 8401

New Zealand
TMVC See above
IAMAT PO Box 5049, Christchurch 5; web: www.iamat.org

South Africa
SAA-Netcare Travel Clinics PO Box 786692, Sandton 2146; fax: 011 883 6152; web: www.travelclinic.co.za or www.malaria.co.za. Clinics throughout South Africa.
TMVC 113 DF Malan Drive, Roosevelt Park, Johannesburg; tel: 011 888 7488; web: www.tmvc.com.au. Consult the website for details of clinics in South Africa.

Switzerland
IAMAT 57 Voirets, 1212 Grand Lancy, Geneva; web: www.iamat.org

First-aid kit
A basic first-aid kit could sensibly include the following:

- antiseptic wipes
- plasters/Band-aids, and blister plasters if you're hiking
- wound dressings such as Melolin, and tape
- sterilised syringes and needles
- insect repellent; antihistamine cream
- antiseptic cream
- oral rehydration sachets

In Ukraine
'Don't drink the water' fully applies to Ukraine and is the best advice to follow for a healthy trip. Never mind the lead pipes, dodgy sewage systems and a menagerie of gastrointestinal ailments, the water just tastes bad and will make you sick. Drink bottled or boiled water only; tea and hot drinks served in restaurants are safe.

Accept that you will get diarrhoea at some point and then you won't be so unhappy when you do, although good hygiene such as scrubbing your hands regularly with soap may help prevent infection. New food and new bacteria are the usual cause of diarrhoea in Ukraine and the condition should last only 24 hours. Even if you are taking anti-diarrhoea tablets like Imodium, be sure to drink lots of clear fluids to avoid dehydration. Rehydration sachets can be purchased in most pharmacies, but you can make the solution yourself with a teaspoon of salt, eight teaspoons of sugar and a litre of safe water. Bacillary dysentery usually fails to settle after 24 hours, and the diarrhoea may contain blood and/or slime or you may have a fever. This may be difficult to distinguish from amoebic dysentery. The latter is a much more serious ailment passed by contaminated food or water and human contact. Besides severe and bloody diarrhoea, there may be constant vomiting, stomach pains and a high fever. Another unpleasant, though rare, illness is giardiasis, caused by the protozoan *Giardia lamblia*. This gut infection includes greasy, bulky and often pale stools, stomach cramps and characteristic 'eggy' burps. It requires prompt treatment otherwise chronic infection may occur. Replenish all your lost fluids by drinking about four litres of rehydration fluid a day. Doctors in Ukraine will also prescribe antibiotic treatments, but if you think you will not be near medical facilities then carry your own supply. Ciprofloxacin (one 500mg tablet repeated 6-12 hours later) will usually work for bacillary dysentery. Suspected amoebic dysentery or giardiasis, should be treated with 2g of tinidazole (Fasigyn) taken as four 500mg tablets in one go, repeated seven days later if symptoms persist. If your tummy feels fine, but your stool appears dark red, don't panic – you are probably eating a lot more beets (*borscht*) than you are accustomed to.

Chernobyl

Chernobyl does not pose a serious health threat for travellers in Ukraine unless you plan on camping next to the reactor for an extended period of time. The general advice cautions against eating local food known to contain radiation, namely mushrooms and berries gathered from the Polissyan woods. Also, avoid freshwater fish from rivers, as they are known to carry worms.

Animals

In urban areas, stray dogs move about in large packs and scavenge for food. Even if you think the puppies are cute, and others seem to be feeding them scraps of food, remember that these are wild animals that have been known to attack individuals. They also carry disease, rabies being the most obvious risk. Whether or not you are vaccinated, you are at risk of contracting rabies from being bitten, scratched or licked over open wounds. Wash the area immediately with soap and water then apply an antiseptic (or alcohol if you don't possess any antiseptic), then go as soon as you can for medical help. Having pre-exposure rabies vaccine (see above) will reduce the number of post-treatment doses required. If you have had at least two doses of vaccine then you will not need rabies immunoglobulin (RIG). The latter is expensive and often unavailable, so will offset the cost of being vaccinated before departure. Rabies, if contracted and untreated, is always fatal and a horrific way to die.

In cheaper hotels, bedbugs can be a problem, known for the rows of small red bites you'll find in the morning. Bedbugs do not spread disease and there's not much you can do about them, but calamine lotion or a proprietary antihistamine cream such as Anthisan can reduce the itching.

AIDS

AIDS is spreading in Ukraine, mainly through intravenous drug use and prostitution. Be wise. It is sensible to buy condoms before you leave to guarantee their quality, although most kiosks and shops sell good-quality ones in Ukraine.

Ukrainian health care

Socialised medicine once supported a culture of efficient, long-term treatment, but with the current economic situation and severe supply shortages, the quality of care has dropped significantly. Ukrainian doctors are for the most part highly skilled, but paid miserably low salaries. Most continue to work with the incentive of receiving underhand gifts of cash or in kind for medical services rendered. In my experience, travellers are welcome at public hospitals and will often be given priority. Be prepared to pay for any service, but don't be surprised if they refuse your money; there is prestige in treating a foreigner. However, there is a reciprocal health care agreement with the UK, so most medical treatment is free. This may also apply to dental treatment, but you will have to pay for prescribed medicine.

Drunk doctors are a known problem in Ukraine's depressed state, so you might think to check their state of sobriety before they begin to cut. Several private clinics have emerged in the larger cities where the staff speak English and the quality of care is comparable to that in the West.

When Ukrainians go to a hospital, they are often expected to bring their own supplies along, including gauze, syringes and even anaesthetic. Travelling with a small first-aid kit is always a good idea, and it is also wise to take packaged syringes and needles in case you need an injection. These days, Ukrainian pharmacies are well stocked with high-quality medicine and medical supplies. Pharmacists work as over-the-counter doctors. Simply pointing or explaining an ailment in gestures will usually get you the right medicine or ointment.

Ukrainian folk medicine is a fascinating topic and you won't leave the country without being offered some sort of home remedy, some of which involves the supernatural. *Babushki* gather dried herbs and sell them on the street as medicine. List your symptoms and they'll mix a tea infusion that can – they say – cure anything. Mustard plants, powder or plasters are also effective for soothing chest colds.

Cold weather

Ukrainian winters are colder than might be expected, so bundle up with lots of layers and make sure to cover your hands, ears and head, where you lose the most heat. After a while, you'll find your body gets used to the cold, but pay attention to signs like chattering teeth. After being outdoors, drink hot tea or eat hot borscht, for it can help prevent catching cold.

Frostbite is a serious condition where the flesh has actually frozen. The first signs include a 'pins and needles' sensation and white skin. Go inside and warm the affected area with lukewarm water and slowly increase the temperature until feeling returns. Be smart about walking on frozen rivers and lakes. Ukrainians will not step on ice unless the temperature has been continuously below 0°C for at least five days. You can usually see which ice is safe for recreation for all the footprints and fishing holes there. If you do fall through, get indoors, remove the wet (but frozen) clothing and treat for hypothermia.

CRIME AND SAFETY

In general, Ukraine is a safe place to travel, and much safer than most of the neighbouring countries. The anarchy of the 1990s seems to have settled down to a semblance of law and order; however, when riches are flaunted in the midst of poverty, there will be crime. No matter how hard you may try to belong in Ukraine, you will stick out as a wealthy foreigner and be the desired target for petty criminals.

Muggings, pickpocketing and robbery are the most common threats. Bad things tend to happen in train stations, bus stations, and marketplaces where there are lots of people continuously moving about and cash and belongings are shifting hands. Be especially alert when you are in any of these places. Also, people have been known to have their bags slashed while riding crowded subways or trolleys.

Capitalism has not been around long enough to divide cities into 'good' or 'bad' areas so both potentials exist everywhere. Bear in mind that public places are badly lit and that people are often mugged at night or in dark stairwells. Bring a small torch (flashlight). Using a mock wallet with expired cards and a convincing wad of worthless cash is a wise precaution. Local crime also tends to involve alcohol and money. If you are drinking with people you have just met, be on your guard. People have been robbed when they are drunk, or worse, they have been drugged and then robbed. Don't engage with drunk people who approach you, simply get away.

Trains are quite safe. People usually get robbed on trains when they are alone, so travel in groups or else close the door to your compartment with multiple locks. Taxis are also safe, but beware of any suspicious behaviour. If the driver demands you pay up front, get out of the car. If they pull over midway for petrol or to change a tyre, get out of the car and watch them from the roadside. If it feels suspicious, simply walk away. Pay a taxi driver only after you have stepped out of the car and have your bags with you.

Organised crime (the mafia) gets a lot of talk, but is of no real interest to tourists and vice versa. Mobsters in Ukraine fill a very different niche than they do in the West and will not bother you unless you are purposefully trying to undermine their business. Donetsk and Dnepropetrovsk both have reputations as gangster towns but seem to be moving from the shadows into legitimacy.

If you are a victim of a crime, think before you act. If you are staying in an upmarket hotel or are travelling with a tour agency, report it with them first. If your passport has been stolen or the crime is of a serious nature, be sure to make a report at your embassy. The slang term for the police is *musor* ('rubbish') which reflects the reputation of Ukrainian law enforcement. Use your own judgement about filing a police report. Travellers have reported good and bad experiences with the police who may or may not be corrupt. Keep in mind that, as a foreigner, you may fall under more suspicion than the criminal.

Scams and swindles

Ukrainians freely admit that they don't trust their own countrymen, a general fear which contributes to nationwide tension. Remember that Ukraine is a very poor country with high unemployment, so that foreign tourists with hard cash in hand are the sought-for prey of con men. Swindles can take many forms. Offering services for cash, or demanding special fees, are common, and there has been an increase of staged scenarios to attract your attention and then take your money without you being aware. The latest scheme involves someone finding a large wad of money within your view and then forcing you into confidences or using sleight of hand to take or switch real money for fake. Ignore anyone who approaches you with a plan or blocks you from others' view. Extortion and intimidation are often used to get money from foreigners. Use your logic and just say no. There is no legitimate reason to open your wallet for anyone, unless there's a real threat of violence.

Visitors are often shocked by the Ukrainian belief that if a crime has been done to you, it is your fault for not preventing it. Be streetwise. For example, Ukrainians will never simply open a door without asking '*kto tam?*' and checking who's there. You may find that people seem to always be asking you the time or requesting a cigarette. This is a way for them to confirm your status as a foreigner. Their curiosity may be innocent, but it is acceptable to ignore the question and continue

DATING/MARRIAGE SERVICES

In Ukraine, there are more companies that market women to Western men than there are travel agencies. Luring older single men (and their money) over to Ukraine has become a booming, yet unregulated business and sadly, 'romance tourists' seem to outnumber any other kind of independent traveller in the country. Most dating services charge a yearly fee and allow you access to women's pictures, profiles and addresses so that you can pursue a long-distance courtship. Men are then encouraged to send flowers and gifts and spend as much as they can on having letters translated from their Ukrainian girlfriends. Eventually, you are expected to travel to Ukraine to meet the woman, although most men plan an itinerary to visit a dozen or so girls and pick one to marry. It is not for me to question how any two people expect to have a meaningful marriage when they don't speak the other person's language. However, if this is your intent, there are some things you should know:

- Very few of these marriage services are legitimate businesses but instead are temporary internet scams collecting the credit card details of naïve men and milking them for all their worth. I've known people to lose thousands of dollars.
- Obviously, a Western–Ukrainian romance has much more to do with economic disparity than any mystical connection between Western men and Ukrainian women, as is advertised.
- Ukrainian women are not as desperate to get out of the country as they once were. Too many men show up in Ukraine and find they are at the complete mercy of their 'date' who proceeds to spend all their money for them, or else simply robs them and disappears. Set-ups involve multiple accomplices who will know what to do with your wallet and successfully cover their tracks.
- Bear in mind that unless you marry her in Ukraine, getting a return visa to pursue your relationship in your own country will be extremely difficult, if not impossible.
- Ukrainian women may be very beautiful, but they do not make good souvenirs. Many a newly-wed husband has been divorced once his wife has her new passport.
- Today, Ukrainian women make up the majority of (white) prostitutes in European capitals, most of whom are victims of human trafficking. Travelling to Ukraine in pursuit of women is of the same genre. Remember that an estimated 50% of prostitutes working in Ukraine are HIV positive or infected with syphilis.

walking; that's what Ukrainians do. Avoid fortune-tellers who always leave with much more money than you intended them to have.

Internet scams are rife. When making travel arrangements with any Ukrainian company, check their website to see when it was last updated or call them, and refrain from wiring money or sending credit card details. Many 'dating' agencies are high-profile set-ups and romantic meetings often turn into big scams. Realise you are taking a large risk by getting involved with any of these organisations.

Having been warned, know that Ukrainians have a frightfully honest nature and are above all very kind and hospitable. People in the market will refuse to sell you something that isn't fresh, compliments are sincere and sarcasm non-existent. Don't let unnecessary fear lead to a rejection of everyday Ukrainian hospitality.

Bribery

Paying someone a little extra to make sure something gets done became a past way of life when a collapsed legal framework offered no guarantees. Things have changed a lot in a very little time and now most fees come with receipts. Some bribery still exists, but the practice should not be encouraged by foreigners. These days, a sly slip of American cash rarely solves any problems, but it will draw undue attention.

On the street

Driving in taxis can be plain scary, but most survive the experience by looking out the side window. Cars often drive down sidewalks, so be aware when walking. Always look both ways when crossing tram tracks in the city, even if they appear old and unused. In crowded transport, it is fairly easy to get shut in the doors. Simply yell, and others will alert the driver to stop.

Women travellers

On the surface, Ukraine's many decades of communism erased sexism to the point that women doing anything on their own – including travel – is now the norm. Females may find that they feel more vulnerable as a foreigner than as a woman. It would also not be facetious to say that a certain solidarity exists among women in Ukraine so that you should feel protected when other women are around. The most obvious risk is travelling alone on overnight trains, where even in first class you may be sharing a compartment with an unknown traveller. Nine times out of ten, you will befriend the stranger and it will be a great experience, but the odd smarmy passenger is not unheard of. You always have the option of buying out the tickets for an entire compartment, which is still a rather cheap way to travel if also a slightly lonely one. Otherwise, there is safety in numbers, and travelling in a four-person *coupé* will increase your odds of someone else looking out for you. If you find that you are expected to share a train compartment with three other men and they all give you the creeps, simply ask the conductor (almost always a woman) to change your place. You will find however, that most men follow train etiquette, allowing women privacy to change clothing and offering the lower berths for sleeping.

Overall, follow your intuition and take the same precautions you would in your own country. Don't walk alone in dark secluded streets. Think ahead and have a contingency plan for ways out of various situations (ie: alternative means of transportation, alternative accommodation). Professional taxis (with signs and phone numbers listed) are normally safe for women. Let others know where you will be travelling and if you are planning on going out at night, tell them when you hope to be back.

Ukraine's dating protocol is mysterious, although acting helpless and flirtatious will attract men who will expect more than you may be prepared to give. Accepting drinks from strangers is always a bad idea, as is going back to their apartments. Telling a persistent man that you are Orthodox Christian (*Ya Verushaya*) will get him off your back.

Racial minorities

Racism is another unfortunate aspect of Ukraine, although cities like Kiev and Odessa appear to be rather multi-cultural. In Ukraine, racist mindsets are linked to the general animosity of the poor against the rich as some find it hard to grasp that someone of a different race earns more and lives better than they do. If you are not the same colour as they are, you may suffer double the attitude, but rarely aggression. Expect to be stared at a lot and periodically stopped by the police for passport checks.

PACKING

It is difficult to pack light for Ukraine, where a wide range of situations demands different things. However, Ukraine is not so barren these days. In big cities you can find most consumer goods, so leave the contingency items at home and bring extra money. Some things you can't get in Ukraine are: (good) toilet paper, a Swiss army knife (with screwdriver head – you'll use it), powdered milk for your tea or coffee, nail clippers, hand sanitiser or packaged wipes. You'll use a small torch (flashlight) more than you expect – for unlit stairwells and when the electricity goes out. You can buy all toiletries in Ukraine, including designer razor blades. Contact lens solution is just hitting the big shops in Kiev, but is non-existent elsewhere, so bring it all with you. If you are travelling during the coldest part of winter, you may find your contacts (especially hard ones) have a hard time staying in and you'll wish you had your glasses. If you normally wear glasses, bring an extra pair. Many people also find they need sunglasses in summer. Bring a small first aid kit with anti-gas, anti-diarrhoea pills such as Immodium-D, aspirin, syringes, bandages, Neosporin (or other antiseptic cream) and tweezers. Instead of the pre-packaged travel sewing kits, make your own: bring one spool of dark thread (blue of black), a pack of needles and a fair number of buttons (it is uncanny how they fall off in Ukraine). Depending on which part of the country you are going to, bring a small Russian dictionary, a Ukrainian one, or both. Also, Ukrainians love business cards and use them passionately. If you have them, bring lots.

Luggage

The nicer your luggage, the more people will have their eye on you. Having beat-up bags makes you less of a target for theft. A hard-sided suitcase with wheels is best as large soft-sided bags can be (and have been) slashed open. Much depends on the nature of your trip, be it an organised tour or if you are on your own. If taking the road independently, pack light and inconspicuously. Dark duffle bags, simple backpacks, or a small, wheeled suitcase are best. The giant, brightly coloured backpacks you see all over western Europe are still too loud for Ukraine and you will only draw attention to yourself. The exception would be a planned hiking trip. Army/navy surplus stores always sell a good variety of heavy canvas bags, and their colour scheme will help you blend in better in Ukraine. Padlocking bags is also a good idea.

When touring during the day, refrain from using a 'fanny' pack ('bum bag') or fancy camera bag. Carry your belongings (including camera) inside a simple plastic shopping bag like you see all the Ukrainians using. It's all you need and a thief won't think to grab it.

Clothing

You are judged by what you wear in Ukraine, and Ukrainians will wear their very best clothes and shoes in public no matter how intense their poverty. The Western impulse to dress down on the road comes as a shock, since Ukrainians assume all Westerners are rich and therefore should be travelling in designer labels and diamond bracelets. To the other unnecessary extreme, many travellers are loaded down with pre-conceived images of a desolate land and pack for Ukraine as if they were going camping. Comfort should be your main aim, but men should bring at least one pair of nice trousers and a button-down shirt, and women should have one 'semi-nice' outfit (ie: skirt and blouse or dress). You will be surprised how a change of clothes will bring you increased respect when needed.

Bring comfortable and sturdy walking shoes, but avoid flashy white trainers which are coveted merchandise. Sturdy clothes are best for daytime activities. Even if it's normally not your style, bring a pair of loose-fitting pyjamas to wear on overnight trains, or a T-shirt and running pants. You will be more comfortable and its *de rigueur*. Keep in mind that you can buy any kind of clothing in most large Ukrainian cities.

Ukraine gets very hot in the summer (+30°C) and people's clothes come off. Women tend to dress skimpily and a lot of men will work in the fields wearing nothing but their underwear. Travellers in public are still expected to keep covered, except for beaches and parks. In other seasons, you will be amazed at how women in high heels never fall on the ice and how men keep mud off their trouser legs, two feats that set the Ukrainians apart.

Winter wear

Ukrainian winters are bitterly cold, with temperatures down to –30°C plus severe wind chill. If you are travelling from November to March, pack warm clothes. The streets are never cleared when it snows so that thick ice forms on all roads and sidewalks which later turns to grey slush and goopy mud in the spring. A pair of sturdy **insulated, waterproof boots** will prevent you from being cold, wet, dirty and miserable. A hat is also vital – bring something warm that covers your ears, like a woollen beanie. Ukraine knows its weather best, so a lot of travellers purchase their hat after they've arrived. You may have your stance about fur, but the classic Russian *shapka* is still the preferred head covering in winter, and it makes a lot of sense in the cold and wind. If you do choose to buy one, go with rabbit, mink or astrakhan wool – all made from farmed animals.

Several layers will keep you warm inside and out (proper indoor heating has only just been introduced). A wool sweater is nice and warm unless it gets wet (hang it outside to dry, let it freeze and then beat out the ice crystals). Cotton dries quicker indoors. Wear a thick and heavy coat or parka that is extra long (and preferably water-resistant). Bring at least one pair of long underwear during the coldest part of the year and wear long thermal socks that come up to your knees. To keep the wind out, wear a long scarf that you can wrap several times around your neck.

If you are going hiking in the Carpathian or Crimean mountains, bring layers of clothing that can be easily added or removed to match the erratic weather. A waterproof windbreaker is also a good idea, even in summer.

Electricity

AC is 220 volts and outlets fit the same plugs used in continental Europe. Unless you are staying in very posh hotels (which have their own power systems), make sure to unplug appliances that you are not using. Frequent electrical surges can destroy your television, iron or hair dryer. The electrical outlets on trains are for small razors only. Frequencies are also different (50 hertz), so in certain cases you will require an adapter as well as a converter. Keep in mind that certain electrical appliances will cost much less in Ukraine than in your home country.

Toilets

Pack at least one roll of toilet paper with you for the trip. Ukrainian toilet paper is a tribute to recycling with rough chips of pulp still visible (and tangible). Nine times out of ten there will be no paper in your toilet stall so saving paper napkins from restaurants in your pocket is a worthwhile precaution. When in search of a toilet, think like a socialist (train and bus stations, large public parks, city squares).

MAKING THE BEST OF YOUR TRAVEL PHOTOGRAPHS
Nick Garbutt and John R Jones

Subject, composition and lighting
As a general rule, if it doesn't look good through the viewfinder, it will never look good as a picture. Don't take photographs for the sake of taking them; film is far too expensive. Be patient and wait until the image looks right.

People
There's nothing like a wonderful face to stimulate interest. Travelling to remote corners of the world provides the opportunity for exotic photographs of interesting people, intriguing lifestyles and special evocative shots which capture the very essence of a culture. A superb photograph should have an instant gut impact and be capable of saying more than a thousand words.

Photographing people is never easy and more often than not it requires a fair share of luck. Zooming in on that special moment which says it all requires sharp instinct, conditioned photographic eyes and the ability to handle light both aesthetically and technically.

- If you want to take a portrait shot, it is always best to ask first. Often the offer to send a copy of the photograph to the subject will break the ice – but do remember to send it!
- Focus on the eyes of your subject
- The best portraits are obtained in the early morning and late evening light. In harsh light, photograph without flash in the shadows.
- Respect people's wishes and customs. Remember that, in some countries, candid snooping can lead to serious trouble.
- Never photograph military subjects unless you have definite permission.

Wildlife
There is no mystique to good wildlife photography. Look for striking poses, aspects of behaviour and distinctive features. Try not only to take pictures of the species itself, but also to illustrate it within the context of its environment. Alternatively, focus in close on a characteristic which can be emphasised.

- Focus on the eyes, make sure they are sharp and contain a highlight.
- Look at the surroundings – there is nothing worse than a distracting twig or highlighted leaf lurking in the background. Although a powerful flashgun adds the option of punching in the extra light to pep up the subject, artificial light is no substitute for natural light, and should be used judiciously.
- At camera-to-subject distances of less than a metre, apertures between f16 and f32 are necessary to ensure adequate depth of field. This means using flash to provide enough light – use one or two small flashguns to illuminate the subject from the side.

Landscapes
Good landscape photography is all about good light and capturing mood. Generally the first and last two hours of daylight are best, or when peculiar climatic conditions add drama or emphasise distinctive features. Never place the horizon in the centre – in your mind's eye divide the frame into thirds and either exaggerate the land or the sky.

Equipment

Keep things simple. Cameras which are light, reliable and simple will reduce hassle. Extreme cold can play havoc with electronics.

For keen photographers, a single-lens reflex (SLR) camera should be at the heart of your outfit. Remember you are buying into a whole photographic system, so look for a model with the option of a range of different lenses and other accessories. Compact cameras are generally excellent, but because of restricted focal ranges they have severe limitations for wildlife.

Always choose the best lens you can afford – the type of lens will be dictated by the subject and the type of photograph you wish to take. For people, it should ideally should have a focal length of 90 or 105mm; for candid photographs, a 70–210 zoom lens is ideal. If you are not intimidated by getting in close, buy one with a macro facility which will allow close focusing.

For wildlife, a lens of at least 300mm is necessary to produce a reasonable image size of mammals and birds. For birds in particular, even longer lenses like 400mm or 500mm are sometimes needed. Optics of this size should always be held on a tripod, or a beanbag if shooting from a vehicle. Macro lenses of 55mm and 105mm cover most subjects and these create images up to half lifesize. To enlarge further, extension tubes are required. In low light, lenses with very fast apertures help (but unfortunately are very expensive).

For most landscapes and scenic photographs, try using a medium telephoto lens (100–300mm) to pick out the interesting aspects of the vista and compress the perspective. In tight situations, for example inside forests, wide-angle lenses (ie: 35mm or less) are ideal.. These lenses are also an excellent alternative for close ups, as they offer the facility of being able to show the subject within the context of its environment.

Film

Film speed (ISO number) indicates the sensitivity of the film to light. The lower the number, the less sensitive the film, but the better quality the final image. For general print film, ISO 100 or 200 fit the bill perfectly; under weak light conditions use a faster film (ISO 200 or 400). If you are using transparencies just for lectures then again ISO 100 or 200 film is fine. However, if you want to get your work published, the superior quality of ISO 25 to 100 film is best. Try to keep your film cool – it should never be left in direct sunlight (film bought in developing countries is often outdated and badly stored). Fast film (ISO 800 and above) should not pass through X-ray machines.

Different types of film work best for different situations. For natural subjects, where greens are a feature, Fujicolour Reala (prints) and Fujichrome Velvia and Provia (transparencies) cannot be bettered. For people shots, try Kodachrome 64 for its warmth, mellowness and superb gentle gradation of contrast; reliable skin tones can also be recorded with Fuji Astia 100. If you want to jazz up your portraits, use Fuji Velvia (50 ISO) or Provia (100 ISO), although if cost is your priority, stick to process-paid Fuji films such as Sensia 11.

Nick Garbutt is a professional photographer, writer, artist and expedition leader, specialising in natural history. In 1996, he was a winner in the 'BBC Wildlife' Photographer of the Year Competition.
John R Jones is a professional travel photographer specialising in minority people.

Only newer restaurants feature public toilets. The letter (М) is the Gents and (Ж) is the Ladies. Most public toilets are of the stand or squat variety with raised porcelain footsteps. The cost ranges from 30 to 70 kopecks so always keep a single hrivna ready to pay the attendant. Ask for *bumaha* (paper) if you see that the attendant has some and be prepared to fork out some kopecks for the privilege. Each wagon on a train has its own toilet at the end of the car, although it is better to use them closer to the beginning of your journey while the floor is still dry. Long bus rides will stop at least once every two hours for a break. If you tend to be fussy about clean toilets and you are only travelling in bigger cities, McDonalds almost always guarantees a hygienic experience.

MONEY
Ukraine is still a cash economy, but credit and debit cards are making headway as banks stabilise. Travellers' cheques are often more of a pain than their security warrants in Ukraine, although some banks and most luxury hotels accept them. Diversifying is the best method of carrying your money: bring a fair amount in cash, use a debit card for withdrawing more cash, bring a credit card for certain hotels and as a safety measure, and take some travellers' cheques if you really like them.

Cash means US dollars or EU euros. British pounds are usually accepted by banks only and will not give you a competitive exchange rate. Go to the bank in your home country and ask for crisp, mint condition bills printed after 1995 as Ukrainian moneychangers often refuse a bill showing any sign of wear. Foreign citizens bringing more than US$1,000 cash (travellers' cheques included) must fill out a special declaration form. These days it is not necessary to carry that much and you only increase your chances of being robbed if you do. US$300 to $500 is more than enough. Wearing a hidden moneybelt is wise, but don't keep all your cash, cheques or cards in one place. Spread them on your person and in your luggage and don't forget where you've put it all. Stuffing bills into shoes or socks is a bad idea as they often tear or get sweaty. Smart travellers will always carry an emergency stash of a US$100 bill or euro equivalent. If you do have old or damaged money, some large banks will take it, but for a lower rate.

Paying with credit cards is still a new phenomenon saved for luxury hotels, nice restaurants and posh stores in Kiev and a few large cities. Visa, MasterCard, Maestro and Cirrus are generally accepted, Diner's Club and American Express less so; check the stickers in the window or the establishment. When paying with plastic, be patient. Sometimes you may even need to show the attendant how to process a credit card transaction. Credit card fraud is a known problem in Ukraine, so be conservative in your payments and hold on to all receipts as a precaution. It is best to reserve your credit card for big transactions with reputable businesses. Instead, use debit cards to draw cash from machines (and keep your statements). This gives you the best exchange rate and limits the amount of money you are carrying on your person at any one time.

When needed, money transfers are convenient. Western Union has been in Ukraine for ten years and now has literally hundreds of offices all over the country. Call 8 800 500 1000 from anywhere in Ukraine to find the closest point. The main office is in Kiev at Proreznaya 15; tel/fax: 044 228 1780; email: office@ westernunion.org.ua; web: www.westernunion.org.ua or www.westernunion.com.

Currency
The hrivna (abbreviation UAH, plural hriven), was chosen as the new currency because the soft 'h'/hard rolled 'r' diphthong can only be pronounced by the most nationally astute Ukrainian of Ukrainians.

Hrivna bills come in denominations of 1, 2, 5, 10, 20, 50 and 100. The 100 kopecks are the very cute coins that jingle in your pocket; 100 kopecks make one hrivna. Inflation has stabilised to the point that for the past year (2003) the US dollar has been worth about 5.3UAH and the euro worth slightly more. In hotels and some very expensive shops, prices are often listed as *y.e.* (standard equivalent) which is Ukraine's politically correct term for the US dollar.

Exchange booths are ubiquitous, recognisable for the daily rate chalked in next to the various flag symbols. It is illegal, unwise and unnecessary to change money anywhere else. Gone are the days when foreigners could pay for things in small US bills: people prefer hrivna (or euros!). Even though everyone deals in it, there seems to be a perpetual lack of small change. Always carry a fair stash of 1, 2 and 5 hrivna notes for buses, toilets and entrance fees (taxis normally have change). The couple of hundred hriven you are carrying in your pocket may not seem much to you, but it is a month's salary for some. Save the big bills for big purchases. Kopecks often seem a nuisance, especially when you consider their worth, and shop attendants will sometimes round up to the nearest hrivna. Always keep at least 50 kopecks just in case; it is better to have some coins in your pocket than to rummage through your bills trying to determine if that's a 1, 10 or 100 note.

How much?

This is a question only you can answer as only you know your spending habits and the level of comfort you demand. Ukraine can be incredibly cheap without too much effort. Train, plane and bus travel are all very inexpensive, going to a museum or to the opera is cheap and nice restaurants cost so little that the poorest travellers can eat well. In fact, Ukraine is arguably the only country left in Europe where travelling can be cheaper than staying at home. Travellers can skimp by on US$15 a day, by choosing the cheapest hotel rooms (without individual plumbing), buying food in markets, eating in cafeterias and travelling on trains. Most independent adult travellers I've met (who don't speak any of the language) budget around US$50 a day.

Accommodation and extra services (taxis, interpreters) will eat up most of your budget, as many hotels charge per person and a lot of 'tourist' services intentionally overcharge. Ukraine's tourist industry now caters for US$100 and US$200-a-day budgets and you can easily spend that much per day on hotels. Travelling by aeroplane and chauffeured car will increase the price tag further. Organised tours usually charge US$400 to $500 a week and include hotel accommodation, meals, transport and guide.

Tipping

Tipping is not a traditional practice, but it's slowly making headway with the market economy. In sit-down restaurants, a service charge of 10% will be included in your bill. Otherwise, if you like your service, 15% is the unwritten rule. Taxi prices are usually negotiated beforehand, so a tip might be defeating the purpose of your bargaining. You might find that you have a hard time convincing some people to accept a tip as they don't see why they should accept extra cash for just doing their job. Explain that it is *na chai*, which is the Russian/Ukrainian expression 'for tea' from the old days when servants were given a little extra to spend on meals. Anything up to 5UAH is enough. Tipping with US dollars is simply gauche.

Travelling in Ukraine

TRAVEL CULTURE IN UKRAINE
Even after a decade of independence, foreigners are still something of a novelty in Ukraine (apart from in Kiev). To avoid frustration, it's a good idea to consider the local mentality regarding travel and tourism and don't discount recent history.

Soviet influence
For the past 70 years, people living in Ukraine were subject to totalitarian management of their lives. Individuals were told where they could and could not go, what they could experience and what was forbidden. All citizens were issued 'passports' that served as a control mechanism to keep people in place. These documents marked which city a person was allowed to be in and what they were allowed to be doing there. Travel within the USSR was highly restricted and holiday opportunities were usually granted through a person's workplace. This did not mean that people never travelled but rather meant that travel was purely functional. The Soviet Union spanned 12 time zones, and its citizens were jostled from one end to the other in order to make socialism work. Ukrainian geologists were sent to research Kamchatka's volcanoes, while an Estonian family would be given work in a Zaporizhzhya factory. The gigantic Soviet military was the largest mechanism of travel, where new recruits were given assignments that usually tended to be very far from home. (Ask any man over 30 where he served in the army and you'll get a lesson in Eurasian geography.) Besides the military, only the party élite and very few others were permitted to make trips beyond the border. Soviet citizens showing interest in foreign countries were under suspicion of wanting to defect and all Westerners were dubbed spies. Needless to say, the concept of independent travel was non-existent.

Inturist
'Inturist' was the established government section in charge of all tourist affairs both for incoming foreigners and Soviet citizens. As the ultimate award for work or political achievements, Ukrainians could go on specially designed tours to other parts of the communist world such as Bulgaria or, in very rare cases, Cuba, and only after completing intense background checks. For the few foreign visitors that did get into the Soviet Union, Inturist acted as an 'anti-travel agency' to prevent them from actually travelling. Tours, hotels, and itineraries were set up to let foreigners see as little of the country as possible and go home with decent (albeit fake) impressions of the Soviet Union.

A two-tiered system evolved that kept foreigners and locals segregated in their leisure. Foreigners paid six to ten times the price for any tourist service, despite the false exchange rate of the command economy. There were plush 'foreign' hotel rooms, restaurants and fancy shops where only foreigners could go, and train tickets for higher, foreign prices. Most of the country was completely off-limits.

Today, this two-tiered system is slowly crumbling, and most proprietors now pride themselves in charging foreigners the same price as Ukrainians. Still, the unfortunate belief pervades that foreigners need to be catered for separately. Travellers will feel confined if they do only what is expected of them. This also means luxury treatment at luxury prices, and at first you may be refused a budget room simply on the pretext that you are a foreigner and should pay more.

In addition to keeping the outside separate from the inside, Inturist served to keep track of foreigners' movements. Visas were (and technically still are) issued for individual cities, not the whole country. Upon arrival in a city, registration with the local authorities was mandatory and checks were put in place to trace the traveller's path. You had to show your visa and have the details copied before being issued a room key or buying a train ticket. Many of these protocols still remain but have more to do with ticket sellers being able to read your name in Cyrillic than having a bored bureaucrat in Kiev tracking your moves.

The most unpleasant leftover of the Inturist days is the mentality that travel exists in an institutional medium granted from above. According to this mindset, there are no travellers, only tourists; and tourists only go and see what is offered them. Experiences are either purchased or permitted and there is little room for free movement or free interpretation. Much of Ukraine's tourist industry still caters to this philosophy out of bad habit and independent travellers will get lots of quizzical looks. You may be told that what you are doing is *nel'zya* ('forbidden'!) or just impossible. It *is* possible, and legal, and everyone else is missing out.

Ukraine unveiled

Beyond the Soviet experience, Ukrainian traditions are closer to a traveller's heart. Historically, Ukraine's *kobzari* roamed freely across the land singing long ballads and reciting poetry to villagers in exchange for their hospitality. Pilgrims spent lifetimes walking the thousands of miles between the sacred sites of Orthodoxy, the very voyage becoming a spiritual act. These are traditions that deserve remembrance today as more people travel to Ukraine and more Ukrainians begin to travel in their own country. The suspicion surrounding foreigners is lessening and now there is a sincere curiosity about the rest of the globe. You may still be stopped by police who want to see your *dokumenty*, but they are most likely to be interested in chatting with a foreigner rather then causing you problems. Indeed, the interest of the outside world in Ukraine is a boost to national self-esteem following a slump. In response to Ukrainians dreaming of the tropics, one Ukrainian traveller said, 'Why go and see sand? We have everything here: forests, rivers, lakes, fields, mountains, and the sea.'

Organised travel versus independent travel

This may be an easy choice for some to make, but it is worth pondering seriously. If you want to see the main tourist sites in a short time, or else you are looking for a specialised itinerary, such as Jewish heritage sites, an organised tour would be best. If you are keen to wander across the countryside and enjoy the process of discovery, do it yourself. Keep in mind that preconceived notions about either form of travel do not apply in Ukraine because 'travel' is still so young. The new group tours on offer have not been around long enough to be cheesy, and if you pick the right tour agency, the trip will definitely prove adventurous. Most people choose organised tours for the convenience of having someone else deal with the visa and internal transportation arrangements, as well as the fact that this eliminates the feared language barrier. Ukraine is much more ready for foreigners travelling in a group than it is prepared to deal with independent travellers. The real Ukraine

– the hilariously rude women behind counters, the all-night train rides, and picnics in the forest – are beyond the coach's windows and tour guide's umbrella. Independent travel ensures intimate interaction with the people, which is easily Ukraine's greatest attraction. There are still certain activities that will require someone else's help, eg: a trip to Chernobyl or serious hiking in Crimea, and these are best arranged prior to your trip. If you are travelling on your own, remember that you are a pioneer of sorts, reinventing a lost concept. Move wisely and enjoy the bumps.

TRANSPORTATION (GETTING AROUND)
By air
Flying between cities in Ukraine can save a lot of time and is usually quite cheap (around US$60 one way). Lviv, Donetsk, Dnepropretrovsk, Kharkiv, Odessa, and Simpferopol have year-round air connections, but travellers often have to change in Kiev. Remember that domestic flights almost always go through Kiev Zhulyany Airport and that, if connecting to an international flight, you will have to transfer to Borispol. Even though many other cities will boast an airport, they may not actually have any flights, and schedules depend on the season. The summer months offer a wide range of flights, and during the tourist season in Crimea there are direct daily flights between Simpferopol and all major cities. Most local travel agencies can book and sell tickets, as can any of the upscale hotels in cities where there is a functioning airport. Take note that domestic flights have a much lower service standard than international flights and stricter luggage requirements.

Aerosvit is an established domestic carrier with internal flights between Kiev, Kharkiv, Simpferopol, Odessa, and Dnepropetrovsk. The main booking office in Kiev is at Vulitsa Vasylkivska 9/2, Office 7A; tel: (044) 490 3490; email: vvtls1@aerosvit.com; web: www.aerosvit.com/eng.

Kiy Avia offers the widest range of destinations (including Ivano-Frankivsk and Chernivtsi). In Kiev, 4 Vul. Horodetskoho, tel: (044) 490 4949; or 1 Vulitsa Dmytrivska; tel: (044) 490-4907; email: info@kiyavia.com; web: www.kiyavia.com.

Ukraine International Airlines has domestic flights between Kiev and Lviv, Dnepropretrovsk, Donetsk, Odessa, and Simpferopol. In Kiev, 14 Prospekt Peremohy; tel: (044) 461 5050; email: uia@ps.kiev.ua; web: www.ukraine-international.com/eng.

There are other airlines that fly domestically, such as Air Ukraine and ICAR, but these smaller companies tend to be in constant flux and have a less reliable record. Regional airlines are mentioned in their respective chapters.

By rail
While most Soviet institutions dissolved in a flash, the trains kept running. Ukraine has inherited its own portion of the vast rail network that once connected the entire Soviet Union (at its height it was the largest railroad in the world) and although it is the slowest way to travel, it is the most reliable way to criss-cross the country. Trains are comfortable and cheap, and Ukraine's present rail system is far more efficient than those of Britain or America.

Technically, you can get anywhere by train, but it is best for long distances between larger cities. Train routes were built towards Kiev and Moscow as focal points, so north and south lines tend to be quicker than the east–west trains which have to zigzag across the country. Schedules were designed so that a journey between two major cities would last the night and travellers could awake at their destination. As distances vary, these overnight trips may have to leave in the early afternoon or else closer to midnight in order to make travel time end closer to morning. Thinking in terms of train travel time, Ukraine is 'two days' wide, with Kiev in the centre. Lviv–Kiev is one overnight journey, and Kiev–Kharkiv is another night's journey. Dnepropetrovsk and the Black Sea cities are overnight journeys from Kiev, while far eastern Ukraine (Luhansk) and Crimea are one and a half days, meaning a long night and then a half-day more.

Every large city has at least one train with a daily connection to and from Kiev. These 'company' trains are a little nicer and faster than the regular trains and christened with cute names to represent the region of Ukraine it serves (the train to Donetsk is called *The Little Lump of Coal*). The *Capital Express* is a new 'European' train that speeds between Kiev and Kharkiv twice daily, stopping in Mirhorod and Poltava on the way. The journey takes only five hours. Cities closer to Kiev can be reached on daytime trains, or else you can wake up in the middle of the night to quickly get on or off during a two-minute stop.

Smaller *elektrichki* connect rural areas to regional urban centres and leave from a smaller *vokzal* usually located next door to the main station. These trains are used primarily by people who live in the country and come to trade in the town markets, or else during the summer when they are packed full of city dwellers brandishing hoes who faithfully tend their individual plots. This is a completely separate rail system with its own ticketing. The trains are dismally slow and, even with the tight rows of upright wooden benches, the cars are crowded. *Elektrichki* are hot and airless in the summer and absolutely freezing in the winter. If you want to go out to the countryside, you may be better off taking a bus, although you'll be missing another bright bit of the real Ukraine.

In the station

The вокзал (*vokzal*, station) embodies all the excitement of travel under one great roof. The buildings tend to be more grandiose than the functional Soviet style since many of them were built by the Germans during the occupation. Inside, the commotion never stops. Hustlers and pickpockets are always at work in the larger stations, so be on guard.

Довідко (*dovidko*, Ukrainian), Справочная (*spravochnaya*, Russian), is the information booth and may or may not be marked with the little 'i' symbol. It is more identifiable as the window where the woman has a microphone. Finding out about train timetables and prices has to be done separately from the actual buying of the ticket, and your sincerest question at the каса (*kasa*, ticket counter) may be met with a finger pointing you to the information counter. If you require any information to be written down they will charge you for it (around 2UAH).

New to many refurbished *vokzal* are plush first-class lounges with an entrance fee of around US$1. Passengers rest here after arriving in the middle of the night or before leaving sometime before dawn. This closed-in lounge is guarded, heated in winter, air conditioned in summer and there are lots of big cushy chairs to sleep on. If you can sleep sitting up and don't mind the TV blaring all night, it's a cheap night's rest.

Some remodelled stations also have flashy 'Service Centres' which were designed as a separate information/ticket booth for Western tourists. In some cities, foreigners are required to buy their tickets here. The attendants rarely speak English but can be helpful. It is still easier to chance it and get in the regular queues with everyone else.

In every station there is a secure room where you can leave luggage for up to 24 hours and sometimes longer. Look for the камера схову (*kamera skhovu*, Ukrainian); камера хранения (*kamera khraneniya*, Russian) with the symbol of a suitcase in a box with a key above it. (Sometimes it is a short walk to the side of the station.) Larger stations will have automatic lockers that work with tokens purchased at a booth nearby. Set your own combination on the inside, drop in one token and shut the door. To open, set the combination on the outside, drop the token and pull. If there are no automatic lockers or your bags are too large, the left-luggage room with shelves is perfectly safe. You may be horrified at the thought of leaving your things with seemingly impoverished strangers, but I have never heard of anything being stolen from these attended rooms. The service costs up to 4UAH a bag and you'll be given a flimsy bit of paper that you need to show when you come back.

Train schedules/buying tickets

Kiev's main station is the only one in Ukraine that posts both Cyrillic and Latin spellings for its train schedule. This should be a strong incentive to learn the alphabet. If you can read the cities and know the words відправлення (*vidpravlennya*, departure), and прібуття (*pributtya*, arrival), you should be able to understand the timetables. Only final destinations and origins are listed so think regionally. Find the closest city to your desired goal or else look at a map. Trains leave щоденно (*shchodenno*, every day), or perhaps on even парні (*parni*) or odd непарні (*neparni*) days. Remember that you can get anywhere on a train, but it will take time.

There are generally three different class tickets for a train. CB (*es-vay*) is luxury class and means the compartment will have only two bunks inside. Not all trains have these first-class spaces. Купе (*coupé*) is still considered comfort-class with four bunks inside. Плацкарт (*platskart*) is the lower-class car packed full of rows of small bunks. (There is an even lower-class ticket occasionally sold, but it is like travelling in a cattle car.) Not all trains have luxury compartments so sometimes taking a *coupé* is the most obvious option. A typical overnight ride in a *coupé* costs US$8 to $12, while a luxury ticket from Lviv to Kiev will be under US$30.

Some train stations will have only one functioning ticket counter, while others seem to have a hundred, all with different specifications on who is allowed to buy tickets there (eg: war veterans, parents with children, invalids, etc). Go to the longest queue, or ask which *kasa* sells to foreigners. If you do not speak any of the language, say the city, or else write down the date you want to travel, your destination and which class. You will have to show the visa page of your passport in order to be issued a ticket, and you must pay in cash. Outside of the station, there are central offices selling rail tickets in larger cities, and some of the former Inturist offices can also do bookings. It is best to buy tickets a few days in advance, but if you are an impulsive traveller, you will most likely be able to get tickets on the day of departure. You may be told there are no more tickets and to come back later. Last-minute free spots only show up on the computer a few hours before the train leaves and may cost a little bit extra. Some travellers want to buy out a whole compartment either for privacy or security. This works sometimes, but you cannot prevent the conductor from sticking somebody in with you when they see your *coupé* is empty. Your belongings are probably safer when there are other people around. Don't ever buy from touts, even though they rarely approach foreigners. In the early post-Perestroika days it was easy to bribe your way onto a train, even across a border. Those days are long gone and a foreigner without a legitimate printed ticket will pay heavily.

Spaces are usually assigned. Lower bunks (*nyzhniy*) are considered more favourable than the upper (*verkhniy*) and it is normal to request your preference when you buy the ticket. Your luggage is more protected under the lower bunks. *Coupé* train cars have seven compartments, and #4 in the middle of the car has the most sought after tickets. If you end up in the upper right-hand bunk in #7 you will know that you did not make a flattering impression at the ticket counter or else you were the last one to buy a ticket. The toilet is on the other side of the wall and the door bangs all night long. Going *platskart* is hardly worth the few hrivna you save, but if you want to try it out, take extra precautions. Travel with someone else and don't carry valuables with you. The people in *platskart* are not significantly more dishonest, but there are so many people in one space that it is more difficult to keep a watch out for the one thief that may be lurking.

Train schedules seem to be the one thing that never changes in Ukraine and trains always run on time. If the train is originating from your location, board early, around 15 minutes before departure. Platform numbers are listed no more than 20 minutes before the train leaves. If the train is only stopping by, be ready to get on fairly quickly. Read your ticket to know which car (*vagon*) you are in and be standing near where you judge that car will arrive.

On the train

A rush of legs and bags will follow the train's shining headlight down the platform, even though there may be plenty of time before it leaves. Early boarders get to stake out the better storage spaces and tend to roost supreme in the *coupé*. Each *vagon* has a uniformed conductor who checks your ticket before letting you on, distributes bedding, and serves tea and coffee. These conductors are usually young women who work a gruelling schedule. Get on their good side and your trip will be nicer.

Don't expect to 'see Ukraine' from your seat on the train. Years of dirt and smoke have misted up the windows, causing the view to be more obscured than mystical. In addition, the Soviet government planted trees along the major rail lines to prevent travellers from seeing politically sensitive bits of the country. In summer, it may seem you are riding in a green tunnel. Still, there will be gaps when a glance out the window will meet a fantastic view of golden sunflower fields or an ice-encased forest.

Where you will see Ukraine is *inside* the train. Life on the train car is as real as it gets, and you'll find that trains are a great way to become intimately acquainted with people. A range of customs sets the atmosphere on Ukrainian trains. For the duration of travel, the stress and hard work of daily life have ceased, and the mood is laidback and celebratory. If you are sharing a *coupé* it is polite to introduce yourself early on and participate in the conversation. Food is shared, stories are swapped and the party will drag on late into the night. This is a great time to practise your language and interact freely. In almost every case the other passengers will be excited to have a foreigner in their car and they will look out for you. A *coupé* generates a sense of solidarity and befriending your fellow travellers is the best way to ensure you don't get anything taken and that you feel safe. In these circumstances, it is fine to leave your things while you explore the rest of the train.

Early in the trip, the conductor will come by to check tickets and distribute bedding. This is mandatory and costs extra (around 8UAH). The conductor also serves coffee, tea, or mineral water upon request, each for a handful of kopecks. It's a good idea to bring an extra bottle of water with you as the windows are permanently screwed shut and the air gets rather warm. Restaurant cars are present but rarely serve the lavish cooked meals they once did. Things are quick and casual now: soup from a packet, instant coffee, dry rolls etc. The train will stop at many towns along the way, and *babushki* jump at the doorway to sell you *pirozhki*, hot *varenniki*, drinks, or even whole smoked chickens.

Each car will have a WC at one end, equipped with a toilet and small sink. Push on the lever under the faucet to make the water run. When you flush, you'll catch a glimpse of the tracks whizzing beneath you. This is the very obvious reason that the WC is locked when the train is not moving. Smokers must use the small space at the end of the car right before the coupling joints that connect the cars. Watch your fingers and toes when crossing from one car to the next. Before going to sleep, lock the door of your compartment. One lock is the turning handle and the conductor can open this with a key. The other lock is a metal clip on the upper left-hand side of the door. This sticks out and blocks the door from opening all the way and is not entirely necessary.

If you are on an overnight train and your stop is not the final destination, the conductor will make sure you are awake. Be ready to hop off quickly. In the smaller stations, trains stop for one to two minutes. Otherwise the whole train wakes up together with lights and loud pop music. You'll find that mornings are busy with people brushing their teeth and shaving in the corridor, changing clothes and re-packing bags. It may have taken you 12 hours to go just 300km, but you will have slept most of the way and experienced Ukraine's grandest travel tradition.

By bus

Much quicker, much less expensive, but a little less comfortable is the *avtobus*, which can be a plush coach, a bouncy 1960s bus, or a claustrophobic minivan. The bus travels at about 100km/h so it cuts train time in half (Odessa to Kiev takes only six hours). The bus also allows a great view of the countryside, and this is how most people travel to the rural areas. It is the main form of transport around Crimea, as well as the preferred method of travel between the many mountain villages of the Carpathians. You can go literally anywhere on the bus, but schedules change frequently so it becomes a task of going to the station and finding out how soon you can leave. The main *avtovokzal* (bus station) is located on the far outskirts of town in big cities or else right next to the train station in very small towns. When there are multiple bus stations, locate the one closest to the direction of your destination. Tickets can be bought in advance, or on the bus. Sometimes there are assigned seats, sometimes not, and sometimes seats are assigned but people sit wherever they want anyway. Hold on to the minuscule bit of paper that is your ticket. Buses and minivans will stop and pick up every person that flags them down so things can get fairly claustrophobic, if not chaotic. In the dead of winter, buses can be extremely cold and you'll pray for a large *babushka* to come sit next to you. In the summer, you'll want a window seat. When the bus does make a stop, keep a sharp eye out for your bags. Theft on buses is uncommon, but then, so are you.

The exception to the above is a new range of private companies that charge a little more than the train, but will get you there quickly and in relative comfort:

Avtoluks is a quality coach company that offers regular daily connections across all of Ukraine with offices in each regional centre. They have an English website: www.Avtoluks.ua. Central Office: Kiev, V. Chistyakovskaya 30; tel: (044) 536 00 55; email: info@Avtoluks.ua

Gyunsel is another company with good service. They are based in Kiev and have daily services to and from Dnepropetrovsk, Donetsk, Khar'kiv, Kherson (via Uman), and Kosiv (via Vinnytsya and Chernivtsi). There are additional lines to Crimea in summer. In Kiev's central *avtovokzal*, tel: (044) 488 88 01/ (044) 265 03 78; email: office@gunsel.com.ua

By car

There are not enough pages in this book to list the reasons you should not want to drive in Ukraine, and yet people do it. Touring Ukraine behind the wheel is more stressful than it is adventurous and paranoia about your car getting stolen or wrecked will quickly replace the joy of being able to roam freely. For the few who still dare to drive, consider the following:

If you are driving your own car, have every possible bit of paperwork and registration with you, especially your customs declaration form. You must have an international driver's licence. A very solid anti-theft device (eg: steering-wheel lock) is mandatory, and a car alarm is highly recommended. Foreign cars are known targets. Park only in guarded, fenced-in car parks and avoid driving between cities after dark as this is when most car-jackings occur.

Ukrainian roads are abominable. Often there are more holes than there is road and it is common to get stuck doing 30km/h just to keep the shocks intact. Every season has its perils: deep sticky mud in spring, ice in winter and dust and pebbles in summer. Cracked windscreens are very common. Petrol stops, road-stop cafés and motels are becoming more regular but only accept cash. International road signs apply and most Ukrainian bookshops sell good quality road atlases, some with Roman spellings.

Highway roadblocks are also a favoured pastime of the Ukrainian police (aka 'auto-inspection officers'). Drivers in the other lane will flash their front beams to warn of an upcoming block and to slow down. A patrol will signal you to pull over by holding out a black-and-white stick. If you do get pulled over at a roadblock, the best strategy is shrugging your shoulders and speaking only in English. Usually this gets you waved on. If not, be co-operative in showing them the requested documents and don't try anything silly like bribing them.

Car rentals are a fairly new possibility and are available in a few cities. Prices are two to three times higher than what you would expect at home, and this is not including the additional, higher than average insurance. Professional auto thieves target rental cars so take every precaution for security. Rental companies offer chauffeur-driven cars as well, which can be a much less stressful option. **Europcar** (www.europcar.com), **Hertz** (www.hertz.com.ua), and **Avis** (www.avis.com.ua) are the most established. Specific information is given in the regional chapters.

Hitching

There is no such thing as a free ride in Ukraine. Waving down a car for a ride is normal, but the driver is stopping in the hope of getting some cash from you. Out in the country this is sometimes the better way to travel. In cities, hitching works as an informal taxi system. Stop a car by sticking your right hand out palm down. Many drivers will take whatever you give them, but it is best to make a deal beforehand.

Near the bus station there will always be a few men trying to fill their cars up with passengers going to the same destination. This way they cover their gas costs and can make a bit of money on the way. You may sit for a long time until the car is absolutely crammed before you leave. Still, it can be a quicker way to travel and usually costs the same as the bus. Make sure the price is understood and don't pay until you've reached your destination and stepped out of the car with your bags. Women travelling alone should obviously avoid hitching.

TRAVELLING IN THE CITY
Taxis

Taxis are generally easy to find and use, but keep in mind that in Ukraine taxi drivers have the reputation of minor league con men so it pays to be savvy. They are doing it for the money and some will double the price when they encounter a foreigner. It never pays to be too paranoid about getting ripped off, but bargain all the same. Excluding Kiev, a trip anywhere inside a city should never be over US$2. (Kiev, followed by Simpferopol and Chernivtsi, are the worst cities for overpriced taxis.) If you have the choice, go for the little guy – meaning the beat-up Lada and

Zhigulii with self-positioned taxi signs. These are entrepreneurial taxi drivers who must still pay off a higher hand for the privilege to be working. They cost less than the larger taxi companies and tend to be of more honest character. Always agree on a price before sitting in the car and don't get talked into paying more. If you are planning on taking a taxi on a long trip outside the city, the general rule is 1UAH per km. Often the driver will offer to wait, or else you will have asked him to make the return journey. He will charge you extra for the wait so make sure you have agreed on the price.

Public transportation within towns and cities

Communism granted Ukraine an exceptional system for moving lots of people around quickly. Decades of wear and tear have slowed things down a bit, but it will always be the best way to go from A to B in a bustling city. Most people travel only by public transport and you'll be amazed at the number of bodies squeezed into a single car. Things can get very cramped during rush hour (07.00–10.00, 16.00–19.00) so keep your purse or backpack against your chest and breathe slowly. Before a stop, individuals inch their way to the door, asking each person in their way if they are getting off. If someone taps you on the shoulder and mutters something, move out of the way or else nod if you are getting off. At times you will have no choice but to be ejected. Learn to be pushy and fight your way on and off transport.

Subway

Kiev, Kharkiv, and Dnepropetrovsk each have a metro, open from 05.30 until midnight. Tokens cost 50 kopecks and can be bought in a booth at the entrance or sometimes from the small orange machines hanging on the wall. One token buys one trip to any other station. Drop the token in, and the metal gates open up. When things get really crowded, make sure to allow the doors to close after the person in front of you before dropping your token and walking through. Getting shut in the doors really hurts.

Ability to read signs is helpful, especially when changing lines, but a good map will do the trick. There are maps in this guide and most subways will have maps posted at the entrance and in the cars. If in doubt, follow the largest crowd.

Trolleys, trams and buses

The *tramvai* and *trolleybus* are an Eastern European institution and good for going short distances in town. Signs mark the stops. People are usually packed on too tightly for you to just walk on and pay. The best method is to hold a 1UAH note in your hand as if you are ready to buy a ticket. The conductor will come and sell you one for between 40 and 60 kopecks. Otherwise, people pass money hand over hand all the way to the driver, and the change is passed all the way back. A ticket is ripped or hole punched to show that its been used. Hold on to it in case of random checks by the controllers. If you are carrying heavy luggage, you may be expected to pay extra. It is safest to buy one ticket per bag and avoid the likes of big-city controllers who enjoy fining foreigners. The word for fine is *straf* and if it's over US$2 they are making it up.

Marshrutka taxis are both public or private minibuses that run maze-like routes through the city. They use the regular bus stops, but you can also flag them down anywhere you see them. In smaller towns, these will be the most reliable way to get between city centres and train and bus stations. The number and route are usually posted in the window, but always check with the driver by stating your destination and waiting for a *da* or *nyet*. The cost is usually 1–2UAH. They can get crowded and your view may be blocked. Ask someone next to you to let you know when to get off or just call out *na ostanovkye!* ('next stop!').

ACCOMMODATION
Hotels

Transition is the best way to describe Ukraine's present state of accommodation. Until recently, hotels were either bawdy hangouts for the Soviet *nomenklatura* or basic dormitories to house the travelling proletariat. Major refurbishing has turned a few crumbling buildings into shiny, high-standard hotels in the largest cities and among the traditionally approved tourist spots, otherwise, expect hotels to be fewer and standards to be lower than back at home. (What's on offer will tell you how far off the beaten path you are travelling.) Most Soviet-era hotels are in the midst of staggered reconstruction. The push to make everything *Evro* (European) standard has generated higher prices and some saccharine décor, while often overlooking the essentials. Awareness of the following realities will help:

Plumbing is not a Ukrainian forte, and enquiries about water can incite a frank display of optimism. ('No, we don't have hot water, but we *do* have cold water!') In luxury hotels, there will always be hot water, but in middle-range and budget hotels, be sure to check, even if it means visiting the room and turning on the faucet. Countrywide, hot water is usually turned off sometime in late spring and then comes back on in October. During the winter months, most hotels will post hot water schedules in the lobby (usually early morning and late evening). 'European' showers are often perceived to be more upper class than bathtubs, and so remodelled rooms will often have showers. Budget rooms also sometimes have a 'shower' which is a drain on the bathroom floor and a hose coming out of the wall. *Lux* rooms will have both.

The concept of double beds is fairly unknown. Normally, a 'double' room means twin beds. You'll have to make a special request for 'a single bed for two people', and even then, this is usually two single beds joined together. The very nicest hotels will have real queen-size beds, but this is still a new thing. Traditional Ukrainian bedding consists of a two-sided sheet covering a thick woollen blanket, much like a duvet, and most pillows are filled with goose down. During colder months, you can always find extra blankets stuffed in the cupboard.

Central heating and air conditioning have also just made their debut in Ukraine, and many hotels will advertise that their nicer rooms have *konditsioner*. If travelling in winter among the humblest of hotels, you can stay warm by stripping the bedclothes and mattress and making your bed next to the heater on the floor.

Ukrainian rooms are traditionally classified as *odnomestny* (single, *one place*), *dvukhmestny* (double, *two places*), *pol-lux* (junior suite) and *lux* (suite). Suites can be much nicer, or simply more complex, with multiple rooms, multiple TV sets or multiple toilets; however, value-for-money, it is sometimes better to get a *lux* or *pol-luks* in an average hotel then to get the double room in a more expensive hotel. This may have something to do with the fact that Ukrainians rarely stay in a hotel for functional reasons, but usually hold parties in larger suites.

Classification

Establishing a fixed system for grading Ukrainian hotels is impossible since price, quality and service vary so much from place to place (even floor to floor). Ukraine's star-rating system should also be ignored since it is inconsistent and irrelevant. Never trust outside appearances: the hotel entrance may sport a gold-emblazoned 'Reception' sign (in English) over smiling uniformed staff, while two floors up the rooms lack hot water; meanwhile, the dingy grey concrete block down the road may turn out to have comfortable luxury rooms. This book classifies hotels by room price, and there is some correlation to standard, but not always. The general rule is to always see a room before you take it.

Luxury

Most of Ukraine's poshest hotels have been open only two or three years and range from an élite corporate standard to very opulent palaces that would easily classify as five-star in the West. Anything upwards of US$100 a night is considered luxury, but in cities where there's a choice (Kiev, Odessa, Crimea) you'll find the value of US$100 highly variable. Ukrainians expect all foreigners to stay only in luxury hotels, but the rooms don't feel very Ukrainian. All luxury hotels have their own private source for hot water and electricity and usually feature very nice restaurants (the staff will also speak some English). Mafia culture has encouraged the latest fad: sumptuous 'rest cottages' managed by luxury hotels out in the countryside.

Middle range

The nebulous in-between means anything that is neither obvious luxury hotel nor of the lowly Soviet variety. Prices range from US$40 to US$90, and this is where tour groups usually stay. Most middle-range hotels are in flux, meaning some rooms have been remodelled, many have not, instilling a two-tiered pricing structure for 'standard' rooms of lower quality, and the better 'comfort' rooms. Middle-range rooms will have their own bathrooms that usually feature hot water and since most of these were former Inturist hotels, they offer convenient services for travellers.

Budget

Overall, most hotels in Ukraine are fairly inexpensive, but because of the push to modernise, wealthier markets are taking over. Ukraine's budget hotels mainly consist of the old Soviet hotels that have not been bought up by business developers, and charge US$5 to $30 for a very basic room. In some places, this will be all that is available, and you should relish the experience. A lot of middle-range hotels will also have cheap rooms, which are simply not yet remodelled, so it is always worth checking. Budget travellers can knock a fair amount off the room price by differentiating between a room with *udobstv* ('conveniences') or *bez udobstv* ('without conveniences'). Getting a room with sink only and no toilet or shower means sharing a communal facility in the hall for which you normally pay 3 to 5UAH each time for a hot shower. Smaller budget hotels will also clean clothes and shine shoes for minimal fees.

Security

Middle-range and luxury hotels always have a security guard posted at the entrance or near the lift to prevent non-residents from entering. Hotel management also have a secure safe, and some upmarket rooms will also have their own safes. Leaving things in your room is normally fine – the cleaners will dust underneath the wad of bills you left on the night table and put them right back as they were. The real threat is people from outside the hotel who know you are staying there. Stash valuables away in different places in your room. Always lock the door behind you when you enter the room. If someone knocks, ask who it is (*kto tam?*) and if it is not a sweet old lady with cleaning supplies, then don't open.

Payment

Making a reservation (*bronirovaniye*) usually means contacting the hotel ahead of time and paying a non-refundable fee equal to half the price of the room upon arrival. As of yet there is no norm for price: some hotels charge per person, others charge per room. Aside from luxury hotels, all amenities are considered added extras and will be included in your bill: telephone, refrigerator, television. Hotels usually specify if breakfast is included in the price (normally it is). Even though laws and protocol have changed, some hotels still charge foreigners at least twice as much as Ukrainians for the same room, although the practice is fading away as Ukrainian travellers become much wealthier than foreigners. Most lower-standard hotels will charge you in advance for the whole duration of your stay.

Other options
Most train stations have small sections of rooms with beds that function like a hotel. Follow the bed signs, normally up to the second floor. In small towns a room costs around US$7 while in the biggest cities, the standard is much nicer and rooms cost around US$20.

Another good way to save money is to rent a private apartment, for one night or for a month. The quality of accommodation is often much more comfortable than any budget hotel (hot water, bathroom and kitchen) and can cost around US$18 and up a night. Private companies will advertise short-term apartment stays, or you can find women outside the train station who are yelling *kvartira* (apartment) or *komnata* (room). Ask the price, see the apartment, and then make a deal and get the keys. The best cities for apartments are Yalta, Kiev, and Odessa. Arrange beforehand if you will pay up-front or pay per day.

Country home stays
Inspired by foreign development projects, 'rural tourism' is evolving in certain regions of Ukraine (eg: the Carpathians and Crimea) allowing a bed-and-breakfast style home on rural farms for between US$5–10 a night. Keep in mind that these programmes are in their earliest stages of development, so the experience can be raw but invigorating. If you want to see life on a farm and make friends with the people who live there, it should be encouraged. Information on green rural tourism is found in the appropriate chapters.

Camping
Camping in Ukraine can be more institutionalised than travellers wanting to camp are used to. Often signs for camping will bring you to hotel-like accommodation with hotel-like prices. In the Carpathians, most campsites include a *kolyba* (mountain hut), while in Crimea, campsites tend to be near caves of some sort. If building a fire near proscribed sites, always use the metal rings provided. Camping in the wild should not pose a problem, but keep in mind the general mindset of suspicion towards foreigners and check beforehand to make sure you are not entering a restricted area.

EATING AND DRINKING
Drink
Drink is synonymous with alcohol in a country where vodka is the national pastime and a cultural rite. All holidays, birthdays, weddings (and funerals) are celebrated with *horilka* (vodka). Business dealings are done over a vodka toast, and new friends are made to feel welcome with '100 grams'. In the dead of winter, a stiff swallow at breakfast keeps workers warm as they set off into the cold, but only when followed by frequent doses throughout the day. Without a doubt, vodka is imbibed in alarming quantities in Ukraine. Hetman is the most refined brand, but there are more brands of vodka than there are first names in Ukraine, and vodka takes up the

most shelf space in food shops. *Samogon* is a homemade vodka brew and each family has its own special method for distilling it. Only drink *samogon*' if it is offered to you in someone's home or in a restaurant. The stuff sold in the open-air market is not regulated and is often laced with lethal ingredients (like anti-freeze) to increase its volume and potency. *Pyvo* (beer) is the most widespread 'soft' drink, with varying strengths of alcohol content (up to 12%). Chernihiv and Rogan are the most beloved Ukrainian brands. Foreigners take differently to Ukrainian wine, but if wine-tasting is your thing, there are a few Crimean and Tavrian wines with reputation, in particular those from Massandra. Georgian and Moldavian wines are next in popularity and *Sovietsky* champagne is uncorked at the slightest allusion to festivity.

The national non-alcoholic beverage is *kvas*, made from old black bread and sugar. It has a malted flavour and tastes best cold and homemade. Ukrainians also bottle *kompot*, a light drink made from their homegrown fruit and boiled water. Cherry is the best. A very wide selection of juice (pear, peach, plum, grape, etc) is available in restaurants, kiosks and shops.

Mineral water is always available, and it is a good idea to become acquainted with the Ukrainian springs and choose one you like. Evian and Volvic are sold in the fancier marketplaces, but locals will insist you benefit from the healing qualities of their own mineral water. Ukrainian brands tend to be a bit saltier than you may be used to. Mirhorod and Truskavets are the most well-known. If you want less mineral taste and no fizz, ask for Bon Akva Negazova.

Coffee (*kava* in Ukrainian, *kofye* in Russian) will be on offer in the humblest of circumstances, and instant flavoured coffee seems to be the latest fad. *Chai* (tea) is revered in Ukraine almost as much as it is in England, and is usually served with lemon and sugar. Having milk with your tea is a foreign concept and may be treated as an impossible request; bring your own milk powder if it is important. Herbal teas (*chai iz trav*) make a nice hot drink, and for every ailment Ukrainian *babushki* have collected some twig or flower that will cure you. Everyone collects *lipa* from the flowering lime trees after which the month of July is named. Mint and camomile are also popular. In homes, homemade jam or natural honey is served with tea to be stirred into the cup or else eaten plain by the spoonful.

Food

Ukrainian cuisine is such an honest expression of the land itself, and a traditional meal can teach you more about Ukraine than any guided tour in a museum. The richness of natural ingredients comes from centuries of growing things in fertile soil and an intimate relationship with the woods and steppe. Poverty, shortages, and political turmoil prevented store-bought goods from being used in recipes. The heavy workload of the peasant lifestyle with the added stress of severe winters and repeated famine meant food's main function was to fill empty bellies and keep bodies warm. This it does.

Borscht is the mainstay of the Ukrainian table and is probably the number one connotation foreigners make with Ukraine. It is not simply 'beet soup' as it tends to be known, but rather an important staple made with anything that grows in Ukraine. The bullion base is boiled with meat or vegetable stock, and then the various ingredients are slowly added one by one to bring out each flavour. Cabbage, potatoes, onions and dill are a must, and the beet is added to give colour. Everything else is thrown in at the discretion of the cook. A good bowl of borscht will consist of more vegetables than liquid and have a tangy aftertaste. The proven rule is that your spoon won't sink when placed in the centre of the bowl. As the ultimate comfort food, borscht is boiled in massive proportions in Ukrainian homes and served for breakfast, lunch, and dinner. It always tastes better after a day in the pot.

In restaurants, the soup will usually come with soft buns called *pampoushki* to dip into garlic sauce, or else black bread and *smetana*, a rich and flavourful cream.

Varenniki are large stuffed dumplings and considered *the* national dish of Ukraine. Generally, they are filled with potatoes and smothered in fried onions and *smetana*. They can also be filled with meat or farmer's cheese, and in spring they are stuffed with cherries, apples or strawberries and served for dessert. *Holubtsi* is another traditional dish of meat and rice rolled up in cabbage leaves and covered with a creamy tomato sauce. Technically from Siberia, *Pelmeny* are meat-filled ravioli.

Meat is treated as a luxury even though most people can afford it now. The traditional Ukrainian recipe is to stew it in little clay pots with potatoes, mushrooms and black pepper. Pork dishes are the most popular. *Balyk* is smoked pork tenderloin with very little fat, while *Salo* is pure smoked pork fat carved right off a pig's back. Ukrainians love the stuff and there are many jokes about how wonderful a thing it is. (When a beautiful woman lands on his desert island, a stranded Russian calls to a stranded Ukrainian on another island telling him to come quickly, the thing he wants has just arrived. The Ukrainian jumps into the sea and swims furiously, gasping 'Salo, Salo!') The lard is usually cut in thick slices and served as a snack with bread or whole raw garlic cloves. Sausage tends to be very fatty and usually eaten cold with bread.

Chicken Kiev is a legitimate Ukrainian dish but ordered only by foreigners. Fish abounds on restaurant menus, but skip anything from Ukraine's polluted rivers. Also, do not order *osetrina* (sturgeon) or black caviar. Sturgeon is an endangered species, and both of these Russian delicacies kill its chances for survival. (Red caviar is from salmon and is OK to eat.) Sardines and anchovies on toast are popular party fare.

What food you will eat depends largely on the time of year you are travelling, although imported produce is quickly becoming the norm for the new élite. Generally, market tables are laden with fresh fruits and vegetables – sweet peppers, cucumbers and every form of squash imaginable. All summer long, Ukrainians work in their country plots and then preserve the food for the barren winter months. These bottles of fruit, relishes and pickles spruce up the potatoes and soured cabbage. If you don't pucker up when you bite into a Ukrainian pickle, then it isn't Ukrainian. Fistfuls of salt, homegrown garlic and hot peppers give the piquancy. Ukrainians also take their mushroom and berry collecting seriously, using them in all kinds of traditional dishes (mushrooms sold in the market are safe and tasty).

Vegetarians need not fear as abstaining from meat has been a necessity for Ukrainians during lean years, and is also a religious practice for faithful Orthodox believers fasting for Lent and other holy festivals. Keep in mind that eating and serving meat of some sort is perceived as a sign of status, while lack of meat at a dinner table is a reluctant admittance to poverty. If you do turn down meat offered by a host, make sure to sincerely compliment another part of the meal. Traditional vegetarian staples include *deruny* (potato pancakes), buckwheat (*kasha*) and various vegetable stews and soups. *Mlyntsi*, or *blyni* in Russian are pancakes, sold like crepes in outdoor stands with either jam or savoury meat and cheese. If you want truly good Ukrainian cuisine, do what you can to be invited into someone's home for a meal. No restaurants can imitate the cooking of a Ukrainian *babushka*.

Street food

Food sold on the street is usually safe and very tasty (if its steaming or smells fresh, it won't come back to haunt you). *Babuskhi* are always selling hot *pirozhki* filled with potatoes, seasoned cabbage, or meat and you'll soon recognise their universal

BREAD

Bread *is* life in Ukraine, and you'll find it an important staple on your travels, by itself or else with cheese, *smetana* or sausage. Buy bread in the morning as all bakeries are sold out by early afternoon. *Baton* are the short white loaves that resemble oval French bread except much heavier. You can also find sourdough (square loaves) and all kinds of braided varieties for festivals. The traditional Ukrainian loaf is black bread (*chorni khlib*), made with buckwheat and rye flour and tasting slightly of vinegar. As a rule, one round loaf should weigh exactly one kilo. Black bread was the main staple of peasant diets far into the 20th century (and again during the last stretch of national poverty). The rallying cry and slogan of the first Russian revolution was 'Bread, Peace and Land' and the central role of wheat in Ukraine means that bread has always been a symbol of food, independence and wealth. Ukrainian tradition welcomes guests of honour in a ceremony of 'bread and salt' where a decorated loaf and a small bowl of salt are presented on an embroidered cloth. Originally, guests were meant to break off a piece, dip it in the salt, eat and nod. Nowadays, the loaf is usually spared for a later meal, so simply nod or bow in recognition of the ceremony.

call and learn to buy a few of these stuffed buns for the road. Modern street cuisine reflects the 'friendship of the nations' or multi-culturalism of Soviet days. Originally from Crimea and the Caucasus, *chebureki* pastries are stuffed with spicy meat and onions but their nourishing value comes from the heavy grease left on your fingers. In restaurants and homes you'll taste *plov,* a rice and mutton dish from Central Asia and *adzhika,* a spicy Georgian sauce made of herbs and tiny peppers served with meat or potatoes.

It is a sin to travel without food in Ukraine and people you've just met may pack elaborate hampers for the next leg of your journey, even if it's only just a two-hour bus ride. Train and bus stations sell more and more candy and alcohol and fewer staples, but a stop at any food shop (*gastronom* or *produkty*) can stock you for a journey. Fresh fruit, yoghurt, cheese, sausage, rolls, juice and water make good reserves for train trips. For long hikes, Ukrainians normally pack canned goods, chocolate, bread and bottled water.

Thank goodness the fall of the Soviet economy did not end Ukraine's faithful sweet production. The brightly wrapped candies are sold in bulk on the street, in shops, and even from restaurant menus. Try *byelochka* (chipmunk), a delicious hazelnut cream chocolate, or the crunchy *metior,* little balls of nuts and honey covered with black chocolate. Ukrainians like ice-cream year round, and it is sold and eaten on the streets even on the most frigid of January days (if it doesn't melt in your mouth, chew it).

Restaurants and cafés

Eating out is still considered a luxury for most Ukrainians so that you'll often find you're the only patron(s) in an upscale restaurant or that the only other guests are there for a wedding, birthday or business deal. Varied interpretations of European cuisine predominate and chefs will add pizzazz by naming their classiest dishes *syurpriz* (surprise!) or *lux* (deluxe). The latest rage is the restoration Ukrainian folk restaurant and if you are part of an organised tour, you are bound to see lots of these, as well as other themed dining: pirates, the Wild

West or the mystical East. Pizza and fast-food joints have also secured a corner in most cities; however, the norm is still the generic Soviet-style restaurants with names like Irina or Elit. Disco décor and live synthesised music are part of the experience, so enjoy it.

Upscale restaurants will have an English menu, and it is always worth asking for one, even in a small café. Otherwise, never let the fact that you can't read the menu be a deterrent. Ask what something is, sound it out or take a stab in the dark. Restaurant menus will appear incredibly inexpensive at first glance, which they are. The budget-conscious can still eat elaborate dinners for practically nothing; however, the accepted restaurant tactic is for bills to add up quickly. Menus usually state the price of a food next to its allotted quantity (in grams) – you pay separately for any extras, and everything is extra. Also, you may often find that the menu is several dozen pages long, but when you start ordering you are told that everything you want is unavailable. In such a case, find out what the kitchen is prepared to make or ask about the house specialties (firmeny blyuda).

The best way to judge a restaurant is by the price of a bowl of borscht, a universal common denominator in Ukraine. US$1 should be standard. Anything more than US$3 means the restaurant is pretentious and if it costs below one dollar, the general food standard may be lower than your stomach can handle. Travellers with small pockets or the simply curious can get a hearty and affordable hot meal at the stolovaya (cafeterias). If you are afraid of getting a bug, stick to hot staples like borscht and avoid the cold fried breaded bits of meat.

There exists no traditional concept of breakfast and Ukrainians eat much the same food in the morning as they do for lunch and dinner. Hotels generally offer a 'Swedish table' in the spirit of a smorgasbord with smoked meats or sausage, cheese, bread, coffee and tea. Cafés are just beginning to offer continental-style coffee and croissant.

THE BANYA

Ancestral tradition and a lack of hot water helped to make public bathing a favoured pastime in Ukraine and a cultural institution. A sauna is a dry sweat-bath of the Finnish variety, usually accompanied by a small pool of freezing water for intermittent dips followed by much yelping. The Russian banya is more traditional in Ukraine, and resembles a Turkish bath. As the whole ritual usually takes place in the nude, men and women visit separately. A stone oven in the parilka generates incredibly hot steam and people stand or lie down on the varied levels. Once your body is running with sweat, bunches of lime, birch or oak branches (depending on what effect you want) are used to whip and beat you until the green gel of broken leaves, bark and dead skin cells stands out against your red back. Traditionally you are supposed to scream for more (yescho!) until you almost pass out. Stepping out of the parilka, you should immediately immerse yourself in cold water, rest a bit, and then go back for more. Going to the banya also includes taking a series of showers at various temperatures, scrubbing yourself with soap, getting a massage, shaving, drinking lots of fluids (non-alcoholic) and engaging in vigorous conversation with the lads (or the girls). The experience is very communal, not least for the fact that people must partner up to beat each other. You emerge feeling clean inside and out, revived and ready to take on anything. In winter, regular visits to the banya will prevent catching colds.

Entrance normally costs less than US$3, although private rentals cost much more. The experience is meant to last several long hours, if not the whole day. You'll be given a white sheet as a wrap, and you can buy veniki (branches) there. Most hotels will have a sauna, which can be rented out by the hour, but for the real thing ask around for a traditional *banya*. In Ukraine's large cosmopolitan cities, authentic communal baths have given way to élite private clubs, but in the outskirts, people still follow a weekly tradition of going to the *banya*. Here are a few in Kiev:

Solomenskye Bany (Solomon's Baths) Urytskovo 38; tel: 044 244 0198. Communal and historic.
Troitskye Bany (Trinity Baths) Krasnoarmeiskaya 66; tel: 044 227 4068. Private and luxurious.
Tsentralnye Torgovye Bany (Central Trade Baths) Malaya Zhytomyrskaya 3A; tel: 044 228 0102. Huge and famous.

ARTS AND ENTERTAINMENT

How rare it is that a country with so little material wealth should sustain the arts with such passion. Ukrainians love art in all of its forms: theatre, dance, music, painting, etc and nobody should go to Ukraine without taking in a performance at the opera or ballet. Tickets are incredibly cheap (a private box in the Kiev Opera will cost under US$10) whereas the show's quality is always outstanding. The longstanding traditions of Russian and Ukrainian ballet have not faltered and many a traveller who thinks ballet is not his/her 'thing' gains a new fascination with dance. Opera is just as invigorating, and most theatres will rotate a very large repertoire over the course of the season. Even if you don't understand what a play is about, there is something about watching Chekhov performed in the country where he wrote. Also, part of the fun is watching all the families and young children who come dressed up for an affordable night out. Ukrainians of all ages enjoy even the most serious of plays, and to be seen at the theatre is a sign of one's cultural prestige. To complete the experience, eat red caviar toast during intermission, bring flowers for the ballerinas and shout 'bravo' louder than anyone else.

Films are always badly dubbed into Ukrainian or Russian, with the very rare exception of a Russian film, and Russian mafia culture (or lack of it) has introduced a whole new series of casinos and tawdry nightlife. Striptease has become the mistaken trademark of a 'classy' restaurant or club, and you might be surprised at a seemingly 'nice' restaurant in the middle of the day. Most of these dancers are underemployed ballerinas. Go to the ballet instead!

Museums

Ukrainian museums are always run by pleasant ladies and old men who normally did some related degree at a Soviet university and now earn kopecks managing the displays. Ask a question and you'll be astounded by the knowledge you gain. You'll find that the same authoritarian attitude about travel exists within museums and you'll be vehemently commanded where to go and what to look at. Free wandering is a no-no and if you skip a room or go in the 'wrong' direction you will face the wrath of a *babushka*. Because of a lack of money, there is rarely any heat inside museums and the attendants will not turn on the lights until you walk into a room.

Nearly every town has a natural history museum that tells the socialist history of the town from prehistoric times to the revolution and on to the Soviet era with displays on local achievements in agriculture and industry, as well as natural history, local dress and regional arts and crafts. Some museum attendants will be selling their own souvenirs or museum booklets which help to supplement their meagre incomes. Smaller towns rarely get foreign guests, so you may be asked to sign a guest book with your impressions of their museum.

SHOPPING

You can buy anything in Ukraine, which is quite a statement since only five years ago, there was quite literally nothing in Ukrainian shops. Posh shopping centres now grace the streets and underground passages of Kiev where foreigners are meant to buy things like crocodile handbags and US$2,000 shoes. At the other end of the spectrum are grannies who sell shoelaces or sunflower seeds on the street. During the early transition years, the commerce that was not conducted on the street corner was based in temporary metal kiosks, which you still see in residential neighbourhoods. Everything that's for sale will be hung in the window so you only have to point and pay. You can still buy magazines, drinks and snacks in kiosks, but most have been phased out in favour of normal shops. With stable currency and some law and order, typical shops appear in all cities. The traditional Ukrainian *rynok* (market) should be a part of the travel experience: taste-testing honey or cream on your knuckle, tumbling through rutabagas and sniffing smoked chickens. Don't start bartering for something simply because it's an outdoor market. Fixed pricing is more and more regular in Ukraine and the tag will usually tell you how much it costs. Food is the exception, and if you are indecisive, you may be offered a discount, or you can request a deal.

Souvenirs

With the new rise in tourism comes the advent of mass-produced 'Ukrainian' goods, many of which are not Ukrainian at all. Everyone thinks first of the *matroshka* doll, the wooden personage inside another inside another inside…These days, *matroshka* have turned into a comic venture, often painted with the faces of foreign politicians but traditional dolls are painted with family faces and flowery designs (there should always be an odd number). Ukraine's traditional hand-embroidered clothes – *narushniki* – should be made of long white linen or cotton with ornate stitching on the ends. Those in the know can tell the difference between machine-spun and authentic hand designs. Red, brown, orange, yellow, black and blue are traditional colours, although some regions vary. Ukrainian folk painting uses ornate bright flowers or fairytale themes on a black lacquered surface, usually on a bowl, platter, round jewellery box or wooden egg. Woodcraft is also genuinely Ukrainian: combs, ornate spoons, pipes, plates and bowls; small clay pots are also very authentic. Religious icons are traditional and some very beautiful modern examples can be purchased at most churches, however it is illegal to export any antique icons so don't try it. Ukraine enforces very strict laws about keeping national art treasures, historic coins and medals in their country. Make sure and ask the buyer if you will be allowed to take your purchase outside of the country, as they are somewhat responsible under the law.

Buying fur should be discouraged all round; however, if you really must have that Russian fur coat or *shapka* choose wisely as buying fox, beaver, lynx or sable will further deplete endangered species. Ukraine (and Russia's) red and silver fox population is slowly disappearing due to unregulated trapping for the cash foreigners will spend. Know what you are buying: you can always find *shapkas* made of farmed rabbit and mink, or even dog.

Avoid getting roped into visiting Ukrainian 'souvenir art galleries', which usually include a vast collection of kitschy canvases: flowers in a vase, naked women or old-time Kievan street scenes that resemble Montmartre. Also, the days of buying *real* Soviet paraphernalia are also finished, although someone might make you a gift of some personal item. The stuff in the markets emblazoned with red stars is made in China.

TAKING PICTURES IN UKRAINE

Kodak Express shops are on the high streets in even small Ukrainian cities, so getting filmed developed anywhere quickly is not a problem. City camera shops sell quality equipment in case you lose a lens, but it's all a lot more expensive than back home. Sadly, the old Soviet photographic equipment recently gave way to a wave of Japanese products, meaning you can no longer buy or develop the ultra-grainy black and white film. In fact, generic 400 ISO colour film is all you'll find. Slide film, unusual speeds or any form of black and white is almost impossible to buy in Ukraine. Photographers should remember that deep white snows and the slant of winter light make overexposure the biggest danger. (No, the radiation of Chernobyl will not do anything to your film or camera.)

Although this is really not a problem any more, don't run around taking pictures of military subjects (tanks or marching soldiers) unless there's a parade. You'll only appear suspicious. Everyday Ukrainians have no stigma about having their picture being taken, but you should be sensitive and ask permission first. (If you say you will send them copies, then get their address and *do it!*) You'll find that the minute you put an adult in front of a camera, their smile will fall into a serious grimace, presenting the ever-solemn 'Soviet passport' face. If you want to get someone to smile, hold the camera and aim, but talk to them for a long while until they do smile, or pretend you've already taken it, say *vsyo* (that's all), and when they smile in relief, click the shutter.

Also bear in mind that under-funded churches, museums and tourist sites supplement their revenue by charging photographers *per frame* that they shoot. This can cost from 3–5UAH.

BUSINESS

Business hours are normally 09.00 to 18.00 with a lunch break between 13.00 and 14.00. That said, you'll find many places are open until very late, and many food shops, hotels and stations are open 24 hours. Museums and other tourist spots usually have one or two 'days off' when they are closed. Check before you go somewhere.

MEDIA AND COMMUNICATIONS
Newspapers and magazines

Welcome to Ukraine magazine is a unique English-language travel magazine with well-written stories and artistic photography focusing entirely on Ukrainian destinations and local history. The publication is sold in most bookshops in Kiev. *Panorama* is Ukraine International Airline's in-flight magazine published monthly with a back section on visiting Kiev, and some articles on travel within Ukraine. *The Ukrainian* is a progressive, Kiev-based business magazine that addresses current affairs and the Ukrainian business climate but not much else. For details of publications specific to Kiev, see page 106.

Telephone

Ukraine's country code is 380 (although the zero is normally included with the city code). Some public pay phones still take 50 kopeck pieces, but most accept only UTEL cards that can be purchased at any post office. These are only worth using for domestic calls. Most hotels will let you make international phone calls from your room, but tend to charge a fair amount (at least US$2 a minute to Britain,

GIVING SOMETHING BACK

Travelling is always a two-way experience, where visitor and visited make all sorts of exchanges, both intended and subconscious. As you take in all that Ukraine offers, consider how your presence affects this country and what you can do to help during your travels. Just being in Ukraine and spending money at local businesses is a positive move, even if it is only sunflower seeds from a *babushka*. However, in the regional chapters I have listed certain opportunities where travellers can actively participate in local projects. I also ask that you please contact me with your experiences and any future suggestions of organisations or means for giving something back.

US$1 to USA and Canada). Most post offices will also have international phone booths, where you pay a deposit, make a phone call at regular rates and then retrieve your balance. Some international phone cards are now sold in big cities, but the least expensive way to call internationally is to find the rare internet café that offers web phone access. This halves the cost and the connection is clearer.

To call within Ukraine, dial 8 (for long-distance), then the city code (eg: 044 for Kiev) and then the number. In this book, all phone numbers are listed with their city codes for calling from outside the city. For local calls, just dial the last 7 digits (sometimes there are only 5 or 6, depending on the size of the town). When calling internationally, dial 8, wait for the tone, then dial 10, followed by country code, city code and so on. Sometimes it takes a few tries.

Post

Traditionally, the *poshta* (post office) was for paying electricity bills and receiving pensions. Travellers can get confused by the dozens of queues and windows. If you want to buy stamps and mail a letter, go to the window with all the colourful envelopes and cards. Always send letters *avia* (airmail). Traditionally, letters were addressed in the opposite manner to European post (first line: postcode, city; second line: street address; third line: surname, name), and you may still see some post addressed this way. However, most of Ukraine has now changed over to the standard European fashion (name, address, city and postcode, country). The sender's address goes in the upper left corner and the receiver in the middle. Note that postcards can be sent as open cards only within Ukraine; if you are sending them internationally you must put them inside a red-and-blue striped airmail envelope. Receiving letters in Ukraine by *poste restante* has become a less secure option in recent years. If you are going to be in the country for a while, getting a post office box is cheap and reliable. Otherwise, it's better to use email on your travels. Letters from Ukraine to Europe take around ten days to arrive and to North America at least two weeks.

Parcels

DHL has offices all over Ukraine: in Kiev, Vasylkivska 1; tel: 044 264 7200. FedEx works through the local Elin Inc, Kiev, Kikvidze 44; tel: 044 495 2020; fax: 044 495 2022; email: fedex@elin.kiev.ua. Inside Ukraine, you can send parcels on trains or buses, and it is a lot more secure than it sounds, as long as you have someone picking it up at the receiving station.

Internet

Ukraine is more internet savvy than certain Western nations and you'll have no problem getting access in computer clubs, internet cafés and hotels in cities. In smaller towns, ask at the closest post office. Either they will have a computer or can direct you to an internet club. Charges range from US$1 to $2 per hour. Cyrillic letters are printed beneath the Latin letters of the QWERTY keyboard, and you can change the typing language by clicking the prompt at the bottom right hand corner of the screen.

The email and websites listed throughout this book were checked at the time of writing, but you may find that it takes a while to get a response from the other side. Be patient, as communicating in English is not a given.

Part Two

The Guide

Kiev Київ

As the capital and largest city, Kiev usually grants visitors their first impressions of Ukraine in a vivid show of stateliness and energy. First-time guests seem most surprised by the tall government buildings that line Khreschatyk, the old palaces and the exquisitely reconstructed churches, as well as the burgeoning shopping centres and flashy business presence. This *is* a beautiful city. Even more picturesque is Kiev's simple geography, built on a series of steep wooded hills that rise above the wide channel of the slow-moving Dnepr with its long islands. Flowering chestnut trees cover the streets and riverbanks for half of the year, and during this time, no other city could seem so green and full. Despite a population of three million, Kiev feels very natural, and each of the hundreds of golden church domes rises up in just the right place.

Kiev occupies a strange mental space in the world's mind: those who know the city feel an intense affection for the place, while 'Kiev' remains otherwise unknown except for vague connotations of a distant eastern capital or else a buttery piece of chicken. No songs or stories romanticise Kiev (in English) and so most people hark back to Soviet recollections when Kiev completed the triad of great Slavic capitals – placed third after St Petersburg and Moscow. Fortunately, Kiev experienced a much more tasteful resurrection than the other two cities, and today the Ukrainian capital stands alone as the most ancient and least politicised of the three – upheld by a somewhat separate history and unique glory that visitors find so attractive. There is the Kiev of monuments and vistas, churches and statues, all of which fits nicely into a bus tour or a few days of walking. Then there is the city of Kiev comprised of several highly individualised neighbourhoods, some of which are over a thousand years old and others that only came into existence during the past 25 years. Each quarter preserves its own personality, defined over the years by who has lived there and what has happened on those streets. Getting to know Kiev requires a bit of targeted wandering.

Kiev is still the easiest city to travel to in Ukraine and the capital has become the number one tourist destination in the country. For organised group tours, Kiev is included on almost every itinerary, even if it seems out of the way or out of context with the subject of the visit. The simple fact remains that there is an amazing amount to see and do in this city and it would be a pity to come all this way and miss the place Ukrainians enjoy showing off the most.

HISTORY

Kiev is where it all began – Russia, Ukraine, and all that came with it. The city confesses a turbulent past but also employs its colourful history to reinforce a positive identity. Legend presents a touching beginning with the advent of one

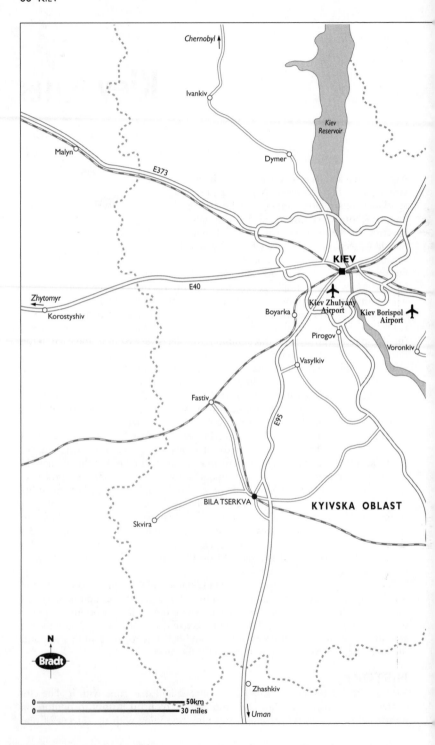

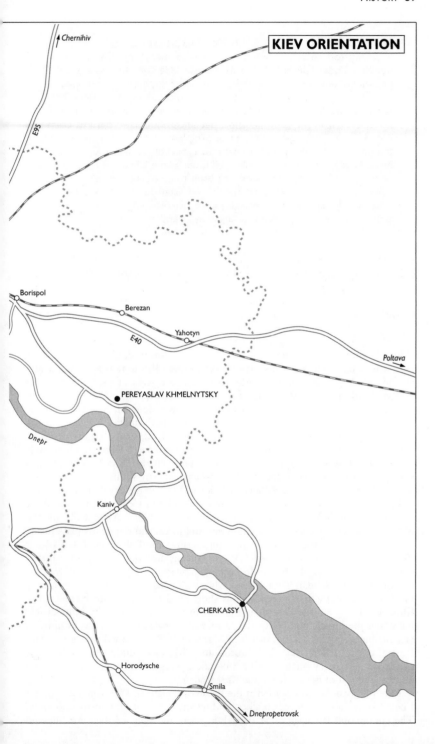

HOW DO YOU SPELL КИЇВ IN ENGLISH?

It seems too short a word to warrant so many spellings, but new transliterations of the ancient Cyrillic name include *Kyjiv, Kiyiv, Kyiv,* and the time-honoured *Kiev* (apostrophes and silent letters add exponential combinations). The inability to canonise a correct Latin spelling stems from contested Cyrillic spellings that would denote either a Russian or Ukrainian preference. It might seem pedantic, but since both Slavic cultures claim Kiev as their founding hearth, even spelling becomes a touchy subject. In this book and in most people's heads the capital of Ukraine is *Kiev,* but to be politically sensitive you would spell it out as the Ukrainian *Kyiv.* If you pride yourself as a cultural purist and want to pronounce the city's name 'right', go to the central train station and listen to the robotic female announcer list all the trains departing from *Kyh-Yeev.* Whoever she is, hers is the kindly voice of government-approved Ukrainian.

early Slavic family to these hills in the 6th century AD. Of the four siblings, the oldest brother was named Kiy, hence *Kiev.* Through the centuries of tribal warfare and peace, the group of forts on the Dnepr evolved into a lively and secure trading post eventually ruled by Varangian (Viking) princes. As the capital of all the lands between modern-day St Petersburg and Moldova, Kiev was one of the largest and most powerful cities in Europe.

Probably the most influential event in Kiev's history came in AD988 when Prince Vladimir dramatically baptised his entire nation in the Dnepr River. This new state religion and a universal law allowed Kievan Rus to flourish at home and abroad, and the 11th century marks Kiev's longest years of glory. St Sophia's cathedral and the Pechersky Lavra date from this period.

This same wealth and fame also led to the city's downfall in 1240 with the devastating Mongol invasion by Batu Khan. The city never fully recovered, and was eventually annexed to the Lithuanian principality in 1362. At the beginning of the 15th century, Lithuania granted Kiev the Magdeburg Law, a Germanic legal code which granted autonomy to prominent cities. Under self-rule, Kiev benefited from a strong urban development and vibrant cosmopolitanism similar to the cities of western Ukraine, but alas, the Mongol invasion of 1482 cut the city down once more.

Poland began ruling Kiev after the Union of Lublin in 1569, which changed the demographic of the city with a large influx of Poles and Jews. Meanwhile, the age of the Ukrainian Cossacks was coming into full force, and the towns just outside of Kiev began to witness periodic uprisings against the Polish nobility. Cossack Pyotr Sahaydachny is remembered for supporting the Ukrainian and Orthodox community in Kiev, all the while keeping peace with Poland, but it was the Cossack hetman Bohdan Khmelnytsky who finally drove the Poles out of the city in 1648. The moment of freedom was short-lived for Kiev's inhabitants, since Khmelnytsky signed the Pereyaslav Agreement in 1654 and the city immediately fell under the jurisdiction of Russia. At first Moscow's influence was minimal, a fact attributed to Cossack hetman Ivan Mazepa who had formed strong ties with Russia but guarded the city's autonomy. Mazepa funded a plethora of constructions in Kiev (including the walls and towers of the Pechersky Lavra) and donated the rest of his wealth to the Kiev academy.

Kiev's Russian fate was settled at the Battle of Poltava in 1709 when Tsar Peter I beat Mazepa and his Swedish allies, ending any hopes of Ukrainian autonomy. The culture and language of St Petersburg were the signs of the new élite and

Russians were added to Kiev's diverse population. When Russia took control over 'right bank' Ukraine in 1793, Kiev was no longer the peripheral city of other empires, but a central metropolis, albeit in 'Little Russia'. The Magdeburg Law was only revoked in 1835 and the autocratic government introduced the centralised legal system. Despite present-day anti-Russian sentiments, the period of Russian rule during the 18th and 19th centuries turned Kiev into a beautiful and booming modern city. Ukraine's sugar trade was the first of many large industries to be based in Kiev, and the fever of industrialisation spread quickly. In 1900, the population had reached 250,000; ten years later, it had doubled.

Kiev's intellectual tradition and large labour population made it an important city in the dissent and popular revolt against the tsar. With both nationalists and workers challenging St Petersburg's authority, Kiev was targeted by the Black Hundreds and made an example of a rebel's fate. During the Russian Revolution and subsequent civil war, Kiev changed hands 18 times until the final Bolshevik victory in 1921. The capital of the Ukrainian SSR was moved from Kiev to Kharkiv, where there was greater support for the Bolsheviks, but then moved back to Kiev in 1934. As the second largest 'republic' in the Soviet Union, Kiev wielded significant political power, but this was severely curtailed in Stalin's purges of the Ukrainian communist leadership, followed by the Nazi occupation in June 1941. The defence of Kiev in World War II was perhaps less heroic than is portrayed in the city's memorials. Over half a million Red Army troops immediately surrendered to the Germans, which was soon followed by the ordered execution of 180,000 civilians at nearby Babi Yar. When the city was liberated in November 1943, it was estimated that half of Kiev's population had been killed.

Kiev's real heroism lies in the city's ultimate survival and total reconstruction following the war. Of all the cities in the USSR, Kiev was revered for its beauty, art, culture and especially people. Famous Kievans include Mikhail Bulgakov, Golda Meir, Mikhail Hrushevsky, Sholom Aleichem, Isaac Babel, and more recently statesman Yevgeny Primakov and actress Milla Jovovich.

The last tragedy to take place in Kiev was in 1986 with the explosion of the Chernobyl nuclear power plant 90 miles north of the city. The citizens of Kiev were not informed until more than a week after the event, and the patterns of chronic illness are only now being recognised. At the height of Perestroika, the catastrophe widened the split between Kiev and Moscow. The city witnessed many active protests on the Maidan Nezalezhnosti in the final months of the Soviet Union.

Now the capital of an independent country, Kiev is establishing itself as the most prosperous and developed city in Europe-conscious Ukraine, but don't expect the rest of the country to look so flashy. A host of renovations makes the city skyline a little more impressive each year, and a swift improvement in guest services has increased Kiev's esteem under international scrutiny. Kiev's post-Soviet makeover relies heavily on historical references (the birthplace of Slavic Orthodoxy, Kievan Rus and the Cossacks) as well as fuzzy perceptions of Western culture. These days it is hard to visit the city and not be impressed by these conceptions of the past.

GETTING THERE AND AWAY
By air
Obviously, Kiev is the main entry and exit point for air travel to Ukraine and there is more information in *Chapter 4* about particular routes. Direct flights link Kiev with most European and Central Asian capitals while almost all domestic flights connect to Kiev.

Airline offices in Kiev

Aeroflot Saksahanskovo 112A; tel: 044 245 4359
AeroSvit Chervonoarmiyska 9/2; tel: 044 490 3490
Austrian Air Chervonoarmiyska 9/2; tel: 044 244 3540
British Airways Yarsolaviv Val 5; tel: 044 490 6060; web: www.britishairways.com/ukraine
Czech Airlines Ivan Franka 36; tel: 044 246 5627
Lithuanian Airlines Dmitrivska 1; tel: 044 490 4907; tel: 044 490 4907; email: info-ukraine@lal.lt
LOT Polish Airlines Ivana Franko 36; tel: 044 246 5620
Lufthansa Khmelnytskovo 52; tel: 044 490 3800; email: kiev@lufthansa.com.ua
Malev Hungarian Airlines Hospitalna 12 г; tel: 044 247 8672
Ukraine International Airlines Peremohy 14; tel: 044 461 5050
KyiAvia Peremohy 2; tel: 044 490 4902
KLM Ivana Franka 34/33, 2nd floor; tel: 044 490 2490; email: kilm.Ukraine@klm.com; web: www.klm.com.ua
Transaero Chervonoarmiyska 9/2, office 1; tel: 044 490 6565
Turkish Airlines Horodotskovo 4; tel: 044 229 1550

Borispol Airport – Бориспіль

Communist logic dictated that a city's international airport should be built incredibly far away, and Borispol is no exception – located 40km away from the city centre. Luckily, transferring between the airport and the city has become much easier. Expect to pay around US$25 for a taxi from the airport into the city, while the journey from Kiev to the airport costs half the price (logically). Catching a bus is just as easy and much less expensive. The **Polit airport bus** travels from Peremohy Square in the centre of Kiev to Borispol and back, leaving every 15–20 minutes from 05.00: with the last bus leaving at 23.15; tel 044 296 7367, cost US$2. The journey takes about one hour. The private bus company Avtoluks has all of its transit journeys pick up and drop off between Borispol and Kiev's Central Bus Station. This is the most comfortable option and takes only 35 minutes. Other regular buses serve both airports from the Central Bus Station at Moskovskaya Square.

Kiev Borispol has a bad reputation, which it only half deserves. A major refurbishment has helped improve things, but the immigration process can still seem a bit tangled and highly chaotic. Upon arriving, passengers are hoarded into several very long and very slow queues that creep towards a row of surly guards waiting to stamp your visa. Your bags will be waiting for you after the first checkpoint, having long beaten you to the spot. With bags in hand, enter the new line at customs. You'll have already been given a customs declarations form before landing, which should be filled out clearly and honestly (paying more attention to detail than normal). Hand it over to a customs officer, and be fully prepared to have your bags tumbled through. Once you've been waved on (making sure you have your customs form stamped and on your person) you will exit into the main hall, where there is an information booth if you're feeling a little bit overwhelmed. The shortest time anyone gets through this process is one hour.

The Ukrainian answer to all the hustle and bustle is a newly introduced VIP service, where foreign visitors can circumvent the dismal wait by paying up prior to arriving. As a Very Important Person at Borispol, you'll be whisked off to a separate terminal and allowed to quickly pass through. As advertised, the US$80 fee helps save time and 'reduces scrutiny' by customs officers. If it seems appalling to pay someone else in order to be treated civilly, that's because it *is* appalling, but then so are the queues. Usually the VIP service is an option offered with group tours, but if you are travelling on your own, contact your airline or the Borispol Information Service; tel: 044 296 7243.

Zhulyany Airport – Жуляни

The lesser of Kiev's two airports is actually a more convenient location to fly into since it is closer and therefore more accessible by public transportation and city taxis. Traditionally, the smaller city airport has dealt mainly with domestic air traffic, although technically, any flights from former Eastern bloc countries will come in here (Aeroflot and Czech Airlines both have international flights to Zhulyany).

The airport is 7km southeast of the city centre. To travel on public transportation, take trolleybus #9, or much better marshrutka #568 which goes to Prospekt Shevchenka, although with luggage a taxi would seem the best bet (around US$5–7). Transferring between Zhulyany and Borispol is not too difficult. A taxi between the two is US$30. The phone number at Zhulyany Airport is 044 242 2308.

By rail

All train tracks lead to Kiev, making it the easiest destination in Ukraine and the easiest place to leave. In fact, even if you don't want to come to Kiev, you may have to stop over in order to get somewhere else.

On any given day, you can get a train to anywhere and come to Kiev from anywhere. Whether or not there are any spaces is the catch – especially during holiday seasons. The earliest you can buy tickets is one month before you travel, but many people wait until a few days before, or even on the morning of travel. You should also check times and length of travel, since this can vary a great deal. Trains to Crimea either go to Sevastopol (2 daily; 18 hours) or Simferopol (4 daily; 16 hours). There are also plenty of trains to Lviv (5 daily; 11 hours) and Odessa (5 daily; 11 hours). Travel to and from Kharkiv (5 daily; 5 or 9 hours) has recently become easier with the advent of Ukraine's first luxury train, the Capital Express, which makes two daily connections with stops in Poltava and Mirgorod and gets to Kharkiv in five hours. There is only one daily train to and from Donetsk (12 hours), and one to Dnepropetrovsk (8 hours), although many other trains pass through Dnepropetrovsk on their way to Kiev. The train's departure platform number is posted in English and Ukrainian 30 minutes before departure.

International routes to and from Kiev are numerous and rather inexpensive. Russian destinations are usually listed as domestic routes, with 14 daily connections to Moscow (14 hours) and just one to St Petersburg (via Chernihiv; 24 hours). A few cars leave from Kiev every other day to be connected to Ukraine's Trans-Siberian railroad all the way to Vladivostok (via Kharkiv; 7 days). Other trains come and go from Minsk (twice daily, via Chernihiv; 12 hours) and Kishinev (twice daily; 14 hours) while train schedules to Riga (24 hours) and Vilnius (18 hours) constantly change. The most popular international routes are between Kiev and Warsaw (1 daily; 20 hours; US$50), Berlin (1 daily; 24 hours; US$100) and Prague (1 daily; 34 hours US$120).

Kiev's train station is actually two stations joined by a causeway crossing all the tracks and platforms. Vokzalna metro station is the closest public transportation access. The closest main entrance is the 'Central' Station, the other side is the South Station. If you have a talented taxi driver who knows the trains, he will drop you off at the side closest to your train; otherwise, it's a matter of walking over the long causeway terminal to your platform. An impressive renovation has turned Kiev's station into the most modern and user-friendly station in Ukraine, and visitors will be grateful for the English signs and listings.

There are over 100 ticket counters in Kiev's main station, all for different purposes. Counters number 41 and 42 (2nd floor of the South Station; open 07.30–20.00) are designated to sell to foreigners and the attendants speak limited English. You can still buy tickets elsewhere, but it is to your advantage to use these attendants since they are more flexible, have special access to better seats and give foreigners priority on full trains. The other ticket office in central Kiev is located at Prospekt Shevchenka 38/40. Dialling 005 on any Kiev phone will put you through to the train station, but if you don't speak Russian, the lady on the other end is not much help. Most Kiev hotels will have agents who can also book tickets for you.

There is a left-luggage office in the basement of Kiev's South Station. Pay your money to the nice old woman and you'll get two tokens – one that locks the locker and another to open it later. Set your own combination on the inside (and write it down somewhere), drop in the token, and shut it firmly while it's buzzing. To open, set the outside combination to match, drop in the token and carefully yank it open. You are allowed to leave luggage for 24 hours before it's cleaned out. The lockers are safe and well-guarded and using them can give you some peace of mind. This helps if you want to check out of a hotel and spend the day around Kiev before boarding a night train to somewhere else.

Getting a taxi from the train station can be overpriced. If you are trying to save money, take the metro one stop to the station Universitet and you'll be able to catch a cab there for much less.

By bus

Like the train, you can catch a bus from anywhere to get to Kiev and vice versa, but you must ask yourself if this is the best way to meet your particular travel goals. Schedules change daily on the smaller lines, so if you like to have set plans beforehand, you will be limited to the new private companies.

Bus routes spread out in a radial pattern from Kiev, divided into five directions: Zhytomyr, Chernihiv, Uman, Cherkassy and Poltava. The Central Station is at 3 Moskovskaya Square; tel: 044265 0430; best reached by travelling to Lybidska metro station and then taking a bus (#4 and #11), taxi, or walking to the next junction. Western destinations leave from Dachna Terminal; Peremohy 142; tel: 044 444 1503; eastern destinations leave from Darnytsya Terminal (near the metro station Darnytsya) Gagarina 1; tel: 044 559 4618. Northern destinations leave from Polissya Terminal; Shevchenka Square; tel: 044 430 3554 and southern destinations depart either from Podil Terminal (Nyzhny 15A; tel: 044 417 3215) or Pivdenna Terminal; Glushkova 3; tel: 044 263 4004. If in doubt, go to the Central Bus Station where many long-haul routes still originate. Bus tickets can also be purchased at the central bus office; Lesi Ukrayinki 14; tel: 044 225 2066.

Regular buses are cheap, slow, and bumpy. The most popular routes go to Zhytomyr (3 hours) and Pochayiv (12 hours). Shorter bus rides visit the tourist sights just outside of Kiev, such as Kaniv or Pereyaslav. A few private bus companies run out of Kiev's Central Bus Station and travel as fast or faster than the train, are very comfortable and charge about the same amount as the train. **Avtoluks** has the most widespread service, with buses to and from Lviv (10 hours), Yalta (17 hours), Odessa (8 hours), Kharkiv (7 hours), Zaporizhzhya (9 hours) and every city in between. Besides their office at the station, their central office is at Chistyakovskaya 30; tel: 044 536 00 55; email: info@Avtoluks.ua; web: www.Avtoluks.ua. **Gyunsel** has good connections between Kiev and the east (Kharkiv, Dnepropetrovsk, and Donetsk) as well as the Carpathians; Novopolevaya 2; tel:044 488 88 01/ 044 265 03 78; email: office@gunsel.com.ua.

International bus routes to and from Kiev include Paris, London, Rome, Antwerp, Athens, Prague, and the Baltic capitals. For now, the best international coach in Ukraine is **Lviv Inturtrans**; Reitarska 37/401; tel: 044 212 3340. As a non-Ukrainian, make sure you know the route of travel and have made prior arrangements (ie: transit visas) for the countries you'll be passing through. Taking a bus to Kiev from another country is only worth it if you are really trying to save money on the international journey; otherwise, just cross the border and then take a train to Kiev. Remember that inside Ukraine, if the trip is over six hours by bus, consider the train as a more comfortable, albeit slower, option.

GETTING AROUND
Metro
Construction of the Kiev metro was begun only after World War II, in 1949, and many of the oldest stations (on the red line) exhibit classic examples of socialist realist design, some of which are remarkably beautiful. Because Kiev is built on top of the Dnepr's ravine, the metro stations are dug extremely deep, and this may be the longest escalator ride you've ever been on. During the five minutes it takes to descend, everyone stands and stares at every one else before zooming off into different directions. You haven't seen Kiev unless you've been underground.

Currently, there are 41 stations divided into three separate lines, coloured blue, green and red. The routes were designed to transport people from home to work and so the metro is not always the best way to go from one tourist attraction to another; however, it is the quickest way to get around the city.

The metro is open from 05.30 until midnight every day with constant and frequent trains all day long. During rush hour (from 07.30 and 16.30), things get very tight and pushy. Move with the flow of people and don't be afraid to shove. Politeness never got anyone very far on the Kiev metro and at times this is the only way you'll ever get on. Keep bags and wallets close at hand and be alert.

Finding your way underground is yet another incentive to learn Cyrillic. Look at a map and think out your journey before descending. In the actual tunnels, arrows show the direction the train travels as well as the remaining stations on that line. When transferring from one station to another, read the signs, ask, or in some cases, simply follow the crowd climbing the stairs from the middle of the platform rather than moving to the ends of the hall.

For now, one ride on the metro costs 50 kopecks, including transfers. The orange machines in the entrance of the stations take 1 and 2UAH notes and give you plastic tokens in return, or just wait in line and buy them from the cashier. For longer stays you can purchase unlimited travel on a monthly card.

KIEV BY BOAT
Taking the funicular or the metro to the station Poshtova Ploscha brings you next to the **River Terminal**; tel: 044 416 1268. Pleasure cruises originate and end here, many of which travel all the way down the Dnepr to Crimea. There are also basic passenger services available to other Dnepr towns and short boat tours of Kiev, as well as short transits to some of the islands and beaches in summer. Ice covers the Dnepr for about three months a year, and the river terminal is in full swing only from May until October. Schedules change all the time, either check out the terminal, or else contact one of the tour agencies that organise river tours (eg: SAM, Mandrivnyk).

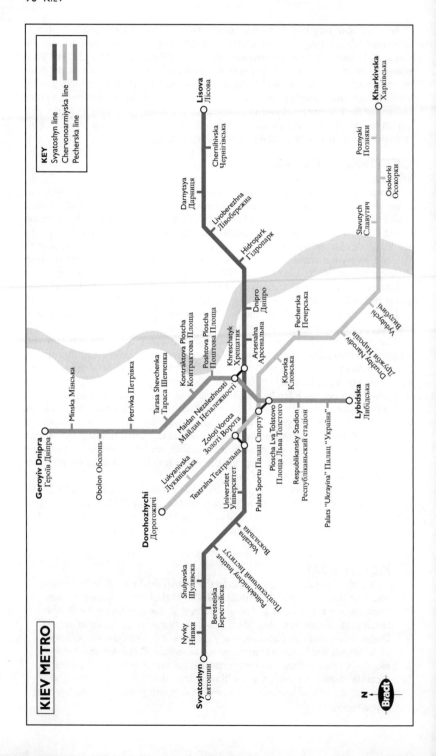

KIEV METRO

KEY
Svyatoshyn line
Chervonoarmiyska line
Pecherska line

Taxi

Riding in Kiev's traffic cures atheism – sidewalks can become an extra lane, and lanes will suddenly change direction. Furthermore, Kiev's taxi drivers are picky about who they pick up – if traffic is bad they'll tell you by refusing to go, although occasionally money talks.

Dialling 058 on any phone will give you a voice that can get you a cab – but flagging one down is quicker and more negotiable. Hail a cab outside your hotel and you'll be charged at least two times the normal price; walk down the street and the price goes down. As a foreigner, you'll always be expected to pay more. US$3 to $4 is normal for two or three people travelling a good distance across the city, but taxi prices change by the minute. Most cabbies in Kiev are fair, especially those driving beat-up jalopies. Talking to the driver during the ride (or even trying to) can teach you more about Kiev than most tour guides.

For a no-nonsense pay-and-just-get-there ride, try one of Kiev's private companies:

Radio Taxi Tel: 044 240 1036
Taxi Blues Tel: 044 296 4243
Art Tel: 044 229 8543

Trolleys, trams, buses, marshrutka

Following years of complete apathy, Kiev's trams and trolleys now feature vigorous ticket controllers that seem to be making up for all the lost time. As a foreigner, they will be especially keen to check your ticket and fine you for something or other. Make an effort to buy a ticket (50 kopecks) from the driver upon boarding, or keep some change out for a ticket seller. In addition, buy a ticket for every large suitcase you may be carrying. Nodding your head and saying you don't speak Russian won't help the situation. A *straf* (fine) costs around US$2 and you'll wish that you'd just taken a taxi. Tram and trolley routes are usually depicted on city maps, albeit very badly. Pure trial and error or local advice are more trustworthy references.

There are over 400 official *marshrutka* routes through Kiev and not one of them goes in a straight line. These minibuses are the cheapest and fastest way to move above ground, once you get the hang of it. A major central pick-up stop is in front of Universitet Station (and all other metro stations) although you can flag one down anywhere. If you can't read the signs in the windshield telling the destinations, simply ask. Fellow passengers tend to be very helpful as well. Costs range from 1 to 2UAH.

Car rental

Kiev is leading the way for Ukraine's new car rental industry, and most upmarket hotels will offer some sort of car-hire services, although usually with a chauffeur. Until very recently, driving on your own in Kiev (especially in a rental car) has always been perceived as foolhardy. That said, many still do it and things may be changing with the advent of so many international companies. Here are a few reliable leads:

Avis Kamyshynska 4; tel: 044 490 9890; email: avis@avis.kiev.ua
Europcar Gorkovo 48A; tel: 044 238 2691; email: ua@europcar.relc.com
Hertz Muzeiny 4; tel: 044 296 7614; email: hertzua@i.kiev.ua

WHERE TO STAY

If only the Ukrainian economy had made the same swift conversion that Kiev's hotels have recently experienced! In less than five years, the capital's illusions of grandeur have helped churn out a pile of very swish hotels that smell of money and new paint. The high-reaching standard is slightly problematic, since every hotel wants a piece of the luxury market and subsequently prices their rooms as such – whether or not their facilities are actually upmarket. Even though few hotels merit the price, offering US$100-a-night rooms has become the ultimate status symbol. Such inflation is the curse of capital cities but in future years, where foreign visitors choose to stay will hopefully push supply and demand curves back into sync.

Luxury
The following accept credit cards and feature private hot-water systems.

Premier Palace Shevchenka 5–7; tel: 044 244 1200; fax: 044 229 8772; email: info@premier-palace.com; web: www.premier-palace.com. Since completing a brand new renovation, the Premier Palace has been crowned with five stars (the only one in Kiev) but in pre-revolution days, this really was a palace. Rising up from the crossroads of Kiev's most impressive boulevards, few superlatives need be spared on this hotel. The simple and elegant rooms would rival most upmarket European hotels, and an excellent health club and competent business centre complete the atmosphere of posh comfort. A classy mood is reinforced by the hotel's Latin creed reminding visitors that their 'name tells all'. The palace's panoramic restaurant, 'Imperia', offers a pleasant setting for top-quality meals with a fantastic view of Kiev at night. All the hotel staff really do speak English. Rooms start at US$370 a night.

Vozdvyzhensky Vozdvyzhenska 60; tel/fax: 044 531 9900. This small and quiet hotel is tucked away just off Andreisky Spusk, making it a perfect hotel for first-time visitors to Kiev. Vozdvyzhensky is also the rare Ukrainian hotel where you actually get what you pay for. Professional management and big, brand-new, fully equipped bathrooms put this hotel a step ahead of the rest. A double room (with king-size bed) is US$180; large suites cost US$290, but there are a few 'tourist class' rooms that are much cheaper (around $60). Personal attention to guests is everyday policy.

Dnipro Hotel Khreschatyk 1/2; tel: 044 229 8450; fax: 044 229 8213; email: reservation@dniprhotel.kiev.ua; web: www.dniprohotel.kiev.ua. Once upon a time, this was the only hotel foreign visitors were allowed to stay in, meaning the Dnipro has a slight advantage in working with group tours and taking care of all travel arrangements. Attempted grandeur make it a pleasant enough hotel to stay in, but it is difficult to mask the Soviet construction, meaning rooms tend to be very small, except for the larger and more expensive suites. The division between superior and standard rooms further complicates pricing. Single superiors cost US$135, a double, queen size room costs US$205; suites are US$300. Only double superior or higher have baths; otherwise, all rooms are equipped with showers. Standard (meaning Soviet) rooms are about US$40 cheaper, but if money is a concern, there are cheaper and nicer rooms elsewhere. Two pluses are the Dnipro's advantageous location at the end of Khreschatyk, and the very entertaining restaurant run by a highly ambitious Ukrainian chef.

Domus Yaroslavska 19; tel: 044 490 9008; fax: 044 462 5145 email: postmaster@domus-hotel.kiev.ua; web: www.domus-hotel.kiev.ua. Located in the heart of Kiev's historic Podil neighbourhood, the pale pink Domus hotel is thoroughly quaint and favoured by businessmen. The comfy beds and tactful renovation deserve mention. Singles/doubles cost US$140/$190, suites are US$250 a night.

Hotel Rus Hospitalna 4; tel: 044 294 3020; fax: 044 220 4396; email: reservation@hotelrus.kiev.ua; web: www.hotelrus.kiev.ua. Considered upmarket in Kiev, the Rus is a behemoth hotel tower with hundreds of clean and orderly rooms, used frequently for conferences and group tours. Visitors will probably find that the service and standard is just about average compared to back home. The location is somewhat central and prices are per room, meaning singles or doubles cost US$120 and suites are US$150; a few travellers have mentioned this hotel was overpriced.

Hotel Kozatsky Mykhailivska 1/3; tel: 044 229 4925; fax: 044 229 2709; email: kozatsky@ukrnet.net; web: www.kozatsky.kyiv.ua. Not so much a luxury hotel as a luxury location, the Kozatsky stands right above all the action on the Maidan Nezalezhnosti. Most rooms for foreigners (ie: lux) cost US$100 a night although there are some nice rooms for around US$75. The Kozatsky is owned and operated by Ukraine's Ministry of Defence, so your neighbours will always be interesting.

Middle range

Staying farther out from central Kiev can knock US$30–40 per night off your hotel price, but remember to take transportation into consideration; most of the following are located in Kiev's left bank, sometimes near a metro station. These middle-range hotels cover a varied quality spectrum so make sure you always see the room first.

Adria Raisy Okypnoi 2; tel: 044 516 2459; fax: 044 517 8933; email: reservations@eurohotel.com.ua; web: www.eurohotel.com.ua. A Polish–Ukrainian joint venture, the Adria offers the same quality and comfort as any of Kiev's upmarket hotels, but is located further from the centre. This is the private 'luxury' part of the giant Turist complex. Rooms cost around US$90. Major credit cards are accepted.

Turist Raisy Okypnoi 2; tel: 044 517 8832; fax: 517 6243; email: hotel-tourist@uprotel.net.ua; web: www.hotel-tourist.kiev.ua. Officially Kiev's largest hotel (next to the Adria), this 27 storey building is not unlike the millions of Soviet apartments that house most of Eurasia today, although slightly nicer inside. The left bank location may seem dissuasive, but the Livoberezhna metro station is literally next door, the river and Hydropark are close by and, after all, one should be able to enjoy the real life of residential Kiev. Rooms cost between US$45 and US$55 per person.

Bratislava Malyshka 1; tel: 044 559 6920; fax: 044 559 7788; email: Bratislava@ukrti.com.ua; web: www.bratislava.com.ua. Rooms are quite modern, all with showers and new bathrooms. With singles US$40, doubles US$60, this is probably the best deal on the left bank. Darnitsya is the closest metro station.

Express Shevchenka 38/40; tel: 044 239 8995; fax: 044 239 8947; email: hotel@railwayukr.com; web: www.railwayukr.com. A spectrum of economy rooms to lavish suites means the Express doesn't really fit in any one category. The hotel charges per person in the room, so standard singles/doubles are US$20/$30, while the nicer rooms cost US$50/$60 up to US$100 for wannabe suites. From the outside things look dismal, but a massive remodelling has really turned things around on the interior. The ground floor is also the central office for booking rail tickets and the train station is a direct walk down the boulevard.

Sport Chernoarmiyska 55A; tel: 044 220 0252; fax: 044 220 0257. Another towering Soviet high-rise with decent rooms, known for its casino. Singles cost US$45, doubles are US$65, and there are also few suites for US$75 and up. The price is a good deal for the close location, just south of the centre and right next to the Respublikansky Stadion metro station.

Budget

Finding a cheap night's stay in Kiev is becoming more of a nightmare since foreign travellers are perceived as wealthy and spendthrift. The few remaining discount hotels illogically charge foreigners the same Ukrainian price but in dollars. Be prepared to spend at least US$20 a night.

Hotel Kiev Hrushevskovo 26/1; tel: 044 253 0155; fax: 044 253 6432; email: kievhtl@ukrtel.com; web: www.hotelkiev.com.ua. Located directly across from the *rada* (parliament), president's house, and the Marinsky Palace, Hotel Kiev is operated by the presidential administration and often used by government employees. The structure and atmosphere are not unlike most renovated Soviet buildings, but at the time of writing Hotel Kiev is the best deal for budget accommodation in terms of location, price, and standards (there is hot water). A nice room for two costs around US$50, while the cheaper, lower standard rooms go for around US$20–30.

St Petersburg Shevchenka 4; tel: 044 229 7364; fax: 044 229 7472; email: s-peter@i.kiev.ua. Across from the Premier Palace, the St Petersburg has seen better days, but the old building means rooms are spacious and hallways creaky. Rooms cost from US$10 to US$40 depending on the extras you want with your room – and everything is extra, especially any form of plumbing. A double with toilet costs US$26.

Slavutych Entuziastiv 1; tel: 044 555 3859; fax: 044 555 5637. The hotel has both standard (old) rooms and new (refurbished) rooms, indicating a two-tiered price structure. The old rooms rent for US$18 to US$30, while everything else is around US$50. One must decide if the cost of the cab ride offsets the money saved for a somewhat mediocre hotel. The left bank location is no treat in terms of access, but from this side there are some great views of the Pechersky Lavra and all of Kiev. The closest metro is Livoberezhna.

Railway station

Every railway station in Ukraine used to have its own small hotel where late-night arrivals could sleep on until the next day or stay the night before a long journey. The nicest of these is in Kiev's South Station (the *Pivdenny Vokzal*) at the more modern end of the main rail terminal on the 4th floor – just follow the 'bed' signs. Everything is sparkling new, and the rooms are heated in winter, cooled in summer. None of the rooms are en suite, but the bathrooms are new and clean with continuous hot water. US$18 a night per person, breakfast included.

Renting apartments

One option for a reasonably priced stay in Kiev is renting a private apartment, which may be worthwhile if you are planning on staying for more than a week. Traditionally, the square in front of the Central Train Station is busy with female agents who either advertise their own apartment or arrange rentals for a range of accommodation. For now, the going rate is about US$20 a day for a decent one-room apartment with double bed, kitchen and bathroom. If making arrangements on your own, use caution, since prices will already be jacked up a bit and this is a black-market trade where foreigners can be targeted for swindles.

You might consider going the legal route and use one of Kiev's many apartment rental agencies. A good company can do all the hard work for you and meet you at the airport with keys in hand. This is rarely the cheapest option, but it is much less expensive than hotels, while the housing situation is often much nicer. Try **Avanti** apartment services; tel/fax: 044 247 0558; email: hotel@avanti.kiev.ua; web: www.avanti.kiev.ua; or try **Absolut**; Tsvetayevoyi 10/87, office #17; tel/fax: 044 530 1310; email: hotel@hotelservice.kiev.ua; web: www.hotelservice.kiev.ua. Both can arrange secure and comfortable apartments for around US$500 to $600 a month.

WHERE TO EAT

Kiev has more restaurants per capita than any other Ukrainian city, a feat inspired both by the general demand for nice places to eat and an entrepreneurial explosion that introduced a lot of gaudy décor (like mermaid waitresses or motorcycles hanging from the ceiling). Kiev's eating establishments often seek an exotic approach and follow scattered trends – for a while, Mexican restaurants were popping up everywhere, while the next big thing seems to be sushi.

Eating out in Ukraine can be ridiculously cheap, but in Kiev, food prices are comparable to other European countries. These days, you can find anything from exquisite French dining to Ukrainian fast food served in plastic – with the advent of corporate culture most central restaurants will advertise a *'byzness lanch'*. As a general rule, if a restaurant has seats to sit down in, they most likely have a menu in English and will accept credit cards. The following are all open until at least midnight:

Ukrainian
Pid Osokom Mikhayilovska 20. This small café caters mainly to the Ukrainian business set, seating people together on long wooden benches. It can get crowded because it is so popular, though the aromatic food is worth it. Authentic and inexpensive Ukrainian cuisine is served hot by a matronly staff.

Kozak Mamai Prorizna 4; tel: 044 228 4273. Ukraine's Cossack past is relived in a series of decorated rooms just off Khreschatyk, but the Ukrainian food is exceptional and the atmosphere more peaceful than would be expected if the uniformed waiters really were Cossacks. Expect to spend around US$20.

Pechersky Dvorik Krepestnoi Pereulok 6; tel: 044 253 2667. Representing a turn-of-the century Kiev salon, the well-lit and open space of the Dvorik offers a relaxed atmosphere and a creative menu. Food is mainly Russian/Ukrainian, with a few recipes borrowed from the earliest Slavic chronicles. Located close to the Pechersky Lavra; main dishes are US$5–10.

Tsarskoe Selo Sichnevoho Povstannya 42/1; tel: 044 573 9775. Located right between the Pechersky Lavra and the giant motherland statue, this complex of Ukrainian huts was built with tour buses in mind. The only things that makes this theme-dining experience different are the very high prices and the local clientele who can afford it. At night, the Selo turns into quite a jazzy party place.

Hunter (Myslyvets) Saksahanskovo 147/5; tel: 044 236 3735. A wild mountain theme is reinforced by lots of fur and dried plants hanging from the walls. Food is Carpathian style, specialising in wild bird and game. Around US$30.

Kniazhy Grad Velika Zhytomyrska 2; tel: 044 228 3729. Someone had the sense to focus on Kievan Rus when searching for a colourful theme for their restaurant. The 'Princely city' is located near some of Kiev's oldest monuments and serves sophisticated Ukrainian food without any gimmicks. Under US$15.

International
Le Grand Café Muzeiny 4; tel: 044 228 7208 www.legrandcafe.kiev.ua. Both pricey and élitist, this French-style café is Kiev's flashiest hangout. The menu explores some interesting Ukrainian-French hybrids (like vareniki with foie gras) while the drinks are more sturdy and conventional.

Concord Pushkinskaya 42/4 8th floor; tel: 044 229 5512. A posh and comfy interior, the Concord features unique French-Asian fusion cooking. Expect to pay US$40 a head.

Mimino Spasska 10A; tel: 044 417 3545. This cosy restaurant in the heart of Podil serves not-entirely authentic Georgian food, but dishes are still spicy and delicious. Prices are average.

Himalaya Khreschatyk 23; tel: 044 462 0437. Kiev's only Indian restaurant for the time being. The location is convenient and visible, the atmosphere pleasant enough, and the chef *is* Indian. Fixed lunches cost around US$8.

Makabi Kosher Rustavelli 15; tel: 044 235 9437. 'Kosher food for kosher prices' so says the slogan. Located next to Kiev's central synagogue, authentic Israeli fare and delicious vegetarian food attract both Jew and Gentile. A meal costs US$5.

Vostok Naberezhno-Khreschatytskaya; tel: 044 416 5375. A tribute to eastern exoticism, this Chinese restaurant stands out from the rest for its sense of style and authenticity.

Diverse chefs from various regions of China serve up unique and unfamiliar dishes. If you order fish, you'll be asked to pick it out of their small pond before it wriggles off to the kitchen. Main dishes cost US$10–20.

011 Ilinska 18; tel: 044 416 0001. Tasty Yugoslavian cuisine served in an ambient hall or out on the covered terrace; (011, incidentally, is the telephone code for Belgrade). Medium prices.

Antalya Fedorova 10; tel: 044 220 6157. Refined Turkish food outside Kiev's centre. Under US$20 a meal.

Svitlytsya Andreyevsky Spusk 13B; tel: 044 416 3186. This rustic French café is right off the major tourist street and serves wonderful meat fondues, crêpes and light meals for generally low prices.

Quick meals
Non-Stop Prospekt Peremohy 6; tel: 044 216 4073. As the name implies, this bar and grill is open 24 hours, offering a broad vegetarian menu, fantastic barbecue, and lots of drinks. Prices range from kopecks up to US$15.

Chateau de Fleur Khreschatyk 24; tel: 044 228 7800. Looking on to Kiev's main drag, this is not a French restaurant, but more of a modern cafeteria serving soup, salad, pancakes, and almost anything. Known for the view; under US$15.

Kyivska Perepichka Khmelnitskovo 3. Without shame or modesty, I confess that this is my favourite place to eat in Kiev and it is the only food stand to have remained open for the entire decade since independence. The Perepichka is a quintessentially Kiev snack similar to a sausage roll; hot dogs are covered in Pirozhki pastry and then deep-fried (of course!). The hot, hand-held treat costs about US$0.20 and you'll find it impossible to eat just one.

Uno Pizza Volodymyrska 40/2; tel: 044 228 4362. Real Italian pizza for about US$7. Next door to one of Kiev's loudest Irish pubs.

Cafés and bars
Passazh Khreschatyk 15; tel: 044 229 1209. Kiev's coolest coffee house with high ceilings, small tables and only the necessary frills. Serves pancakes of all sorts.

Marquise de Chocolat Prorizna 4; tel: 044 235 4546. This rather new dessert café has already made its name in Kiev with an advertisement of a woman covered in melted chocolate. Besides all things dark and delicious, the menu offers colourful cocktails and a range of coffees.

Moda Bar Naberezhno-Khreschatytska, Pier #6; tel: (04) 416 7388. Known for outlandish parties, daily fashion shows and bartenders who perform dazzling tricks. Open all night every night with very loud live music.

Sapphire Bar Shevchenka 5–7; tel: 044 244 1262. On the second floor of the Premier Palace hotel, the bar is sophisticated and the drinks overpriced, but you can watch BBC World.

Hotel restaurants
Whether or not you are staying at either hotel, the **Empire** (Premier Palace, Shechenka 5–7, top floor) and the **Dnipro** (Khreschatyk 1/2) both feature remarkable restaurants for travellers who enjoy long and sumptuous meals. Without drinks, meals run to between US$30 and $50.

WHAT TO DO
Theatre
The true Kiev experience should include a show at the **National Opera and Ballet** (Volodymyrska 50; tel: 044 224 7165). Tickets sell for US$3–20 for a range of classics like Swan Lake and Rigoletto. Just down the block is the traditional **Russian Drama Theatre** (Khmelnytskovo 5; tel: 044 224 4223).

For Ukrainian language theatre, try the historical **Ivan Franko National Drama Theatre** (Ivana Franka 3; tel: 044 229 5991). Performances tend to be diverse and innovative. The **Podil Drama Theatre** (Kontraktova Ploscha 4; tel: 044 416 5489) is world famous and very entertaining, doing everything from adapted Shakespeare to poetic Ukrainian pieces. You can buy theatre tickets at the respective theatres, or at the central booths on Khreschatyk 13 and 21; tel: 044 228 7642.

Shopping

Never fear, these days you can find anything in Kiev. All along Khreschatyk, the formerly dingy underground passages have been transformed into sparkling luxury and high-tech shops that sell perfume, teeny bathing suits, diamonds and laptops. The largest of these 'malls' occupies the space beneath the Maidan Nezalezhnosti, offering two floors of wealth and glamour year round. The old Soviet state department store ЦУМ (for Central Universal Store; Khmelnytskovo 2; tel: 044 224 9505) once offered everything the USSR produced; now it's looking more and more like Harrods of London.

For a more traditional Ukrainian shopping experience, try the **Bessarabsky Rynok** at the corner of Khreschatyk and Prospekt Shevchenka. This is the way people have been shopping in Kiev from the beginning, only now the products have changed. All the vegetables and fruit are imported and picture perfect, as are the flowers and jars of caviar. The name of the market comes from the Bessarabian (Moldavian) merchants who lived and worked in this section of town. Lots of noise and free samples are part of the act. Everyday open-air street markets are more commonplace by the metro stations further outside the city.

If you're looking for souvenirs, there tend to be quite a few street vendors on the Maidan Nezalezhnosti who sell music, books, flags and Ukrainian-themed knick-knacks. Most people find general gifts among the markets on Andreyevsky Spusk, but there are a few upmarket souvenir shops around the city. For decorative crafts, try **Gonchary** (Andreyevsky Spusk 10A; tel: 044 416 1298). In the centre, **Sia** (Kreschatyk 46A), or **Silk Route** in Pechersk (Suvorova 4; tel: 044 295 0324). For a wide variety of books and magazines in Russian, Ukrainian and English, try **Mystetstvo** (Khreschatyk 24; tel: 044 228 3668), **Planet** (Khreschatyk 30), or **Orfey** (Chervonoarmiyska 6; tel: 044 224 0001).

OTHER PRACTICALITIES
City tours and travel assistance

Kiev now has a roaring business in guided group tours, fixers, and other travel services, many of which are semi-reliable. Here are a few reputable companies that have a proven record and English-speaking guides.

Albion Chervonoarmiyska 26; tel: 044 461 9746; email: Info@albion.com.ua; web: www.albion.com.ua. Does group tours of the city, has constant buses leaving across from the train station.

Mandrivnyk Poshtova Ploscha 3; tel: 044 463 7604; email: mandrivnyk@adam.kiev.ua; web: www.mandrivnyk.com.ua

New Logic Mikhayilivska 6A; tel: 044 462 0462; email: incoming@newlogic.kiev.ua; web: www.newlogic.com.ua. Young and vibrant, with good sightseeing packages in Kiev and low-cost trips to Chernobyl.

Olymp Travel Kreschatyk 21; tel: 044 228 1650; email: welcome@olymp-travel.kiev.ua; web: www.olymp-travel.kiev.ua. Professional staff, has a good knowledge of Kiev,but focuses on longer package tours of the country.

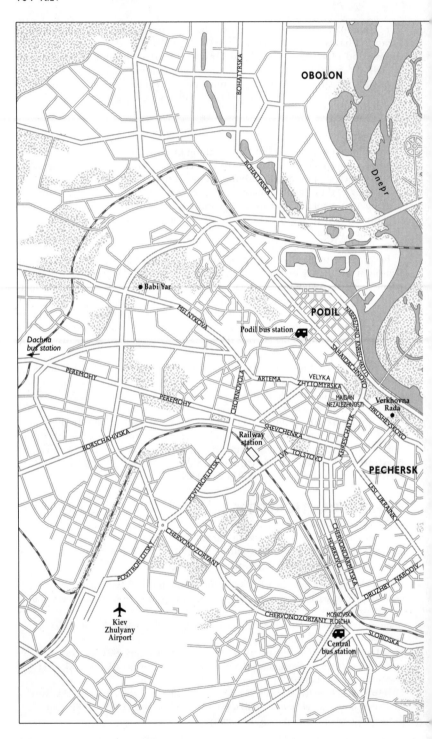

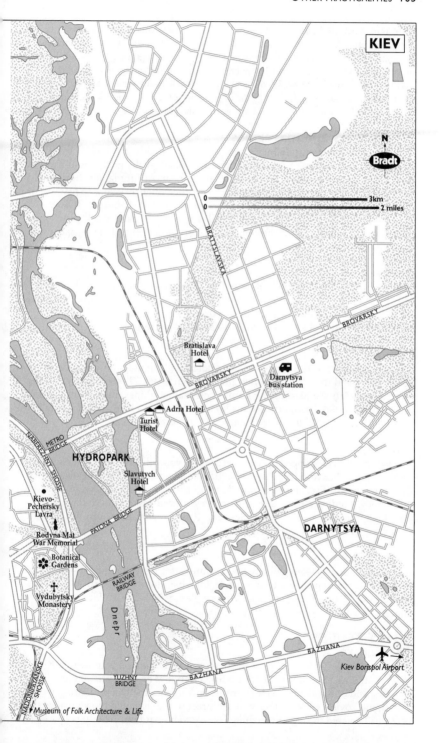

SAM Ivana Franka 40B; tel/fax: 044 238 6959; email: raskin@samcomp.kiev.ua; web: www.sam.com. The biggest and most established incoming tour operator in Ukraine. Good for contacting before your trip or when you show up. Besides organising guides, hotels, and interpreters, SAM is known for its Dnepr cruises and very full day trips to Chernobyl.
Ukrzovnishintour Khmelnytskovo 26; tel: 044 229 8464; email: uit@uit.kiev.ua; web: www.uit.com.ua. Don't be daunted by the unpronounceable name; this company gives good tours of Kiev and specialises in day trips to Kaniv, Uman, and Chernihiv.

Newspapers and magazines

The *Kyiv Post* (web: www.kpnews.com) is not just the ex-pat weekly, but a rare bit of free press offering a reliable insight into what's really going on in Kiev, in English. The newspaper is available free in most upmarket hotels and restaurants or for sale at any newsstand. The other English-language newspaper is the pro-government *Kyiv Weekly*, also widely distributed. *What's On* (www.whatson-kiev.com) is a colourful English-language weekly detailing restaurants, nightlife, and entertainment. For more general newspapers and magazines, see page 82.

Internet

Internet cafés are not lacking in Kiev and the English-language signs will point the way. Prices hover around US$1–2 an hour. Try **Overgame** (Maidan Nezalezhnosti 2, 2nd floor; tel: 044 229 0253), **Pentagon** (Khreschatyk 15; tel: 044 228 2182), or **Cyber Café** (Prorizna 21; tel: 044 228 0548).

Post

The central post office occupies an impressive building on the corner of Khreschatyk and the Maidan Nezalezhnosti (open 08.00–21.00 every day; closing Sunday at 19.00). Besides buying stamps and mailing things, there is an internet café and a number of international phone booths that charge about US$.60 a minute for calls to North America and US$1 to western Europe.

Banking

So many banks have popped up around Kiev that you will have no problem getting cash or finding out your bank balance in hrivna. There are also banking facilities at the central post office, and most middle to upmarket hotels will have an ATM in their lobby. Finding a place to change money is even easier than finding a bank. Just look for the signs with American, Russian and European flags, with correspondent currency rates chalked in.

Telephone

Kiev's city code is 044 and all city phone numbers are seven digits. Within Kiev, just dial these seven digits; from outside Ukraine, drop the 0, dial 38 (country code), 44, and then the seven digits. All pay phones in Kiev take Utel cards only, which you can buy at the post office.

WHAT TO SEE
The centre

The first place you'll be shown, or the first place you'll find on your own, is Kiev's most central north–south boulevard **Khreschatyk**. The road was one of Kiev's very first and once followed a clear stream flowing into the Dnepr. During World War II, the Soviets sabotaged most of the street so that it would blow up after the Nazis had entered the city. Everything you see today has been rebuilt; people may

A WALK THROUGH KIEV

If you take the time to visit each place mentioned, this itinerary will take a day.

* Starting at Universitet metro station, cross the street to **St Vladimir's Cathedral**.
* From St Vladimir's walk down Leontovycha to Khmelnystkovo, turn right and walk one block.
* Cross the street and you are in front of **Ukraine's National Opera House**. Book tickets for a night performance.
* Walk up Volodymyrska (north) to the green park where you see the remaining '**Golden Gate**' (**Zoloti Vorota**) of Kiev's pre-Mongol fortress and a monument to Yaroslav the Wise.
* Continue down Voloymyrska to **St Sophia's Cathedral**.
* In the middle of Sofiyska Square is the monument to Bohdan Khmelnytsky. Cross the park/thoroughfare to the opposite St Mikhayil's Square and the bright blue **St Mikhayil's Monastery of the Golden Domes**. On the way you will pass the monuments to Princess Olga, saints Cyril and Methodius and the Apostle Andrew, and near the entrance to St Mikhayil's you see the monument to the victims of the Ukrainian famine.
* The stately white building across St Mikhayil's Square is Ukraine's Ministry of Foreign Affairs. Walk past it and down Desiatynna, to the ruins of **Desiatynnaya Church**, the **History Museum** and the ancient tree.
* Continue down Desiatynna past the art galleries and to the turquoise **St Andrei's Church**. Begin your descent on **Andreyevsky Spusk**, (which can take a whole day if you want to see everything). At the base of the hill, walk one block into the heart of **Podil** at Kontraktova Ploscha. Take the metro back.
* If you still have time in the evening, get off the metro at **Maidan Nezalezhnosti** (two stops from Kontraktova Ploscha). Enjoy the sights and grandeur of the square, then start down Khreschatyk (south) past all the government buildings, city hall, the shops and restaurants, and end your day by shopping at **Bessarabsky Rynok**.

criticise the pomp of post-war Stalinist architecture, but these monumental structures define Kiev today. The central focal point of the boulevard is the **Maidan Nezalezhnosti** (Independence Square) that seems to be moving in the direction of Times Square in New York with its large-scale electronic advertising. This was once the Place of the October Revolution but now features Kiev's largest shopping centre (underground), a chic McDonalds, the central post office, and lots of friendly Ukrainian nationalists selling flags, books, and music. On the opposite side of the street is Kiev's newest monument, a white and gold pillar erected in 2001 to celebrate a decade of independence. Down below, on the left side is another recent bronze sculpture showing the heroes of Ukrainian folklore.

Where Khreschatyk begins its descent to the river stands a giant titanium arch over the brawny statues of two 'brothers' – Ukraine and Russia – raising fists in union. Of course, the monument to the 'Friendship of Nations' is controversial today, but the space has remained, probably for its wonderful view of the river and the city. The park continues south all the way to the Caves Monastery, *Rodyna Mat*, and botanical gardens.

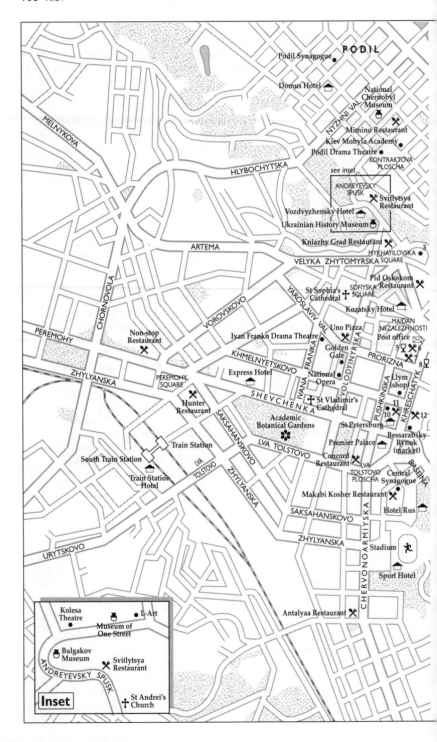

Podil Synagogue

PODIL

Domus Hotel

National Chernobyl Museum

NYZHNI VAL

Mimino Restaurant
Kiev Mohyla Academy
Podil Drama Theatre

KONTRAKTOVA PLOSCHA

HLYBOCHYTSKA

see inset

ANDREYEVSKY SPUSK

Svitlytsya Restaurant

Vozdvyzhensky Hotel
Ukrainian History Museum

MELNYKOVA

Kniazhy Grad Restaurant
MYKHAYILOVSKA SQUARE 3

ARTEMA

VELYKA ZHYTOMYRSKA

Pid Oskokom Restaurant

St Sophia's Cathedral
SOFIYSKA SQUARE

Kozatsky Hotel

VOROVSKOVO

YAROSLAVIV VAL

Uno Pizza
MAIDAN NEZALEZHNOSTI

Non-stop Restaurant

CHORNOVOLA

PEREMOHY

Ivan Franko Drama Theatre

Golden Gate

Post office
5 6
7
8

PRORIZNA

ZHYLYANSKA

KHMELNYETSKOVO

Express Hotel

IVANA FRANKA

National Opera

VOLODINYRSKA

Llym (shop)

PUSHKINSKA

PEREMOHY SQUARE

SHEVCHENKA

St Vladimir's Cathedral

11

10

KHRESCHATYK

12

Hunter Restaurant

SAKSAHANSKOVO

Academic Botanical Gardens

LVA TOLSTOVO

St Petersburg

Premier Palace

Bessarabsky Rynok (market)

Train Station

South Train Station

Train Station Hotel

IVA TOLSTOVO

ZHYLYANSKA

Concord Restaurant

LVA TOLSTOVO PLOSCHA

Central Synagogue

BASENA

Makabi Kosher Restaurant

SAKSAHANSKOVO

Hotel Rus

ZHYLYANSKA

CHERVONOARMIYSKA

URYTSKOVO

Stadium

Sport Hotel

Antalyaa Restaurant

Inset

Kolesa Theatre

I-Art

Museum of One Street

Bulgakov Museum

Svitlytsya Restaurant

ANDREYEVSKY SPUSK

St Andrei's Church

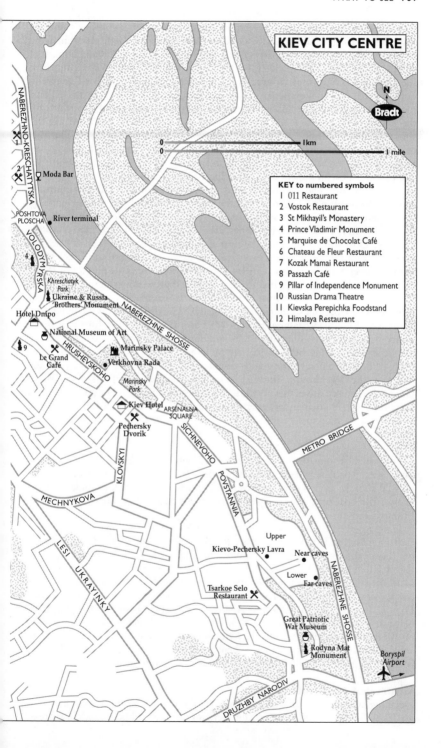

KIEV CITY CENTRE

N

Bradt

0 ———————————— 1km
0 ———————————————— 1 mile

KEY to numbered symbols
1 011 Restaurant
2 Vostok Restaurant
3 St Mikhayil's Monastery
4 Prince Vladimir Monument
5 Marquise de Chocolat Café
6 Chateau de Fleur Restaurant
7 Kozak Mamai Restaurant
8 Passazh Café
9 Pillar of Independence Monument
10 Russian Drama Theatre
11 Kievska Perepichka Foodstand
12 Himalaya Restaurant

NABEREZHNO-KRESCHATYTSKA

1

2 Moda Bar

POSHTOVA
PLOSCHA River terminal

VOLODYMYRSKA

4

Khreschatyk
Park
Ukraine & Russia
'Brothers' Monument NABEREZHNE SHOSSE
Hotel Dnipo

National Museum of Art

9
Le Grand
Café

HRUSHEVSKOHO

Marinsky Palace

Verkhovna Rada

Marinsky
Park

Kiev Hotel ARSENALNA
SQUARE
Pechersky
Dvorik

KLOVSKYI

SICHNEVOHO

METRO BRIDGE

MECHNYKOVA

POVSTANNIA

LESI UKRAYINKY

Upper
Kievo-Pechersky Lavra Near caves

Lower
Tsarkoe Selo Far caves
Restaurant

NABEREZHNE SHOSSE

Great Patriotic
War Museum

Rodyna Mat
Monument

Boryspil
Airport

DRUZHBY NARODIV

Volodymyrska runs parallel to Khreschatyk and has emerged as Kiev's embassy row. Central to the boulevard is the **Golden Gate** (Zoloti Vorota), a last remaining portion of Kiev's original ramparts prior to the Mongol invasion, although much of what's on display has been added. Further down the street at 50 Volodymyrska is the **Ukrainian National Opera**, an incredible building from Kiev's *belle époque*, built in 1901. (Taras Shevchenko's name and bust have been added to this national monument as well.) The building's interior hall is just as beautiful, renowned for the 1911 assassination of Pyotr Stolypin, prime minister to Tsar Nikolai II. He was shot point blank during the second intermission of Rimsky-Korsakov's 'The Tale of Tsar Saltan'. Nobody has died here since, and it is quite easy to get tickets for any of the shows – the ballet and opera boast an amazing repertoire. Few things in Kiev compare to an evening spent in this building.

At the opposite end of Volodymyrska is Sofiyska Square with the landmark tower of **St Sophia's Cathedral** and the mighty statue of Bohdan Khmelnytsky. From here it is an easy walk across the park to Mikhayilovsky Square, the monastery and Vladimir's Hill, where the famous statue of Prince Vladimir holding a cross still stands above the river as he did in legend when all of Kiev was baptised. From here it is an easy walk to the very vibrant and artsy street **Andreyevsky Spusk**, or else a quick funicular ride down to the quarter of **Podil** in the north. Both places are tied to Kiev's past and present intellectual life.

The seat of the Ukrainian government is based along the blocks of Hrushevskovo that run south from Khreschatyk. The most picturesque building is the rococo **Marinsky Palace**, built in 1752 as a royal residence for the Russian aristocracy. Today the blue and white building is used only for the president's private state functions, but tourists may walk the grounds, although you will most likely be hurried along by the guards that stand on every corner. Next door to the palace is the **Verkhovna Rada**, the national parliament of Ukraine. All of Ukraine's representatives meet beneath the big rounded glass dome and it is in this building that Ukrainian independence was declared on August 24 1991.

Much of what there is to see and do in Kiev lies outside the city centre.

Podil

Kiev's funicular joins the original 'upper city' with Podil, the Dnepr flood-plain-turned-residential-neighbourhood. The ride is fun, the view is good, and it costs only 50 kopecks. Pick it up behind St Mikhayil's Monastery of the Golden Domes or near the boat terminal. Otherwise, take the metro to Kontraktova Ploscha or Poshtova Ploscha.

Long ago, Podil was the nitty-gritty part of Kiev where foreign merchants and craftsmen lived and worked away from the more refined churches and palaces on the hill (hence the river port, contract house and large market spaces). A cosmopolitan flair is still in place and a visit to Podil gives a good impression of what Kiev used to look like before all the turmoil of the 20th century. What was once Kiev's outer quarter now features some of its best architecture and most candid street scenes. Podil is also home to **Kiev Mohyla Academy**, probably the most prestigious place of learning in Ukraine, founded in 1615. The prominent building is the main feature on Kontraktova Square. As with all city quarters made famous by the students, no students can actually afford to live here any more. Artsy and historic, Podil is becoming a gentrified neighbourhood for Kiev's newest professionals.

Churches and holy sites

Detailing Kiev's hundreds of churches would require a multi-volume set of guidebooks, and then a few years later there might very well be a hundred more to write about. Even if churches are not your thing, it would be a pity to miss what Kiev does best. For now, these are the sites that fascinate the majority:

Kievo-Pechersky Lavra

The 'Caves Monastery' is Kiev's number one tourist attraction both for Ukrainians and foreigners. The enormous ensemble of white church halls with green and gold rooftops has come to represent the spiritual heart of the country and symbolise Kiev's survival throughout a millennium of adversity. Officially, the monastery is defined as a government Historical-Culture Preserve, but this area – and the caves in particular – are a national religious shrine and the headquarters for the Ukrainian Orthodox Church (Moscow Patriarchate). Over 100,000 pilgrims come every year to pray and worship and tourists should visit only in the spirit of reverence and modesty. That said, the Lavra is beginning to show signs of tourist trap development that already detract from the mood, including abundant souvenir shops and multifarious money-making devices.

The history of the Lavra dates back to Prince Vladimir's introduction of Christianity as the new state religion of Rus. Following this event St Anthony of Lyubech left Mount Athos in Greece and settled in Kiev in 1051. He lived on the banks of the Dnepr in a manmade cave where he became known for his strict asceticism and spiritual powers. With the help of his devoted follower St Theodosius, Anthony was able to expand the caves by a series of tunnels and cells to accommodate more disciples, leading to the formation of an extensive underground network where monks spent entire lifetimes meditating, praying and writing. Ukraine's (and Russia's) earliest historians, scholars, and icon-painters were all attached to the Kiev's Lavra, including the author of the *Chronicle of Bygone Years*, Nestor. This heritage, and the advent of a printing press in 1615, made Kiev the intellectual centre of Christian thought for all Slavic lands.

The stunning buildings on the surface were begun as early as the 11th century, and while a few exhibit the simple rounded domes of Byzantium, the majority of the architecture reflects mid-18th-century baroque styles employed to rebuild the monastery after a devastating fire in 1718. (The Mongol invasions of 1240 and 1480 – as well as an earthquake in 1620 – had already destroyed the older portions of the monastery in stages.) The area was made a cultural preserve in 1926 after the Soviet takeover, but long periods of neglect and the destruction of the war left a series of odd museums surrounded by rubble. Gorbachev returned the monastery and Far Caves to the Church in 1988, followed by the Near Caves a year later, while the Ukrainian government gained control of the upper churches after independence. Most of the glistening structures you see today were only just restored.

A visit to the monastery and caves can be as short or as long as you want. The ticketing system is as Byzantine as the architecture. General admittance to the Upper Lavra is 10UAH, but every church, exhibition and museum sells separate tickets – it does not take long to collect a pocketful of ripped paper. On occasion, foreigners are charged about ten times more and the right to take photographs costs an additional 12UAH. If you find this troublesome, you can sometimes avoid the maze through a personal guided tour, which will cost around US$30. Freelance tour guides will approach you with lower prices upon entering, or you can make prior arrangements; tel: 044 290 3071. To get to the Pechersky Lavra, take the metro to Arsenalna, then cross the road and take trolley #38 or bus #20 to the fortification walls at Ivana Mazepa 21. Marshrutka #163 also travels between the Lavra and Khreschatyk.

If you are in a taxi or with a tour group, you will most likely get dropped off outside the light blue **Troitskaya Church**. Now used as a gatehouse, the original church was built in 1108 but now features classic examples of Ukrainian baroque. Before rushing inside, be sure to enjoy a long look at the murals of the outer walls, painted in 1900. The main path leads to the **Great Belltower**, the tallest Orthodox structure in the world at 96.5m. For 3UAH you are allowed to climb to the third highest level and take in a fantastic view of all the domes, the park and the river. Directly across from the belltower is the **Church of the Assumption** (**Dormiton Cathedral**), which is technically the oldest church (above ground) in the Lavra, completed in 1077. The original structure was blown up by retreating Soviet forces in 1941 and was only rebuilt in the year 2000 with its seven gold turrets and marvellously detailed design. To the north is the **Church of All Saints** built at the end of the 17th century by the Cossack hetman Ivan Mazepa. It's known best for its vivid interior of gold and painted portraits. To the south of the Dormiton Cathedral is the **Refectory**, built at the end of the 19th century when the community of monks was sizeable enough to require such a large dining hall. The accompanying Byzantine dome is almost more impressive than the interior **Chapel of Saints Anthony and Theodosius**, although some of the original 19th-century painting still remains.

The rest of the Upper Lavra is comprised of several remarkable buildings housing slightly unremarkable national museums. Each is open 09.00–17.00, most are closed on Tuesday, and entrance is 5UAH. The **Museum of Historical Treasures** is in the far rear of the Lavra and shows all the jewellery and metalwork from the Scythians to the present. Directly behind the Dormiton Cathedral is the early 17th-century print shop that now houses the **Museum of Books and Printing** which exhibits some unique illuminated manuscripts dating back to Kievan Rus. The **Museum of Theatre, Music and Cinematography** is located at the back of **St Nicholas Church** with the star-studded blue dome. The exhibit is mostly nostalgic paraphernalia from Kiev showbiz days. Directly south of the belltower is the **Residence of the Metropolitan** where the head of the Ukrainian Church once lived. Today it is the **Museum of Ukrainian Decorative Folk Art** that is slowly accumulating its collection of national costume and craft. Directly across is the **Museum of Micro-miniatures**, a remnant of the Lavra's Soviet period. There is little historical value in this off-the-wall display except maybe to better understand the Soviet cultural mentality of the 1970s. Through a row of microscopes visitors can view things like a chessboard on a pinhead, the word 'Peace' written on a human hair, the portraits of famous Soviet heroes etched into poppy seeds, or golden horseshoes on a dead flea. Several other halls are open and advertised as art galleries; however, the exhibits consist largely of conveyor-belt paintings churned out and sold to tourists.

Visiting the caves

Sadly, most tourists wander for hours in the Upper Lavra looking for the caves and seeing everything but. What your guide won't tell you is that you can visit the caves on your own for nothing, since the entrance to the tunnels and the present-day monastery (the Lower Lavra) are holy sites that exist outside the realm of entrance fees. To get to the caves from the Upper Lavra, walk under the white flying buttresses of the old print shop and descend to the right and through the gate. This brings you to the Lower Lavra. To get to the caves from the street, walk down the long descent outside the fortification wall – this is where most of the Russian-speaking crowds will be headed.

The caves are open to the public from 09.00 to 16.00. There is no admission fee, but it is customary to purchase a beeswax candle at the entrance to use as

THE BODIES OF THE SAINTS

After the monastery moved above ground, many of the caves became virtual necropolises – underground cities with marked 'streets' where the dead were laid. While some of these saints died nearly one thousand years ago, their bodies have been preserved without any form of embalming. The church claims this to be the miracle of saints, and pilgrims still come to touch the shrouded bodies and partake of this life power.

Soviet scientists were employed to disprove the miracle and deride any supernatural belief in the caves. Their studies concluded that the caves' total lack of moisture prevented organic decay. Now in the post-Soviet era, these same studies are being used to support the mystical power of the saints' relics. Supposedly, the Soviet scientists had also found that radiation from the bodies was emitted in elliptical patterns somehow linked to the magnetic poles of the earth. An experiment with wheat plants then proved the saints emitted a 'bio-physic' power that directly influenced the nuclear level of living matter. This research was especially useful following the Chernobyl disaster, when it was 'scientifically proven' that this holy radiation protected against atomic radiation, especially when prayers were offered to the saints.

Many other miracles are addressed to the bodies of the saints, but the biggest miracle is that the bodies are still there. Seventy years of atheist Soviet rule did much to destroy the Ukrainian Church, but somehow the caves survived with their saints. There is evidence that many of the bodies were moved or hidden to confuse authorities, though the accepted story is that the Soviet government tried to empty the caves and failed. After piling all the saints into the back of a truck, the driver found he could not start his engine. The officials tried everything, but they could not move the vehicle. The patriarch was summoned and told of the dilemma, to which he responded that, try as they might, the saints' bodies would never leave the monastery. After three weeks of sitting outside, the bodies were brought back into the caves, the truck's engine started, and there was no more meddling with anything subterranean.

your light in the tunnels. Visitors are asked to whisper only, and women are asked to cover their heads and to not wear heavy make-up. Few places in Ukraine grant a better view of Orthodox spirituality than these caves. Both church and lay people come to pray, to sing, to meditate and to pay homage to the oldest saints of Ukrainian Orthodoxy, whose bodies are preserved in the tunnels. Darkness, gold, incense, icons, and skulls add to the solemn and mystical aura of the caves. As the popularity of this holy site increases, certain sections of the tunnels and underground chapels have been barred off, for the use of pilgrims only. These are usually the most beautiful and interesting parts of the caves, so be a pilgrim if you want and enter through the wooden doors; just be silent and circumspect.

The caves are divided into two separate networks, *Blyzhny* (Near) and *Dalni* (Far). The **Near Caves** date from the 11th century and contain the very sacred **Vedenska Church** with its gold iconostas. St Anthony built these tunnels for himself to find solitude from his original community that had expanded in the older caves. His tomb lies in these caves, as well as that of Nestor the chronicler. Once your eyes get used to the darkness, you can see the fragments of original frescoes above most of the tombs. The entrance to the Near Caves is slightly hidden, since the real entrance is used for guided group tours only. If you are on your own, go to the **Khrestovozdvyzhenska Church** (18th century). The entrance to the caves is in the fore chamber, the exit is in the chapel.

The **Far Caves** comprise the original underground monastery from 1051 and centre around the **Church of the Annunciation** with its immaculate gold doors and incredible painting. St Theodosius is buried in his own chapel, as well as many other saints and those church leaders killed during the Russian Revolution. The Far Caves also join up with the legendary Varangian cave, where the Vikings hid their booty back in the 10th century. If you think you suffer from claustrophobia, think long and hard before entering the Far Caves. Most tunnels are fairly deep underground and barely measure six feet high and two feet wide. The influx of large tour groups can easily place over a hundred single-file people between you and the surface.

Entrance to the Far Caves is through the **Annozachatiyevskaya Church** at the furthest southeast corner of the Lavra. The green-roofed walkway connects the exit of the near caves to the entrance of the Far Caves. The towering gold-domed church across from the Far Caves exit is the **Church of the Birth of the Blessed Virgin**. Built in 1696, the only remaining painting dates from the 19th century, while the exterior uses examples of traditional Ukrainian folk art. Nearby is the **Far Caves Belfry**; with its sharp spires and classic Ukrainian baroque style, this is one of the better restored buildings in the Lavra.

St Vladimir's Cathedral

Kiev's most artistic church is also one of its youngest constructions, built to commemorate 900 years of Christianity in Rus. Started in 1862, the cathedral took over 30 years to complete due to some overly ambitious architects. In one of his last displays of public duty, Tsar Nikolas II presided over the cathedral's christening in 1896. The final design reflects the basic Byzantine style of seven black domes, but the lemon yellow exterior and colourful interior make this a much lighter and more decorative church than is typical in Orthodoxy. Stepping inside will trigger some very sincere 'oohs' and 'aahs' and some fulfilling moments can be had from staring at the colossal paintings that cover much of the walls and ceiling with depictions of Kiev's spiritual history. On your right, upon entering, is the painting of Vladimir's baptism in Chersoneus in Crimea. On the left is the baptism of Kiev, with the citizens of Rus descending into the Dnepr. Most of the interior of St Vladimir's was painted by the Russian artist Viktor Vasnetsov who belonged to a 19th-century circle of artists known as 'The Wanderers'. The faces and human figures reflect an art nouveau and pre-Raphaelite influence, but the themes and composition are expressly Slavic (the colours look best in winter sunlight). Facing backwards exposes the rather dark and ominous representation of Michael the Archangel in the Final Judgement. This is the church most frequented by the citizens of Kiev and therefore the best place to experience any number of daily services with music. The cathedral is located at Shevchenka 20, across from Universitet metro station.

St Sophia's Cathedral

Grand Prince Yaroslav the Wise built St Sophia's in 1037 to thank God for defending Kiev against the Pecheneg invasion of 1024. The church was modelled after the Hagia Sophia in Constantinople, but now bears the external trappings of the baroque era. Today the entire complex functions as a museum of Kievan Rus, exhibiting hundreds of original frescos and some very well-preserved Byzantine mosaics. The sarcophagus of Yaroslav 'The Wise' is located in the north chapel (along with his bones) and he is still revered as a positive political role model for Russians and Ukrainians. The old chronicles report that he was a diplomatic and judicious leader whose reign marked the height of Kievan Rus. In his memory stands the church's landmark blue belltower from the 17th century. The cultural reserve is located at Sofiyska Square; open 10.00 to 18.00, closed Thursday. Tickets to get on the grounds are 2UAH, everything else is priced separately, although the church is really the only building worth touring, entrance 5UAH.

St Mikhayil's Monastery of the Golden Domes
This sky-blue sanctuary rises up in a pyramid of bright domes directly east from St Sophia's belltower. Several different monasteries stood on this spot from the 12th century onwards, but this newest version was only just completed in 2001. During Stalin's destructive wave of 1937, St Mikhayil's was completely blown up and the lot left empty until President Kuchma supported its reconstruction. The complex is now owned by the more nationalist Ukrainian Orthodox Church (Kiev Patriarchate) meaning this is one of the few places in Kiev where you'll actually hear Ukrainian being spoken. Both architecture and artwork are true to Ukrainian style and few churches in Kiev are so delicate and bright.

Outside the monastery walls are two meaningful monuments. The iron and stone cross that forms the shadowed outlines of humans remembers the victims of the Ukrainian famine of 1932–33. The larger white marble sculpture shows Princess Olga in the centre with the Apostle Andrew on her right-hand side, and the founders of Slavonic literacy on her left, St Cyril and St Methodius. None of these characters were ever alive at the same time, but the figures represent Kiev's spiritual, political, and artistic forebears.

Vydubytsky Monastery
Located on the banks of the Dnepr within the botanical gardens, this monastery was founded at the spot where the pagan effigy of Perun floated to the surface after having been dumped into the water upriver. For much of Kiev's history, the monastery controlled the Dnepr ferry that crossed here. St George's Cathedral (1701) features as the most prominent structure, but the other buildings echo a smaller version of the Caves Monastery. You can reach the monastery by taxi to Vydubytska 40 or from the metro station Druzhby Narodiv, but this also makes a nice walk from the top of the botanical gardens; tel: 044 295 4713.

Jewish sites
Kiev's **Central Synagogue** was built in 1898 in the very heart of the city; Shota Rustavelli 13; tel: 044 235 9082. The building was used as a puppet theatre for the duration of the Soviet regime. Today the metro station Palats Sportu is just across the street and next door to the synagogue is a popular kosher restaurant where people from all over the world enjoy very delicious food. The older **Podil Synagogue** is on Schekavytska 29; tel: 044 416 2442. The façade was built to look like two separate houses with a clandestine entrance at the back.

Prior to World War II, there were over 150,000 Jews in Kiev who made up 20% of the city's population. Before the Nazi advance reached Kiev in 1941, some 100,000 of Kiev's Jews had already fled deep into the Soviet Union, many of them into Central Asia and Siberia. On September 29, only ten days after Kiev had fallen, the Nazi Einsatzgruppe ordered all Jews to report near a grassy ravine that lies just outside the city limits, **Babi Yar**. Here the people were gathered in groups and then shot en masse. On the first day, 33,771 people were killed, and throughout the

KIEV IN MINIATURE: ANDREYEVSKY SPUSK

According to the Bible, Andrew was the first apostle to be called to follow Christ, and according to legend the saint sailed up the banks of the Dnepr and landed in this particular spot, prophesying that on these hills a great city would rise up (legend also claims he landed in Crimea). The saint supposedly climbed this particular hill in Kiev and fixed a cross in the ground; a curved and narrow lane now twists from this spot and follows St Andrew's path down to the Dnepr. After Kiev adopted Christianity, the great pagan idol Perun was tied to a stag and dragged down 'Andrew's descent' (*Andriyivsky Uzviz* in Ukrainian), beaten with sticks, and shoved into the river.

Today the sea-green and dark teal **St Andrei's Church** crowns the top of Kiev's favourite street with spindly turrets and a fanciful baroque dome. The unique design is the work of Italian architect Rastrelli who had already built St Petersburg's most famous buildings, the Winter Palace and Tsarskoe Selo. The church in Kiev was his last masterpiece, completed in 1762, after which he was fired by Catherine the Great. The church was turned into a museum of architecture to avoid the wrath of Stalin and remains a museum today. The interior has only just been renovated and is still rather empty, except for the two very interesting paintings of St Andrew and Prince Vladimir. Open 10.00–18.00, closed Wednesday; entrance 5UAH.

By the time you get to St Andrei's, someone will have tried to sell you something to remember Kiev by. In the 19th century, Andreyevsky Spusk was the proud domain of artists and writers and since then, the street has harboured Kiev's more Bohemian elements. Today, souvenir markets and so-called art shows run along the entire length of the street and this is where most tourists are directed to buy gifts. Most of the stuff for sale is mass-produced, but it is what most people want: matroshka dolls, fake Soviet paraphernalia, machine-stitched Ukrainian embroidery or T-shirts with Lenin making obscene gestures. Further down the street the bits and bobs become more varied with woodcarving, home-knit wool, old prints, books, and coins. The festive bazaar is kept alive with the help of musicians, street poets and mimes. Much of the art consists of rows upon rows of kitschy painting, but there are still a few authentic galleries on the descent. Have a look in **Gallery 36** (Andreyevsky Spusk 36; tel: 044 228 2985; email: infor@Gallery36.org.ua; web: www.Gallery36.org.ua), a private gallery that features quality work by contemporary Ukrainian artists. For more traditional Ukrainian themes and Socialist Realist painting, try the very professional **L-Art** (Andreyevsky Spusk 2b; tel: 044 416 0320; web: www.lartgallery.com) at the bottom of the hill.

From the top of the street, you will spot the modest white statue of Apostle Andrew. This marks the beginning of the old residential area, and most of these homes are architectural monuments, including the wooden house at #34, known as 'Noah's Ark' for its wooden exterior and a history of cramming lots of poor starving artists onto its floors. Every building has a story; the seven-

occupation, Babi Yar was used for executing Ukraine's gypsies, nationalists, communists and more Jews. Few knew about the tragedy of Babi Yar until after liberation. A Soviet monument was dedicated to the 'Soviet citizens' who perished, and the massacre was remembered in the poem by Yevgeny Yevtushenko. However, it was only in 1991 that a Jewish memorial could be built, and in 2001 another monument was dedicated to the memory of all the children who had died here.

storey yellow edifice (#15) with one single tower is known as 'Richard's Castle', named after King Richard I in *Ivanhoe* by the children who once played on the street. These were once the favoured flats of Kiev's more prestigious artists.

The famous Russian writer Mikhail Bulgakov was born in Kiev, and moved to house #13 with his theologian father at age 15. Here he attended high school and medical school and then worked as a doctor during the revolution. The **Bulgakov Museum** (Andreyevaksy Spusk 13; tel: 044 416 3188; open 10.00–17.00, closed Wednesday; entrance 5UAH, 12UAH for a guided tour in English) now occupies his home. The ghostly surrealist exhibit incorporates ideas from all of his well-known works, but mainly from his autobiographical first novel *The White Guard*, which recounts his experiences in Kiev during the Russian civil war. Any object that is not painted white is an original object from the Bulgakov family. Enthusiasts of *The Master and Margarita* may find less allusions to this book than might be hoped for, but a general knowledge will help in understanding some of the stranger features in the house. Bulgakov spent most of his writing career in Moscow but published very little in his lifetime due to harsh censorship.

It's not too hard to find food on the Spusk, but if you want to sit down for a bit, the place next door to Bulgakov's house is worth trying out (Andreyevsky Spusk 11; tel: 044 416 5123). The restaurant has no name so as to reinforce its mysterious nature, but the building is recognised for the black metal cat outside, with the tail of a snake – a character remembered from Bulgakov's *Master and Margerita*. The chef is Armenian so of course the food is wonderful, and live piano and violin music add to the semi-spooky atmosphere. A full meal costs around US$12–18.

Across the street is the **Kolesa Theatre** (Andreyevsky Spusk 8; tel: 044 416 0422), a small avant-garde playhouse that already has an established following in Kiev. The upstairs theatre produces more well-known pieces (eg: Henry James, Ionesco, Flaubert) while the lower floor is a working café with interactive theatre every night of the week. Somehow or other, patrons will get roped into the performance art.

Last but in no way least is the delightful **Museum of One Street** (Andreyevsky Spusk 2B; open 12.00–18.00, closed Monday, entrance 3UAH) at the very bottom of the descent. Breaking away from the stifling mould of Soviet museums, the ingenious display recounts the story of this one street through a meticulous collection of objects gathered over the ages from each address. Simple treasures like old clothes, spectacles, dishes, and books are arranged in artful installations to represent all that has happened in these homes during the past century. Visitors need not speak Russian to enjoy the visual history of the lives of this neighbourhood: the circus performer, the Orthodox priest, the Jewish rabbi, the composer, the writer and soldier. (In breach of inscrutability I will reveal that this is one of my favourite museums.)

Visiting Babi Yar today requires taking the metro out to Dorohozhychi station. The southern park shows the very tragic-looking Soviet memorial; the northern park and forest is where the actual massacre took place. The children's memorial is next to the metro station and the Menorah monument is at the base of the ravine. Following the path south will take you to Kiev's **Jewish cemetery** on Melnikova.

Museums
The Great Patriotic War Museum

In Russian, World War II is remembered as the great patriotic struggle for the motherland. The **Rodyna Mat** (Nation's Mother) is the titanium goddess that towers above Kiev's right bank with a sword and shield in hand, commemorating the defence of one's country. Don't even think about comparing it to the Statue of Liberty, although there are elevators going up inside and a staircase to a viewing platform in her right hand (Brezhnev built it). The museum is located inside the pedestal and an adjoining hall, telling the story of Soviet Ukraine's victory over the Nazis in panoramic displays. A separate exhibit details the struggle of socialism in the Soviet wars of the Third World, including Angola and Afghanistan. The letters, pictures, and old uniforms are sobering.

The surrounding park is a popular place for a stroll and offers a great example of vast Soviet public space. Paths lead past the eternal flame, the tomb of the unknown soldier and two graffiti tanks tied together in peace. Another trail leads down to the ruins of the Pechersk fortress, the main tsarist defence for Kiev in the 19th century. Getting to the *Rodyna Mat* is just a few more stops from the Caves Monastery. Go to Arsenalna metro station and take bus #20 to the very end, or else a marshrutka or taxi to '*Rodyna Mat*'.
Sichnevoho Povstannyaa 44; tel: 044 295 9457; open 09.30–17.00, closed Monday; entrance 3UAH

The Museum of Folk Architecture and Life

Of all the recreated village-museum preserves in Ukraine, the assembly near Pirogov is the largest in size, the broadest in culture, and the liveliest. Over three hundred original pieces of folk architecture have been gathered to represent every traditional region of Ukraine and now comprise a 'national village'. Visitors are allowed to roam freely and enter the wooden churches, windmills, thatched cottages, and barns. The attention to detail on the inside is impressive, as are the craft displays. Costumed peasants play the part and answer questions. During warmer months traditional craftsmen work in the open and sell wild honey, woodcarving, pottery and embroidery. The outdoor fairs (in late spring and early fall) are a lot of fun if you can make it.

Most people visit the museum with a group tour ordered through any local company. Plan on at least four hours to see the place. Pirogov (Pyrohiv) village is directly south of Kiev on the right bank of the Dnepr, and thus outside the reach of most public transportation. On your own, take bus #27 from metro station Libidska to the village of Pirogov (Pyrohiv in Ukrainian). The ride takes about 30 minutes. Otherwise, you can choose to spend your money on a cab or an organised tour (around US$15 either way).
Pirogov; tel: 044 266 2416, open daily 10.00–17.00; entrance 10UAH

The National Museum of Art

This classical building was once the museum of history, and any art on display was a mere illustration of the past. Later, all artwork was nationalised by the Soviet government, leaving the museum with the largest collection of Ukrainian art in the world. Establishing a well-rounded display that defines the country's art has been difficult. For now, you can see medieval icons, 18th- and 19th-century romantic art (some Shevchenko sketches) and some of the most well-known pieces of Soviet-era socialist painting, including original poster art from the revolution. If you prefer sport to art, across the street is the playing field of Kiev's famous 'Dynamo' football team.
Hrushevsky 6; tel: 044 228 6429, open 10.00–18.00, closed Friday, entrance 5UAH

National Chernobyl Museum

One of Kiev's newest museums, the Chernobyl display in Podil explores the human side of a most devastating nuclear tragedy. Probably the most haunting sight in the museum is the hundreds of old signs from cities that were made ghost towns after evacuation. A model of the reactor and a detailed pictorial account of the accident help explain the event to non-Russian speakers (at present there are no English tours offered). The rest of the exhibit deals with the pain and trauma of Chernobyl in a series of highly surrealist art installations.
Provulok Khorevy 1; open 10.00–18.00, closed Sundays, entrance 5UAH

National Museum of Ukrainian History

Ukrainian independence is the prominent theme of the museum, from pagan Slavic times to the political struggles of the last decade.

In the open square next to the museum lie the foundation stones outlining the first stone church in Kiev. The Desyatinnaya (Tithing) Church was built in AD989 in honour of Prince Vladimir's promise to give one tenth of the state income to the new church. However, the building was razed by the Mongols in 1240 and never rebuilt. Shading the ruins is an 800-year-old *lipa*, or lime tree, a plant revered by Ukrainians who use the leaves and flowers as a cure-all.
Volodymyrska 2; tel: 044 228 6545, open 10.00–18.00, closed Wednesday, entrance 4UAH.

Parks

So many parks to choose from, and all of them so nice. **Krheschatyk Park** between the street and the river makes a good beginning for a walk above the Dnepr. The road and path connect to over five different parks, including the exquisite **Marinsky Park** once used for tsarist military manoeuvres. At the end of the road are the expansive **National Botanical Gardens** near Vydubytsky Monastery. A more central forested space are the other **Academic Botanical Gardens** behind the metro station Universitet.

The feel-good Soviet recreation zone **Hydropark** can be reached by the metro station of the same name. Spanning two long islands, the park is comprised of small forests, marshes, and natural sand beaches, constantly reshaped by the Dnepr. Plenty of trails allow for some interesting walks and views of the city, and in summer the place is filled with sunbathers, swimmers, and ice-cream vendors – reminiscent of beachside amusement parks. In winter, the islands are an offbeat but strategic spot to see the gold domes of Kiev, to watch the ice-fishing and to step out on the ice yourself.

OUTSIDE KIEV

There are plenty of interesting destinations just outside the city limits, and a few that are a bit further but can be fitted into one day. **Pereyaslav-Khmelnytsky** (Переяслав-Хмельницький) was a vital city in Kievan Rus and a seat of its own principality. However, the town went down in history in 1654 when Bohdan Khmelnytsky came to this spot and swore allegiance to the tsar, fatefully tying Ukrainian lands to Moscow. Today the town brings in tourists interested in the Cossacks, ancient Kiev, and the Pereyaslav Agreement. The entire town and adjacent countryside now make up the Pereyaslav Historical Preserve, which includes the Museum of the History of Ukrainian Folk Architecture, similar to the one in Kiev (Pirogov) and St Michael's Church. In contrast to big urban Kiev, a day trip to this left bank settlement offers a fair introduction to the old country.

Pereyaslav is also the birthplace of Jewish writer Sholom Aleichem (Solomon Rabinowitz) whose famous stories candidly portrayed *shtetl* life in tsarist Russia. A principal character in these tales was one Tevye the dairyman, and collectively these writings formed the plot for the musical *Fiddler on the Roof*. The home where the writer was born is part of the preserve and now houses a museum of his life. On the road to Pereyaslav from Kiev, you will pass near Voronkiv, the village where Sholom Aleichem attended school and later based his fictional town of Kasrilevke (Anatyevka in the musical). Travel to Pereyaslav takes about one and a half hours and is best done by bus or taxi. Most tour agencies also offer Pereyaslav as a day trip.

Bila Tserkva (Біла Церква) is another town made famous by Bohdan Khmelnytsky when he signed his treaty of Bila Tserkva with Poland in 1651, cutting back on Cossack rights and allowing Polish gentry to regain their lands. Khmelnytsky broke the treaty within the year, eventually driving the Poles out. Bila Tserkva, (literally 'white church') is a popular day trip for its quaint churches and pleasant tree park. Travelling to Bila Tserkva is easy since it falls on the well-travelled southern route from Kiev to Uman and Odessa. Joining an organised tour of the town can be done with any Kiev agency and there are plenty of direct buses from the Central Bus Station. The drive is about one hour.

Chernobyl (Polissya), **Kaniv** (Dnepr), and **Uman** (Podillya) are also popular day trips from Kiev. Each is included in its respective regional chapter.

Polissya Полісся

The north central region of Ukraine is clad in thick forests, hence its name *Polissya*, or 'in the woods'. Ironically, the pristine nature of the egion was permanently marred by the Chernobyl nuclear disaster in 1986, which adds to the difficulty in getting around this very rural area. Because of its proximity to the capital, most independent travellers venture north in a series of day trips from Kiev, although as more outsiders gain interest in Ukraine, they are likely to choose Polissya as an unlikely bit of wilderness open to discovery.

The very earliest of Slavic tribes settled among Polissya's trees and rivers and were brought under Kiev's jurisdiction during the 7th and 8th centuries, meaning the oldest of Ukraine's towns and villages stand between the mixed oak and spruce forests. Tour groups most often visit the ancient churches and pre-Christian fortress of Chernihiv, while the other most popular excursion takes in the barren shell of Chernobyl's nuclear power station and the quietest miles of Ukrainian countryside.

Getting around

The capital Kiev is technically a part of Polissya and acts as the central transfer point for each outlying area. While there are frequent trains to both Zhytomyr and Chernihiv, these are usually long-haul transits that don't mind taking their time getting there. Bus travel is quickest for either city, while anything in between is simply not possible due to the controlled 'zone', the Kiev reservoir and border with Belarus. Getting to Chernobyl involves more precise plans, usually with an organised company.

CHERNIHIV – ЧЕРНІГІВ

For its concentration of ancient churches and holy spots, Chernihiv joins UNESCO's list of World Heritage Sites and has been called the 'open air museum'. From over 20km away, the golden cupolas and towers of several cathedrals and monasteries come into view so that even from a train, you're hit with the same sense Orthodox pilgrims might feel as they approach such a destination. Chernihiv offers an interesting and primeval retreat from the big city, and the countryside surrounding Polissya's Desna River warrants long gazes followed by long walks.

Most people believe the city's name comes from either the black forest surrounding the original settlement – hence *cherny* ('black') – or from *Cherniga*, the prince of the Severian forest tribe who lived here. By the 7th century, the Polissyan tribes had already joined with Kiev to form the basis of the Rus civilisation, and the line of Chernihiv princes became instrumental in the political process. Chernihiv

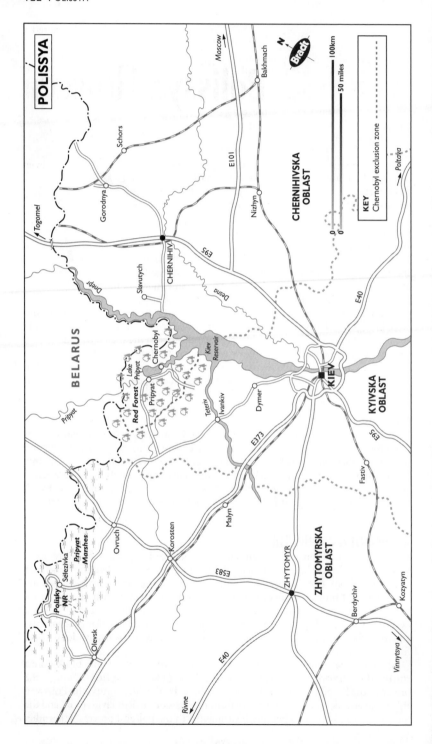

became an official Kievan principality in the early 11th century and covered a territory almost the size of Texas. Large tribute payments and trade with Byzantium funded the several churches built in honour of Kiev's new religion. Prince Svyatoslav (son of Yaroslav the Wise) was the first Kievan prince to rule this region permanently, but the city's golden age was cut short by two hundred years of Mongol attacks. After brief Lithuanian rule, the lands and city came under the jurisdiction of Moscovy. As the closest Ukrainian city to Moscow, Chernihiv played only a minor role in the struggle between Russia, Poland and the Cossacks but thanks to these uneventful years, Chernihiv preserved its best architecture when other cities were decimated. The lack of industrial development instigated by the Russian Empire and the USSR was yet another favour. During the Soviet age, *Chernigov* was the brand name of the country's best beer, and the breweries still make the stuff today and sell it under the Ukrainian label *Chernihiv*.

Independent Ukraine reveres Chernihiv as a lost city that conveys the way the whole country used to look. While so many Ukrainian cities had their churches destroyed and were overcome by Soviet industry, Chernihiv has kept its original face. Orthodox pilgrims have begun to pay homage en masse and secular tourists come this way to witness the provincial glory of Kievan Rus. In one day, most people tend to see all the churches and historical sights they care to see, but staying in Chernihiv allows a pleasant alternative to just another night in Kiev. Despite its proximity to the capital, Chernihiv remains beyond the normal tourist circuit, so a trip this way becomes rather intentional or, for the brave few, a point of transit to and from Belarus.

Getting there and away
Made to accommodate day trippers, the daily train leaves Kiev every morning at 09.00, arrives at 12.00 and returns at 19.00 in order to get travellers back to their hotel by 22.00. Few visitors can resist photographing the cherry-red train station. Other rail connections do exist en route between Kiev and Minsk, so the stop at Chernihiv tends to be in the late evening or early morning and takes up to four hours to get to Kiev; depending on the border, Minsk is nine hours away. The other domestic line creeps west from Sumy (7 hours) and Kharkiv (10 hours). By marshrutka, the trip from Kiev takes about two-and-a-half hours and three hours by bus.

Where to stay and eat
The city's largest and most central hotel is the 18-storey high-rise **Gradetsky** (Mira 68; tel: 0462 245 025). The location falls within walking distance of most of the city's churches, and guides can be arranged at the main desk. Some rooms are renovated, meaning a whole range of rooms, prices and comfort levels is available. A typical double with bath costs US$40. The restaurant on the top floor is known for its view of the city and for the time being is considered the best dinner option in the city. The **Pridesnyanksy Hotel** boasts a more corporate flavour (Shevchenko 99A; tel: 04622 954 905). Nice doubles and suites are around US$50 to $70, while the regular singles make a comfortable option and cost US$25. The least expensive choice is the **Slavyanksy** (Mira 33; tel: 0462 274 604) with very basic rooms for US$15 to US$25 a night.

What to see
The oldest part of the city lies in the '**Val**' next to the Desna riverbank, surrounded by earth mounds once used to defend the settlement in prehistoric times. These ramparts and complex of churches make up the **Dytynets** stronghold and present-

day cultural preserve. Remnants of the fortress date back to the 16th century, although the original structure was built in the 12th century and subsequently destroyed by the Mongols in 1240. The **Cathedral of Boris and Hlib** commemorates Ukraine's first Christian saints, the two brothers of Yaroslav the Wise who were killed by their eldest brother, Prince Svyatopolk. This small white church was built in 1123, and features the stunning, pure silver Tsar's Gate, doors recast from a single pagan idol that was found near the church in the 17th century and melted down. Next door is the first building of the **Chernihiv Collegium**, founded in 1701 and one of the first secular schools in Ukraine. Across the green on Pidvalna stands the **Cathedral of the Transfiguration of Our Saviour** (Spaso-Preobrazhenskya), Chernihiv's oldest and most visited church, built in 1036. Most of the early Kievan princes are buried here, including the son of Yaroslav the Wise, Svyatoslav (note the highly baroque iconostas). South of the Dytenets is the 18th century gold-domed **Katerynynska Church**, funded by a Cossack colonel in thanks for his victory against the Turks. The building now houses a small museum of Polissyan folk craft and souvenir shop. The **Chernihiv Historical Museum** is next to the small **Art Museum** in the neo-classical building by the river. An informative exhibit tells the history of the town in pictures and objects, and displays some remarkable religious treasures.

The city branches out from its own **Red Square** in front of the Chernihiv theatre (citizens now refer to the square as *krasna* in Ukrainian, which means 'beautiful', instead of the Russian *krasnaya* for 'red'). In the park behind stands **St Parasceve's Church**, fashioned from brick in the most basic of Byzantine styles during Chernihiv's 'golden age' of the 12th and 13th centuries. The chapel is famous for its perfect acoustics, a feat attributed to early craftsmen who placed overturned clay chamber pots in the corners of the church and periodically rung them to test resonance. The interior is still quite bare, since the church was closed for much of the Soviet era.

The **Yeletsky Uspensky Monastery** is on the southern side of the town, centred around the flowing towers of the **Uspensky Cathedral**. Founded by Prince Syatoslav in the 11th century, the first Christian monastery in the provinces of Kievan Rus has become a popular pilgrimage site. The nearby mound is the **Chorna Mohyla** (Black Grave), an early Slavic burial mound, much like the barrows of Celtic civilisations. Most of what's in the museum was found here. The hills continue with **Boldyna Hora** (old Slavic for 'Oak Hill') that cover the **Caves of St Anthonius**, built by the same Saint Anthony who founded the Kiev Pechersky Lavra. This underground city of monasteries, catacombs and churches is the largest of its kind in Ukraine with an intricate floor design on four separate levels. The perfect white, green and gold turrets of the miniature **Ilyinska Church** mark the entrance to the caves, open 09.00 to 16.00. Following the winding path leads to the **Troitsky Monastery**, the best preserved of Ukraine's religious buildings, often used as the model by which so many other structures follow in their present-day renovations. The murals inside the **Trinity Cathedral** are rare originals from the 18th century.

CHERNOBYL – ЧОРНОБИЛЬ

The site of the world's very worst nuclear accident now peaks the curiosity of tourists who probably knew about the event before most Ukrainians ever did. For all there is to see and do in Ukraine, Chernobyl is on its way to becoming the country's leading 'I was there' destination. Practically every Ukrainian tourist agency offers a day trip into the 'zone', trading the would-be environmental attractions of Polissya for a post-apocalyptic view of a tainted landscape.

The town of **Chornobyl** (in Ukrainian) lies 20km south of the Belarus border on the Pripyat River. Few foreigners realise what a giant operation Chernobyl was and how central a role it played in the region. A massive artificial lake was formed to cool the four reactors and nearly everyone living in the nearby town of **Pripyat** was somehow connected to making the nuclear energy that kept Kiev's metro running and streetlights aglow.

Unfolding the fateful events of April 26 1986 now sounds like a too-often told campfire tale: the number 4 reactor of the Chernobyl nuclear power plant was to be shut down for routine maintenance and it was decided to test the electrical system to determine if it could keep the reactor's regular cooling system running in the event of a power loss. Obviously, the experiment failed, and this was exacerbated by the fact that the emergency cooling system had been shut off, allowing the overheated system to continue to overheat. The initial explosion at Chernobyl was actually pressurised steam in the cooling system, followed by a genuine nuclear detonation a few seconds later. Two plant workers were immediately killed by the blast. Open to the air, the burning reactor shot nine tonnes of dematerialised waste a mile skyward, followed by a giant radioactive cloud of xenon and krypton gases.

Chernobyl's real heroes were the very first firemen sent in. A lack of preparation and a general failure to grasp the seriousness of this type of accident led to the firemen receiving lethal doses of radiation within a couple of minutes. For two weeks, the reactor continued to burn while workers tried to counteract a myriad of chemical fires. A modern monument to the 31 firemen who died was recently erected in the town.

The double tragedy of Chernobyl was the Soviet Union's attempt to keep it quiet. The towns close to Chernobyl were only evacuated two days after the explosion, and the Ukrainian public were not notified until nearly a week after Swedish scientists had identified the radioactive cloud blowing north. Contaminated rain fell on southern Belarus soon after the explosion, so that this and the environment around Pripyat are considered the worst-hit areas. Soviet logic deemed Polissya a safe place for a nuclear plant due to its low population density and relative proximity to Kiev. The Pripyat marshes and woodlands of Belarus and Ukraine are still considered an exceptionally rare ecosystem, but the woods around Chernobyl will be forever poisoned. The famous '**red forest**' surrounds the southern and western sides of the site and forms a creepy landscape of barren trees sprouting from thick sand that was imported to stop ground radiation. All the small mammals died within the first year after the accident and new fauna has only recently ventured into the area. As Chernobyl's cooling system once flowed directly into the Dnepr, the water has higher than average radiation levels that decrease as you move downstream (this is the real reason you shouldn't eat river fish from the markets).

For Ukrainians, the most direct consequence has been a jump in thyroid cancer among children, as well as the thousands of stillbirths and deformities in newborns following the first year after the accident. Since then, thousands more deaths have been blamed on the nuclear disaster, but it is hard to prove any correlations. The government supports involved compensation schemes with discounts and regular health treatments for registered 'invalids', but sadly, Chernobyl has become the national excuse for any form of malaise.

After repeated requests and cash payments from the EU and the United States, Chernobyl's last reactor was shut down permanently in the year 2000. Thousands remain jobless. Over 120,000 inhabitants were permanently evacuated, and to house them the government built the town of **Slavutych** on the northern banks of the Dnepr. For those keen to see Ukraine's youngest town, Slavutych is not in the 'zone' and can be reached by bus from Kiev or Chernihiv. Chernobyl is still an open wound for Ukraine, so that many Ukrainians still don't know how to react to a rise in travel interest. International agencies and the government hope that frank and open tours to the site will take away some of the stigma at home and abroad.

Visiting Chernobyl

You will not become sterile or get cancer by visiting Chernobyl. In fact, you are more likely to ingest radioactively contaminated foods in Kiev (like mushrooms, berries and vegetables) than to be negatively affected by the site. The restricted exclusion 'zone' is cordoned off by two concentric circles 10km and 30km from the plant. The only thing to see in the zone is that there is nothing to see. Landscapes are barren and overgrown, and the villages eerie and empty. A few die-hards (literally) have returned to their country homes, but for the most part things are left as they were at the time of evacuation. Entering an area frozen in 1986 USSR feels a lot like time travel.

Anyone is allowed to contact the appropriate government ministry and apply for the necessary passes to get into the 'zone', but going through a private tour agency is a lot less hassle. Getting to Chernobyl is not so tricky if you're with a group. The drive from Kiev takes two-and-a-half hours and passes checkpoints at the 30km and 10km zone (the guards' posturing and flustered paper checking is a bit of show to recreate that special Soviet mood). Although clearly unnecessary – except for the obvious dramatic effect – visitors are fitted with special jumpsuits and shoes at the 10km checkpoint, then periodically checked with a Geiger counter during the tour.

A visit to the site comes down to staring at the giant concrete sarcophagus that supposedly stops the 180 tonnes of festering nuclear fuel from harming anyone. As a rule, you must stay at least 100m from the building. Organised trips tend to include a sobering tour of the ghost town Pripyat and other villages where radioactive buildings were buried under mounds of earth, and children's toys abandoned in the streets. Most tours also require a feel-good luncheon when visitors are expected to engage in limited dialogue about nuclear safety and world peace.

Organised trips leave out all the bureaucracy, and make it a lot easier to plan from abroad. Large groups of ten or more tend to get deals charging US$30 per person, but if you are on your own expect to pay at least US$150. Trips also have to be planned three to five days in advance as tour agents must apply for clearance beforehand. The company **SAM** (in Kiev: Ivano Franka 40B; tel: 044 238 2060; fax: 044 238 6952; email: main@samcomp.kiev.ua; web: www.sam.com.ua/eng) is the best-known provider for Chernobyl and charges around US$200 for a one-on-one private guided tour, decreasing in price as group numbers increase (a group of five cost $60 each). **New Logic** (Mikhailivska 6A; tel/fax: 044 462 0462; email: incoming@newlogic.kiev.ua; web: www.newlogic.com.ua) caters to young and professional travellers and can do a private day trip for US$120. Another trusted company is **Sputnik Kyiv** (Pushkinskaya 9; tel: 044 228 0938; fax: 044 464 1358; email: income@sputnik.kiev.ua; web: www.sputnik.kiev.ua).

If you are one of these fiercely independent types who wants to discover Chernobyl on your own, you are free to go the government route, although it takes longer and you will be without your passport for a few days while you are 'processed' (document clearance requires a minimum of seven days). Ukraine's

Ministry of the Chernobyl Catastrophe (Velyka Zhytomyrska 28; tel: 044 216 8472; fax: 044 216 8546) has a much longer name in Ukrainian and carries an official mandate of dealing with requests to visit the 'zone' and the site. You can also contact **Chernobyl InterInform** directly, based at the actual site. They can issue passes and arrange for a longer stay if you want. Write (in English) to: Director of the State Department and Administration of the Exclusion Zone, Chernobyl, Khmelnytskovo 1A (tel: 029 352 553; fax: 029 352 205). There is no public transport to Chernobyl, so independents will have to arrange their own (which means additional documentation for drivers, etc). An alternative to all the trouble is to visit the Chernobyl Museum in Kiev (see page 119).

ZHYTOMYR – ЖИТОМИР

Zhytomyr pinpoints the 'in between' zone of changing landscape where the forests of Polissya turn into the fields of Podillya, and the suburbs of Kiev are traded for rural existence of western Ukraine. The name 'Zhytomyr' reflects the poetry of Ukrainian folklore: *zhyto* is rye, *myr* is peace. A large rock in the main park commemorates the founding of the city in AD884, when local tribes joined with Kiev, albeit reluctantly. Wedged between Kiev and Polish lands, Zhytomyr was never one or the other, but in 1804 the city was made the capital of the new Russian province Volyn, which incorporated all the land between western Volhynia and Kiev. In the new jurisdiction was one Countess Hanksa of Zhytomyr, who began an affair with the French novelist Honore de Balzac. The two eventually married and the writer came often to Ukraine, living out his last days near Zhytomyr. Today the city is still the primary point of transit to and from the west and a predominantly Ukrainian-speaking area.

The city lies on the Teteriv River that cuts through channels of rocky cliff formations. In summer, the beaches and rocks above the city dam are a popular place to swim and sunbathe. The city's main historical sights are concentrated on the **Zamkovy Maidan** (Castle Square), including **St Sophia's Cathedral** and the Natural History Museum; however, the region's countryside is much more worthy of flattery. There are no organised tours in this area, nor any typical travel infrastructure, but that should be encouragement to those who seek to discover a natural and under-appreciated corner of Ukraine. For those hardcore wanderers who seek the unknown path, the **Polisky Nature Reserve** is in the farthest northern corner of Zhytomyr region and encompasses beautiful virgin forest near the village of **Selezivka**. Bird lovers will see some rare owls and the area has known populations of wolves and lynx.

Getting there and away

The train station is on the eastern side of town on Vokzalna. Contrary to logic, the main railroad from Kiev does not come straight to Zhytomyr, so that getting back and forth to the capital usually takes four hours and makes a very indirect transit. There are trains to anywhere, but south–north connections tend to service Zhytomyr regularly, eg: daily connections to Vinnytsya ($2\frac{1}{2}$ hours), Odessa (12 hours) and Zaporizhzhya (15 hours).

Zhytomyr lies on the main highway from Lviv to Kiev, so travelling in either direction is quick and convenient. The central bus station is at Kyivska 93 and buses to Kiev ($2\frac{1}{2}$ hours) and Vinnytsya (2 hours) are the most obvious choices. The private company **Avtoluks** (at the bus station; tel: 0412 360 257) has three daily buses back and forth from Lviv (7 hours) Rivne (3 hours) and Kiev (2 hours). Marshrutka zip back and forth to Kiev in under two hours, usually dropping off at the Dachna Bus Station. A taxi to Kiev would cost around US$40.

Where to stay and eat

The aptly named **Hotel Zhytomyr** is located near the main square (Ploscha Peremohy 6; tel: 0412 228 693; fax: 0412 226 772). It's the usual story of some renovated rooms and some still in their former state, but overall this is the most comfortable option in the city. New rooms with 24-hour hot water cost US$45 singles/US$60 for doubles. Bare-minimum rooms cost much less (around US$7). The restaurant and café provide nourishment and the former Inturist office can take care of all travel bookings. **Hotel Zhovtnevy** is also central, but less new (Kyivska 3; tel: 0412 375 083). Rooms cover the whole gamut of amenities and cost from US$5 to US$55 and the restaurant is not bad at all.

Podillya Поділля

Discovering the 'real Ukraine' is an elusive goal, but Podillya will most likely satisfy any such longings. The traditional region fills in a comfortable distance between Kiev and the far western fringe and also represents the happy medium of an honest but moderate cultural revival without the political edge. The cities hold some historical importance but are pleasantly run-of-the-mill, while the active rural areas are less tainted than average. It is no strain to wax romantic about these lands – for all that has transpired here and the simple natural beauty of the place. In the southwest the hills of the Carpathian plateau begin to flatten out into one eternal field stretching all the way across the country. The landscape appears monotonous at first glance but unique to this area are the river gorges that cut through the low hills and expose the layered bedrock under grassy bluffs.

Historically, Podillya has been the centre of 'right bank' Ukraine – the land between Galicia-Volhynia and the Dnepr River. On the edge of both Poland and Muscovy, Podillya developed on the fringe and was therefore never very Polish nor very Russian. This borderland existence led to two phenomena: firstly, the long war between Poland and Turkey inspired a ring of fortresses to be built which in turn demarcated Podillya as a region. These medieval castles are still a common sight around the larger towns and their architecture reflects a continual change in ownership. Secondly, lawlessness characterised the shifting periphery. Bohdan Khmelnytsky began his campaign in Podillya and liberated the right bank from any rule before marching on to Poland. Minorities suffered tremendously, especially the local Jewish population. Later, Russia returned the area to Poland's jurisdiction, but repeated peasant uprisings prevented the Polish nobility from any firm hold. The *haidamaky* movement continued in Podillya until the mid 1770s with small peasant bands violently attacking landlords and merchants. The largest rebellion in 1768 had the peasants in complete control of the fortress and city of Uman. When the *Rzeczpospolita* finally collapsed, the western parts of Podillya came under the Austro-Hungarian Empire and Russia took the rest.

The identity of these lands did not change, even throughout the Soviet era. Wheat has made Podillya what it was for the Poles and what it is today. Here, the image of a golden field under a blue sky is delivered as promised by tourist brochures, and wheat is still the focus of so many traditions. During the Podillyan harvest, the labourers hold work contests and present the winners with elaborate necklaces, bracelets and crowns braided from blades of wheat, and a symbolic sheaf of wheat is usually displayed in the home. A little-known fact is that most of the wheat covering the great plains of Canada is a hybrid from a single plant brought over from Podillya; local farmers swear that Podillya has the best soil in Ukraine

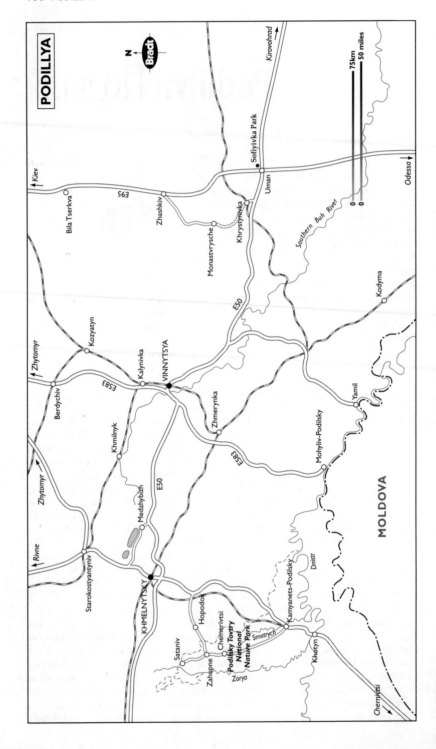

and a walk through any field will reveal mucky black *chyornozom* wanting to stain your hands.

Podillya's greatest appeal is that it has stayed so average. As one of Ukraine's traditional regions it has kept its own customs, dress, dialect and *pysanky* designs which now set it apart from the surrounding areas. In addition, the Jewish heritage sights and castles make it an intriguing destination and a worthwhile stop between Kiev and the west.

Getting around

The major transport hubs are Vinnytsya, Khmelnytsky and Uman. Major train lines to the west (Galicia and the Carpathians) and to Odessa all pass through Podillya and several trains originate in each of Podillya's cities. Still, getting around Podillya is best done by motor transport, since the trains are quite slow and usually run only during the night on their way to a long-haul destination.

VINNYTSYA – ВІННИЦЯ

Podillya's largest city is built on the banks of the Southern Buh River and is the gateway to the west as well as an up-and-coming centre for Ukrainian culture. Wandering the streets may seem aesthetically disappointing due to severe damage during the war, but the parks and churches are pleasant and the surrounding villages endearing. While Podillya is known for its wheat, Vinnytsa has built its reputation on sugar refining and the fields outside town still feature leafy green sugar beet. Agriculture, and the home base of the Ukrainian Air Force keep the city alive today.

This site first belonged to Kievan Rus but the city was founded only in the 14th century by the Lithuanian princes. A few small castles were built, raided, and reinforced; the latest was constructed in the 16th century on the small island in the middle of the river. Vinnytsya is remembered best for its role in the Ukrainian 'liberation' movement led by Bohdan Khmelnytsky. In 1651 the Cossack regiment defeated the Polish troops for which the obelisk monument stands today. The scene was repeated during the *haidamaky* uprising when the city was taken over by the peasants. When Podillya was declared a Russian province in the 18th century, Vinnytsya was made its capital and quickly assumed its role in providing the empire with sugar. The railway from Kiev to Odessa was built in the 1870s which linked the city to the rest of urban Ukraine and boosted the local economy to light industry. Vinnytsya only came back to Russia's attention during World War II when the Nazis quickly occupied the city in July 1941 and began construction of their eastern front command centre. The 'Wehrwolf' compound was visited twice by Hitler during his campaign and the ruins of the sizeable underground base can still be visited. During Soviet times Vinnytsya's population nearly reached 400,000 but has been declining since independence. These days travellers come to Vinnytsya in remembrance of the Jewish past and to visit the outlying rural areas.

Getting there and away

As the major hub for the south and west, trains to and from Vinnytsya are very frequent but all are passing through to another location. The train station is on Ploschad Geroyiv Stalingrada on the far eastern side of the city and a trolley goes down Kotsyubinskovo and Soborna to the centre. Larger train schedules will usually list Vinnytsya as a stopping point on any particular route but it pays to be picky about which one you take. In the worst case you will be on a very slow train that leaves or arrives in the middle of the night. Travel time from Kiev is over three hours and a little less by bus. The luxury bus companies also stop in Vinnytsya on their long-haul routes to and from the Carpathians. Avtoluks has an office on 50 Rokiv Peremohy; tel: 0432 554 078; open 09.00–20.00. In any case, getting a bus to Kiev, Zhytomyr, Khmelntysky, Uman, Chernivtsi or Odessa is never a problem from the central bus station on Kievskaya 8. The east (Batutina 18) and west (Khmelnytske Shosse 107) stations are more likely to service the local villages. There is a functioning airport in Vinnytsya but flights are few and irregular. Currently, there are occasional flights to Kiev and in the summer there is a flight to Crimea every other day. Check with the local office of *Kiyavia* on Soborna 101; tel: 0432 355 022; email: vinnitsa@kiyavia.com

Where to stay

Podillya Pushkina 4; tel: 0432 327 596. Podillya is the hotel most frequently visited by foreigners visiting Vinnytsya and deserves its solid reputation. The modern building is right off the very central *Maidan Nezalezhnosti* (Independence Square) and has quality accommodation with showers and toilets in every room. Refurbished rooms cost US$30 for a single, US$45 for a double. Suites are US$50.

Ukrayina Kozitskovo 36; tel: 0432 321 771. Once known as the very posh 'Savoy' this hotel occupies one of Vinnytsya's remaining historical buildings in the heart of the city. They also have a nice sauna. Regular rooms are about US$20 per person while the very nice deluxe rooms cost US$50–70.

Zhovtnevy Pirohova 2; tel: 0432 325 663. This hotel is close to the city centre, across from Park Gorkovo. Recently privatised, the rooms have been remodelled on two floors with private bathrooms. Rooms range from US$30–60, but there are some singles for under US$20.

Pivdenny Buh Ploschad Zhovtnya 1; tel: 0432 359 061. Located across the river, near the small island, 'Southern Buh' is a short walk from the Central Bus Station. Rooms are simple but not too bad. US$10 for singles, US$15 for doubles.

Profsoyuzov Khmelnytske Shosse 2a; tel: 0432 352 308. This is a typical Soviet-style hotel with the usual basics but it is secure and cheap. Rooms cost $10 to $15.

Where to eat

The **Podillya Hotel** has a nice restaurant with traditional Ukrainian food. The other hotels **Ukrayina**, **Zhovtnevy** and **Pivdenny Buh** also feature in-house restaurants. **Stara Vinnytsya** (Kositsovo 14) rejoices in the old world splendour of the city with pretty typical cuisine. Otherwise there are a few good cafés and bars along Teatralna and Soborna.

What to see and do

Vinnytsya is a straightforward town without too many frills. A good walking tour will take in most of the sights. Crossing south on the Kositskovo Bridge brings you to the **old city**, now a collection of hilly streets including the former Jewish quarter, 'Yerusalimka'. The Vinnytsya **Ukrainian Drama Theatre** (Teatralna 13) is one of Ukraine's better playhouses and has a varied repertoire of entertaining shows even if you don't understand the language. The **Museum of Local Lore** (Soborna 19) is like most other folklore/natural history museums in Ukraine but with a better collection of Podillyan artefacts. The **Pirogov Museum** in the southeast of the city is a memorial to Russian medicine if you have the time and the interest. The churches of Vinnytsya are surprisingly well preserved in spite of heavy bombing in World War II; most were built during Catholic Polish rule. The yellow, Orthodox **Church of the Transfiguration** is at Soborna 23 and not far is the **Dominican Cathedral** (Soborna 12) built in 1624. The Orthodox **Church**

NIKOLAI IVANOVICH PIROGOV (1810–81)

Vinnytsya is very proud of its museum and church dedicated to the surgeon Nikolai (Mikolai) Ivanovich Pirogov. He was born in Moscow in 1810 and completed medical school by the age of 17. By age 26 he was teaching surgery in Germany and he was world-renowned when he travelled to Sevastopol to treat soldiers during the Crimean War. The battlefield offered ample opportunity for experimentation and his contributions to medicine include the plaster cast and the Pirogov method for amputation where the heel bone is left as a walking support. He also perfected the use of ether as an anaesthetic. In the small village of Vyshnya just outside of Vinnytsya, Pirogov opened a free hospital to treat all the local peasants. A prominent medical academy was built in Vinnytsya in the doctor's name and he has been glorified with Soviet grandeur. His home is now a museum on Pirogova 155 (in the Botanical Gardens). The church is in the nearby village and serves as a tomb. His body is still on display, embalmed by a method that he invented.

of **St Mikola** (Mayakovsky 6) is probably the last remaining example of Podillyan wooden architecture, built in 1746.

Getting to Hitler's bunker, **Wehrwolf**, is easiest by taxi. The 8km journey north to the village of Stryzhavka should cost around US$3. The local government and private investors have been debating as to the status of the site, so access may or may not be limited. At the time of writing, parts of the underground fortress were freely accessible and due to some heavy explosives, pieces of the 4m thick concrete wall were jumbled about the surrounding fields. Over 14,000 Ukrainians were shot and buried here after they were used as slave labour to build the complex.

UMAN – УМАНЬ

It is sad to think that some travellers take in Ukraine's largest cities but miss the very heart of the country. Uman is the right place to come and get a glimpse of small-town Ukraine without going through the business of getting stranded in a tiny village. The strange-sounding town is considered the gateway between west and central Ukraine and is named for the Umanka River which crosses the Kamyanka River and forms a natural barrier against the south. The natural landscape inspired the Polish *rzeczpospolita* to station a regiment here in the 1600s that proved effective in warding off the Tatar invasions but failed to stop the Ukrainian Cossacks and the rebel peasant bands of the 18th century. Taras Shevchenko's famous poem *Haidamaky* tells the story of the 1768 Uman massacre in which 20,000 people were killed – most of them Jews seeking protection from the Poles. The extremely wealthy Pototsky family ruled Uman until 1834 and their greatest contribution was the extravagant garden covering the northeast side of the town. The contrast of boundless luxury in such common environs has made the exceptional park a major attraction for Ukrainians. The town itself is honest, if not slightly bare. If you find you're trying to kill time in Kiev, Uman makes a distinctive day trip into rural Ukraine. The central location also makes it an ideal quiet stop for any cross-country itinerary.

Getting there and away

Uman's fame means several Kiev-based tour agencies run day trips from Kiev with return coach travel included (see page 103). For the sake of convenience, these pre-arranged tours are the best option for visitors.

Uman is the primary junction for road trips to Odessa from Kiev, so the quickest and most comfortable way to get here on your own is by long-haul luxury bus. A Kiev–Uman ticket with a company like Avtoluks should cost US$6.

The train station is located at Maidan Gagarina in the southwest corner of the town. There is a daily train to Kiev, but the other trains to Cherkasy and Vinnytsya are very slow and inconvenient. Instead, regular buses come and go from Vinnytsya (1½ hours), Cherkasy (2 hours) and Kirovohrad (2½ hours) at least twice a day. From Kiev's central *avtovokzal* there are two daily buses and the trip takes three hours. Uman is the primary junction for road trips to Odessa from Kiev so the long-haul luxury buses are the quickest and most comfortable way to get here on your own. A Kiev-Uman ticket should cost US$6.

Where to stay and eat

If you choose to stay the night, the austere **Hotel Uman** on Maidan Lenina is the most likely choice with a fairly decent restaurant. The annual influx of Jewish pilgrims has established a steady market for staying with locals. Ask around for anyone with a room (*komnata*) or flat (*kvartira*). Depending on what time of year you are there, a room for the night will cost US$10–20. A few cafés line Sadova on the way to the park and for food essentials there is the central market (*rynok*) at the bottom of Radyanska.

Sofiyivka Park

Back when Imperial Russia had an inferiority complex against France, a common expression stated that 'Sofiyivka is no worse than Versailles!' The lavish gardens occupy a quarter of Uman and bear no resemblance to French symmetry and splendour. Instead Sofiyivka is designed in the romantic style aiming to imitate natural landscapes. Trees, rocks and water are the prominent media and the original architects redirected the Kamyanka River in order to fill the artificial pools and miniature waterfalls that cut through the gardens.

Count Felix Pototsky began construction of the gardens in 1798 as a gift to his new bride, the legendary beauty Sofia. Greek by birth, Sofia had been sold into slavery by her parents as a 12-year-old girl. The Polish ambassador to Turkey bought her in Istanbul as a present for the Polish King Stanislaw August; however, while travelling back through Ukraine she met the son of the Polish army commander Jozef Witte, who fell in love with the 15-year-old and bought her from the ambassador. The newly married Madame Witte quickly became a celebrated society figure among the Polish gentry. She soon took up delivering diplomatic mail and was rumoured to use the opportunity for spying for the Polish king as well as Catherine the Great. Sofia eventually left her husband and two children but was soon remarried to the Polish Count Pototsky in Uman. He adored Sofia and designed the park as a memorial to her beauty incorporating the mythology of ancient Greece: the 400-acre park has its own Isle of Lesbos, a terrace of the muses, red poppy 'Elysian' fields, a Cretan labyrinth and an underground stream called Styx. Sadly, long before the park was finished, the Count uncovered an affair between his son from his first marriage and his young wife. Broken-hearted, he grew seriously ill. Sofia supposedly spent two days on her knees begging to be pardoned but the count died without forgiving her. She finished the park herself during a brief affair with the Russian Count Potemkin, then lived out her days in melancholy. The fact that a freak earthquake actually pushed her grave out of the Uman churchyard has the locals convinced that she was a witch.

The park is well maintained and it is easy to spend up to a day walking the paths. The best time to visit is in September, when the colours are extraordinary and the white swans are still about, but the park is open all year and is still worth a trip even in the dead of winter. Horseback riding tours can be arranged at the park, and there are boat tours through the river Styx and on the largest lake. A taxi from the train station is US$2 and the park entrance is an easy walk from the bus station. Entrance costs US$1.

Uman's Rabbi

The Breslov movement of Hasidism was inspired by Rabbi Nachman who was himself the great-grandson of the founder of Hasidism. Born in Medzhybizh in 1772, the Rabbi spent most of his life in the village of Bratslav (near Vinnytsya and from which comes the term 'Breslov') where he preached a religion based on joy and spiritual freedom. Modern-day Breslov Hasidic Jews follow a principle of living life to the fullest and practise a unique form of free-flowing prayer where the devotee 'chats' openly with God for one hour each day. Rabbi Nachman died young of tuberculosis having expressed the desire to be buried in Uman, next to the victims of the 1768 massacre. In his writings he promised to pray for the success of any pilgrim that came to his graveside and recited the ten psalms of the *Tikkun K'lali*. Breslov Hasidic Jews feel the need to make the journey to Uman at least once in their lifetime, which usually takes place on the Jewish new year and the commonly heard Breslov chant is 'Uman, Uman, Rosh Hashanah'. Uman's local Breslov community has quickly recovered in spite of decades of near extinction and the yearly pilgrimage is now the crowning event for the town. The Rabbi's grave is located in the Jewish cemetery on the corner of Belinskovo and Pushkina.

KAMYANETS-PODILSKY – КАМ'ЯНЕЦ-ПОДІЛЬСЬКИЙ

The 'museum city' is renowned for its diverse historic architecture but the real 'wow' factor is the immense canyon that completely encircles the old city. Nature's sense of strategy could not have been more deliberate: the rocky island is high and inaccessible, except for one very tiny causeway leading to the site of Podilya's largest medieval fortress. Down below flows the narrow River Smotrych, so named because the transparent water allows you to see the bottom (*Smotry* is the Ukrainian imperative 'Look!'). Most of the new city is covered with thick tree cover and the castle faces west so the sunsets are spectacular. Kamyanets represents the historic and cultural heart of Podillya and in terms of things to see and do, the city is Podillya's main attraction.

Nobody knows for certain when Kamyanets came into being, but the valuable landscape was already protecting humans in the first millennium. Legend states that after Kievan Rus lost Galicia-Volhynia, a Lithuanian prince passed through this area and shot three deer within minutes. Three plaster-like deer by the gorge commemorate the event that convinced the Lithuanians to move here. They were followed by 350 years of Polish rule (less 25 years of Turkish occupation). The massive stone fortress with pointed towers replaces the original 11th-century wooden structure which had burned down. Changing ownership and numerous reconstructions have turned it into a sprawling fortification and none of the seven towers resemble each other (the Turks built the square-shaped ones, the Russians built the round ones).

Because the fortress and town were made of stone instead of the usual wood, the town was called Kamyanets (from the Slavic *kamen'*, stone); the suffix Podilsky was added when the city was made the capital of Podillya by the Poles. The castle made the city an impenetrable safe haven and a developed centre for trade. Since Kamyanets fell under the Magdeburg Law, each ethnic community

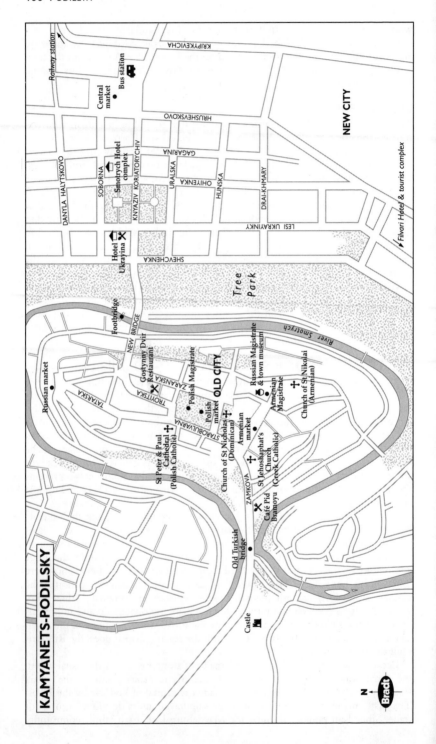

Previous page The refectory (AD1696–1701) in Kiev's Cave Monastery and the Dnepr River, Kiev (MW)

Above Kiev suburb at dawn (AE)

Right St Andrei's Church, Kiev (MW)

could have its own legal authority and all religious traditions were self-ruled. Cosmopolitanism became the norm and today the locals will state a different number for how many nationalities claim Kamyanets as their home (I've heard between seven and seventeen). The Armenians, Jews, Poles, Romanians, Azeri, Greeks, Bulgarians, and every other group each built their homes and places of worship so that Kamyanets looks like no other place in the world or every place in the world depending on how close you are standing. UNESCO declared the old city a World Heritage Site because of its high concentration of preserved architecture styles and the Ukrainian government has ranked it third in cultural importance after Kiev and Lviv.

There are currently 25 working churches, which is a record in this country, while the legacy of defence remains with the prominent Kamyanets-Podilsky military academy. On weekends the streets and parks are filled with camouflaged soldiers strolling under the chestnut trees and this is one of the few Ukrainian-speaking cities where Soviet war monuments are still revered. Polish and Ukrainian visitors are legion, but to all others Kamyanets is a well-kept secret. The old city is a bit of a shambles due to lack of funds and the tourist infrastructure is still very basic, but overall the city is a refreshing destination with a very separate take on Ukraine's past and present. (The strange smell in the air comes from the city's largest industrial enterprise – the vodka factory.)

Getting there and away

There are two overnight trains to and from Kiev every day. The later *Bukovina* train starts in Chernivtsi and arrives in Kiev at a more reasonable hour, and vice versa. These and a number of other trains go through Khmelnytsky, which is three hours away. Travel to Chernivtsi is five hours (!) by rail so motor transport is the better option going south. The train station is on Pryvokzalna in the far northeast corner of the city; a taxi into town should cost US$1–2. Kamyanets is much more conducive to bus travel. The station is right behind the central market on Pershotravneva Vulitsa in the new city. There are four daily buses to Kiev, and frequent, quicker links with Khmelnytsky and Vinnitsya. Routes to western Ukraine and the Carpathians are also plentiful but long; a better option would be going to a larger city first, like Chernivtsi. By bus or car the trip to Chernivtsi (via Khotin) is under two hours and a shared taxi from either bus station will cost under US$5. In the city, the bus #19 and frequent marshrutka run between the old and new cities.

Where to stay and eat

It might seem stupefying that a town with such tourist attractions offers so few amenities but for all of its sights and history, modern-day Kamyanets is still a simple place that avoided Ukraine's first wave of 'development'. Let's hope it stays that way to some degree. **Hotel Ukrayina** (Lesya Ukrayinka 32; tel: 03849 391 48) is the fundamental hotel of the city once managed by Inturist. The cheapest rooms are only US$6 with bed and sink while a limited number of refurbished rooms have hot water and individual bathrooms for US$35. **Restaurant Ukrayina** is on the ground floor of the hotel and is treated as the most luxurious of the city with its gold and scarlet décor while its menu and prices tend towards the typical: borscht is 50 cents and most of the larger dishes are under US$2. You'll find the chef friendly and willing to make anything you ask for and they do accept credit cards. One block east in the city's highest building is the **Smotrych Hotel Complex** (Soborna 4; tel: 03849 398 06; email: hotel_tl@ukr.net). It's an odd post-Soviet set-up where the hotel occupies the 6th floor, a travel agency and internet café are on the 5th and a bar is to the right of the ground floor bank lobby. Don't be put off by looks, just take the lift to the 6th floor – the rooms are new and comfortable, and astonishingly inexpensive (about US$10 per person). The hotel always has hot water and each room features an en-suite bathroom. The café/bar serves typical Ukrainian food. **Filvarki Hotel** (Lesi Ukrayinky 99; tel: 03849 383 37; email: fcenter@kp.km.ua; web: www.filvarki.km.ua) sells itself as the classiest place in town but its standard is pretty much identical to Smotrych and its location is less central. Rooms are US$10–20 and suites US$40. The restaurant **Gostynny Dvir** (Troyitska 1) is in the old city and serves classical Russian food in a more showy setting.

Tourist information

Tourist TI is the tour agency running out of the Smotrych Hotel (Soborna 4th, 5th and 6th floors; tel: 03849 377 42). They are good for putting together local tours and have good contacts. **Filvarki** also has a very professional agency (see telephone and address above) offering excursions outside the city and outdoor activities including mountain bike rentals and fishing.

What to see

The **castle** is the focus of the city's attractions and a walk from the new city will take you past most of the sights. The castle was begun in the 11th century but most of what we can see today was built between the 14th and 18th centuries (the wooden version burned down). The greatest thing about Kamyanets-Podilsky Castle is that you can climb on everything freely. All the towers and ramparts are open as well as the various dungeons and the incredibly deep well. Things are so accessible in fact that a little precaution is in order when romping about; the ascents can be a little precarious but allow some lofty views of the fortress and city, as well as the surrounding landscape. The castle was first defeated by the Turkish invasion in 1672 and in their short reign, the Turks added some stylistic changes that are still in place. Peter the Great visited the castle after the Russian takeover and the beloved bandit Ustym Karmalyuk (one of many Ukrainian Robin Hoods) was a prisoner here on three different occasions. But the castle is best remembered as the set for the old black-and-white film version of *Ivanhoe*. The castle is open from 09.00 to 17.00 every day; entrance costs 3UAH or US$4 for foreigners; guided tours can be arranged in English, Russian, and Polish. A museum of folklore occupies one side of the castle with a permanent exhibit of local crafts, traditional objects, and artwork displays about life in Podillya.

The bridge connecting the castle with the old city is one of the oldest in Ukraine and can only be crossed on foot as it is structurally unsound for cars. It was the Turks who filled in the arches and pillars with stones. Be it rumour or history, when the Turks finally found themselves fleeing from the castle, a cart filled with gold was overturned spilling over the bridge into the Smotrych. Treasure hunters have dug deep into the riverbed but nothing has been found. Now, the hole is a popular fishing spot.

The **old city** is confined to the steep island and serves as an effective display of the Magdeburg Law: each ethnicity has its own quarter, magistrate and churches. The Russian magistrate is on **Armenian Square** and houses the **town museum** (open 09.00–17.00, closed Monday, 1UAH entrance). The exhibit is small, consisting of religious paintings and a collection of weapons used by each army that has passed through Kamyanets; the museum's greatest piece is the Soviet-era statue of a monk carrying a basket. When plugged in, the statue turns to reveal an unclad girl inside the basket – at one time these were mass-produced as atheist propaganda but know appear as rare curios. South of the square is the **Armenian magistrate** with its white-and-black square tower. The Armenian **Church of St Nikolai** (built in the 14th century) is next door. The Greek Catholic **St Jehoshaphat's Church** is closest to the bridge and was the central building of the old Ruthenian community. The Poles lived in the central part of the island, defined now by the two tallest steeples of the **Polish magistrate** and the **Church of St Nicolas** at the Dominican Monastery. The largest church is the Polish Catholic **St Peter and Paul Cathedral** which incorporates a remaining minaret from the Islamic past now topped with a golden Virgin Mary. The pale orange church has a black and gold interior and features the rare statuary of Christ sitting with his head in his hands.

Sadly, parts of the old city are in a serious state of disrepair; the colourful buildings and bare parks make for a sobering but intriguing walk. The old synagogue has been turned into a flashy restaurant and most of the open empty cellars mark the former homes of Kamyanets-Podilsky's Jewish population. The main bridge into the new city is at the top of the island but a few small footbridges also cross the Smotrych and lead to a lot of winding trails through a shady park on the right bank. Above the new bridge is a waterfall seeping down the wall of the gorge and a long stone staircase descends to the river. The new city is much less dramatic but just as quiet. Most activity surrounds the **central market** on Prospekt Hrushevskovo.

The **Podilsky Tovtry National Nature Park** covers the southwest corner of Podillya and is part of the **Medobory Ridge**, a 100km-long mound following the north bank of the Dnistr River outside Kamyanets. The scenic countryside is a blend of green forests and rocky steppe scattered with villages and several smaller parks. The term *medobory* means 'honey-drinking' since the area is a known spot for collecting medicinal herbs and flowers. The area is open for exploring, but the two agencies in Kamyanets can help arrange specific visits and activities for the region.

KHMELNYTSKY – ХМЕЛЬНИЦЬКИЙ

The capital of the oblast bases much of its glory in Kamyanets-Podilsky to the south and in the Podillyan countryside. On its own, the city of Khmelnytsky could very well be the least exciting place in western Ukraine. Travellers in Podillya will end up here on their way to Medzhybizh or moving south, but will find the city fulfils a very functional role for the area and not much else.

In 1954, the city's name was officially changed in honour of the legendary Cossack hetman Bohdan Khmelnytsky but this was little more than a Soviet political gesture. Before, the city was known as Proskuriv, a derivative from the name of the River Ploska. The Cossacks did pass through in 1648 taking the small wooden fortress on the Southern Buh from where they prepared further onslaught of the Polish army, and Bohdan Khmelnytsky made his base here in the summer of 1653, rousing the local peasants to fight with him. Excluding moments of massive uprisings, the Polish noble family Zamojski ruled the territory until Russia annexed the city in 1793 along with the rest of the right bank. Hit particularly hard during the Russian civil war, Khmelnytsky has since followed the path of most industrial Ukrainian cities and was known best in Soviet years as the home of a pasta factory. In light of the current cultural wave, Khmelnytsky fares well as a genuinely Ukrainian city that stands a better chance for foreign investment because of its steady economic past.

THE BA'AL SHEM TOV BESHT (1700–60)

Yisrael Ben Eliezer was born in 1700 in the Podillyan village of Okopy. Orphaned as a young boy, the local Jewish community took charge of his education and welfare. He was a dedicated student but also a dreamer who disappeared into the forests and countryside for weeks at a time. Widowed at a young age, he was married a second time to a Rabbi's daughter and the pair moved to the Carpathian Mountains where, legend states, he spent most of his time meditating in the forest. He enjoyed interacting with the poorer people whom he claimed were 'limbs of the divine presence'. By the time he had moved to Medzhybizh he had the reputation as a healer and holy man and was called the Master of the Good Name, or Ba'al Shem Tov (BESHT is an acronym of the Hebrew letters). He dedicated his life to spiritual work from which modern-day Hasidism was born. Denouncing self-mortification in favour of rejoicing, the BESHT taught of the divine presence in all things and that performing the normal tasks in life was a form of devotion. Song and dance became important rituals of worship and he loved simple stories as the primary means for spiritual learning. He died in 1760 leaving many followers but none of his own writings.

Getting there and away

Khmelnytsky is the link between Ternopil, Vinnytsya, and Kamyanets-Podilsky. Three daily trains connect with Kiev (8 hours), each along a different route, costing US$10–15 for a coupé. There are also daily trains to Lviv via Ternopil and Chernivtsi via Kamyanets-Podilsky. The train station is at the end of Shevchenka on the city's eastern side. The intercity bus station is on Vinnytske Shose 23 with routes to everywhere imaginable, but the East Bus Station (next to the train station) is more convenient. Numerous shared taxis also leave from here. Vinnytsya and Ternopil are both around two hours away by car; Chernivtsi is five hours. The train would be better for any longer trips.

Where to stay and eat

Podillya (Shevchenko 34; tel: 0382 610 83) is midway between the train station and the city centre. It is currently the most comfortable hotel with low-to-middle-range rates. **Zhovtnevy** (Proskurivska 44; tel: 0382 647 23) and **Tsentralny** (Gagarina 5) offer nothing special except for a more central location. These two hotels follow the Soviet protocol of hospitality with low prices (under US$15). All three hotels have their own restaurants which is your best bet for a meal. The city's other more established restaurants are on the far outskirts of the town. Centrally, there are smaller cafés off the Maidan Nezalezhnosti on Gagarina and Soborna.

OUTSIDE KHMELNYTSKY

Medzhybizh – Меджибіж

This small town is one of Ukraine's true gems and is rightfully becoming a more celebrated destination in Podyllia. On the bank of the Buh River stands a stocky medieval castle dating from early Lithuanian times, now surrounded by quiet farms. Medzhybizh fortress was just one of a circle of castles employed by the Poles in their defence against the Turkish slave raids. The Zaslavksy family lived inside the walled palace and made their fortune from the surrounding land. As members of the Polonised Ruthenian nobility, they ruled the local territory and were rumoured to be wealthier than the King of Poland. The impressive outer wall has remained, along with the palace, stable ruins, dungeon, and a Polish Catholic chapel to which the conquering Turks added a minaret.

The town's name means 'between the 'bizh' – a combined form of Buh and Buzhok, the two rivers that meet here. The nearby rivers and outlying fields are idyllic so it seems appropriate that a spiritual movement was born out of such a place. Jews made up the majority for over two centuries here; most visitors to Medzhybizh are on a pilgrimage to see the grave of the BESHT, the founder of Hasidism. The town's old Jewish cemetery is one of the better preserved in Ukraine and many prominent Hasidic leaders are buried here. Outside the town is the site where 3,000 Jews were massacred in one night by the Nazis. The mass graves are marked with a monument.

Getting to Medzhybizh is an easy bus trip from Khmelnytsky's East Bus Station (by the train station). If you choose to go by taxi, bargain beforehand. The general rule is around 1UAH per km, and Medzhybizh is about 35km away. There are also buses to and from Vinnitsya.

Bradt Travel Guides is a partner to the 'know before you go' campaign, masterminded by the UK Foreign and Commonwealth Office to promote the importance of finding out about a destination before you travel. By combining the up-to-date advice of the FCO with the in-depth knowledge of Bradt authors, you'll ensure that your trip will be as trouble-free as possible.

www.fco.gov.uk/knowbeforeyougo

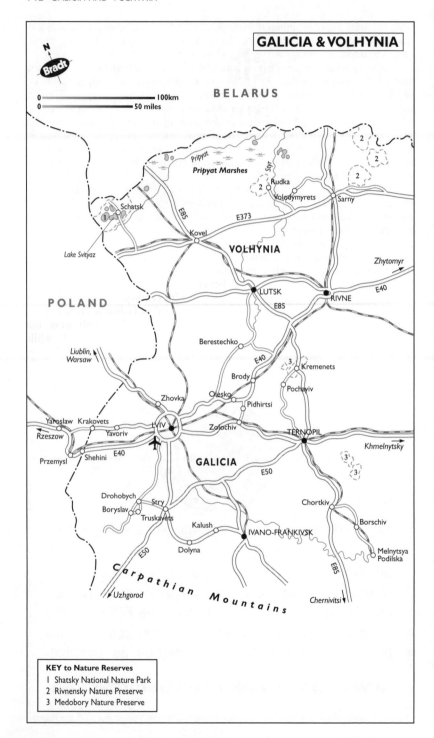

GALICIA & VOLHYNIA

N

Bradt

0 ————————— 100km
0 ————————— 50 miles

BELARUS

Pripyat
Pripyat Marshes

Schatsk

2

2

2

2
Rudka
Volodymyrets
Sarny

Styr

E85

E373

Lake Svityaz

Kovel

VOLHYNIA

Zhytomyr

POLAND

LUTSK

RIVNE

E40

E85

Berestechko

*Liublin,
Warsaw*

E40

3
Kremenets

Brody
Olesko
Pidhirtsi
Pochayiv

Zhovka

Yaroslaw Krakovets

Rzeszow
Yavoriv

LVIV

Zolochiv

TERNOPIL

Khmelnytsky

Przemysl
Shehini

E40

GALICIA

E50

3

3

Drohobych
Boryslav
Truskavets
Stry

E50
Dolyna

Kalush

IVANO-FRANKIVSK

Chortkiv

Borschiv

Melnytsya
Podilska

C a r p a t h i a n   M o u n t a i n s

Uzhgorod

E85

Chernivitsi

KEY to Nature Reserves
1 Shatsky National Nature Park
2 Rivnensky Nature Preserve
3 Medobory Nature Preserve

Galicia and Volhynia
Галичина & Волинь

Known for its fiercely independent nature and quirky traditionalism, *'Halychyna'* (Galicia) sounds like 'Wild West' to the Ukrainian ear and is regarded with both wonderment and suspicion. At heart though, Galicia is a curious relic of old Europe, both sophisticated and nostalgic. Travelling in this region is a delight; the landscapes are picturesque and the people's mentality is markedly different, meaning things tend to work better.

The two regions have been paired since the 12th century, but each is distinct: Volhynia is covered with tall forests and dotted with lakes, Galicia is a blend of soft brown fields and little green knolls. Polish influence marks both areas, but Volhynia in the north was more oriented towards Prussia and Lithuania, while some of Galicia's charm stems from its provincial role in aristocratic Poland and the Austro-Hungarian Empire. The architectural leftovers make Lviv a highly decorative regional capital and everyone I've met agrees that this is Ukraine's most beautiful city. The growing popularity of tourism in the west seems to be based on its proximity to 'Europe' and the mistaken belief that dipping across the border into Lviv will fulfil the traveller's urge for a taste of the once-forbidden USSR. Any such desires are hopelessly outdated, if not slightly misdirected, since Galicia has always been a place unto itself. Entering Galicia feels more like dropping back a few centuries into a world where people still live closely to the earth and custom and superstition rule (the evil eye is a common sufferance in these parts). The countryside here is especially rustic and quaint: tin-roof farms, churches made of hand-cut logs, split-timber fences and ducks waddling through vegetable patches. This was the one part of Ukraine that was never really collectivised by the Soviets, so the life and landscape are more rugged and unchanged.

Ukrainian nationalism burns brightest in the west. The oldest Slavic traditions are still followed religiously and it's worth planning a trip to coincide with a holiday to witness the vivid spectacles and haunting music. Outside most villages is a steep mound topped with crosses of tied tree limbs, flags and banners; these are burial sites to mark the graves and memories of partisan fighters who died in the struggle for Ukrainian liberation. A heritage of resistance has Galicians thinking they are the most Ukrainian of all, but the rest of the country secretly pokes fun at their Polish accents. (With the commercialisation of Poland, the region has seen a massive influx of Polish tourists coming to see what their own country used to be like.) Group tours are likely to include some time in the west since Lviv is such an attraction and individual itineraries should sway westward for the cultural riches and the simple fact that Ukraine is not Ukraine without Galicia.

HISTORY

In a historical context, Galicia and Volhynia have always been the exception to the rule, which is why it feels so different from the rest of the country. When Kievan Rus began to weaken in the 13th century, the joined principalities (based in Halych and Volodymyr) became an autonomous kingdom that endured the Mongol invasion in 1240 and continued for over a century as an independent polity. Many consider this brief interlude as the first true Ukrainian state. Poland occupied Galicia in 1349 (Lithuania had already invaded Volhynia) and introduced the Magdeburg Law in 1356 as a set of rights by which a city was self-governed. Beneath the princes and boyars, the 'burghers' evolved as a new social class of wealthy leaders that regulated Lviv's growing trade. Economic opportunity attracted Jews, Germans, Greeks, and Armenians to Galicia's cities, while the Ruthenians (Ukrainians) had limited access to urban areas by law. Polish language and culture dominated and the Greek Catholic Church was born as a compromise between papal authority and Ukrainian Orthodoxy.

After the collapse of the Polish *rzeczpospolita* in the 18th century, Galicia found itself a part of the Austro-Hungarian Empire while Volhynia was annexed to Russian right-bank Ukraine. 'Galicia' is actually the Austrian name given to the province that stretched from Krakow (in present-day Poland) to Kolomiya in the Carpathians. Austrian rule proved politically and financially beneficial and like most of central and Eastern Europe at the time, Ukrainian national consciousness was sharpened. The uprising of 1848 solidified a new ideal for the Ukrainian people and their petition for more recognition and cultural freedom was granted. (This was a noted difference from the rest of Ukraine, where use of the Ukrainian language was officially banned under Russian rule.) Great Britain was the only country to support the idea of an independent Western Ukraine forming in the Treaty of Versailles in 1918 and so the following year Galicia found itself once again a part of independent Poland. This ended with the Ribbentrop-Molotov Pact which sanctioned the German invasion of Poland in 1939 and subsequent Soviet occupation of the eastern half of Galicia. Stalin's attempt to help the area 'catch up' with Soviet Socialist Ukraine was a murderous disaster brought to a halt by the Nazi invasion in 1941. Jews made up 10% of Galicia's population and those who did not flee to Central Asia were the first to be killed. Like the Baltic states, Galicia became an official part of the Soviet Union only after the war in 1945 and there are stories of Ukrainian partisan bands still fighting 'the Russians' in the hills of southern Galicia until the 1960s. Active cultural resistance never ended and the final push for Ukrainian independence was kindled in Galicia with the demonstrations in 1988.

The utterly turbid and separate history of the far west is a primary source for Ukraine's divided self-image today. Galicia is praised for the way it has protected the Ukrainian language and culture, but resented for its militancy. Even while Ukraine tries to orient itself towards the EU, the European traditions of Galicia conflict with the post-Soviet ways of the east. Travelling in this area, you cannot help but notice the nationalist fervour, as well as the difference in attitude and service.

Getting around

Lviv is the largest city in western Ukraine and the central transportation hub for getting anywhere in Galicia and Volhynia. From Lviv there are separate train lines and bus routes to all major cities: Lutsk, Rivne, Ternopil, Ivano-Frankivsk and Uzhgorod. Keep in mind that these cities also have their own direct links to Kiev and other Ukrainian cities. Lviv has an efficient local transportation system with frequent minibuses to all the villages and regular routes to the Carpathians. Like most of Ukraine, getting around in Galicia is a question of supply and demand: for US$5–10 you can go anywhere. Volhynia is a little less direct since the main rail line is the route between Kiev and Warsaw. Travelling between Galicia and Volhynia, you might want to take the quicker motor transport because you'll miss the dramatic scenery on the train.

LVIV – ЛЬВІВ

Ukraine's most elegant city, Lviv is a promised cure for any sceptics still entrenched in negative images of post-Soviet cities. Instead of rusted smokestacks, Lviv stands as a beautiful and eclectic monument to art and history. Each building is like a fossil of Lviv's past reincarnations and recent development assures this city will become a fashionable destination. Among Lviv's open squares and wide boulevards, visitors will recognise bits of Paris, Florence, Krakow, Vienna, and old St Petersburg. Attention to detail is imperative: the relief on door panels, the shaped iron gates, the graceful balconies and ornate stonework reflect centuries of luxurious craft. Right now it's all a bit rough and unpainted but the breadth of structural art makes such a romantic ensemble that people should feel a sense of urgency to see Lviv in its natural state before the city gets covered in billboards and neon (although locals laugh and tell me that Lviv is immune to tastelessness).

Prince Danylo of Halychyna (Galicia) founded the city in honour of his son Leo, hence the name Lviv from the root for 'lion'. The symbol of the city is a lion and an interested person could spend weeks discovering all the lions that feature on doorknobs, cornices, gates, keystones, and just about every façade in the city centre. The prince built his castle at the top of the conical-shaped hill, known today as Vysoky Zamok ('High Castle') which is also the name of the leading Ukrainian-language newspaper. With Galicia's annexation to Poland, Lviv grew into a vital metropolis of very wealthy foreign merchants and churchmen as well as Ruthenian and Polish labourers. Polish rule contributed the cobblestone streets and baroque architecture as well as the still-present Polish language and Roman Catholic faith.

Lviv's real building boom took place in the 16th and 17th centuries and was heavily influenced by the Italian renaissance. Architecture students from Europe and America are now coming to study in Lviv for its wealth of pure Italian design. Under the Hapsburg Empire Lviv (then known as Lemburg) developed into a more progressive, intellectual, and artistic city. The university was founded and architects from Vienna and Prague introduced art nouveau to the city's collage. Lviv soon defined its own style and was the birthplace for various artistic and literary movements largely unknown in the west. The rise of Ukrainian national consciousness in the 19th century was centred in Lviv and a whole new set of monuments are dedicated to these writers. Lviv emerged relatively unscathed from the wars of the 20th century and since independence the city has developed in leaps and bounds. UNESCO has just designated the entire city as a World Heritage Site and the Ukrainian government claims that over half of Ukraine's recognised architectural monuments can be found in Lviv. The recent praise is worthy but says little about Lviv's brooding personality. Whether or not you believe in the supernatural, there is something very mysterious and Gothic about the city. The medieval quality seems to be part of the attraction. Lviv is flaunted as Ukraine's number one destination and group tours stop here for a minimum of two full days. If you are on your own, you'll find it difficult to pull yourself away simply for the quantity of things to see and the richness of aimless urban exploration; a person could easily spend an entire two-week holiday in Lviv and still feel all the contentment of travel.

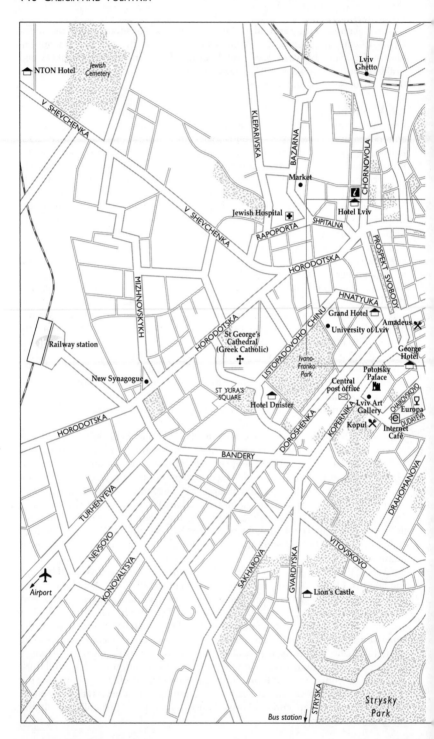

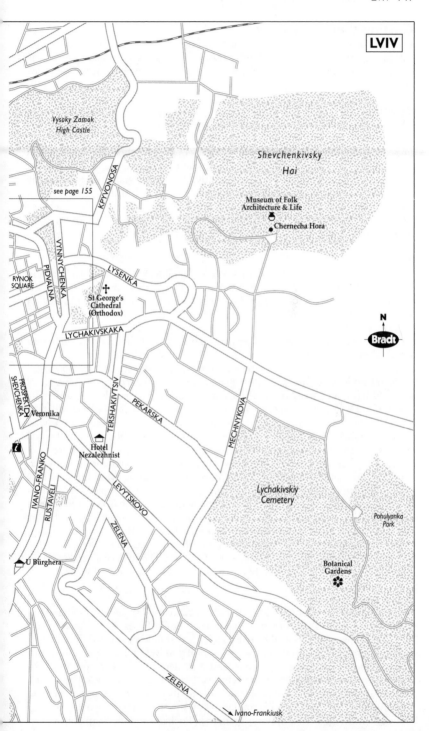

Getting there and away

Lviv is Ukraine's European gateway and for obvious historical reasons, the major routes are oriented towards Poland, meaning this is a good place to enter the country, to begin or end a trip. It is also an important stopping point between Kiev and the Carpathians.

By air

The airport is located 3km to the southwest of the city centre and is best reached by taxi or marshrutka. Trolleybus #9 also connects the airport to the city. At present, daily flights serve Kiev and Warsaw (LOT) and there are two flights a week to Frankfurt (Lufthansa). Other European connections are less predictable. Domestic destinations also change frequently, the most regular carrier being Kiy Avia. Their Lviv office is at Prospekt Shevchenka 11; tel: 0322 743 027; email: lvov@kiyavia.com. Aerosweet (Nalyvaika 3; tel: 0322 978 190) also has flights to Odessa and Kharkiv. For airport information call 0322 692 112, otherwise most upscale hotels have their own air ticket booking office.

By rail

Lviv is the largest train station in western Ukraine and a common junction between domestic routes and international (mainly central European) destinations. The train station is at the end of Chernivetska; tel: 0322 748 2068. A taxi from the centre should be around US$3 or take tram #6 or marshrutka #2 to the city centre.

There are five daily trains between Lviv and Kiev, each along a different route, some of which are very indirect and long. The trip should take around 12 hours. There are two city trains: *Lviv* is the quickest and most direct, while *Halychyna* has stops in Khmelnytsky and Ternopil. (If you want to travel in style, the Grand Hotel has a plush private carriage that does the journey back and forth to Kiev as part of the *Lviv* train.) Daily trains also service Dnopropetrovsk, Odessa, Donetsk and Kharkiv. These longer routes can take up to 20 hours and first-class tickets cost around US$25; a coupé is under US$10. Trains to Ivano-Frankivsk (4 hours) and Uzhgorod (6 hours) normally travel during the day and cost under US$5. As always, you can get to any other city on a train from Lviv but you need to find out the particular schedule, time and route and make sure its worth your while. Most hotels in Lviv have travel offices that can book train tickets, or at least give you the current timetables. Otherwise the most convenient place to buy railway tickets is the central booking office at Hnatyuka 20. From Lviv, international routes service Berlin, Warsaw, Prague, Budapest, Rzeszow, Przemysl, Kosice and Bratislava. Just south of the main train station is the local train station with the small *elektrichki* branching out to Galicia's villages. Here it's a matter of reading the timetable or finding a trustworthy soul to lead the way, but it's a lot easier to stick to the village buses.

By bus

Lviv's bus station is at Stryska 189 (tel: 0322 632 473) and is another busy conjunction for local and international transit. Trolleybuses #5 and marshrutka #71 go to the station from the centre and a taxi should cost US$3. You can go anywhere on a bus, but you must ask yourself if you want to. It does not help that Lviv's station is notoriously chaotic and travellers can have a real time co-ordinating their schedule with the vehicles. Don't hesitate to ask someone at a window, stating your destination and having them write down the time of departure and the platform. From Lviv, bus travel is best for going to other Galician cities (eg: Ternopil, Ivano-Frankivsk, Pochaïv) and the Carpathians.

THE POLISH BORDER

Lviv is the gateway for most European traffic into Ukraine and is less than an hour from the Polish border. Horror stories you may hear about this crossing reflect a different era. These days Poland is too busy convincing foreigners how European it is to give anyone too much hassle while the Ukrainian side is still regimented but a lot more relaxed than it was five years ago. Compared with your other options (consider Romania or Russia) Poland is the least problematic. The biggest problem is the wait, which if you come at the wrong time can last more than six hours; a 'quick crossing' is anything under an hour. If you are travelling to or from Warsaw, it is often better to just go on the train, but if you are simply crossing the border, take one of the short bus connections to Rzeszów (Zheshov) or Przemyśl (Permishl). These can take between two to three hours to do the whole trip, and since they are regular and frequent, there seems to be a more established protocol with the checkpoints (sometimes).

The 'luxury' Ukrainian coach lines serve Lviv and are nice for getting to other places in western Ukraine. Lviv-Inturtrans (Kuznevycha 2; tel: 0322 676 769; email: intur@mail.lviv.ua) has an established international route between Kiev and Antwerp, and a domestic route to Dnipropetrovsk; they also do a variety of bus tours in Galicia. Avtoluks has two offices in Lviv: on Sakharova 42; tel: 0322 345 021, and next to the bus station, tel: 0322 632 464. Their bus to Kiev travels through Lutsk, Rivne, and Zhytomyr and takes the exact same time as the train. Longer routes on an overnight bus can be tedious and you'll wish you had a bed on the train, but if you want to see the scenery of western Ukraine, take the bus and travel during the day. There are also plenty of buses crossing the Polish border all day long (see below).

The local marshrutka buzz about the city like flies but there are a few well-known pick-up spots and each minibus is usually well-marked with its destination. Travel to western Galician villages picks up in front of Shevchenko 24; eastern Galicia buses pick up at bus station #6 on Lychakivska. It is still often safer (in terms of confusion and success) to find transport going to your local destination at the main bus station.

By car

If you're driving from Kiev or Poland, all roads lead to Lviv; just follow the signs. The E-40 goes east to Kiev, westbound crosses the Polish border at Shehini (to Przemyśl) and continues all the way to Brussels. The E-50 goes south to Uzhgorod, crossing the Hungarian border at Chop; the T-1402 goes southeast to Ivano-Frankivsk. Lviv's streets are tight (and bumpy) and auto-theft common, so use only guarded parking lots. There is one in the city centre (tel: 0322 974 114) and some hotels have secure areas for cars. Car rental is new to Lviv but the nicer hotels sometimes offer chauffeur-driven rental cars. Negotiating your own long-haul taxi is not difficult.

Getting around

Even the locals seem bewildered by Lviv's public transportation system, but compared to most, it's a good place for first-time foreigners to give it a go. A wrong move is easily forgiven since Lviv is really a walking city. Trams run along the larger boulevards and to the train station. You are most likely to use #1, 6, 7 and

9. A central tram station is behind the theatre, diagonally across from the opera. From here, most cars go along Horodotska to the main train station. Trolleys have a tough time on Lviv's cobbles and so few venture into the centre, but there is the #5 that goes to the bus station. Lviv's taxis are user-friendly and more honest than usual, so this is really the best way to see the parks and city sights that are farther out. A ride to anywhere in the city, including the airport and train station should be about US$3 or less.

Tour operators

Being the progressive city that it is, Lviv has a central **Tourist Information Centre** that offers very useful information to visitors about hotels, restaurants, attractions, and everything that is going on in Lviv (theatre, festivals, exhibitions). This is the best place for city maps and brochures and they can also co-ordinate walking tours, arrange English-language guides and local excursions. (A private guided tour of the city in English costs US$10 per hour, and there are two group tours every day except Sunday.) The centre is open from 10.00 until 18.00 and is located at Pidvalna 3; write to Lviv Tourist Board, Pidvalna 3, 79006 Lviv, Ukraine; tel/fax: 0322 97 57 51/67; email: ltb@mail.lviv.ua. They have an exceptional website: www.tourism.lviv.ua.

Meest-Tour is a well-known international travel company based in Lviv, particularly specialising in outdoor pursuits in Ukraine and throughout Eurasia. The Ukrainian–Canadian joint venture has been around longer than most and has built a strong reputation for local knowledge and adventurous tours. This is a good company to contact when planning a trip from outside Ukraine since they are comfortable communicating in English and are capable of taking care of lots of particulars in advance (hotel, transportation, visas, etc). Besides offering unique tours in Lviv, they do a variety of local excursions to Galicia's monasateries and castles, and if you want to head to the Carpathians, these are the right people to contact for organising long treks, mountain biking and river-rafting. Located at Prospekt Shevchenka 34; tel: 0322 970 852; email: office@meest-tour.com; web: http://www.meest-tour.com.

Yunta (Prospekt Shevchenka 23; tel: 0322 728 710; email: yunta@mail.lviv.ua) is a private company run by former members of Inturist, so they have access to much of the infrastructure for dealing with incoming tourists. They do more relaxed trips to the Carpathians as well as local excursions in Galicia.

Where to stay

Lviv's hospitality industry is a step ahead of the rest of the country in quality while still avoiding the rush of overpricing that afflicts Kiev. Take note that the water situation has never been good in Lviv so the more plush hotels will advertise their separate water systems and lower-end hotels will post schedules predicting when the hot water will be flowing. Also, Lviv is not exempt from the general rule in Ukraine regarding accommodation: price rarely indicates quality, making it difficult to rank Lviv's individualistic hotels. If you're trying to make your money stretch, don't write off 'luxury hotels' that may have a variety of rooms, some at lower prices.

Luxury

'Luxury' here means they have their own water systems and accept credit cards.

Grand Hotel Prospekt Svobody 13; tel: 0322 724 042, 727 665; fax: 0322 769 060; email: grand@ghgroup.com.ua; web: http://www.ghgroup.com.ua. This classy hotel deserves its sumptuous name and is by far the most tasteful upscale hotel in Lviv, not forgetting that they also have real double beds that are very comfortable. The baroque building has just been remodelled and the 'grand' company works as a conglomerate of luxury services in Lviv, including an indoor pool, health spa, private clubs, a private train car, a business centre, and an in-house tour agency that can arrange any kind of trip to anywhere. Somehow the place avoids being too snobbish: the walls feature changing exhibits of local art and the staff speak manicured English. Single rooms are US$95–105 per night, doubles are US$120–135. Larger suites are US$150–170 per night. Best of all is their elegant restaurant with live harp music every evening. Accepts credit cards.

Hotel Dnister Mateiko 6; tel: 0322 974 305/06; fax: 0322 971 021; email: dnister@cscd.lviv.ua; web: http://www.dinster.lviv.ua. The outside structure reveals this to be Lviv's fomer Inturist hotel, but now the Dnister functions as a quality corporate-style hotel for business travellers and large tour groups. The refurbished rooms are comfortable and clean, albeit a little small. Based on single/double occupancy, regular rooms are US$48/$54, a little larger rooms are US$78/$84, 'semi-luxury' are US$100/$106, and large suites are US$130/$136. All rooms have showers, except for the suites, which have baths. The Dnister does have a good view of the city and has kept all its Inturist connections, meaning they can book air and train tickets and offer private tours. The large restaurant on the second floor serves typical Russian fare with a separate vegetarian menu and a breakfast buffet. Accepts some credit cards.

Lion's Castle Glinki 7; tel: 0322 971 563; fax: 0322 351 102; email: Lions_castle@org.lviv.net. If my parents were coming to Lviv, I would want them to stay in this converted Austrian mansion. Situated in one of Lviv's quiet and traditional neighbourhoods, the Gothic hotel characterises the city better than most. Visiting dignitaries from the Hapsburg Empire used to stay here and it was the first to be open after independence. There are only fourteen rooms (each very individual and spacious) and the hotel functions as a bed and breakfast. There are five categories of rooms, but the nice ones (in the older building) are US$80–120 per night; a regular double is US$50. They also co-ordinate airport and train station pick-ups, have a guarded car park and a nice garden in the back. Their ground-floor restaurant is a bit glitzy but it's only a 10-minute walk to the city centre. All credit cards accepted.

Middle range

George Hotel Mitskevycha Square 1; tel: 0322 974 255; email: geoh@mail.lviv.ua. This pink and white baroque hotel has a fantastic location in the heart of the city and is becoming more popular with foreign tourists, particularly Germans. The grand staircase, high ceilings, and chandeliers pay tribute to a distinguished past, but the years have left the spacious rooms slightly tattered and smoky. 'Tourist class' rooms are US$30–40 with a shared bathroom; nicer rooms (meaning better beds and private bathrooms) are US$60–70; a very large suite is US$80. The bathrooms are average, but there is always hot water and through constant effort the hotel stays clean. No credit cards.

U Bürghera Ivano Franko 73; tel: 0322 761 251. Modern and cosy, this brand new complex is named after the old burghermasters that ruled Lviv in Magdeburg times, though the lurid décor confirms the new business élite ruling Lviv today. This is honest-to-goodness Western-standard accommodation; there are very comfortable double rooms for US$40/night and real double beds for US$50 and at present this is probably Lviv's best value for money. All rooms have internet access and there are some really amazing luxury suites with private swimming pools and/or jacuzzis for only US$70–80. The restaurant and bar are known party areas. Outside the city, the hotel owns a luxurious country resort with the unfortunate name of 'Burger Club'. The hotel staff can arrange rooms and transportation if you fancy getting out of town. Accepts credit cards and has no problems with water.

NTON Hotel Shevchenka 154; tel: 0322 333 123; fax: 0322 981 753; email: hotelnton@ukr.net; web: http://www.hotelnton.lviv.ua. If you are driving from Europe, this is a good motel to stop at, since it is right off the main road, has a large guarded parking lot and is only a short tram ride into the centre. From the centre, take tram #7 to the end. To the hotel's advantage is that everything is new, including the furniture and plumbing (meaning 24-hour hot water). Rooms are US$30–40 with individual showers, US$50 with a bath, and US$60/$80 for a suite.

Budget

Hotel Lviv Prospekt Chornovola 7; tel: 0322 792 270; fax: 0322 792 547. Hotel Lviv is a soot-covered, Soviet-style hotel offering a straightforward crash pad for travellers in the city centre behind the opera house. The rooms are small and beds are solid; you pay for any extras (eg: hot showers cost $0.40). The clientele tends to be Ukrainians 'doing business' and large Polish tour groups. Prices vary depending on whether or not you have 'a view' and how many stairs you have to climb to get to your room: a single without a view costs US$7, with a view is US$14; doubles are US$10–25. (If you are trying to stretch your money by staying in a budget hotel, the view is not worth the price of an extra night's stay.) A group of three or four sharing a room costs US$4 per person. Hot water is available 06.00–11.00 and 17.00–24.00, and the sauna is US$3 for a 2-hour session. The ground-floor restaurant is open from 08.00 to midnight and serves inexpensive and filling meals.

Hotel Nezalezhnist Tershakivtsiv 6; tel: 0322 757 224. On the eastern side of the city, this hotel appears perpetually closed from the outside, but in fact it is always open; sneak through the many doors until you get to the administrator. The interior atmosphere is reminiscent of an early 1970s TV show, but the rooms are inexpensive and the hotel is secure. The best deals are for couples, since a single costs US$16 and a double is US$17. Their 'lux' room is a good deal at US$24 and is an honest replica of the apartments that most Soviet citizens used to live in. For a Soviet leftover, the staff are uncharacteristically friendly. Hot water runs in the early morning and late evening.

Hotel Kiev Horodotska 15; tel: 0322 728 571. Not Lviv's fanciest, but definitely the cheapest. The spooky grey building is one of the only Stalinist structures in the city, which should be enough 'character' for those who want it. Right in the very city centre, the crumbling walls and dingy interior are balanced out by a friendly ambiance among staff and patrons. Singles (with a 'view, TV, and fridge') are US$12, a double puts you up to US$14. For space and decent rooms, choose the 'luxury' option for US$20. Hot water runs from 06.00 to 09.00, and from 18.00 to 20.00.

Where to eat

Lviv is Ukraine's one great hope for perfecting the art of eating out, perhaps stemming from the aristocratic past. Restaurants tend to be simultaneously elegant and laidback, and new places tend to spring up every day. Most of the ones listed here take credit cards. 'Having coffee' is also a common Lviv ritual and the local dialect has its very own word (*kavyarnya*) meaning a coffee shop in Lviv.

Restaurants

Oselya Hnatyuka 11; tel: 0322 72-16-01. Ukrainian theme restaurants are suddenly ubiquitous but this one stands above the rest; the dishes, tables, waiters' clothes and drying flowers build an authentic representation of an old Ukrainian cottage. The food is also genuinely Ukrainian as well as sophisticated. If you are not lucky enough to be invited to someone's home for dinner, this will do. The menu is very traditional and a two-course meal with drinks runs to around US$10.

Kupol Chaikovskovo 37; tel: 0322 744 254. Run by three sisters who relish the joy of old things, the restaurant is fashioned as a quaint Polish tea salon. In fact, this hilltop house was once the home of a famous Lviv art salon and many of the relics on display belonged to the renowned Volsky family. The antique collection is as impressive as the exquisite food; a good look at the walls and artefacts tells you much about Lviv's history. The atmosphere is warm (candlelight, lace and framed Polish love letters) and the cuisine is a mix of Polish and Austrian dishes; the chicken and bacon rolls are a popular choice. A flowery outdoor patio is a nice place for tea and a view of the city. Open 09.00–23.00.

Amadeus Katedralna 7; tel: 0322 978 022. Already famous for its grilled food and big servings, Amadeus is a very cosy upscale restaurant right next to the Latin Cathedral near Rynok Square. The clientele leans towards 'yuppie' with dishes like 'the hungry husband' (a hefty portion of grilled meat and potatoes) and flame-broiled salmon. Live performances of romantic jazz every evening; open 11.00–23.00.

The Grand Restaurant Prospekt Svobody 13; tel: 0322 72 40 29. On the main level of the Grand Hotel, but with a separate entrance around the corner, the restaurant is both simple and very classy, with refined food and a gentle atmosphere. European dishes and pasta predominate the menu. Despite posh appearances, all budgets can afford to eat here. Open 08.00-23.00.

Olmar Krakivska 2; tel: 0322 798 542. The restaurant has a central location next to Rynok Square but follows the more typical post-Soviet model of forced grandeur in order to wow the local mafia. Take away the glitter and what's left is a light and airy restaurant that serves remarkably inexpensive food. The service is also better than average. Open 'til midnight.

Diva Dudayeva 5; tel: 0322 745 022. The menu is chic Ukrainian, the décor an almost-convincing imitation of art nouveau. Salads, soups and pasta dominate; they also do breakfast and some hearty dinner dishes. Open 11.00–23.00.

Cafés and bars

Europa Shevchenka 14; tel: 0322 725 862. This is not just a bar serving Ukrainian beer, but a very personal place serving breakfast, lunch and dinner. The menu is diverse and inviting and this is a common meeting place and the large TV attracts football fans.

The Italian Yard Rynok Square 6 0322 720 671. Mid-morning to late evening coffee inside Lviv's most memorable piece of architecture. Go through the museum entrance into the courtyard.

Veronika Shevchenka 21. Upstairs is a candy-striped, Viennese-style café serving fancy coffee, sweet and savoury pastries, rich cakes, truffles and bonbons. Down in the cellar is a dark and smoky bar. Open from 10.00 until midnight.

The ONU Vynnychenka 10. This is an attempt to have a combined bookshop/café serving coffee, tea and ice-cream and is aptly located right beneath Lviv's headquarters for the ONU, the right wing nationalist liberation army-cum-political party. Its worth a cup of tea to see the paintings of Ukrainian freedom fighters like Stepan Bandera and the displayed uniforms for partisans of Ukraine's Galician Army. Ukrainian history and folk books are for sale at the counter. Open from 10.00 to 22.00; try to order in Ukrainian.

The Milk Bar Corner of Kopernika and Svobody. This is the place to come if you are really on the cheap, or if you want to see where the real Lviv hangs out. The city's labour force and students come here for lunch and after work for drinks or meals so the atmosphere tends to be relaxed and jovial. Besides milk and ice-cream, the café serves a variety of soups, pancakes and homey food that fits the local income. Nothing on their menu costs more than US$1 and if you can't read that, then pointing works well. Open until 22.00.

Dzyga Virmenska 35. Part café, part art gallery, part antique dealer, this is the commercial side of Lviv's avant-garde scene. The café inspires some interesting and vivacious gatherings and also features regular local art exhibitions, installations and photography. The building is at the end of one of Lviv's oldest alleys. Open 10.00–22.00.

Food markets

If hotel restaurants and quaint cafés become a drag there are plenty of food markets. The one at Halytska Square is small and central and sells mainly fruit and vegetables; the main market is at the end of Shpitalna/Bazarna and sells everything from frozen chicken thighs to pantyhose and prescription glasses (this used to be the Jewish cemetery). There are also plenty of all-night grocery stores that sell fresh produce, bread, cheese, meat and bottled drinks.

Post and internet
The big beige and tan building on Slovatskovo is the central post office, but there are many visible offices throughout the city. Lviv has more 24-hour internet/international phone shops than any other Ukrainian city. **Internet Klub** (Dudayeva 12; web: http://internetclub.lviv.ua) has a lot of computers and their international phone rates are cheaper than normal. **Nazgul** (web: http://www.nazgul.lviv.ua) has two separate locations: Chornovola 101 and Krushelnitskoi 1 (follow the signs). Schoolboys flock here to play computer games but the club is very accommodating for other services and they serve drinks.

What to see and do
The best thing to do in Lviv is to get lost and enjoy the aimless wandering in the streets. Many of the streets are narrow and there is no better way to appreciate oak timber cobbles than by walking on them. The city centre is compact, so the 'sights' are close together and there's even more to see and do between these sights. If you're not a fan of the urban adventure or long walks, a guide can be helpful and it is easy to pinpoint some target areas.

Architecture
Lviv is synonymous to pretty buildings and this is what most people come to see. **Rynok Square** is bound to become the city's tourist hotspot, but currently dwells in a natural existence with the city administration building in the centre and statues of Adonis, Neptune, Diana, and Amphitrite marking the four corners. 'Market Square' has always been central to Lviv's trade and wealthy merchants built their homes and shops on its edges. The city fire of 1527 burned the original Gothic structures to the ground so that today the square's colour and style reflect baroque and renaissance design from the 17th and 18th centuries. The buildings' uniform width stems from a statute of the Magdeburg Law that permitted three windows tax-free. Larger houses belonged to merchants who were willing to pay the extra fee in order to impress. Each of the 44 buildings has a unique history and there are separate guidebooks (none in English yet) that give the individual backgrounds. Most beloved by Lviv's citizens is the **Italian Yard** (6 Rynok Square; entrance fee 50 kopecks) which was the home of the wealthy Greek wine merchant Kornyakt. The courtyard's simple arches and columns reveal Lviv's romantic past and during the summer, a small café functions on the terrace. The upper floors house one of the city's many historical museums. Number 3 Rynok Square is built in late baroque style and comes with a tale. A poor labourer fell in love with the merchant's daughter who lived here, but her father disapproved and promised her to a man of higher breed. To celebrate the engagement, he threw a ball in the upper floors of the house and the young pauper slipped in uninvited to see the girl. The merchant attacked the boy but he fought back and severely injured the older man in the fight. The merchant grew ill but before he died he forgave the young suitor and gave his blessing to the two lovers. Number 4 Rynok Square is known as the Black Mansion and features an uncomfortably small stoop at the front door that prevented the guard from falling asleep while sitting at his post. The Venice House is at 14 Rynok Square; the Venetian merchant who lived here added the St Mark's coat of arms; house number 32 displays some elements of Lviv's austere art nouveau.

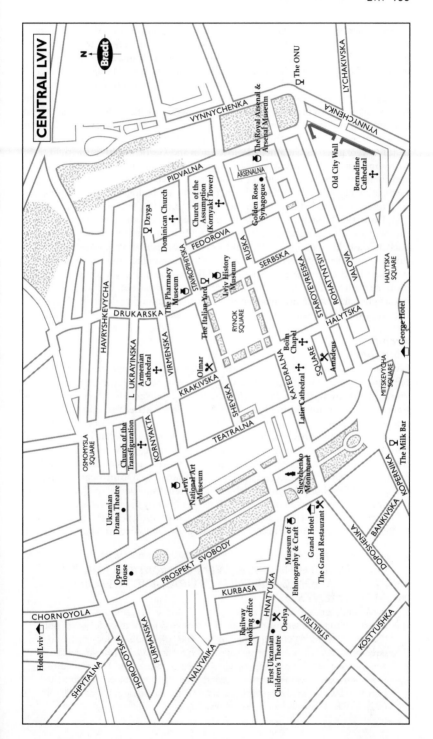

CENTRAL LVIV

The square is but one example of Lviv's architectural wealth and there are some real discoveries to be made in every neighbourhood. These are just a few favourites: the red and grey **Kornyakt Tower** on Pidvalna was built by Lviv's wealthiest benefactor and has been the city's symbol through the ages; Pidvalna 13 is a beautiful example of 19th-century 'Mauritanian' architecture with its brightly painted leaves and carvings (it is now a dentist's office). Peach-coloured **University of Lviv** (Universytetska 1) occupies the old Galician Sejm (parliament) and was founded in 1661. The statue on the top represents Mother Galicia blessing her two children, the rivers Dnistr and Vistula. Traditionally, lectures were given in Ukrainian, Polish, Latin and German. This is the right place for young travellers to meet people their age since the area is buzzing with students and there are some nice cafés in the vicinity. Everything about the building at 6 Listopadovoho Chinu is eye-catching, down to its highly decorated doors; the structure was intended as a casino but is now home to the Lviv Inventor's Club. The **Pototsky Palace** (Kopernika 15) was used for wedding ceremonies during the Soviet era; across the street (Kopernika 22) is the birthplace of Leopold von Sacher-Masoch (who gave us the term 'masochism'). Prospekt Shevchenka underwent a major renovation in 1997 and the white and red towered building was designed by the poet-hero Taras Shevchenko himself. Every Ukrainian city has replaced their Lenin statue with a **Shevchenko monument**, but the one in Lviv is exceptional. Behind the standing poet is a sweeping relief depicting Ukrainian history using religious folk art. The statue was a gift from the Ukrainian community in Argentina and stands in the park on Prospekt Svobody.

Churches

Not only is the number of Lviv's churches astounding, but also the diversity in faith and styles represented. Identifying a church can be difficult since each is known by many different names (for the sake of convenience they are listed by their colloquial names in English). The **Armenian Cathedral** at Virmenska 7 is one of the oldest in Lviv, built in the 14th century by the still-present Armenian community. The church is open only for services, but the courtyard is open, paved with headstones (they say it is good luck in Armenia to have many people walk over your grave). A large wooden sculpture of Christ stands outside which is in pretty good shape after 150 years of snow and rain. The **Dominican Church** is the one at the end of Ukrayinka with the big green dome and is the legendary site of Prince Lev's palace (son of Danylo). This was built by the monastic order in the 18th century using a toned-down baroque, but now belongs to the Greek Catholics. The interior is beige, decorated with gold-covered wooden statues.

GIVE SOMETHING BACK: LVIV FOUNDATION FOR THE PRESERVATION OF ARCHITECTURAL AND HISTORICAL MONUMENTS

Lviv's architectural wealth is indisputable, and a fair amount of foreign investment has allowed some level of restoration work to go forward, but the work is never-ending and costly. The Lviv Foundation is a non-governmental, non-profit organisation with a mission to preserve, restore, and popularise Lviv's monuments of culture, history and architecture. Donations are obviously appreciated as well as any form of assistance to promote Lviv's greatest resource. Contact 1 Rynok Square, Office 104; tel: 0322 975 852; email: foundation@mis.lviv.ua.

LEOPOLD VON SACHER-MASOCH (1836–95)

Lviv is proud of its citizens, both the wicked and the holy. Leopold von Sacher-Masoch is remembered best for the clinical term for morbidly obsessive behaviour and is one of the darker characters of the Hapsburg Empire. While he studied and wrote in Prague, Germany and Italy, the novelist's own persona is symbolic of Lviv: his father was Spanish by birth (but from Austrian Prague) and worked as the chief of police in Lemberg (Lviv); his mother was a dainty Ruthenian noble who had her child Leopold nursed by a Russian peasant woman to give him vigour. He studied and practised law but turned to writing stories that dealt with his own childhood fantasies. His novel *Venus in Furs* is a marked expression of masochistic behaviour, as was his violently bizarre marriage – he beat his wife whenever she refused to whip him. The actual term 'Masochism' was derived by the German neurologist Dr. Richard von Krafft-Ebing, who referred to the novelist in his scientific work *Psychopathia Sexualis* and defined Leopold's mentality as someone with an unbearable urge to be controlled by the will of another. Today in Lviv, people are more pleased than ashamed that their city was the birthplace of such a famous psychopath.

Downstairs is the **Museum of Religion** (entrance 1UAH) which used to be a museum of atheism in Soviet times. The church gives organ concerts every Friday, Saturday and Sunday at 15.00; entrance 5UAH. The Greek Catholic **Bernadine Cathedral** is behind the city wall on Vynnychenka and has been under renovation for the past five years. The black and gold interior is both majestic and foreboding; the frescos will be a site to see when they are finished. The **Church of the Transfiguration** (Krakivska 21) once belonged to a Trinitarian monastery as can be seen by the structure, but the violet and blue interior is decorated with traditional Ukrainian embroidery and features an impressive gold ikonostas. This is one of Lviv's better-preserved churches, and staring up into the cupola, one can see the frescos of the writers of the four gospels. There is a sung prayer service from Wednesday to Saturday at 19.00 which is a good initiation into the strong Galician religious tradition. **St George's Cathedral** (5 St Yura's Square) is a canary-coloured assembly of high baroque buildings that make up the ecclesiastical centre of the Greek Catholic Church. It was here that the Pope began his controversial visit to Ukraine in 2001. Before his arrival, the church underwent a costly but tasteful renovation and is now an important spiritual site for many western Ukrainians. The interior is best seen during daylight hours when natural yellow light gives the walls a surreal glow. The view from the hilltop is marvellous. The **Latin Cathedral** occupies Cathedral Square (Katedralna) and is Lviv's largest Roman Catholic church, although here they are called Polish Catholics. The building is 18th century neo-Gothic with a fresh pink and blue baroque interior. Supposedly three bombs landed inside the church during World War II but none of them exploded. This was a repeat miracle from a much earlier battle where cannonballs were unable to penetrate the church (one of these balls is hanging outside the church today). The **Boïm Chapel** is right next door in the corner of Cathedral Square and is a small and dark Gothic building from the early 17th century with a highly detailed exterior. The church is topped with a rare statue of Christ sitting next to his cross above the Latin inscription 'He who passes by, let him ponder if his sorrows are greater than mine.'

Lviv's Orthodox churches are fewer in number, but rich in history. The **Church of the Assumption** incorporates the Kornyakt Tower (the entrance is through the gate at Pidvalna 9; open for services every evening at 17.00). Directly across are the foundations of the first medieval city wall and the statue of Fedorov, who was a prominent figure in Lviv's famous 'brotherhood', a society associated with the church. Fedorov brought printing to Ukraine by publishing the very first Ukrainian Orthodox books in the 16th century. The work of the brotherhoods continued throughout the next century, dedicated to preserving Orthodox learning and tradition under Catholic rule. It now belongs to the Ukrainian Autocephalous church. **St George's Cathedral** (Korolenka 3) was built in the mid 18th century and is now the single symbolic stronghold of the Russian Orthodox Church in Lviv. There are over fifty more churches in the city centre, each featuring extraordinary architecture and open to visitors.

Museums

Some of Lviv's museums have kept the dry Soviet approach for presenting art and history, but the collections are large, money is sparse and most exhibits are under-appreciated. Each institution is still high on being able to print their material in Ukrainian so English labelling is the exception. **The Lviv History Museum** occupies three separate buildings on Rynok Square, numbers 4, 6, and 24; open 10.00 to 17.00, closed Wednesday. Each requires a separate ticket that costs a few hriven and a few more if you want a guide. The exhibit is a little bare but shows the finery of Lviv's aristocratic days. House number 6 is the best choice simply for the interior looking out on the Italian yard. The parquet floor is one of the last true examples of traditional Galician woodcut design. **The Pharmacy Museum** is on the corner of Rynok Square at Drukavska 2; open 09.00–19.00, closing early on Saturday and Sunday; entrance 1.50UAH (displays in English). The pharmacy has been working non-stop for the past 250 years – a real feat considering Lviv's history. The shop in front still works as a chemist and looks like it did three centuries ago with coloured bottles and wooden herb drawers. The tour is self-guided, taking the visitor through the history of early chemistry with collections of old pill presses, balances, mortar and pestles, and alchemy equipment. Things turn a bit Gothic towards the end (follow the green arrows to find your way through the cellars and upper floors) but it is a good way to see the interior of an old Lviv house and there are some magnificent doors featuring Galician art. An interesting fact is that in Galicia (and throughout Poland) the old chemist shops were given names instead of numbered addresses, much like the pubs in England (eg: Under the Golden Deer). **The Royal Arsenal** is the rust-coloured stucco and stone fortress along Pidvalna. This structure was once part of the earlier fortress that surrounded all of Lviv and was where the haidamaky rebels were imprisoned in 1768. The lower floor is an 'art gallery' that sells very large candlesticks and life-size plaster statues of the Virgin Mary while the upper entrance is the actual **Arsenal Museum**; open 10.00–17.00, closed Wednesday; entrance 1UAH. Military enthusiasts will appreciate the diverse collection of swords, uniforms and antique guns. The weapons are not particularly Ukrainian (except for the Cossack war drums), but most of these are genuine artefacts left behind by Lviv's invaders: Hungarian battle axes, Austrian sabres, German crossbows, Tatar shields and glass maces. For something more Ukrainian go to the **Museum of Ethnography and Craft**, Svobody 15; open 10.00–17.30, closed Monday and Tuesday, entrance 5UAH. One exhibit is a hodge-podge of old Ukrainian farm tools but the larger room has a fantastic collection of regional Ukrainian costume. The small shop at the entrance is a good place for buying artsy souvenirs and knick-knacks made by local craftsmen. The **Lviv National Art Museum** (Svobody 20; open 10.00–18.00, closed Friday; entrance 5UAH) has a fine collection of early Ukrainian art, icons, and 19th-century painting. The **Lviv Art Gallery** (Stefanyka 3; 10.00–18.00; closed Monday; entrance 1UAH) features a very large collection of European sculpture, decorative and graphic arts, but the changing 'exhibits' are often big sales of bad art. **The Museum of Folk Architecture and Life** is an amazing outdoor museum-village created from a wide collection of regional folk architecture transported to the city's forested north side. Located in the **Shevchenskyi Hai**, it is more park than museum and it is best reached by taxi (Chernecha Hora 1; entrance 2UAH, children free); the thatched cottages, barns, and schoolhouses are all original structures, decorated inside and out with real artefacts and portraying rural western Ukrainian life over the past two hundred years. The wooden churches are most remarkable, and some are adorned with old-fashioned folk ornaments and are still open for worship.

Theatre

Most visible is Lviv's grandiose **Opera House** at the end of Svobody, a true Viennese masterpiece, beautiful both inside and out, and the focus of community activity. Tickets for the performances (ballet and opera) can be purchased inside at the *kasa* on your right. Across the street is the pale green **Ukrainian Drama Theatre**, the oldest theatre in Ukraine (L. Ukrayinka 1). All performances are in Ukrainian, but the pieces range from Shakespeare to Chekhov. Tickets can be purchased 11.00–14.00 and 17.00–19.00; the repertoire is posted outside. Lviv's **Voskresinnya Theatre** (Hryhorenka Square 5; email: goldenlion@litech.lviv.ua) dabbles in the experimental and has built up a worthy reputation offering unconventional dramas. For the young at heart there is the **First Ukrainian Children's Theatre** (Hnatyuka 11) where you can hear the laughter on the street. A frequent performance is King Lev, a fairy tale about the founding of Lviv. They also do Ukrainian folk tales and some better known classics, like Cinderella.

Jewish sites

The oldest Jewish quarter centres around the end of Fedorov Street and along Staroyevreiska (literally 'old Hebrew Street'). The bare park at the end of the street was commonly known as the 'Square of Weeping' for the tragedy and violence suffered in this neighbourhood. The small houses look much like the rest of Lviv, except inside many of the doorways you can see a few remaining mezuzah (the encased scroll planted in the doorpost of faithful Jews when their homes are dedicated). At the end of Staroyevreiska and beginning of Arsenalna are the ruins of the old city Synagogue called the **Golden Rose**. There are some ghostly outlines of the back wall, the foundations and pillars, as well as the ritual baths now overgrown with grass and shrubs. The working synagogue is on the corner of Mizhnovskykh and Korotka, built back in the '20s but only just remodelled. Almost all of Lviv's Jews were killed in local concentration camps in the early years of World War II. Many Holocaust victims are buried in the Jewish cemetery towards the end of the tram stop on Vulitsa Shevchenka, formerly known as Janowska. Further down Shevchenka is the **Kleparivska Station** from where Lviv's Jews were deported during the war as well as the remains of the **Janowska concentration camp**. The older Jewish cemetery is now the site of Lviv's largest market on Bazarna; at the top of the hill is the old **Jewish hospital** (Rapoporta 8), an expressive piece of Moorish architecture in brick, now used as Lviv's general maternity ward. The **Lviv ghetto** was on the northern side of the city, now marked by the railroad bridge over Chornovola. A large monument

IVAN FRANKO (1856–1919)

In 1875, Ukraine's most famous scholar came to Lviv to study philosophy at the university that now bears his name. Two years later he found himself in prison under false accusations that he was part of a subversive socialist plot against the empire. His published work often met with such reaction, and he served another term in prison with the charge that his stories encouraged the peasants' civil disobedience. Thus, the Soviet regime flaunted Ivan Franko as a martyr 'for the masses', while these days it is the nationalists who worship his brazen 'Ukrainian-ness'. Neither camp suits him really. Ivan Franko was a truly gifted intellectual with a talent for adapting his ideas to all forms of thought and letters. He is well loved for his vivid tales of peasant hardship, his satires, lyrical poetry and powerful essays. Ideologically, his real contribution to the country was his call for solidarity among all Ukrainian people, despite the foreign borders that divided them (his poem 'Moses' is a parable of the Ukrainian people in bondage). He also wrote in Ukrainian, which was a revolution in itself at a time when German and Polish were the only languages of the educated élite in Galicia. In spite of an additional arrest and prison time, Ivan Franko managed to finish a doctorate, be awarded two more, run for a seat in the Viennese parliament, and produce an astounding amount of published work (one piece for every two days of his life). He was nominated for the Nobel Prize in 1910 and it is a chip on many a Ukrainian shoulder that he did not win. He died in Lviv and is buried in Lychakivsky cemetery. It is easily spotted by the abundant blue and yellow flowers on top.

commemorates the victims; the Lviv ghetto was cordoned in 1941 as one of five such places, including the Warsaw ghetto. Lviv's present-day Jewish community is based at Sholom-Aleichema 12.

Parks

For all of Lviv's manmade beauty, the natural elements have not been forgotten and dozens of parks break up the run of buildings. On the northeast side is the **High Castle** (*Vysoky Zamok*) and a climb to the top of the hill gives the best panorama of the city. **Ivano-Franko Park** fills a square hillside with very tall trees, right across from the university around the city's largest monument to the poet Ivano Franko. By far the most romantic is the extensive green area of **Strysky Park**. By tradition, newlywed couples come here after the ceremony to take pictures and dance under the trees, and the small lakes and shady lawns make it a relaxing escape from the city. Other than a resting place for Lviv's past heroes, **Lychakivsky Cemetery** is a hilly forest with big ancient trees towering above the crosses and mausoleums. The park is serenely Gothic with lots of crumbly statuary and giant crows leaping about the graves. A good look at the headstones gives a fair impression of Lviv's last one hundred years; Polish aristocrats, Soviet soldiers, Ukrainian freedom fighters, Jews, and famous writers are all buried together. The entrance to the cemetery is at M and Pekarska; open from 09.00–20.00 between April and September, 09.00–18.00 from October to March; entrance costs 4UAH and a guided tour of the 'famous' graves costs US$2 (Ivan Franko is buried here). **Lychakivsky Park** is behind the cemetery (off Lychakivska Street) as is the **Botanical Gardens** and the much larger Park **Pohulyanka** ('Strolling' Park) made especially for long leisurely walks.

OUTSIDE LVIV

The wonders of the Galician countryside deserve some attention since this is a 'happening place' in rural terms and the villages are a more honest expression of what life is like in western Ukraine. Getting to and from villages is not difficult: buses regularly leave from the main station, and there are plenty of marshrutka that connect villages to the city (schedules and pick-up points can change – simply ask). Lviv's tour companies also specialise in short local trips (see *Tour operators*, page 150), as do most hotels and some bus companies (eg: Lviv Inturtrans). It is also easy to negotiate a driver for the day.

Galician castles look more like chateaux than fortresses; most began as early medieval defence posts that were later turned into lavish palaces for the Polish aristocracy. These chateaux are now Ukraine's greatest claim to old European grandeur and they tend to be more popular with Ukrainians than foreigners. A rise in Lviv's tourism has sparked regional interest and you may hear talk of the mystical-sounding 'Golden Horseshoe'. (This is not a historic chain of fortresses and monasteries, but a recent boardroom ploy to develop the less-visited territories en masse; visiting them all does not make the experience any more endearing.)

Only 30 minutes north, **Zhovkva** makes a good day trip from Lviv. The town's varied buildings have miraculously survived centuries of onslaught and now form a state historical site. The castle was originally 16th century but has been repeatedly changed by each Polish family that has reigned over this area. The city gates are also impressive, as are the numerous churches that avoided destruction by the Soviets. The Christmas Church (on Ivan Franko) is a light wood church built over 300 years ago and this style is currently copied for all the local church reconstructions. The dark wooden Trinity church on St Trinity is used by the local Greek Catholic community and has kept the original iconostas. Another 'must see' is the ornate pink synagogue on Zaporizhka, built in the 17th century and one of the few still standing in Galicia.

Olesky Castle is 70km west of Lviv and features a large park as well as an eclectic museum filled with medieval art, religious artefacts and 16th-century furniture. The white chateau is perched on a small knoll and is treasured as the palace where the Cossack Bohdan Khmelnytsky spent his youngest years. Not far from **Olesko** is **Pidhoretsky Castle** (in Pidhirtsi village). Part bastion, part palace, the bare interior is offset by the luxurious marble designs. Also worth noting is the sagging wooden church in Pidhirtsi which is said to have been divinely 'transferred' to the spot in 1720.

Historically, **Drohobych** has always been an important regional town that has kept a quintessentially Galician feel in spite of its industry. The town was established during Kievan-Rus over 900 years ago and was first known for its salt mines and then later as the centre for oil refining during the Hapsburg Empire. The old city is especially beautiful and there are four original wooden churches, each built in a different age of folk tradition. Drohobych can be reached by train or bus from Lviv and is a very convenient point from which to venture into the surrounding countryside and the amazing Carpathian foothills. Just south is Ukraine's most famous spa town, **Truskavets**, reached via Drohobych or by direct train from Lviv or Kiev. Throughout Ukraine, kiosks and restaurants sell Truskavetska mineral water, which is slightly more salty than most and is used locally to treat digestive problems and to increase metabolism. Visiting the spring's source is typical of the Soviet health holiday. There are plenty of sanatoria (health resorts) but these cater to serious long-term water drinkers. If you are looking to stay a shorter time, the **Hotel Beskyd** and restaurant is the town's best offer; Drohobytska 33; tel: 03247 543 23; web: http://www.beskyd.com.ua. Rooms cost

US$30–50 a night, but they might convince you to take the relatively inexpensive twelve-day package which includes science-fiction-like spa treatment.

TERNOPIL – ТЕРНОПІЛЬ

Galicia's 'other' city has lived the same turbulent existence of changing power (five different countries have ruled over it in the last century alone) but is considered a young town, founded only in 1580. There is no pressing need to visit Ternopil, but the city does fulfil its role as regional centre for the more appealing outer parts of Ternopil region. These are the borderlands between Galicia and Podillya (and Volhynia in the north); the area is virtually unknown to non-Ukrainians. Anyone looking for an original outdoor experience would do well to include these small and serene national parks, and Ternopil's gargantuan caverns attract hard-core spelunkers. The villages of Ternopil oblast have always played a significant historical role in Ukraine's history (eg: Kremenets, Buchach, Berezhany) and it seems uncanny how many foreigners come here to track their ancestors, not to mention the number of Ukrainian celebrities from the area. Nevertheless, Pochaïv Monastery is the main attraction and so Ternopil has become the most obvious stopover in terms of accommodation and transportation.

Getting there and away

Most trains from Lviv going east pass through Ternopil; there are over 15 connections between the two cities everyday and the trip can take two to three hours. Khmelnytsky is about an hour and a half in the other direction with frequent train and bus connections; Chernivtsi is another close link to the south (usually around three hours). Many of the trains from Kiev use Ternopil as a junction for their international links and as the last stop before Lviv, so travel to and from the capital is never a problem; the train station is on Khmelnytsovo. Regional travel is not that simple, since the railroad tracks follow communist logic and miss all the places you want to go and see.

The main bus station is on Obolonya on the south side of the town. There is a one-and-a-half-hour bus to Pochayiv that runs back and forth throughout the day. The link gets crowded with tourists in summer and with pilgrims on religious holidays (especially Ukrainian Christmas and Easter), but a constant supply of transportation appear to meet the demand.

Where to stay and eat

In spite of the city's appeal, Ternopil is slightly lacking in the basics and is far from fitting into the developed tourist's path. **Halychyna** (Chumatska 1; tel: 03522 533 595) is the hotel and is still not in great form even after some renovations. The concrete high-rise is next to the manmade lake with a restaurant by the entrance; costs around US$20/night. **Hotel Ternopil** (Zamkova 12; tel: 03522 224 397; fax: 03522 229 360) is the most centrally located (by the castle) but does not have a great track record. They have a reputation for charging foreigners more and providing less (water problems are a frequent complaint); they also have a strange pricing scheme: it is a better deal to pay for the suite (around US$50) and get the better room than haggle over their bare US$30 rooms. They do, however, have one of the city's better restaurants. In the centre (along Ruska and Shevchenka) there are few cafés and nice shops.

What to see and do

The castle looks more like a Stalinist administration building, since it was remodelled in the 1950s (the armaments were removed back in the early days of

Polish rule). This is the 'sight' of the town, along with the artificial lake. Even so, Ternopil is far from depressing, with a genuine quaintness including 'Podillyan' architecture and very colourful streets. Lovers of small-town adventure can take buses out to **Berezhany** or **Buchach**, both very old towns with castle ruins and numerous churches. Around 80km north is **Kremenets**, one of Ukraine's oldest settlements with remains of the 12th-century castle still standing on a windswept hilltop.

The **Medobory Nature Preserve** is a national park of rocky bluffs along the high ridge overlooking the Podillyan steppe. 'Honey-drinking' park is made up of six different parts concentrated in two disparate areas: one is an hour southwest of Ternopil (by Khorostikiv), the other is in the north by Kremenets and is more frequently included in group tours. The protected spots feature indigenous Ukrainian hardwood trees and forest flowers as well as springs and caverns. It is also the best place in Galicia to see wildlife and birds. Getting there on your own is tricky, although it is an easy matter to take a bus to either place and simply walk from the village. Doing a day trip with a local agency is a lot less headache. Ternopil's Hotel Halychyna can arrange a visit, as can Meest-Tour in Lviv (page 150) and the agencies in Kamyanets-Podilsky (page 138) who are also experienced in arranging guides and transportation for spelunking in Ternopil.

There are over 100 caves in the south of Ternopil region; **Optimistic Cave** is considered the longest in Europe with around 200km of gypsum tunnels. **Krystalna** and **Ozerna** are also very beautiful and individual caves. Most of these are close to the town of Borschiv (100km south of Ternopil) which can be reached by bus, or less conveniently on local train. At present, it is best to travel with an experienced guide as the caves are extremely long and maze-like. In Lviv, the Fund of Support for Scientific and Creative Initiatives specialises in longer expeditions to 'Optimistic' cave. Check their website: http://www.cave-ua.narod.ru. They are best contacted by internet (cave-ua@narod.ru, kursor@lviv.farlep.net) or telephone 0322 404 624 and can tailor specific trips for individuals and groups.

POCHAYIV – ПОЧАЇВ

Ukrainian Orthodoxy ranks the exquisite **Pochayiv Monastery** as Ukraine's most sacred site, *after* the Pechersky Lavra in Kiev (it seems a fierce competition). Both monasteries started as secluded caves that evolved slowly into towering baroque edifices, and both monasteries greet hundred of thousands (if not millions) of Orthodox pilgrims each year. The main difference is that Pochayiv lacks the political and tourist façade of Kiev; meaning here, visitors can witness the sincere display of Ukrainian spiritual life in a quaint rural setting. Pochayiv was also a more obscure target for the Soviet authorities and sustained much less damage than Kiev's Lavra. Today, Pochayiv's collection of ancient master icons is revered by all Eastern Orthodoxy.

The mount was first discovered by a group of refugee monks who had fled Kiev's Pechersky Lavra after the Mongol invasion in 1240. They were strict ascetics who envisioned this spot by the Pochayna River as a true wilderness, both physically and spiritually. The community grew and the cave chapels expanded into the complex of larger halls and churches above ground.

Today's pilgrim masses come to look upon Pochayiv's Holy Mother of God icon, a gift from the Greek Church to the local aristocrat Anna Hoiska in 1559. She discovered a healing power within the sacred icon when her blind brother was cured after he prayed to it. Astounded by the miracle, she handed the icon over to the local monks, along with a hefty gift of land and cash. (The icon was later stolen from the monastery by her grandson who had converted to Protestantism but was later returned by order of the court.) The other sacred relic is the leftover footprint of the Virgin Mary in a rock from which a holy spring now flows. The mark was left after the Virgin appeared in a pillar of fire to a monk and a local shepherd, after which the medieval church of the Assumption of the Most Holy Mother of God was built at the base of the mount. The assembly is mostly 17th-century baroque, but for 100 years the church belonged to the Greek Catholic Church, and some Roman features remain. The monastery was given back to Russian Orthodox control in 1831, after which the high belltower was added, followed by the Troitsky Cathedral, a rare example of Russian modernist design. The bright white and gold structures are stunning, and the religious excitement adds to the spectacle.

The monastery's legendary healing powers now draw bus-loads of invalids (sufferers of migraines are promised a cure by praying while listening to the bell ring). Pochayiv's busiest times are during the summer and on Orthodox holidays, especially the day of St Iove (Job) on September 10. Unless you are part of a larger pilgrimage tour, a visit to Pochayiv is best done as a day trip from Ternopil. Orthodox believers can often stay over at the monastery for a small donation, and the townspeople are known to rent out their apartments for a night or two. Otherwise, there are few facilities for travellers and a feeling of contempt towards tourist development. That said, enterprising tour guides will make themselves known to you (negotiate, but don't pay more than US$5 for a tour of all the chapels and grounds) and whenever indoors taking photos costs 3UAH per frame.

Getting there and away

The simplest way to Pochayiv is taking the Lviv–Kiev train to Ternopil, then taking the bus north. There are also direct buses from Kiev to Pochayiv, which can take up to a whole day and costs about the same as the train and short bus (around US$10). Buses from Rivne and Lviv are also somewhat convenient for day trips.

VOLHYNIA – ВОЛИНЬ

Traditionally lumped with Galicia, Volhynia is the forgotten northwest corner of Ukraine that rarely gets included in tours of the country, since Volhynia's best spots are well off the beaten track. This outer territory is characterised by the great northern forests that were home to the earliest Slavic tribes and much of the north is still covered with thick woods and wetlands: wide lakes, marshes and hundreds of rivers and streams that flow towards Belarus. To visit these farthest corners is to travel beyond the normal vision of dry Ukrainian steppe and to get a better understanding for Ukraine's oldest pagan ties to nature.

The original principality of Volhynia was based in Volodymyr and was one of the most ancient Slavic civilisations. The land was joined to Galicia in a shared kingdom in 1199 but Volhynia's separate nature was based on the Lithuanian influence that predominated after the fall of Kievan Rus, and then at a later phase when Galicia remained a province of Poland while the Russian Empire controlled the Volhynia Gubernia from 1795. Today, Volhynia is quiet and remote, proud speakers of the Ukrainian language, but less prone to rabid nationalism. Travelling to or from Poland will take you along the main route between Kovel, Lutsk and Rivne, but these basic cities hold little interest compared to an expedition up north. Such trips are easier said than done, but well worth the effort.

LUTSK – ЛУЦЬК

Volhynia's largest city is not that large: the old city is nestled into the bend in the River Styr and the three castle towers and church domes give Lutsk its traditional skyline, while the newer Soviet suburbs appear less discouraging among all the green. A visit to Lutsk may be a break away from the average tourist logic; the city's thousand-year-old past is more tragic than heroic and not everybody finds the place entertaining. However, Lutsk is destined to become the main base for river and lake excursions up north and there is some appeal in the frank nature of everyday life in this part of the country.

For Ukrainians, Lutsk (historically known as Luchesk) is famous as the home of an early icon-painting school during the 13th and 14th centuries from which survives the Volhynian Blessed Virgin Mary, considered a national treasure, now kept in Kiev's National Museum of Art. Lutsk was also home to an established Ruthenian Orthodox 'brotherhood' that sought to protect local rights and promote their own faith and culture under Polish Catholic rule. Jews played an integral part in the region's long history and once accounted for over a third of the population; most were killed in the infamous Lutsk massacre, while thousands of others were gathered into the lesser-known Lutsk ghetto. Local Ukrainians suffered equal cruelty from the Soviets when over 5,000 were shot in the midst of the retreating Red Army. During the Soviet era, Lutsk was simply known as a production centre for construction materials and the town where poetess Lesya Ukrayinka went to primary school. A legacy of oppression defines one of the more curious sights: an underground labyrinth of old vaults and tunnels dating back to the 16th century, once used for clandestine activities.

Getting there and away

Most of the routes between Poland and Kiev pass near Lutsk, but do not always stop here since Kovel is the main railway junction. Presently, there is one direct Lutsk–Kiev overnight train every other day (12 hours) and two daily Kovel–Kiev connections that also takes passengers to and from Lutsk. The train station is at the end of Hrushevskovo in the northeast corner of the city. The central bus station is not far away, at Konyakyna 23. Frequent buses between Kiev and Lviv pass through Lutsk, and this is the best place to find transportation to the north and other surrounding areas.

Regular buses travel to and from Lviv (3 hours) and Rivne (1 hour), including the nicer 'deluxe' coaches – *Avotlyuks* has an office in Lutsk at Konyakyna 39; tel: (03322) 471 08.

Where to stay and eat

Few people travel to Lutsk which is a good indication of what is available. **Ukrayina** is considered the town's first-class hotel; Slovatskovo 2; tel: (03322) 433 28. Located near the main central square, the prices of rooms vary from very high to lower middle range; the restaurant is a dependable source of meals for all visitors. Their in-house tour agency is also the former Inturist, meaning you can book tickets here, and it is a good way to arrange visits to the national parks. Tour groups often stop at the less expensive **Hotel Luchesk** (Vidrodzhennya 1; tel: 03322 524 96). This is not a bad place to stay, but the location is inconvenient and far from anywhere (take #3 bus or #8 trolley into town). The other alternative is **Svityaz** (Naberezhna 4; tel: 03322 490 00) which is closest to the old city and not far from the banks of the river Styr. The white building just underwent a Las Vegas-type renovation and now advertises a nightclub, swimming pool, a sauna, and an all-too-familiar 'retro' restaurant.

What to see and do

Lutsk Castle, at the end of Kafedralna, is a basic structure with three towers, built in the 13th century and considerably touched up during Lithuanian rule. The old city is fascinating despite its ruinous state: old Polish monasteries and churches line Kafedralna, and the 14th-century synagogue can still be visited at 33 Halytskovo. The Pokrovska Church on Halytskovo was the original home of the Volhynian Blessed Mother icon, and other examples from the Lutsk school can be found at the Volhynia Museum of Iconography (Peremohy 4) along with other exhibits of 16th- to 18th-century religious art. If you want to explore the underground vaults, one entrance is by the St Peter and Paul Cathedral on Kafedralna.

OUTSIDE LUTSK
Berestechko – Берестечко
After freeing Ukraine from Polish rule in a glorious rampage, the Cossacks suffered an exhausting defeat by the Polish army at the Battle of Berestechko in June 1651. The battle lasted for two weeks, during which hetman Bohdan Khmlenytsky was abducted for ransom by his supposed allies. A black-domed church is built over the 'Cossack Graves' and the event is commemorated every year in June with ceremonies and festive re-enactments. Another sad memorial is the 17th-century Thekla's chapel, built over a mass grave of the 500 maidens who were tortured to death by the Tatars. Getting to Berestechko is easiest on a bus or by hired taxi from Lutsk or Rivne.

Shatsky National Nature Park –
Шатський Національний Природний Парк
Ukraine's 'Lake District' is one of the last true wetlands remaining in Europe, and one of the most threatened; the Pripyat River ends in far away Chernobyl and local pollution has proved problematic. The Pripyat marshes consist of the larger Shatsky Lakes, over a hundred streams and rivers, and scattered swamps along the Belarus-Ukraine border. This intertwining of river systems is where the Baltic and Black Sea watersheds meet and by Ukrainian standards the plant and animal life is extraordinary. Svityaz is the largest lake and the serene home of abundant waterfowl and some incredible bits of tall forest. The tourist facilities are in a phase of transition: old resorts are closing down and attempting to spruce things up. Hopefully there will be some more established long-term accommodation in the future. A summer music festival is held on Lake Svityaz every year and camping is usually not a problem, but as regulations tend to be fluid, stay flexible.

Many will say that foreigners trying to get into Shatsky should just go with a private tour. This is the way that things have always been done and it may seem less hassle, but seasoned travellers will have no problem getting there on their own. Either take the train or bus to Kovel and then a bus (1 hour) to the village of Shatsk inside the park, or else go on the direct bus from Lutsk (once a day). Keep in mind that Shatsky is wedged between two international borders (Poland and Belarus) so that your presence can arouse some old-time fears and suspicions. If you are going to get lost in the woods and end up accidentally crossing into another country, make sure that it's Poland.

Shatsky Park is only a small part of what's really out there. Too little is known about northern Volhynia and its ecology – explorers should take note. The Pripyat, Stokhid, Turiya, and Styr rivers are inviting for kayaking or long canoe trips, and the miniature villages of the marshes are wonderfully obscure.

RIVNE – РІВНЕ
Most visitors to Ukraine will pass through Rivne region, but almost none will stop and visit. The territory appears as mere distance on the map, and the city Rivne is often nothing more than a bathroom break between the west and the capital. The

faulty logic has more to do with the way the Soviets built the rail
highways and says little about Rivne itself. The region's best lakes and fc
purposefully made inaccessible but now the area is open, Rivne
'uninteresting' to most tour companies. This borderland between Volh ... and
Polissya is the most heavily forested area of Ukraine today; the lack of development
keeps the region pure but grossly unappreciated.

Rivne's history is average for western Ukraine. The region was imperative to
Kievan Rus, so today many smaller towns feature castles and ruins. The city then
lived under the Magdeburg Law, had its 17th-century peasant uprisings and
suffered occupation by both Poles and Russians (the town is known as Rovno in
Russian). Hitler made Rivne the capital of occupied Ukraine and so the city was
levelled by the end of World War II. A favourable Soviet leftover is the local candy
factory that still makes most of Ukraine's sweets.

Getting there and away

There is an airport in Rivne, but flights are extremely rare. Rivne does not have its
own train to and from Kiev, but the Lutsk–Kiev train makes a stop, as do all trains
that go to or through Kovel from Kiev, including the Warsaw train. This means
that in either direction, the Rivne stop can fall at an awkward time during an
overnight journey. Train time to Kiev averages around eight hours; other train
routes go to Lviv (around 4 hours) and Lutsk (1 hour). Train tickets can be
purchased at the station located at the end of Prospekt Miru, or at the hotel travel
agencies. North–south routes to Ternopil, Kremenets and Pochayiv are best by
bus; the main bus station is at Kyivska 40. Buses go to and from Kiev all day,
including the plush coaches and international bus lines from western Europe. The
trip from Rivne to Kiev takes 6 hours via Zhytomyr.

Where to stay

Rivne has four hotels; two are worth recommending. **Hotel Mir (**Mitskevicha 32;
tel: 0362 290 470) is in the very centre and has comfortable standards and an OK
restaurant. Rooms range from US$40–60, fancier suites are US$80. This is the
former Inturist hotel, so tickets and excursions can be organised with their agent.
Turyst (Kyivska 36; tel: 03622 267 413) is further from the city centre on the road
to Kiev, but conveniently located next to the bus station. The high-rise complex
has many rooms; about half have been remodelled and some are offered at a lower
cost than those at Hotel Mir. Extra facilities include a restaurant and in-house
tourist agency. Rivne's restaurants are few: **Stambul** (Stepana Bandery 31) has an
oriental flare while **Khmil** (Soborna 17) serves traditional Ukrainian food.

Things to see and do

As a city, Rivne is not a particular gem, mostly rebuilt after the war. The standard
tour includes visiting the many open parks and the Church of the Assumption
(built in 1756). A more original structure is the red brick Cathedral of the Holy
Resurrection (Soborna 36); this is a rare and beautiful example of turn-of-the-
century Ukrainian architecture. **Dubno** and **Ostroh** are two nearby towns that
make for interesting excursions. Both have very old castles; the one in Ostroh used
to be a magnificent palace with squat towers and the remaining ramparts all on top
of a shaped 'castle hill'. Dubno's churches and many monasteries are well-situated
in their small-town setting. Take a bus or taxi to either place (45 minutes).

The northern part of the Rivnensky region is naturally beautiful but rather
undeveloped (some areas were subjected to fallout from Chernobyl but are
considered safe). **Rivnensky Nature Preserve** consists of four protected zones in

northern Volhynia, all part of the Pripyat marshes and only just designated a preserve in 1999. These are great birdwatching areas, but getting to the parks is more difficult since there are no major roads like in Shatsky. First take the train north to Sarny (from Rivne or Kiev); from here the far western zone can be reached by bus or hired taxi to the village of Rudka via Volodymyrets. East of Sarny, the town of Klesiv is within hiking distance of another zone, though the other two are extremely remote. The Rivne Inturist office at Hotel Mir organises limited local excursions; a local **tourist company** that may prove helpful is Sport I Turizm at Zhukovskovo 39; tel: 0362243 939.

The Carpathians
Карпати

Untamed landscapes and dramatic scenery make
the Carpathians a chosen destination for nature-
lovers. The significant mountain chain makes
an arch through the southwest corner of the
country and forms a natural border with
Hungary, Romania, Poland and Slovakia. These are
relatively low peaks (Ukraine's highest mountain,
Hoverla, is only 2,061m high) but the unruly terrain has
protected the area from so much intrusion and now it is the
greenest corner of Ukraine. It is also the cleanest; the most breathtaking feature is
the taste of the mountain air, and the shallow braided streams running through the
valleys are pristine. Anyone venturing away from Lviv or the capital should
consider the Carpathians a priority.

The Carpathians are the westernmost point in Ukraine, both in terms of distance
from Kiev and difference in culture. A completely separate folklore makes this a rustic
setting where tradition still dictates a pastoral life. A 'town' is usually a long stretch of
disconnected farms in vague proximity to a minuscule tin-roof church. Horse-drawn
carts are preferred over cars. It is a land of round haystacks, pine-log fences and vivid
folk art – the place in the journey where travellers use up all their film.

Yet the largest cities deserve the same attention as the mountains. Three
traditional regions make up the Ukrainian Carpathians, each of which once
belonged to a bordering nation: Southern Galicia (Poland), Trancarpathia
(Hungary), and Bukovina (Romania). Dressed by an independent heritage, Ivano-
Frankivsk, Uzhgorod and Chernivtsi bear no resemblance to any of Ukraine's
cookie-cutter Soviet towns and the separate culture is still evident in people's
speech and their stylish architecture. This is the youngest part of Ukraine,
completely annexed only after World War II, however its oldest traditions are still
very much alive. Ukraine's most diverse ethnic groups (the Lemko, Boiki and
Hutsuls) evolved in these valleys and still resist national assimilation today.

Unlike the rest of Ukraine, the Carpathians enjoys a solid tourist infrastructure
that dates back to the Hapsburg monarchy and the romantic urge to seek out all
places wild and quaint. A tradition of hospitality sets the region apart and this is still
the place to hike, camp, climb, raft and ski. As a whole, the Carpathians are just
now being rediscovered as the trendy alternative to Europe's more eminent
mountain chains, but Ukraine's 10% of the range attracts the least amount of
visitors. This has everything to do with the hassle of getting an extra visa and
nothing to do with what's actually on offer. In fact, Carpathian Ukraine has fine
mountain resorts for the ready-made alpine holiday, but also caters for the 'no
frills' backpacker wanting to go a little deeper. The lovely woodlands and complete
remoteness mean any experience here is bound to be unique to the Carpathians
and the rest of the country.

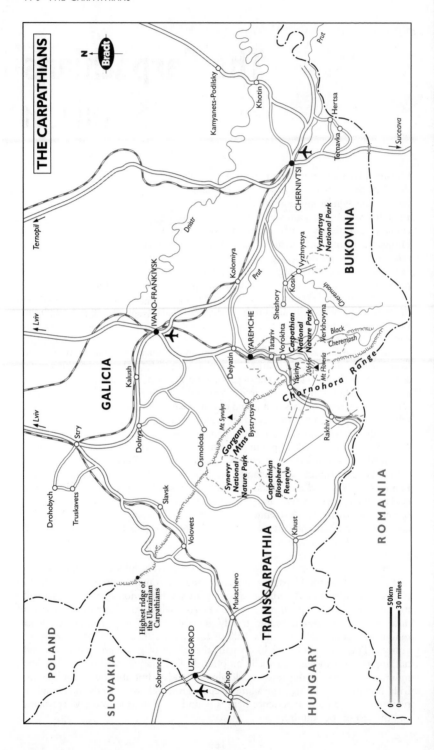

THE MOUNTAINS

The mineral-rich Carpathians are considered Europe's youngest fold mountains that form a landscape of pyramid-shaped peaks and pocketed valleys. In a country as flat as Ukraine, the elevation range of 500 to 2,000m is impressive. Mountain summits are considered sacred places here and most peaks are marked with crosses or patriotic monuments.

Three main recreational ranges make up the Ukrainian Carpathians: the lower hills south of Lviv that include the ski resorts at Slavsk and spa towns like Truskavets; the secluded Horhany range is the least accessible but truly spectacular; and the Chornahora Mountains are the highest, located directly south of Ivano-Frankivsk by the Romanian border. Someone visiting Lviv can very easily do a day trip into the northern Carpathians, but the heart of the Ukrainian Carpathians lies south of Ivano-Frankivsk. A popular mountain circuit starts here, passing through Yaremche, Tatariv, Vorokhta, Verkhovyna, Kosiv, Sheshory, Kolomiya, and finally ending in Chernivtsi and Bukovina. Train and motor transport are available all along, with opportunities for small hikes from each place. Alternative itineraries would allow for long walks in between, such as crossing the Chornohora by foot from Yasynya to Verkhovyna.

Hiking Carpathian peaks is rarely an intense climb, but very satisfying for its unique interaction of natural and human elements. Some areas are empty and forested, in others, the mountain huts and wooden fences add to the view. The hills are also a collector's paradise, with easy-to-find fossils (mainly flowers and fish), and relics from the first and second world wars such as helmets, bullets, and bombshells. Remember that many still harbour the mentality that individual exploration – or hiking without a guide – are not viable actions, especially by foreigners. That kind of caution is unjustified in the Carpathians, where there are plenty of well-worn trails and civilisation is never too far away. In the mountains, use only marked campsites and fire areas; *kolyba* are traditional Hutsul shepherd lodges now built and used as accommodation for hikers; most of these are represented on maps and fall along the trail. All the same, bring a compass. Always travel with sufficient warm clothing. The people who get lost here rarely suffer from hunger or thirst, but from the intense cold at night.

The Soviets were skilful cartographers, but only now is the information from these maps trickling into the public realm. A few private companies have put together decent orientation maps and these are best bought in bookshops in Lviv and Ivano-Frankivsk (yet another incentive to learn Cyrillic). An over-abundance of Ukrainian travel companies are ready to unveil the secrets of the Carpathians for a price but keep in mind that the best aspects of these mountains are freely available. MEEST-Tour in Lviv (see page 150) is best equipped for specialised activities and long group treks.

FLORA AND FAUNA

Carpathian plants and animals form a separate world to the rest of Ukraine and recent years have seen an increased recognition of the region's biodiversity as more people discover one of Europe's most pristine (and most threatened) habitats. The alpine environment and virgin forests form a familiar backdrop for mountain wildlife, but so far the Carpathian's east European location has prevented the over-development of ski resorts and other tourist industry projects that have been the bane of the Alps and Pyrenees. The Carpathians is the last place on the continent with large carnivores, including bears, wolves, lynx and other wild cats.

Ukraine's bear population is nominally small, with only about 1,000 left, but aside from those in Russia and Romania, this is the largest bear population in

THE HUTSULS

Ukraine's very own mountain people create an alternative image to the scythe-wielding peasant of the traditional Ukrainian steppe. In place of the sickle, Hutsuls carry ornate *toporets* (hatchets) for chopping down trees, defending against bears and for their specific style of folk dancing. Although Ukrainian in language, belief, and custom, their unique lifestyle stems from a separate natural world of steep, wall-like mountains and dark pine forests. Felling trees provides lumber for tall-roofed houses that stay dry under the snow, while sheep herding in the mountain pastures offers food, clothing, and income. The traditional Hutsul dress consists of red woollen jackets, red trousers or skirts, wide leather belts and boots; the colours tend to be more vibrant than average. Hutsul cuisine reflects a blend of wild mountain products and Romanian influence. A main ingredient is *smetana* (like sour cream), as are forest mushrooms, corn meal, wild blackberries and sheep and goat products. Brynza (a sharp and crumbly Carpathian goat cheese) is pressed fresh and eaten in large wedges, often as a salty snack with vodka, and mutton shish kebabs are sold in every roadside stand.

Pure Hutsul dialect is a mixture of old Ruthenian mixed with borrowed Romanian and Magyar, and a few of their own expressions. The average Ukrainian cannot understand it. Dances are a show of stationary jumping rather than the spread-out patterns and running so characteristic of Ukrainian dancing in the plains. Hutsuls also play a long alphorn-like instrument called a *trembyta* that can be fashioned only from a pine tree that has been struck by lightning. The horn is held high in the air and when played (at births, deaths and marriages), makes a trumpeting bellow that echoes off the hills. Most revealing of Hutsul mentality are the details, especially in folk architecture: a building's front door is built at chest-level so that guests must bow before the host when entering.

Modern Ukrainians will make proud reference to the Hutsuls but even in the Carpathians, they are still perceived as a caricature rather than a fact of present-day existence. Actually, most of the southern Carpathians are still populated by Hutsuls, whether or not they are on display as such, while the term 'Hutsul' is used as a broad reference to a collective of mountain ethnic groups, including the Boiki, Lemki, and Pokuttians. If you are travelling with a group tour through the Carpathians, much of the journey will consist of pinpointed shopping trips for Hutsul souvenirs. Everything will be touted as genuine Hutsul craft including embroidery genuinely imported from China. The real thing is not too elusive. Look for hand-knit woollen socks, long-hair sheepskins, and simple woodcraft: plates, combs, pipes, and utensils. Authentic Hutsul embroidery is recognisable for its simple repeated diamond or diagonal patterns and for the traditional colours: earthy reds, ochre, dark blue and black. Geometric animal and plant designs are also characteristic.

Europe. The Carpathian brown bear (*Ursus arctos*), a smaller and more docile relative to the North American grizzly bear, spending most of its time rummaging for food, which can include anything from roots and berries to rodents and grubs. (Ukraine's Hutsul shepherds sometimes complain of bears attacking their cattle.) Poachers kill a few dozen bears every year, but the real threat is the destruction of their habitat: Ukraine's small nature reserves are rarely contiguous, meaning that animals like bears, which need wide spaces for roaming and hunting, are forced to make precarious crossings into human territory. Seeing a bear in the Carpathians can't be guaranteed but it is a definite possibility if that is what you are looking for. Local guides, especially those affiliated with the national parks, tend to know where the bears are and when to see them. Mid-summer is best for viewing the animals out in the open; in winter bears go into a state of dormancy; some guides have an uncanny ability to stake out bear dens in the snow and give tourists a peek at the slumbering beasts.

There are only about 500 wolves left but their presence is real in the southern national parks. If you are camping in remote places and are lucky, you will hear them. European lynx are rare, but other types of wildcat are occasionally seen. Ukraine's elk and bison populations are endangered in the Carpathians; most of them are in the tri-country biosphere reserve in Transcarpathia. The most visible local animal species is the Carpathian deer (*Cervus elaphus carpathicus*) which has a unique profile and is easily spotted on wooded slopes and mountain glens all over the area. Fox, marmot, mink and chamois are also prevalent but shy.

Birdwatching in the Ukrainian Carpathians is rewarding with over 280 species, many of which can only be seen in this area. Keep an eye out for mountain wagtail, water pipit, golden eagle, the Carpathian two-tail owl and the white-back woodpecker. Ukraine lacks the organised birdwatching tours of its surrounding neighbours, but the parks support birding and can be helpful with locating prime spots and species identification.

Wildflowers and soft mosses cover much of the open mountain glens. Spring, summer and autumn each exhibit a changed cover of grasses and blooms; crocus, snowbell, violets and monkshood are characteristic for the Ukrainian hills. The mountains on this side of the border are the most heavily wooded of the entire range: beech, sycamore, and tall virgin pines make up the larger forests. The air smells so nice because of all the spruce trees, especially the squat and bushy Siberian juniper, and there are enough deciduous trees to colour things brightly during the autumn. Up in the mountains, many trees are over 30m high and over 400 years old. Only 8% of these forests are under protection, but it is not uncommon to see a swathe of trees cut down inside a reserve. Local tradition and present poverty requires the timber for building and fuel, and enforcement in Ukraine is generally weak. Efforts to protect the area as a whole are complicated by the fact that six different countries share the territory. The area has only recently come under focus by international conservation groups who seek to avoid the same destruction that happened to mountain environments in western Europe.

PRACTICALITIES
When to visit
In general, the climate is much more mild than the rest of Ukraine with a constant flux between sunshine and mist. Snow falls from late November and covers the peaks until May while the lowlands begin a turbulent spring in mid-March. Under snow cover, most peaks are too dangerous to climb, but midwinter (after New Year) is the best time to go skiing. The Carpathian summer is only two months long and this is also when the heaviest rain falls: Ukrainian and Polish tourists invade in August. Like most mountain climates the weather is always changing, so it is wise to wear layers of clothing and carry some kind of waterproof jacket. Hiking is best in late spring or during the long warm autumn (until November).

Getting around

Because of the mountains, local rail access is limited and going by trains to those smaller Carpathian towns with stations is a slow and awkward process. Usually, it is better take a bus, marshrutka or taxi from the larger cities to the rural areas. East–west travel is hampered by topography, so if you are going into the mountains plan your trip along north–south routes. Travel in these parts is also fairly inexpensive: you can go most places by train or bus for under US$5.

Ivano-Frankivsk is the conventional hub for transportation between the main mountain ranges and other towns, as well as Lviv. Comfortable trains also service Chernivtsi and Uzhgorod. Going into the mountains, there are three daily connections via Yaremche (2 hours) to Vorokhta, and two to Rakhiv (5 hours) via Yasynya. A train goes to Kolomiya four times a day (2 hours). The other Carpathian rail line travels from Stry to Mukachevo (and on to Uzhgorod), connecting with Ivano-Frankivsk at Dolyna. Despite all the rail connections, marshrutka traffic between all the Carpathian villages is much more convenient and frequent. The quickest way to and from Vorokhta, Verkhovyna, Kosiv, and Yaremche is by minibus; there is usually one every hour. It is wise to pay attention to where the marshrutka stops, since Carpathian villages can easily occupy a 15-mile stretch of valley. Either specify your exact objective to the driver, who will stop nearby, or get off at the station (usually at the northern outskirts) and walk or take a taxi to your destination. Catching a taxi is pretty much necessary in rural situations. As always, decide on a price before getting in. Taking a taxi can also be a good way to get between towns, or if you are carrying a lot of luggage or equipment. The unwritten rule is about 1UAH per kilometre, but that is highly negotiable. The Carpathians is a locale where hitching is a generally accepted practice, especially in the mountains.

Rural Green Tourism in the Carpathians

International development schemes throughout Ukraine have launched a programme that arranges homestays for travellers in rural areas in the hope that this will create an incentive to preserve the countryside. The Carpathian programme has been successful. Locals (usually on small farms) offer a room in their house for a single night or up to a week in a B&B situation. Prices are low (normally under US$10/night) and staying in a Ukrainian country home is a very unique experience, especially in these very remote Carpathian villages. Individual homes offer different services, but many participants will provide transportation to and from larger towns. The biggest advantage to participating is the raw nature of the visit, although the homes are comfortable. For more information, contact Marko Kotliar (email: mrkotliar@aol.com) and Pavlo Horishevsky (email: inter@il.if.ua); Ivano-Frankivsk Green Rural Tourism Association; tel : (03422) 730 07. Their website is outdated but informative: http://members.aol.com/chornohora/index.htm.

IVANO-FRANKIVSK – ІВАНО-ФРАНКІВСЬК

'Ivano' is the gateway for most travel into the Carpathians and a worthy destination in its own right. Thanks to a complete urban restoration everything is so sleek and new that this could well be Ukraine's most sophisticated town. A series of city squares, pedestrian-only boulevards and small urban trails make it a fun and accessible space, while the old Polish flair provides a romantic backdrop. Art, fashion and business seem to be the town's latest creed and the outer signs show a successful blend of old and new.

The oblast forms the southern reaches of Galicia, and is still marked by pre-World War I borders. Originally, this was the old Ukrainian village of Zablottya, but in the mid 17th century this land (and much of western Ukraine) came under the control of the Pototsky family, the super-wealthy Polish aristocrats who then 'founded' the city and named it in honour of their firstborn son, Stanislaw. The new construction spread out from a six-pointed, star-shaped fortress, bits of which can still be seen in the centre. Under Polish rule the town attracted a variety of monastic orders whose presence is still visible, as well as small merchant communities (namely Jews and Armenians). Stanislaw had a brief moment of glory at the collapse of the Austro-Hungarian Empire, when the short-lived Western Ukrainian People's Republic (ZUNR) proclaimed the city its capital in 1919. Alas, Poland regained control until the Yalta conference when the USSR annexed Galicia. For its 300th anniversary in 1962, the Soviets changed the city's name to Ivano-Frankivsk in honour of the Ukrainian poet and scholar whose sobering statue now stands in front of the Hotel Ukrayina. The change was a feeble attempt on the part of the Soviet government to appease local Ukrainian patriotism: it is in these southern mountains that the Ukrainian Insurgent Army and many other partisan groups resisted Soviet occupation well into the 1960s, the memorials of which are still the visible focus of Carpathian villages.

Many will prefer to simply get off the train in Ivano and directly board a bus for the hills. However, to skip the town is to miss out on the contrast between the modern side of Carpathian life and the rustic ways of the mountains. Ivano is also a good base for getting organised, arranging tours, and enjoying some ease and comfort after extended hikes.

Getting there and away

Ivano-Frankivsk has a functioning airport with one flight to Kiev every three days and the rare flight to Moscow. The airport is best reached by taxi (around US$2) and is located on Konovaltsiya 46. For the present, the train remains the most efficient way to get into the Carpathians, via Ivano-Frankivsk. There are at least three daily trains to and from Kiev; the one via Lviv is the shortest (14 hours) and offers the best time for overnight travel, whereas the link via Chernivtsi can take up to 21 hours. There are also other daily trains to and from Lviv, Odessa, and Kharkiv, as well as Uzhgorod (8 hours via Lviv) and Chernivtsi (4 hours). The train station is located next to the Central Bus Station at Pryvokzalna Square on the eastern side of the city.

Ivano's bus station is frenzied and hectic. Small masses of villagers and their oversized bundles are hustled into compact buses and sent winding off into the mountains. Normally, you'd be clutching onto your bags and ignoring the people shouting to you, but the drivers here are noticeably helpful and honest. Tickets can be purchased inside the station (to the right when facing the train station) or from the driver, if you are simply taking a bus within the Carpathians, it's not worth buying tickets ahead of time; just show up at the station and you will never wait more than an hour for a departing vehicle.

There are dozens of daily buses to and from every village in the Carpathians: Yaremche (1 hour), Vorohkta (2 hours), Verkhovyna (2½ hours), Kosiv (4 hours); all travel times are approximate since much depends on the condition of the mountain roads and the number of stops the bus makes. All the long haul bus services leave from here as well – to Lviv, Kiev, Uzhgorod, and so on – as well as many international buses to Poland and the Czech Republic. A taxi to Lviv will cost around US$30.

City transportation

Ivano is a compact town and most of the streets in the city centre are pedestrian-only. Any taxi around town or from the centre the station should only cost US$1. The number 24 white minibus costs a handful of kopecks and runs a circle between the train station, Hotel Ukrayina, and the airport.

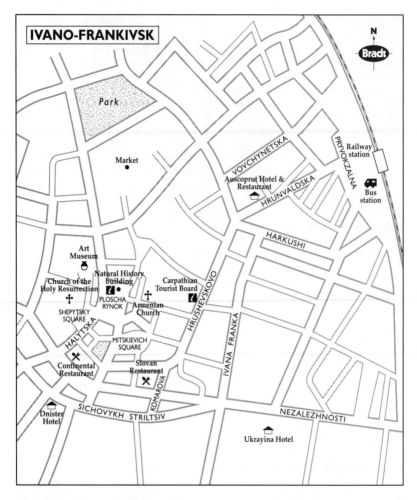

Tourist information

A central **tourist information centre** is located in a corner booth of the central Plosha Rynok (closest to Halytska) where they sell books, pamphlets and maps, and can arrange local guides (in English and Ukrainian). Most hotels will also provide local tours. Because most travel interest is in the Carpathians, Ivano has a plethora of 'agencies' that act as middlemen connecting travellers to tours. **BESHTAU Tour** (Nezalezhnosti 33; tel. 0342 55 30 61) is a local agency that arranges smaller excursions in the mountains, and also does Jewish and Polish heritage trips. Of more help is the **Carpathian Tourist Board**, Hruskevskovo 21; tel: 0342 551 856; email: ctb@trade.gov.if.ua. They have a very good English website (http://www.tourism-carpathian.com.ua) and can provide current information and the right contacts for every kind of activity.

Where to stay

Accommodation in Ivano-Frankivsk has that rare quality of matching diverse needs and budgets without being in a constant state of flux. **Auscoprut**

(Hrunvaldska 7/9; tel/fax: 03422 314 02; email: auskoprut@inf.ukrpack.net) is a light blue Hapsburg mansion that later became the favoured private residence for visiting Soviet *nomenklatura*. An Austrian joint venture has transformed the building into a relatively luxury hotel where rooms have high ceilings, big beds, and spacious bathrooms. Compared to much of Ukraine, this hotel feels enlightened: English-speaking staff, facilities for disabled travellers, and sparkling clean floors. Singles are US$50, doubles US$80 and suites US$100; they also have reasonable group rates and credit cards are accepted. A meal at their classy restaurant is incomparable. **Hotel Ukrayina** (Nezalezhnist 40; tel: 03422 238 00; fax: 03422 247 71) is the former Inturist, now a giant, corporate-style hotel. There is a wide range of rooms, some of high quality: suites cost US$60, remodelled doubles are US$50, and the cheapest 'Soviet' rooms are US$10–20, complete with Soviet furnishings and bad showers. The ground-floor restaurant is unfortunately typical with synthesised music and a slightly generic menu, but their Inturist travel agency can arrange all your travel and book your tickets. The **Dnister** (Sichovykh Stilsiv 12; tel: 03422 279 02) is an old building in the town centre that caters to mostly Ukrainian visitors and offers a cheap night's sleep. A double with private bathroom is US$20, suites are $30. If you choose to use the shared bathroom facilities, a bed is US$7, and the price goes down as the number of people in the room increases. The restaurant is dingy but serves home-style cooking.

Where to eat

Dining out seems to be the favoured pastime in Ivano, and a restaurant culture is emerging. Along Nezalezhnosti there is a string of brand new cafés and pizzerias that always seem to be full, and a few restaurants stand out. Ivano is most proud of the flashy **Slovan Restaurant** (Komarova 4; tel: 03422 225 94) where poised waiters in black tie serve ornate banquet dishes. The atmosphere is calm, the menu 'modern European' and like all such restaurants in Ukraine, the high-style is extremely good value for money; credit cards are accepted. All the hotels also have restaurants open to everyone. **Auscoprut** is the best in town and serves a deadly cup of hot chocolate at teatime. The **Continental** (Nezalezhnosti 4; tel: 03422 552 546) is more typical for Ukraine with abundant decorations and 'peasanty' electronic music. The menu is a variety of intricate meat dishes and salads; a several course meal costs under US$5. If you want to avoid the grandeur, there is a swanky delicatessen to the right of Hotel Ukrayina where you can buy fresh baked goods, meat, cheese, and imported groceries. There is also a market at the end of Sheremety.

What to see

In many respects, Ivano-Frankivsk is a fairly common western Ukrainian city with the exception that it bears a stronger than average resemblance to towns in southern Poland. The streets are paved with cobblestones and the buildings all painted in bright Easter egg colours. **Ploscha Rynok** is the old market square and the evident town centre dating back to the year when Stanislaw was granted the Magdeburg Law. The art deco building in the centre used to be the city hall and is now the regional **Natural History Museum** (open 10.00–16.00; entrance 2UAH). Mammoth bones, iron bits from local burial mounds, and collections from the old Galician kings help tell the story of the oblast, along with some rudimentary yet very sincere displays about local legends. The blue and grey **Church of the Holy Resurrection** (Andrei Sheptytsky Square 22) is a Greek Catholic cathedral built in 1753 and is still a very active church run by local monks and nuns. The original ikonostas is impressive and the glorious musical services attract crowds of townspeople every day. The **Armenian Church** is the pale blue building facing the main square and is owned today by the Ukrainian Autocephalous Orthodox Church. The **Art Museum** (Andrei Shepytsky Square 8; open 10.00–20.00; closed Friday and Saturday; entrance 1UAH) occupies the former collegiate church and is the largest collection of Galician iconography, sacred wood painting and sculptures, including the rare figure of 'Christ in sorrows'. This was the old museum of atheism during the Soviet occupation, and much of the art now on display was hidden from the Soviets in the crypt of the church. The original frescos are just being uncovered and the ceiling is painted with six pointed stars – an old Galician design. English-speaking guides are available. One thing to note in Ivano is the grand example of Ukrainian architecture at Halytska 2: the pink and lavender **medical school**. Across the street and under the bank passageway, you can see the old city wall and part of the original six-pointed, star-shaped fortress.

YAREMCHE – ЯРЕМЧЕ

Yaremche is the tourist centre for the Ukrainian Carpathians – some will be pleased by the relative amount of development, stable accommodation, ease and accessibility, and others will find the gaudy signs and souvenir markets a little disappointing. Either way the surrounding scenery is beautiful and as the main entrance into the Carpathian National Park the town has become a requisite stop and a base for hiking into the Chornohora range. The longest trail to Mount Hoverla begins in Yaremche, and some of the more accessible natural spots are close by, like the Dovbusha cliffs. The Prut River runs rapid and green through the village, forming the gully that made it possible for the railway and the mountain road to pass through here – called Freedom (Svobody) Boulevard in the town limits. A series of bridges (and ruins of former bridges) cross the river at the southern end, and this is where most of the tourist attractions are centred, but there are also few nice trails down to the river. Yaremche is a clear example of modern-day *Hutsulschyna* with its wooden buildings, red clay tiles and steep roofs for the heavy snow and rain of the mountains. The village survives due to tourism and sells itself as a folksy Hutsul backwater, which it actually is despite all the holiday veneer. Traditional methods of herding continue to be the livelihood of many and the customary hospitality comes with a heavy dose of suspicion and curiosity.

Getting there and away

If the mountains are your aim, all paths lead to Yaremche. The best way is driving or taking a bus from Ivano Frankivsk or Kolmiya. The ride into Yaremche from Ivano-Frankivsk is a beautiful little stretch with long reddish wheat fields set before the dark blue patch of the distant mountains; duck ponds and horse-drawn ploughs are prime features. The bus station is at the far northern end of the town; stay on the bus and go further if you need to. Most motor transport continues south to Tatariv, Vorokhta, and Verkhovina. The train station is the adorable peach building near the rather vague town centre. Every day there are four trains to Rakhiv (3 hours, via Yasynya and Vorokhta), one to Lviv (5 hours), two to Ivano-Frankivsk (1½ hours), and two to Kolomiya (1½ hours). The train stops in Yaremche for two minutes only, and the station is open only when a train is passing through, complicating ticket purchases. Marshrutkas and taxis pick up all along the central road and will take you anywhere. There are also plenty of trails so hardcore hikers can make their way to the next town without any problem.

Where to stay

There is no shortage of places to stay in Yaremche, but even with a number of new hotels popping up, things can get crowded in summer. Follow the signs on Svobody to get to **Krasnaya Sadyba** (tel: 03434 222 53), a red-brick, gingerbread-style house on the banks of the river, just opened as a luxury bed and breakfast. Most rooms are US$100/night, though they have a few rooms for US$50. Amenities include heating, cooling, 24-hour hot water, and a high level of security. More of a resort than a hotel, **Karpaty** (Dachna 30; tel: 03434 221 34; fax: 03434 214 72) has adapted from its Soviet past into a thriving private enterprise run by Ukraine's public gas company. The complex is built near the larger souvenir markets; swimming pools, saunas, spas and organised mountain tours attract conference guests and families on holiday. The beds and facilities are clean and comfortable, with varying standards of 'luxury'. Foreigners are charged more than Ukrainians: singles run from US$40–60, doubles are US$50–70. Right across from the Vokzal is **Hotel Prut** (tel: 03434 222 37); a small, century-old Austrian hotel offering low-priced rooms for US$5–10. Most have shared bathrooms and hot water is not a given. A few homey B&Bs in the village offer a very personal stay. The **house at 30B Pushkina** (tel: 03434 214 23) has ten rooms from April until October; the **house at Kamyanka 48** (tel: 03434 332 27) is open year round. Negotiate a fair price and agree on the number of days you will be staying beforehand.

Where to eat

Authentic Hutsul cuisine may seem elusive, but in Yaremche this is what's advertised in most restaurants. **Kolyba** (Svobody 275; tel: 03434 227 08) is the wooden complex near the bridge, named after the traditional Carpathian mountain hut. The log interior and big fireplace make it cosy and there is live Hutsul violin music every night. Food is shish kebabs, fish and salads; a meal costs under US$5. Vodka sells cheap, and Kolyba appears to be the watering hole favoured by villagers. The most recommended restaurant is **Hutsulschyna** (tel: 03434 223 78 email: agenstso@trade.gov.if.ua), another ornate log hut but a tad more contrived: one can't miss the unique rooftop and signs on Dachna. The food is *bona fide* Carpathian fare and delicious: river trout, mushroom soup, pork ribs, brynza, and berries in dessert, tea and salads. A wooden bridge leads from behind the restaurant over a waterfall and into the largest souvenir market. Roadside *shashlyki* (shish kebab) stands are ubiquitous, and most cafés serve the Ukrainian staples borscht and *varennyki*.

Local tourist information

The Department of Tourism and Recreation in Yaremche is located at 266 Svobody, and there are many tourist agencies that offer mountain excursions. One of the oldest private enterprises is **Zori Karpat Tourist Bureau** (Svobody 246, Office 1; tel: 03434 211 82; open 08.00–17.00). This is a mom-and-pop outfit recommended solely for their intimate knowledge of the mountains and its animals. They can arrange English-speaking guides and do special flora and fauna tours, and they often take groups out to collect mushrooms and berries.

What to do

Enjoy the outdoors! There are plenty of trails to follow through forest and over the hills, and the Prut River is a common swimming hole. A small nature park on the southwest side of town acquaints visitors with the mountains and wildlife of the national park; they always have few Carpathian deer living on site. Yaremche has an interesting history of conflict and recreation. The **Carpathian Museum of Liberation** is on Svobody (across from the bus station) and tells the story of the partisans that fought in these mountains, though the museum is open irregular hours and only in season. Most activities centre around the tourist complex of markets and the **Hutsulschyna** restaurant near the short waterfall.

Walks near Yaremche

The Cliffs of Dovbusha is a close and easy walk from the village, but fairly representative of the higher Carpathian forests and quite interesting terrain. The trail is especially good if you are travelling with children or have any health condition preventing a longer hike: the largest loop is under 5km and a thorough slow walk through should take about three hours. From the bridge over the Prut River, walk about 1km south on the main road. The trail starts on the left-hand side and slowly rises up over the rocky drop towards the river. Beech and pine forest covers much of the ridge, and near the turn in the path there's a great view of the valley and the distant Chornohora. The main attractions on the walk are the sandstone 'caves' where the outlaw Oleksa Dovbusha once hid out. These are actually a series of gargantuan boulders tumbled over the summit, with lots of crevices to explore and rocks to climb on. Beneath the spindly trees are a variety of ferns and thick spongy moss. The wild raspberry bushes and blackcurrants underfoot are indeed edible.

No doubt you will hear of the so-called **Ecological Trail** of the Carpathian National Nature Park which is the popular route to Mount Hoverla for those who want to take buses between the towns with periodic hiking in between. Most of the 'trail' follows the road and allows a good view of the scenery while staying close to civilisation; go to Vorokhta, then continue on to the village of Zaroslyak until the end of the road, from where it's a very short 3km hike to the summit of Hoverla. Yaremche is much better for starting or ending long expedition-like walks into the eastern Gorgany and then south into the Chornahora.

CARPATHIAN NATIONAL NATURE PARK

Ukraine's very first national park was established in 1980 and is about 72km (45 miles) long and 20km (12 miles) wide. The park's western border follows the ridge of the Chornohora range south almost to the Romanian border and this area is the most popular place for hiking. Boundaries are marked by the park's painted edelweiss symbol. The park is the most accessible reserve of Carpathian animal and plant life, and the area of the mountains most frequently visited by Ukrainians. Serious hikers will find the trails stimulating and the natural setting is one of Ukraine's best.

The park's **central office** is located in Yaremche at 6 Stusa; tel: 03434 211 57, 228 17; open Monday–Friday, 08.00–17.00. This is the dilapidated white Soviet building with socialist stained-glass at the top of the hill above the marketplace. It may appear uninhabited, but the inside is more lively than the exterior. Technically, all visitors need to register before entering the park, which costs 1.5UAH. This is just a formality, but perhaps a wise one to follow if you are going trekking for more than a few days and if you want to avoid an ugly run-in with bureaucracy. The office offers a fair amount of information about the park and they can sometimes organise individual guides for more specific aims (eg: finding bears). This is *not* the place to get detailed hiking maps: buy those in a bookshop in Ivano-Frankivsk or Lviv.

The park is divided into separate *lisnytsvo*, or wooded areas. Only 20% of the park is completely off-limits to industrial use, and there are certain periods when these protected areas are off-limits to hikers (check at the office). As a rule, stay on the trails: some are dirt roads marked with unsightly cement telephone poles and others zigzag unmarked through the hills. Painted coloured stripes on posts indicate the level of trail you are on: Green is the easiest, with practically no incline,

OLEKSA DOVBUSH

The Dovbusha rocks, cliffs and caves are all named after the most swashbuckling of Ukrainian folk heroes: Oleksa Dovbush. Little is known about his life, for legends prove stronger than fact. Dovbush is known most widely as Ukraine's Robin Hood that stole from the rich foreign landlords (Poles and Hungarians) and spread the booty among the Ruthenian peasants of the Carpathians. His outlaw fame began while still a member of the *opryshki*: small bands of highwaymen with a political agenda to redistribute wealth. Dovbusha's band not only targeted aristocrats, but captured those with a reputation for cruelty and would then hold a trial against them, often ending in their execution. The hit-and-run lifestyle required frequently changing lairs, and legend claims that as a rule Dovbush never stayed in a hideout for more than twelve days, including the boulders and crags near Yaremche.

Although beloved by the poor, the one who supposedly loved him most – a mistress named Dzvynka – betrayed him to a Polish authority (her husband) in the 1740s. Dovbush was captured in the village of Kosmach and quartered in the public square. Pieces of the outlaw's body were hung in villages throughout the Carpathians to discourage future rebellion. As a national hero who stood against foreign oppression, Oleksa Dovbush has regained popular status since independence. Most western Ukrainian towns have a Prospekt Dovbusha running through the centre and his portrait emblazons everything from postage stamps to church banners.

blue trails are found in low mountains, and red is a more intense climb (Hoverla's summit is a red trail).

TATARIV – ТАТАРІВ

Tatariv is on the road to Vorokhta, on the banks of the Prut River. The village is famous for its mineral water springs and the old Hutsul Church of St Dmytry, and this is the beginning of the trail to the top of Mount Khomyak and Mount Synyak. **Hotel Pihy** (tel: 03434 354 04; email: Pigy@jar.if.ua) is a small B&B in the village centre with clean rooms and a constant hot-water supply, as well as a good restaurant. The train from Yaremche stops here, as do all the marshrutkas.

VOROKHTA – ВОРОХТА

Vorokhta is right in the heart of the Chornohora and has a very alpine feel to it. The town was the winter base camp for Soviet Olympic athletes and the giant ski jumps are still in use. There has been a slow conversion into a contemporary ski resort, but 'slow' is the key word – rumours still circulate that lift equipment is outdated and unsafe so skiers are skiing at their own risk. In summer, this is the best base from which to hike to Hoverla in the shortest time, and few consider hiking from anywhere else. The 'town' is stretched over 20km (12 miles) and a steady flow of hikers has kept a few tourist facilities in business. In Vorokhta, take a peek inside the **Christmas Church**, one of the oldest surviving Hutsul wooden churches, built in 1615.

Getting there and away

Vorokhta is a one-hour marshrutka ride from Yaremche and 30 minutes from Verkhovyna; buses do a circle between the three cities throughout the day and

GIVE SOMETHING BACK: ECO-PLAY
The Carpathians are the most 'natural' part of Ukraine and one of the most vulnerable to human impact. Eco-Play was started in Yaremche as a grassroots organisation that strives to promote ecotourism as an alternative to unsustainable use of the environment in the Carpathian National Park. They have regular project days where they clean and maintain the forests and rivers, or plant trees. A foreign visitor lending a hand can be affirming, and it is a fantastic way to see the park. Write, call, or pass by their office. The group's members are all volunteers who are truly passionate about their mountains and know the trails better than anyone else. They can tell you of planned activities, and are experts on local wildlife. Remember that even the smallest financial donation will help them to publish and distribute their environmental awareness literature.
    Contact: Lidiya Fedorivna Hotsul, 6 Stusa, Yaremcha 78500; tel: 03434 211 57; email: Ecoplay-yaremche@ukr.net.

there are longer direct buses to and from Ivano-Frankivsk and to Kosiv and Kolomiya. If you are trying to reach the mountains by train, Vorokhta is the final stop. There are no more than two trains daily to Rakhiv and Ivano-Frankivsk.

Where to stay and eat
Vorokhta was built as a winter sports camp and the hotels used to offer Spartan accommodation for Soviet athletes. Two ski resorts are still working: **Avangard** (tel:(03434 411 44) is at the entrance of the village; **Ukrayina** (tel: 03434 412 70) is in the village centre. Both have a wide range of rooms and prices, but they would rather sell you a week-long package. For the time being, **Ruslana** (tel: 03434 418 40) is the primary restaurant.

THE CHORNOHORA RANGE – ЧОРНОГОРА
The Chornohora are literally the 'Black Mountains' of Ukraine, but under the shifting mist, the colours of the hills change from bright green to dark blue and steely black. These are Ukraine's highest peaks. **Mount Hoverla** (2,061m) is *the* highest, and therefore the most revered and most climbed. The summit is covered with snow from late August to early June so climbing later than early November or earlier than May is foolhardy. The popular trail up to Hoverla starts in Vorokhta and follows a road next to the Prut River to the village of Chornohora where there is a tourist base with unpredictable accommodation. (Take a bus, taxi, or walk this first bit.) From here it is 11km to the summit (around 5 hours), passing through the winter sports camp at **Zaroslyak** where there are camping facilities and an old hotel (tel: 03434 415 91). The path goes through some grand bits of silver fir and birch forest with lots of wildflowers in the spring, and falcons are always swooping above the higher slopes. On a clear day from the summit a fantastic view displays Romania's Marmarosh Alps to the south, the Bila Tysa Valley in Transcarpathia, and the rest of the Chornohora range. Recently, Hoverla's peak has become a bit of a nationalist shrine with its big iron cross and giant Ukrainian flag. Beneath are the words *Ne Maye Natsii, Ne Maye Derzhavy* ('If you have no nation [people], you have no state'). Yet for all the hype of Hoverla, it is by no means the quintessence of the Carpathians: the paths can get crowded in summer, and the rest of the Chornohora are just as beautiful, if not more peaceful. Hikers and climbers like this range because there

are so many peaks so close together, forming a long straight backbone from Mount Hoverla to Pip Ivan. This line of mountains was the post-World War I border between Czechoslovakia and Galicia (Poland) and remaining boundary markers still bear the faded imperial Polish eagle. **Mount Breskul** (1,911m) is 1.5km south of Hoverla, and then it is another 1km to the stunning **Mount Pozhyzhevska** (1,822m) with a trail connecting the peak to Zaroslyak. Further south is **Mount Dantsyzh** (1,866m), followed by the imposing and rocky **Mount Turkul** (1,933m). Trails from Zaroslyak and Rakhiv meet at the peak. In Turkul's shadow is the pristine mountain **Lake Nesamovyte** (1,750m) with a spring from which clean drinking water flows. **Mount Rebra** (2,001m) and **Mount Brebeneskul** (2,037m) are less popular as they are farther away, but as Ukraine's second-highest peak, Brebenskul provides some exciting rocky terrain. Travellers go to the southern Chornohora to climb **Mount Smotrych** (1,894m) and **Pip Ivan** (2,028m). The old meteorological observatory at the top of Pip Ivan looks more like an abandoned castle and now attracts a fair number of hikers who want to check out this spooky Soviet leftover.

Walks in the Chornohora
There are so many trails, mountains and possibilities, it is best to sit down with a good map and plan your own journey. If you are backpacking or simply want to explore the largest amount of terrain, it is best to begin in one town and hike/camp over mountain trails until the next village, from whence it is usually quite easy to get bus transportation onward. Trails leave from Vorokhta and Dzembronya (Verkhovyna) on the eastern side of the range, and from Yasinya and Rakhiv on the western side. Mountain paths tend to be well marked and not too rough except for rocks; however, a lot of lower trails have become overgrown. If you start to think that the trail has simply ended or faded away, walk on a little to see if it doesn't reappear. The main trail between the Chornohora peaks is well-marked by the old Polish border posts. The following are some suggested itineraries that can be amended, cut down, reversed, or added to most of the other walks listed in this chapter:

From Vorokhta to Rakhiv
An extensive, high altitude walk with somewhat rocky terrain; feasible only in fair weather.

Day 1 Instead of taking the main path to Hoverla, leave on the southwest trail out of Vorokhta where you pass through the mountain glade and head uphill for about 6km. From here it is another 1.5km to the top of Mount Kukul (1,539m). You are now on the ridge of the Chornohora and the border of the Carpathian National Nature Park. Take the right-hand trail for 5km; the path descends gently and slowly climbs back upwards towards the peak Velyka Kozneska (1,571m). Spend the night nearby: there is an established campsite about 800m to the right. (*13km; about 7 hours' walking*)
Day 2 Get back on the trail (you should pass the first old Polish border post) and ascend 2km to Mount Hoverla. After taking the requisite snapshots and enjoying the sights, follow the mountain trail south along the eastern ridge to the next three peaks, Breskul, Pozhyzhevska, and Dantsyzh. Continue on to Turkul (5km from Hoverla) and on to Lake Nesamovyte. Stay the night. (*7km; about 4 hours' walking*)
Day 3 Continue south passing Rebra's summit and Lake Brebeneskul, then pass the peaks Brebeneskul, Menchul, Dzembronya and on to the observatory at Pip Ivan. Descend on the western path into the valley. Camp in the glade at the base of Pip Ivan. (*14km; 8 hours' walking*)

Day 4 Follow the path along the stream (Velyky Baltsatul) until the bridge at the confluence with the Bila Tysa, then take the road back to Luhy. Continue to Rakhiv by bus or on foot. (*13km to Luhy; 7 hours' walking*)

On Day 3 there is the option of turning off at Turkul: the right-hand trail will bring you back to Zaroslyak and Vorokhta, the left-hand trail will take you to the village of Hoverla and Rakhiv.

From Vorokhta to Verkhovyna
A lower path that skirts the mountains and then turns back into a cute rural area.

Day 1 From Vorokhta to Zaroslyak on foot or bus, then take the southern path (by the chapel) up to the botanical research station and on to the eastern slope of the mountains. Follow it along the lower sides of Pozhyzhevska and Dantsyzh until Lake Nesamovyte. Take the southern path 1km, until border post #30, turn left and descend to the next peak, Mount Shpytsy. Follow the trail east to the campsite. (*From Zaroslyak: 10km, about 6 hours*)
Day 2 Take the trail across the stream, to the bigger stream into the picturesque valley and village of Bystrets (7km). From here it is another 8km into Verkhovyna (*15km; about 7 hours*)

From Yaremche to Verkhovyna
The proven hiker's route: a week of hearty hiking and mixed scenery in the eastern Gorgany and Chornohora.

Day 1 Take the southern trail from Yaremche to Mount Yavirnyk, then head west/southwest to the camp at the base of Synyak. (*9km; about 5 hours*)
Day 2 Climb to the top of Synyak, then southeast to the Khomyak's peak. Descend to the small road by the stream, turn left and walk to the village of Palyanytsya. Take the southern trail towards the village of Yablunytsya passing Hotel Berkut (tel: 03434 362 30). Stay in the hotel or camp at the site nearby. (*12km; about 6 hours' walking*)
Day 3 Hike from Berkut to Mount Kukul, camp at the base (*14km; 7 hours' walking*)
Day 4 Kukul to Hoverla; descend on the main trail and camp near or at Zaroslyak (*10km; 6 hours' walking*)
Day 5 From Zaroslyak to Mount Brebenskul; descend on the left for 3km to camp. (*12km; 6 hours' walking*)
Day 6 Circle back up to the ridge trail and on to Pip Ivan, then back and east towards Smotrych; 2km west from the peak of Smotrych in the clearing is a campsite. (*14km; over 6 hours*)
Day 7 Hike from Smotrych to Dzembronya and back to Verkhovyna. (*14km; 6 hours*)

YASINYA – ЯСІНЯ
Yasinya is often overlooked on most itineraries, but stands as a worthy destination where many examples of traditional wooden architecture are surrounded by a very beautiful spread of mountains, including the 'back' view of Hoverla. Getting there is easiest by train from Ivano-Frankivsk to Rakhiv (2 daily, 3½ hours). However, the trains tend to arrive at odd hours of the night and barely make a whistle stop. Buses connect to Rakhiv, Vorokhta, and Yaremche. The Soviet ski holiday made this town, but now tourist amenities are scarce; the Zelinska couple run a small guesthouse in the village (Vyzvolennya 243; tel: 03132 431 86).

Left Front door, St Vladimir's Cathedral, Kiev (AE)

Below left Door carving, Lviv, Galicia (AE)

Below right Mosaic, Alexander Nevsky Cathedral, Yalta, Crimea (AE)

Above Broken-down trolley bus in Kharkiv (AE)

Right 'Walrus' swimming in December, Vorskla River, Poltava (AE)

Below Soviet neighbourhood (AE)

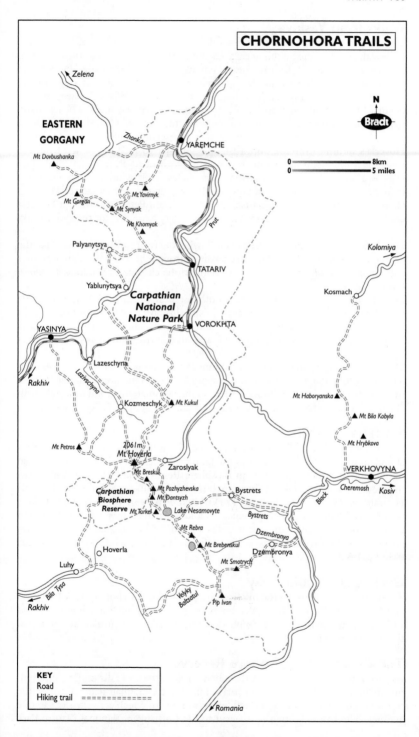

CHORNOHORA TRAILS

N

Bradt

EASTERN
GORGANY

Zelena

Zhonka

YAREMCHE

Mt Dovbushanka

0   8km
0   5 miles

Mt Gorgan

Mt Yavirnyk

Mt Synyak

Prut

Mt Khomyak

Palyanytsya

Kolomiya

TATARIV

Yablunytsya

*Carpathian
National
Nature Park*

Kosmach

VOROKHTA

YASINYA

Lazeschyna

Rakhiv

Lazneschyna

Mt Haboryanska

Kozmeschyk

Mt Kukul

Mt Bila Kobyla

Mt Petros

2061m
Mt Hoverla

Mt Hrybkova

VERKHOVYNA

Mt Breskul

Zaroslyak

*Carpathian
Biosphere
Reserve*

Mt Pozhyzhevska

Mt Dantsyzh

Bystrets

Cheremosh

Kosiv

Mt Turkel

Lake Nesamovyte

Bystrets

Mt Rebra

Dzembronya

Hoverla

Mt Brebenskul

Dzembronya

Luhy

Mt Smotrych

Bila Tysa

Velyky
Baltsatul

Pip Ivan

Rakhiv

KEY
Road
Hiking trail

Romania

Walks from Yasinya

The trail up to the mountains runs south from the nearby village of Lazeschyna. Follow the road by the bubbling river Lazivschyna for about 8km to the mountain base of Kozmeschyk (offering cheap beds in season). Three paths diverge: the central path goes directly south and then rises up the northwest ridge to the summit of Mount Hoverla. The hike is only 7km but relatively steep with a gradual 1,000m climb; the small cluster of huts is the halfway mark. The left-hand trail is a low, forested walk that circumvents the base of Hoverla and ends in Zaroslyak (6.5km), with the option of two intersecting trails that also go up to Hoverla's summit from the northeast. The semi-paved road on the left from the bridge is a mountain path from Kozmeschyk to **Mount Petros** (2,020m). The walk is around 7km, first following a low valley, then winding back and forth before turning off the road and climbing straight up the eastern face of Petros (a 600m climb over 1km). A direct path between Mount Petros and Mount Hoverla complete the triangle from Yasinya and make a very tame two- or three-day walk:

Day 1 Walk from Yasinya/Lazeschyna following the river to Kozmeschyk, take the central path towards Mount Hoverla, passing through the low mountain meadows and into a forest of pine scrub. Set up camp in the clearing by the huts. (*14km; 6 hours*)
Day 2 Follow the trail almost due south for nearly 2km up to little Hoverla (1,850m), then 1km more over high rocks and shrubbery to the summit of Mount Hoverla. Backtrack past little Hoverla and then take the western trail towards Mount Petros. The path meets up with a mountain road and passes a spring. Set up camp at the base of Petros. (*10km; 6–7 hours*)
Day 3 Climb up to the summit of Mount Petros and get a nice view of eastern Transcarpathia: Rakhiv to the southwest and Yasinya to the north. Go back down the same way you came up but take a left on the mountain road and descend north along the winding back road to Kozmeschyk and Lazeschyna. (*12km; 6 hours*)

RAKHIV – PAXIB

Rakhiv is the end of the Carpathian railroad to Transcarpathia with a reputation for abundant wildlife and healthy air as the local health resorts will attest. This is also the headquarters of the Carpathian Biosphere Reserve and quite a sizeable town for these parts. From Rakhiv, there are buses to the villages of Luhy and Hoverla (1 hour) where trails to **Mount Turkul** and **Pip Ivan** begin or end. Hikers wanting the more 'green' experience should start their trek from Rakhiv and choose from a number of longer paths into the Chornohora. The latest and greatest hotel/resort in Rakhiv is **Tysa** (Ivana Franko 1; tel: 03132 226 90; fax: 03132 211 62).

Getting there and away

Three daily trains come to Rakhiv from Ivano-Frankivsk (5 hours), Lviv (9 hours) and Chernivtsi (8 hours); regular buses go to Uzhgorod, Ivano-Frankivsk and Kolomiya about twice a day. Flagging down the smaller marshrutka can get you to the next village and beyond.

The Carpathian Biosphere Reserve

As part of the UNESCO World Biosphere Project, the area falls under a different jurisdiction than most Ukrainian parks. Like most Ukrainian national parks, the territory is divided into six detached 'massifs', none of which are very close to one another. The largest section is adjacent to the Carpathian National Nature Park and protects the western slopes of Mount Hoverla and Mount Turkul. The collective was formed specifically to preserve Ukraine's threatened mountain habitats, and a large number of wild mammals live among these massifs. Attempts to develop ecotourism in the area will require a more active outside interest. For more detailed information, contact the reserve office in Rakhiv: Krasne Pleso 77; tel: 03132 221 93; email: cbr@rakhiv.ukrtel.net

VERKHOVYNA – ВЕРХОВИНА
As a central hearth to the most rural mountain villages, Verkhovyna is a collage of old-time Carpathian imagery that, depending on your view, has either been well preserved or completely forgotten. This is what most tourists were hoping to see in Ukraine all along. Stretched out along the Black Cheremosh River the town branches out into literally hundreds of dirt roads, paths and minuscule villages that extend from the town, dividing the pastures and forests. The mountain town is a good point from which to hike the lower Chornohora (Pip Ivan and Smotrych) and head off on some long and rewarding walks across the most idyllic region of the Carpathian countryside. Although not inside the boundaries of the national park, Verkhovyna is the transfer point between buses and taxis to and from Yaremche and Ivano-Frankivsk with Kosiv and Kolomiya. Eight buses go to and from Yaremche (1½ hours) as well as Kosiv (1 hour) There is no rail link to Verkhovyna. As part of the Rural Green Tourism programme, Verkhovyna offers a prized opportunity to stay with locals. Otherwise, the hotel **Verkhovyna** (Popovycha 9; tel: 03432 215 71) offers Soviet resort-type accommodation.

Walks from Verkhovyna
To head into the Chornohora, walk 9km southwest of Verkhovyna to the scattered village of Dzembronya (the road will follow the Black Cheremosh River; take a left at the Dzembronya tributary). Paths to the mountains also pass from Verkhovyna through Bystrets.

A circular hike
Day 1 Verkhovyna to Dzembronya; follow the trail towards Smotrych for 3km to the camp. (*12km; 6 hours*)
Day 2 Climb to the top of Smotrych, continue on to the highest ridge of mountains. Turn right and climb Pip Ivan. Backtrack north, then proceed to Menchul, descend on the right for 3km to the camp. (*14km; 7 hours*)
Day 3: Follow the trail back through Bystrets and on to Verkhovyna (*15km; 7 hours' walking*)

Verkhovyna to Kolomiya
A less travelled, but highly refreshing walk over hills, passing virgin forest and rural homesteads.

Day 1 The path heads north from the centre of Verkhovyna past the first peak, Mount Hrybkova, and on to Mount Bila Kobyla (1,472m). Continue around the pyramid-shaped Mount Haboryankska (1,445m). Camp at the base. (*10km; around 5 hours' walking*)
Day 2 Follow the trail north all the way to the town of Kosmach. The trail descends slowly and cuts through some lovely forest for the first half, then enters an extended clearing. The minute wooden Paraskivska Church in Kosmach was built in 1718. (*11km to Kosmach; about 5 hours' walking*) From here it is a 1½ hour bus ride to Kolomiya. (There are also buses from Kosmach to Kosiv; 1 hour.)

KOSIV – КОСІВ

The Kosiv bazaar has put this tourist town on the map. Built along the tumbling Rybnytsya river at the base of the Carpathian foothills, the locals make a living by selling Hutsul wood crafts and wool products to unsuspecting visitors. Before buying, compare the trinkets to the real thing in the **Museum of Hutsulschyna Folk Craft** (Nezalezhnosti 101; open 10.00–18.00); a super-decorated log hut houses the collection. The central *pension*-style hotel, **Karpatsky Zori** (Nad Hukhom 15; tel: 03478 216 93) has rooms for under US$40. The town is also part of the rural homestay programme. Multiple buses travel to and from Ivano-Frankivsk (5 hours) and Kolomiya (1½ hours); an overnight bus travels between Kiev's main bus station and Kosiv every night via Chernivtsi (13 hours).

Sheshory Шешори

Sheshory is another small Hutsul village built on the Pistynka River – visitors will enjoy themselves wading in the many pools and waterfalls that run through the village. Getting there is an easy 30-minute taxi or marshrutka ride from Kosiv.

KOLOMIYA – КОЛОМИЯ

Kolomiya is part of the well-trotted tourist trail between the Chornohora range and Chernivtsi – the place where tour buses stop for a convenient half-day display of Hutsul life. The small town is nestled on the plain beneath the distant but still visible mountains. The town's pastel colour scheme puts in question Kolomiya's claim to folksiness, but a serious collection of traditional Hutsul home craft is displayed in the **Museum of Hutsul Folk Art** (Teatralna 25; open 10.00–18.00, closed Monday; entrance 2UAH). Decorated stove tiles, hand-embroidered national dress, ornate wood axes, rugs and wooden dishes exhibit the unique style of Ukraine's hutsuls. In the very centre of Kolomiya is the town's real pride and joy: the museum of brightly coloured Easter eggs built in the shape of a brightly coloured Easter egg. The **Pysanky Museum** (Chornovola 27B; open 10.00–17.00, closed Monday; entrance 5UAH) is a monument to the most Ukrainian of Ukrainian crafts: the intricate, layered colouring of blown-out eggshells. *Pysanky* designs are drawn with melted wax, and then dyed in different colours for each design (usually red, yellow, orange, brown and black). Every region in Ukraine has its own specific colours and patterns and the museum displays them all, as well as some talented submissions by the Ukrainian diaspora in Canada. Sadly, photographs are prohibited.

Getting there and away

Kolomiya is on the main railroad train between Chernivtsi and the west; the station is on the north side of town on Krypyakevycha. Daily trains service Ivano-Frankivsk (4 times a day, 2 hours) , Uzhgorod, Chernivtsi (over 2 hours), and Lviv (6 hours), and there are overnight connections to Odessa and Kharkiv every other day. Kolomiya's excellent connections make it a good alternative base from which to venture into the Carpathians via Kosiv. The bus station is a ten-minute walk from the town centre at the end of Hrushevskovo and this is the more convenient way to zip quickly between the smaller towns. Buses make constant trips to Chernivtsi for around US$1 (1½ hours), Ivano-Frankivsk (1 hour), Ternopil and Kamyanets-Podilsky. Marshrutka also make frequent runs to Yaremche, Kosiv and Verkhovyna. As always, from Kolomiya there is a daily bus to practically anywhere in the Carpathians, it is simply a matter of deciding if that is the best option.

Where to stay and eat
The town's modern hotel is the aptly named **Hotel Pysanky** (Chornovola 41; tel: 03433 203 56; fax: 03433 202 04; email: hotel@yes.ko.if.ua), located directly across from the museum and only recently completed. Rooms are new, light and clean with continuous hot water (showers) and top service; prices are middle range from US$50–80. A less expensive option, **On the Corner** (Hetmanska 47a; tel: 03433 274 37) is a cosy bed and breakfast costing US$15/night per person. **Hal-Prut** at Chornovola 43 is the restaurant next door and serves 'high' Ukrainian food. Another restaurant, the **Karpaty** (Teatralna 15) aims to please the touristy palate with Carpathian dishes.

THE GORGANY RANGE – ГОРГАНИ
For all those travellers who feel they have yet to see the 'wild' part of the Carpathians, the Gorgany range is a place of refuge and complete peace. Far from the paved mountain trails and garish tourist markets (and far from everything else), the Gorgany is Ukraine's most remote area. They are called the 'Gorgons' for the fluorescent yellow-green lichens that grow on the rocky scree on the highest parts of these mountains. Unscathed forest cloak the slopes with hundred-foot pine trees where an active birdlife make the only noise around. The Eastern Gorgany are more accessible to hikers from Yaremche and include the angular peaks of **Mount Khomyak** (1,544m), **Mount Synyak** (1,664m), **Mount Gorgan** (1,595m) and **Dovbushanka** (1,757m). The Central Gorgany are more remote and present splendid views of seemingly never-ending mountains. The main peaks include **Mount Grofa** (1,752m), **Mount Popadya** (1,740m) **Mount Igrovets** (1,804m), and the highest, **Mount Syvulya** (1,818m). Ukrainian partisans fought on these very mountains and the summits of Popadya and Syvulya are still marked by rocky trenches used in the eastern front during World War I. Through this central valley flows the River Limnytsya – a rare and unspoiled waterway that holds the unofficial title as Europe's cleanest river (a taste of the water is convincing).

Access to the Central Gorgany is through **Osmoloda**, a spread of houses over 10km. Osmoloda's name comes from an old Hutsul folk tale: An evil dragon living in the Gorgany looked down in the valley at a young couple about to be married. Jealous, he stole away the maiden and watched the heartbroken young man searching for his *moloda* (betrothed). When he asked the dragon where she was, the dragon turned her into a rock and said *Os* ('There!'). **Mount Moloda** (1,723m) is the drooping peak directly east from Osmoloda. The dirt path into the valley and up to the mountains starts after the entrance sign with the deer on it.

Getting there and away
Getting to Osmoloda is part of the adventure; most Ukrainians have never heard of the village. It is best to take a bus from Lviv or Ivano-Frankivsk to Dolyna (the bus station is next to the bustling market). From Dolyna there are rare but direct buses and taxis to the village of Osmoloda via Yasen, along the Limnytsya River. The journey from Dolyna takes around two hours. If you are going on a long hike with a fair amount of equipment, arranging a car and driver from a larger city may be the best option.

Walks in the Gorgany range
The best walks leave from Osmoloda, but going into the eastern Gorgany is easier from Tatariv. Ambitious hikers can connect the two and walk the entire range from one end to another over a week through the village of Bystrytsya.

Three peaks
A remote hike through the thickest of woods, with steep rises and falls and some incredible vistas.

Day 1 From Osmoloda, take the western trail for 2km. Cross the river at the bridge and follow the trail on the right side of the stream into the forest and up into the hills. As the incline begins to level out at the ridge, there is a dingy mountain hut and campsite. (*11km; 5 hours*)

Day 2 Hike up the steep right hand slope to the top of Grofa. From the top you can see through the twin peaks of Parenky. Go back down to the ridge and hike across towards the top of Parenky (1,737m). From here it is another 5km to the top of Popadya, marked by the old Polish border post from 1923. Return back to the wooded ridge that drops steeply; there is a camp at the top.

Day 3 A long day of getting back to Osmoloda. Descend from the camp and follow the wooded hillside for much of the way. About a third of the way you cross over a top of a small waterfall, loop around and follow the northern shore of the stream until it joins with the river Limnytsia and goes back to Osmoloda. (*17km; about 8 hours' walking*)

Syvulya and Igrovets
Two mountains in two days.

Day 1 Walk south from Osmoloda along the eastern riverbank for 7km, take a left on the trail that follows the stream Bystryk up to the underside of Syvulya where there is a hut and campsite. (*13km; about 6 hours' walking*)

Day 2 Climb to the top of Syvulya, then take the northern trail for 6km to the summit of Igrovets. The path then descends towards the northwest back down through the forest to the river Limnytsya. It is 2km to Osmoloda. (*15km; 7 hours' walking*)

The Eastern Gorgany
Long but fulfilling days.

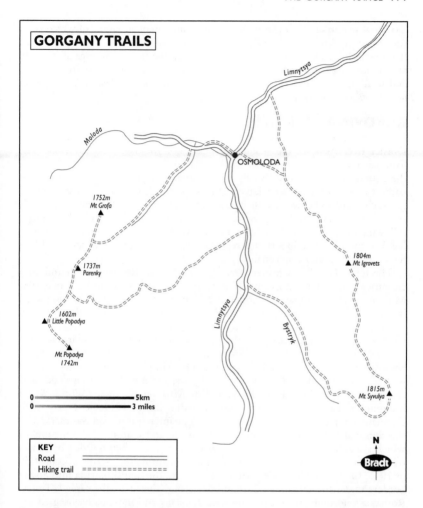

Day trip to Mount Khomyak From the train station at Tatariv, take the fork in the road towards Yablunytsya. Continue for 4km until a bridge turns the road to a hard left – there is a petrol station on the right. Do not cross the bridge, but continue on the right-hand path along the stream for 1km more. Before the next stream there should be a perpendicular trail on the right. Ascend here, eventually crossing over to the left-hand side and into a high mountain glade. Take this trail on the left-hand side up to Khomyak's summit. From the peak, there is a straight view of the three other peaks: Synyak, Gorgan and Dovbushanka. Continue along the opposite ridge towards Synyak, but then drop down on the right-hand trail which goes back to the Zhenets River and on to the main road where there is a bus stop to Tatariv. (*16km; about 7 hours*)

To Synyak and Gorgon Follow the same trail as to Khomyak, but continue on the ridge. You will have to split the trip to at least two days. There are campsites at the northern and western base of Synyak. (*Add 7km one way from Khomyak; 3 hours*)

To Dovbushanka The main trail is 21km from Yaremche, some of which is on uneventful road following the River Zhonka. It is possible to connect to the peak from Synyak by taking the trail that curves along the mountain ridge all the way around the valley and up the west side of Dovbushanka, a 14km hike from Synyak and an all-day feat. (*The trail from Dovbushanka to Syvulya takes 2 days with a stop in or near the village of Bystrytsya*)

BUKOVINA – БУКОВИНА

Charming and eccentric, tiny Bukovina fills the sliver of land between the Prut and Dnister rivers beneath the shadow of next door Moldavia and Romania. The fortunate few who make it this far will be amazed at the quiet, enchanted nature of the countryside. Life passes slowly in this strange corner of Ukraine. Traffic is happy to wait for the conversations of old men to finish and there are more horses, goats, chickens and cows than there are people. Like most of Ukraine, giant fields surround the view, but here they seem to roll away from the road in deep waves, following the rhythm of the nearby mountains. The one exception to Bukovina's hand-to-mouth farm life is the regional capital Chernivtsi, which holds on fervently to its peculiar personality.

The territory's oldest castles were built by Kievan Rus in the 9th and 10th centuries, but after the Mongol invasions the area was incorporated into Moldovia – an event that has defined this land ever since. The Turks conquered in 1504 after which the region was ruled for nearly 300 years by the Ottoman Empire – the eastern flare of Khotin castle dates back to this period. An Austrian victory in 1774 bought the area under the jurisdiction of Galicia and it was made a Hapsburg duchy in 1849, followed by a period revered as the height of Bukovinian culture and advancement. The shifting 20th century caused widespread emigration of Ruthenians and Jews, and it is these groups and their descendants who have mentally kept Bukovina on the map. World War I brought the Eastern Front right into Bukovina and in 1919 the Treaty of St Germain granted the territory to Romania. The inter-war period was marked by the dominant influence of Romanian language and culture, the remnants of which are still in place today. Northern Bukovina was then invaded by Soviet troops in 1940, but went back to the Romanians during the German occupation of 1941. In 1947 Stalin made a secret agreement, moving Bukovina into Soviet borders under the Ukrainian SSR and declaring Chernivtsi the capital. Today, Romania's northern region is still called *Bucovina* and most natives regard the entire area as a single region divided by a false border. On the other hand, Kiev looks proudly upon Ukraine's youngest province as the birthplace of national heroes and a home to Ukrainian patriotism. The reality is that Bukovina is still an odd mix of people and cultures that have more or less gotten along despite the constant shift of power. Variety is the region's most attractive feature, after the landscapes.

CHERNIVTSI – ЧЕРНІВЦІ

You will know when you have met someone from Chernivtsi because they will make sure that you know – the capital and only real city of Bukovina deserves to be proud of its intricate and faded buildings and its diverse citizenship. Even after the most dire economic crises, Chernivtsi has not lost the dignity of its past empire and few urban spaces in modern Ukraine make such an *interesting* visit. Recent ad campaigns have tried to sell the town as 'little Paris' but this is an ill comparison, if not utterly far-fetched. Instead, the locals' conviction that their city is in fact the centre of Europe seems more *à propos*.

The city began as a Galician fortress on the Prut River, soon destroyed by the Mongol invasions. Some say the black oak timber influenced the town's name, others say it describes the black soil of Bukovina; however, in old Ukrainian, *Chern-ovtsy* means 'black sheep' – an apt connotation for this city, whether or not the pun was intended. Among the family of Ukrainian cities, Chernivtsi still stands out as a bit of an odd place (seeing is believing). The city's Moldavian medieval existence was based in steady trade, a feature that attracted consistent ransacking from both friends and enemies and prevented any permanent structures. After gaining control in 1774, the Austrians scheduled Chernivtsi for a makeover. What had been a haphazard gathering of thatched cabins was quickly transformed into an ordered radius of streets lined with exquisite and colourful buildings, including a green opera house, stately pink and blue townhouses, and the magnificent brick residence of the Orthodox Metropolitans (the second highest-ranking officials in the Orthodox Church). Austrian rule over 'Czernowitz' lasted 250 years during which time an extremely cosmopolitan population developed. The city ranked third in size for the empire – after Vienna and Prague – and an independent stock exchange made many inhabitants wealthy. Granted its own university, Chernivtsi offered a home to the rising Ukrainian intellectualism of the late 19th century (this is the 'home' of the present Ukrainian national anthem). The movement suffered during World War I and was all but stamped out during Romania's control of 'Cernauti' from 1918 to 1940, followed by annexation to the Soviet Union. Due to its European past, Russian 'Chernovtsy' was far more advanced than the other Soviet cities in terms of technology (and ideas), and in a way the city was never designated a permanent role in communist society. During the lean years of post-Soviet collapse, Chernivtsi secured its reputation in free trade by starting the largest outdoor market in Ukraine, still booming today. It is no surprise that Chernivtsi was the first city in Ukraine to tear down its statue of Lenin on the main square and replace it with a sizeable effigy of Shevchenko.

Visiting Chernivtsi today is a purposeful venture into the unique persona of Bukovina and western Ukraine. The city still claims almost 100 nationalities as its own; Russians, Jews, Poles and Romanians are the most sizeable and influential minorities. General sightseeing is anything but average and lovers of art and architecture will find contentment in the many churches and museums. Conveniently situated on the route between the Carpathian Mountains and the Black Sea, Chernivtsi makes a gratifying stopover or allows an alternative connection to the mountains from Kiev. If you are entering or leaving the country from the south, the city is the most significant transfer point between Ukraine and Romania.

Getting there and away

One flight per day connects Chernivtsi to Kiev (weekdays only). The airport is rather undeveloped, located in the southeastern outskirts; a taxi into town costs around US$1. During summer, flights serve Kharkiv and Simferopol.

Chernivtsi train station, a noteworthy monument to *belle époque* architecture, was built in 1908 and is located on the northern side of town on Gagarina. Two overnight trains connect with Kiev, one in the early evening and the other around 21.30. The earlier train is longer (around 15 hours) but gets to Kiev the following morning. Both Kiev–Chernivtsi trains stop in Kamyanets-Podilsky, making it an obvious stop along the way. Chernivtsi is situated at an odd rail intersection, increasing travel time to its closest cities. Ovenight trains go to and from Odessa (almost 20 hours) and Uzhgorod (15 hours) once a day. Twice a day there are trains to Ivano-Frankivsk (4 hours) and Kolomiya (2 hours). International train routes leave everyday for Sofia (via Bucharest), Moscow (via Kiev), and Kishinev (Moldavia). A lot of smaller trains enter Romania throughout the day, the border being only 40km away.

Chernivtsi's Central Bus Station at the south end of Holovna offers the most options for connecting locally with two daily buses to Kamyanets-Podilsky (2½ hours), three to Ivano-Frankivsk (4 hours), two to Lviv (8 hours), three to Khmelnytsky (6 hours) and two to Uzhgorod (14 hours). An overnight connection travels back and forth from Kiev (via Zhytomyr) and local marshrutkas go to Kolomiya, Yaremche and Truskavets. Buses into Romania and Moldova are frequent; Kishinev is nine hours away, Bucharest a day and a half.

City transportation
The #5 trolleybus runs up and down Holovna and will take you to most places you want to go. Much of the centre is more accessible on foot rather than rumbling down on cobblestones, but the hotels and some attractions are quite far and will require a taxi. For some reason, the wily taxi drivers of Chernivtsi think they are worth more than any others in provincial Ukraine and often charge Kiev-like prices. Around town, don't agree to over US$2–3; and going out to the countryside will be US$10. Don't be afraid to barter a little.

Internet
Finding access is a bit more tricky in Chernivtsi, hence the listing. **Infocom** is the most central and convenient. Besides fast internet, they offer inexpensive international calls; Central Square 9; email: infocom@chv.ukrpack.net; web: http://www.chv.ukrpack.net;

Where to stay
Chernivtsi is bound to attract crowds of visitors and compared with most of Ukraine, there will be enough decent accommodation for all. **Hotel Cheremosh** (Komarova 13a; tel: 03722 475 00; fax: 03722 413 14; email: cheremosh@intour.chernovtsy.ua) is the tall, modern, high-rise hotel complex on the far southern edge of town. The hotel stands as a rare product of mid-1980s perestroika when a Hungarian-Soviet joint venture embarked on an early investment. The final product is the finest in Communist construction and visitors may feel like they are on a cruise ship with the high atrium, all the in-house amenities and smiley staff. Besides the normal swimming pool, sauna and live shows, the hotel does dry cleaning and supports a strong and creative travel agency that designs personal excursions on a local and national level. Rooms are new and clean with above average bathrooms. Singles are US$45; doubles US$55. The spacious and modern suites cost US$80–90. A very large restaurant is divided into three separate rooms, each with its own décor, music and cuisine: European, Bukovinian and Hungarian. (The Bukovinian menu is convincing and authentic.)

Chernivtsi's new business set claim **Hotel Bukovina** (Holovna 141; tel: 0372 585 625; email: bc-buk@sacura.net; web: www.hotel.cv.ua) as their very own chintzy hangout. Your eyes can't miss the cheery flowerboxes hanging along the bright yellow building, while inside a steady renovation has transformed most of the rooms into comfortable and modern rooms, usually with showers. The new rooms cost US$50–80/night and a range of zany suites go for US$150–300. What the hotel lacks in class, the restaurant makes up for in amusement. The largest dining hall is a memorial to Hapsburg glory, while the backroom is a converted Bukovinian farmhouse, complete with costumed waiters and life-size, papier-mache oxen. The food is traditional and inexpensive. On the second floor, there is

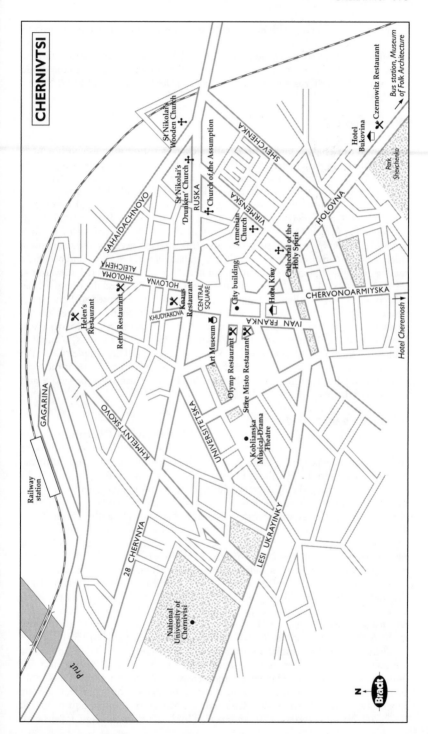

CHERNIVTSI

St Nikolai's Wooden Church

Bus station, Museum of Folk Architecture

Czernowitz Restaurant

Hotel Bukovina

Park Shevchenko

St Nikolai's 'Drunken Church'

Church of the Assumption

RUSKA

SHEVCHENKA

VIRMENSKA

Armenian Church

Cathedral of the Holy Spirit

SAHAIDACHNOVO

HOLOVNA

SHOLOMA ALEICHEMA

Hotel Kiev

City building

HOLOVNA

Helen's Restaurant

Retro Restaurant

Knaus Restaurant

CHERVONOARMIYSKA

KHUDYAKOVA

CENTRAL SQUARE

Art Museum

Olymp Restaurant

Stare Misto Restaurant

IVAN FRANKA

Hotel Cheremosh

GAGARINA

KHMELNYTSKOVO

UNIVERSITETSKA

Koblianska Musical-Drama Theatre

Railway station

LESI UKRAYINKY

28 CHERVNYA

National University of Chernivtsi

Prut

N

Bradt

a walk-in tourist bureau with good connections for making arrangements around Chernivtsi; tel: 0372 585-636.

Hotel Kiev (Holovna 46; tel: 0372 224 83) has the best location in the city centre and is the least expensive. Some of the grand past still clings to the dingy carpets and hot water is a sporadic perk. Singles/doubles are US$12/$17; 'suites' cost US$30.

Where to eat

A wide spectrum of restaurants and a choice of lively cafés mean people in Chernivtsi can enjoy a night out. A rather characteristic eating establishment is **Retro** (Sholoma Aleichema 1; tel: 0372 55 09 62). The restaurant occupies the famous 'Ship' building (constructed to look like a naval craft) and has been open for business longer than anywhere else. The food is mainly Ukrainian and the service quite sophisticated. A person would find it difficult to spend more than US$10 here. **Czernowitz** restaurant is part of the Bukovina Hotel complex (see above) and is perceived to be the city's finest. Besides the super lavish fare, they serve a yummy version of mamaliga, the Bukovinian speciality consisting of a thick, savoury cornflour porridge, similar to Italian *polenta*. *Lederhosen* and beer kegs seem a little out of place in Chernivtsi, but people come to **Knaus** (Khudyakova 4; tel: 0372 510 255) for the lively ambience, real German food and the outdoor beer garden. **Olymp** (Ivan Franka 1-3; tel: 0372 542 979) is supposed to be a Greek restaurant but the Corinthian columns do little to hide the gangster touch. Practically next door is the more intimate and convincing **Stare Misto** (Ivan Franka 7); food-wise, they stick to old favourites. Last but not least is the hidden underground café, **Helen's** (Khelen; Sahaidachnovo 2). This simple 'Christian bar' is universally known for some of the best cooking in Bukovina and is the right place to taste the real thing, especially borscht. The café also lacks the smoke and loud music that usually goes with the territory.

What to see and do

The fanciful brick complex of the **National University of Chernivtsi** should not be missed. Built between 1864 and 1882, the impressive chapel and halls were the official residence for the Orthodox Church leaders of Bukovina and Dalmatia, the two duchies in the Hapsburg Empire with strong eastern rite populations. In this one structure, the Czech architect Josef Hlávka envisioned something remarkably different from his more classical buildings in Vienna, of which there are over 140. Working entirely with standard red bricks and brightly coloured tiles, his design blends elaborate geometric patterns with the traditional Byzantine styles of Orthodoxy into something that resembles a giant Lego castle with hundreds of playful chimneys and miniature turrets. The university was founded in 1875 making it one of Ukraine's oldest, though the school's headquarters was not moved to this location until after the Soviet occupation. Entering the chapel is a highlight of the visit, with its painted mosaics and lofty dome. Behind the main building is a nice garden of rare tree species tended by the university, including the squatty *platan* tree, endemic to Bukovina. For a guided tour, go to the guardhouse at the main entrance gate (at the end of Universytetska), or call 0372 584 821.

The **Kobylianska Muscial-Drama Theatre** is the green opera house on Ploscha Teatralna, famed now for its first public performance of the Ukrainian national anthem, nearly one hundred years ago. Inexpensive tickets to very talented shows can be purchased on site, and the square out front is a busy centre for nightlife. Only one block away is the **Chernivetsky Regional Art Museum**; (Central Square 10; tel: 0372 260 71; open 09.00–17.30; entrance 3UAH). The art nouveau façade with mosaic inlay survives as a work of art in itself while inside a collection of sentimental Bukovinian paintings portrays rural life of the past century. The **Chernivtsi Museum of Folk Architecture** resembles the outdoor museum villages in Kiev and Lviv but with a specific focus on preserving traditional Bukovinian houses and churches; open 10.00–17.00, closed Monday; entrance 1UAH, guided tours 5UAH. To get there take the #4 trolleybus to the end of the line, or even better, a taxi.

The churches in Chernivtsi fortunately missed the wrath of the Russian Revolution and most have undergone recent renovation; a few merit closer investigation than a glance from the street. The **Cathedral of the Holy Spirit** was built in 1844 and stands today as a pale pink, neo-classical cathedral topped with very Polish-looking cupolas. Austrian painters of the late 19th century painted the larger interior murals for which the church is known today. Chernivtsi boasts **two churches of St Nikolai.** The first is an eight-sided log chapel built in 1607, with animal hair and hemp twine still wedged between the cracks to keep out the wind. This is one of the few original wood buildings in Chernivtsi and the city's oldest church; Sahaidachnovo 89. The other St Nikolai was built in the 1930s and boasts five bright blue domes with golden stars. The cathedral's twisted turrets create an optical illusion that has led to this being called the 'drunken church'; Ruska 35. Another block down Ruska is the red-roofed Greek Catholic **Church of the Assumption**. The **Armenian Church** (Ukrayinska 30) is another one of Hlávka's buildings, but was used as an organ hall throughout the Soviet years on the pretext that a suicide in the chapel made it unfit for worship.

If you are tired of looking at old churches and the crumbling glory of the Hapsburgs, a more fresh and lively attraction is **Kalynivksy Market**, just a short trip outside the city. The expansive mile-wide outdoor shopping spread is a testament to the capitalist rudiments of human nature. After Moscow's economic collapse, Chernivtsi was left to fend for itself and would easily have gone the way of so many derelict Ukrainian towns if it had not been for some innovative locals who founded the grand-scale swap-meet in a farmer's field. Now much of Ukraine supplies its own bazaars with hard-to-get luxuries from Poland, Romania and Turkey, all exchanged in Chernivtsi's market. Here, anyone can buy anything, but the recent mood has become more pragmatic and sophisticated: fur coats, designer boots, high-tech kitchenware and *real* Barbie dolls. The change in goods does not detract from the chaos of 50,000 daily visitors. Kalynivsky is the easiest place to get to in Chernivtsi. Most marshrutka head to the *rynok* from all over town and the train station and a taxi costs US$1, or take the #9 trolleybus to the end.

OUTSIDE CHERNIVTSI
Khotyn – Хотин
On the way to Kamyanets-Podilsky from Chernivtsi stands one of Ukraine's more famous castles, fortified by Moldavian prince Stefan III in the 15th century and later occupied by the Ottoman Empire. The Moldavians rebelled against the Turks in 1621 and allied themselves to the Polish king, Sigismund III. Furious, the Turkish Sultan Osman II responded with an overwhelming attack that met its climax at Khotyn. As told, a quarter of a million Turkish troops charged Khotyn Castle on camels, mules and elephants during the famed Battle of Khotyn. The Polish prince, Sobieski, described the battle: 'More than 60 cannons were roaring without cease, the sky was burning, the air was darkened with smoke, and the ground trembled.' The Polish forces quashed the Turkish advance with a measly corps of 35,000 and today the Ukrainians claim it was the strength of 'their' fortress and the cunning command of the Cossack hetman Sahaidachny that granted the Poles a victory and sent the Turks packing all the way to Constantinople. In fact,

the Turks conquered Khotyn in 1711 and the castle flip-flopped dozens of times between the Russians and Turks until 1812 when the Treaty of Bucharest secured its Russian ownership. Visitors can climb the highest towers and sturdy walls to enjoy the view of the Dnistr and the wide Podillyan plain. Almost every group tour in the region will stop at Khotin, and each of Chernivtsi's hotels offer inexpensive day trips to the castle. On your own, Khotin is a one-and-a-half-hour bus ride from Chernivtsi's bus station or one hour from Kamyanets-Podilsky.

Vyzhnytsya – Вижниця

Bukovina's other town attracts nostalgic visitors seeking a glimpse of the poetic *shtetl* life in Yiddish folklore. Quaint and introspective, little imagination is needed to understand the past of the village. However, modern-day Vyzhnytsya appeals less than the surrounding areas south of the Cheremosh River and in the nearby mountains. The bubbly streams, green walks, and traditional Bukovinian farms led to the creation of **Vyzhnytsya National Park** in 1995. Still young and fragile, the protected areas are tough to get to on your own (in Chernivtsi, try the tour agency Navkolo Svitu who offer some trips; Central Square 7/8; tel: 0372 585 263; email: ns@ns-tour.com.ua). Over ten buses a day zip back and forth between Vyzhnytsya and the Chernivtsi bus station (1½ hours) and offer a superb view of the 'real Bukovina'; Kosiv is only 15 minutes away by bus or taxi. The restaurant **Kolyba** in Vyzhnytsya is the regular touristy log-hut setting, similar to those seen throughout the Carpathians – and is the only place to eat in the area.

TRANSCARPATHIA – ЗАКАРПАТТИЯ

Za-Karpattya translates from Ukrainian as 'Beyond the Carpathians', which it is, from Kiev's perspective. From Budapest, this is the borderland between the great

UKRAINE'S ROMANIANS

The extent of Romanian influence among the people of the Carpathians remains a sticky issue for the present fervour of the Ukrainian nationalist renaissance. Bukovina stands out as one definite area where clear signs of Romanian culture and language have held out for over a millennium – an obvious fact for a territory that once belonged to Romania. Today, the densest population of Ukraine's ethnic Romanians reside in southeast Bukovina – just a few miles from the border – but a world apart from the 150,000 who speak Romanian and whose relatives live on the other side. The seemingly inappropriate demarcation can be blamed on Stalin, though. Eastern Europe is generally notorious for mismatched nations and states. The Ukrainian government grants certain privileges to these ethnic Romanians: education is bilingual and special permits allow frequent cross-border travel. At the same time, a central policy of total Ukrainianisation seeks to lessen 'otherness' inside Ukraine's borders. Travellers interested in seeing this unique part of Ukraine should take a taxi (or bus) from Chernivtsi southeast towards the villages of Hertsa, Ternavka, and Dyakovtsy. The trip takes about 45 minutes and passes through some lovely and very remote countryside where change is distinct: only Romanian is spoken, and the separate culture is evident in the food, signs, and memorials that all reflect a very separate culture. A significant number of ethnic Romanians also live in Transcarpathia, while on the flip side over 40,000 ethnic Ukrainians are indigenous to northern Romania.

Hungarian plain and the 'Russian Hills'. A visit to Transcarpathia offers a different take on these mountains and its people, since the region was considered part of the Hungarian Empire for over a millennium. Purposefully left off the larger rail and road networks, the region is often dropped from itineraries through the west, usually because everyone simply passes through the regional capital on to the next place, or else they cross over to 'Ukraine' for a day before slipping back into Slovakia or Hungary. Uzhgorod remains forever the gateway from Central Europe to Ukraine, but the region deserves some deeper investigation than its border city. Not long ago the towns of Mukachevo and Khust offered a picturesque 'European' tour to bemused masses of Soviet day trippers. Today, the really beautiful landscapes stretch along the entire south side of the Carpathian range, just now entering a stage of discovery by foreign travellers and the locals themselves. In the far east of the region, Rakhiv and Yasinya are still known as Transcarpathia's mountain towns, but these are more accessible from (and closer to) Ivano-Frankivsk. The space between the mountains and Uzhgorod is now open for exploration. New national parks (the Carpathian Biosphere Reserve) and recent investment mean there are countless fresh trails to be trodden through Transcarpathia.

After the Hungarian takeover in the 9th century, Transcarpathian history belonged to another country. It seemed that renewed treaties with the Austrians and consistent Ruthenian uprisings characterised the territory more than its natural treasures and Ruthenian people. World War I brought an end to Hapsburg rule, so that from 1919 Transcarpathian Rus fell under the jurisdiction of the fated inter-war Czechoslovak Republic. The confusion in Prague preceding Hitler's invasion allowed a brief taste of freedom when the independent Carpatho-Ukraine was established in 1938. For the non-Soviet Ukrainians of Romania and Polish Galicia, this was a vital step towards a joint Ukrainian state, but the thrill of self-government was ended with Adolf Hitler's support of the Hungarian invasion of Carpatho-Ukraine in the spring of 1939. The local Ukrainians were suspicious of the Red Army's 'liberation' of Transcarpathia and the subsequent 're-unification' to the Ukrainian SSR in 1945. However, as a late arrival on the Soviet scene, Transcarpathia has a very different feel from the rest of the country. This is easily the least Slavic region of Ukraine, and many of the Ukrainian inhabitants can freely communicate in Hungarian, Slovakian or Russian, if not all three at the same time.

UZHGOROD – УЖГОРОД

Transcarpathia's largest city is often a visitor's first impression of Ukraine, although travellers coming from the west would do better to consider this their last stop in Hungary. Uzhgorod's location and history have made the city the travel and trade outpost between 'Europe' and that area now described in euphemisms: the Former Soviet Union, the Newly Independent States, the East, or the CIS).

The town centres on the right bank of the winding Uzh ('Snake') River; 'gorod' is Slavic for 'city'. The *Gesta Hungarorum* ('Hungarian *Chronicle*') mentions the invasion of the Hungarian army into the city of Ung in 872, where the local Slavic prince was killed. Since then, the city has been known as Ongvar, Hungvar, Unguyvar, and Ungvar – all references to the town's Magyar roots. (Backpackers who've just finished a tour through Europe often slap their jaw and exclaim how much Uzhgorod looks like Hungary.) Because of its proximity to 'Europe', Uzhgorod is bound to become Ukraine's busiest entry and exit point, as well as an attractive destination in its own right.

Walking around the town is a pleasure, especially along the *naberezhna*, or riverbank, and around the botanical gardens. When Eastern Europe went free market, Uzhgorod stepped to the head of the class and local *beezness* keeps a swanky attitude in the midst of the city's natural architectural charm – even the Soviet high-rises seem a bit more polished than normal.

Travellers doing a tour of Ukraine by land would do well to consider starting or ending their circuit in Uzhgorod and then returning home via Budapest, only seven hours away by train. Some excursions into rural Transcarpathia begin here, but the transport network means that Mukachevo and Rakhiv have better access to these southern mountains.

Getting there and away

Catching a plane to and from Uzhgorod is easier than most Ukrainian cities of this size. Normally, at least one flight a day travels to Kiev Zhulyany (1½ hours) while links with other Ukrainian destinations vary. The airport is at Sobranetska 145 but air tickets are best booked at the Inturist agency at the Hotel Zakarpattya, or any other hotel in Uzhgorod. The train station is at Stantsiyna 9 at the south end of the town and not far away is the bus station at Stantsiyna 2. Four daily trains rumble back and forth between Kiev and Uzhgorod, always via Lviv, then through Chop or Mukachevo. On average, the rail journey takes 18 hours, and the slowest part is the last link to and from Lviv. Very slow trains also service Chernivtsi (14 hours), Vinnytsya (15 hours), and Kharkiv (30 hours) but Uzhgorod schedules frequently change. Travelling anywhere else in the Carpathians from Uzhgorod is best by motor transport; buses cross the mountains throughout the day to Ivano-Frankivsk (6 hours), Rakhiv (4 hours), and Chernivtsi (9 hours).

Where to stay and eat

The most central hotel off the main bridge is **Hotel Uzhgorod** (Bohdana Khmelnytskovo Square 2; tel: 0312 235 060). Most of the rooms have been renovated and cost about three times as much as the rooms from Soviet days, but there really is something for every budget and expectation of comfort. Regular singles cost around US$12, while the nicer 'luxury' suites are US$80. Hot water runs on schedule for a few hours each day and Hotel Uzhgorod can arrange pickups from either border. The privately owned and operated **Atlant Hotel** (Koryatovycha Square 27; tel: 0312 614 095; email: reception@hotel-atlant.com; web: www.hotel-atlant.com) exhibits the unique style of modern Uzhgorod and offers both security and comfort. Singles are US$25, doubles US$40–55; credit cards accepted. The central location, 24-hour hot water supply and a high standard of service make this the hotel of choice. Atlant's Hungarian restaurant is also a cut above the rest. Most group tours will stay at the towering Inturist hotel, **Zakarpattya** (Kirila i Mefodiya Square 5; tel: 0312 297 510). Location is not great at the far southern side of the city, but the regular Inturist amenities can facilitate travel arrangements and help with local excursions. Hotel prices range from US$25 to $50, while a number of coffee shops and a very large restaurant attract tourist crowds. **Hotel Druzhba** (Vysoka 12; tel: 0312 237 233) is the other Soviet-age hotel, albeit a touch more classy; . The view from the north side of the city means it is a pleasant walk into the city, and the quiet and wooded neighbourhood in the hills attracts Uzhgorod's business crowd for weekend conferences. If you are driving in your own car, this is a safe hotel to park at; prices range from US$20 to US$70. Another car-friendly hotel, **'Eduard'** (Bachynsky 22; tel: 0312 213 355; email: eduard@eduard.utel.net.ua; web: www.eduard.com.ua) is a brand-new, privately owned accommodation northeast of the city centre. Besides very clean rooms and bathrooms with 24-hour hot water, a restaurant, sauna and pool fulfil its description of 'lux'. All rooms are over US$50/night.

CROSSING BORDERS TO AND FROM UZHGOROD

Uzhgorod feels so different from the rest of Ukraine, that many forget they are still in Ukraine; the familiarity also means Uzhgorod is fast becoming the most popular entryway into Ukraine for European travellers. Uzhgorod is right on the Slovakian-Ukrainian border and the willing can simply walk across by following Sobranetska Street all the way to the Slovakian border post in the direction of Sobrance. Otherwise, Kosice is the point of arrival and departure for most public transportation (trains and buses) between Uzhgorod and Slovakia; the train from Kiev to Bratislava stops only in Chop.

The Hungarian border crossing is located at Chop, 20 minutes (without traffic) south of Uzhgorod. Trains to and from Uzhgorod normally pass through Chop (on their way to Kiev for instance) but taking a bus or taxi is the best way to get from the border to Uzhgorod. From Ukraine, the daily rail services Kiev–Budapest and Kiev–Prague pass through Chop, but sometimes you can reduce a long border wait by taking one of many buses from Uzhgorod across the border. From Hungary, the closest stop to the border is at Kisvarda, while the closest junction is at Nyíregyháza; more than three buses a day go to and from these cities and Uzhgorod. The trip between Chop and Budapest takes about seven hours by rail and costs around US$35; Budapest's morning train will put you in Uzhgorod in the afternoon, while a later service arrives in Chop at odd times of the night. Also, I have heard stories of travellers being forced to buy health insurance as they come into Ukraine at this border, but the practice is probably being phased out.

Restaurants have long been integrated with the hotels in Uzhgorod, the Hungarian room at **Zakarpattya** being the most renowned, but sophisticated new restaurants are in the works throughout the city centre and coffee shops along the Naberezhna serve lethal little thimblefuls of Hungarian espresso. Delicious food and a heavy dose of Carpathian mirth are on offer at **Detsa U Notarya** (Gagarina 98; tel: 0312 224 922), Uzhgorod's happiest restaurant. Traditional Transcarpathian food, average prices and lively ambience make it popular among visitors to Uzhgorod.

What to see

Most attractions fill the old city and a walk down Kapitulna will take in Uzhgorod's most famous historical remnants, culminating at the hilltop **Castle** above the bend in the river. The present ruin stands from the 13th century although the construction began in the 9th century and continued well into the 1600s. The glorified pile of stones was a hotbed of Hungarian-Romanian fighting for centuries. Next door to the castle is the **Museum of Local History**; Kapitulna 33. Despite the outdated set-up, a tour of the museum is more stimulating than average, reflecting Uzhgorod's eventful past. The **Museum of Folk Architecture** spreads out just across the street with over 30 examples of traditional Transcarpathian buildings, mostly reflecting the styles of Lemko and Boiki ethnic groups and including the 16th-century wooden **St Michael's Church.** In the summer, frequent festivals and markets in the park play up the nostalgic peasant past.

Uzhgorod's eclectic churches are famous throughout Central and Eastern Europe for their playful design and colour: the twin towers of the **Catholic**

Cathedral on Kapitulna are an Uzhgorod landmark, while the fanciful pink and red **Russian Orthodox Church** resembles a cheerful cake. What is now the very grand, albeit pink Uzhgorod Philharmonic was once the city's elegant **Synagogue** (Yevgena Fentsyka 10).

MUKACHEVO – МУКАЧЕВО

Thanks to recent renovation, the medieval citadel of Mukachevo rests immaculately atop the city's single highest hill, overlooking the green Latorytsya river valley. The red-roofed Palanok castle proved vital in defending the Austrian empire from eastern invasion and it is one of Ukraine's most scenic. During Hungarian rule, the town was known as Munkacs, remembered best as the notorious Jewish *shtetl* from which so many were deported to the camps at Auschwitz. Today, visitors can tour the castle complex and roam through the quiet streets; other sights include the Hungarian Catholic Church and a 14th-century convent.

Getting there and away

Once a day overnight trains from Kiev to Budapest, Belgrade, and Zagreb all make their final Ukrainian stop in Mukachevo, and the reverse is true for the Hungarian and Yugoslavian trains that make their first stop here before heading to Kiev. This means the closest domestic connection is on these routes between Mukachevo, Lviv, and Ternopil. Rail service between Uzhgorod and Mukachevo is usually once a day, usually in the middle of the day on the train from Kiev. A bus or taxi will take under an hour.

Where to stay and eat

Across from the town hall, **Hotel Zirka** (Mir 8; tel: 03131 225 31) is the one and only hotel in Mukachevo for the time being. A nice restaurant, pool and sauna make things comfortable; rooms cost US$30–60.

The Black Sea –
Чорне Море

Half land, half water, Ukraine's southern coastline surrenders vaguely to the Black Sea in a spread of wetlands, estuaries, wide river deltas, sandbar islands and beaches. The country's most diverse and abundant birdlife congregate here, as do a variety of Russian and Ukrainian tourists who flock to the coast in summer, mostly out of habit from Soviet days when Odessa was still the balmy southern capital of a rather cold empire.

The south is still a very friendly place where people are laidback and the sun shines year round over grassy plains and the watery expanse. Ukraine's three largest rivers – the Dnistr, Danube, and Dnepr – all empty into the sea here, so that small-scale farming on the deltas and traditional angling are still the accepted way of life in the country, while shipping has made the cities wealthy. Technically, this convergence of rivers designates the birthplace of human civilisation in Ukraine – a high concentration of pre-historic burial mounds and Scythian relics mark this as a central hub for early human migration from Asia into Europe. The ease of river transportation and the fertile land attracted the ancient Greeks and much later brought the St Petersburg aristocracy to this 'New Russia' where they sought to rise up a great navy. The grandeur remains – along with the Russian language – but the slower pace of life and the warm sky advocate little more than relaxation and a lazy dip in the water.

Getting around

Odessa is the largest and most central transportation nucleus, with the fastest regional trains and buses to Mykolayiv and Kherson. More rural routes towards the Black Sea coast and the Dnepr delta branch out from Kherson, while any travel towards the Dnistr and Danube deltas originates in Odessa. Train and motor routes south towards the Danube are very long and slow; in many ways, this little stretch of land is a piece of 'deep Ukraine'. Getting a taxi, sharing rides, or going on an organised tour can be the best way to access these more obscure destinations.

ODESSA – ОДЕССА

Ukraine's most sociable city deserves all the sunshine it gets, and if you want to see someone smile, simply mention Odessa to a Russian (or Ukrainian). Behind the busy seaport and frantic holiday zone lingers a childish energy seldom known in big cities. Much of Odessa's jubilant reputation lies in the fame and glory of Russia's past, when the empire was endeared towards the peace and renewal found in the south. The city still holds true to these customs of diversity, culture and hospitality, yet even without the historical context, Odessa is a beautiful city by the sea that should naturally attract visitors. Tall trees shade the cobblestone

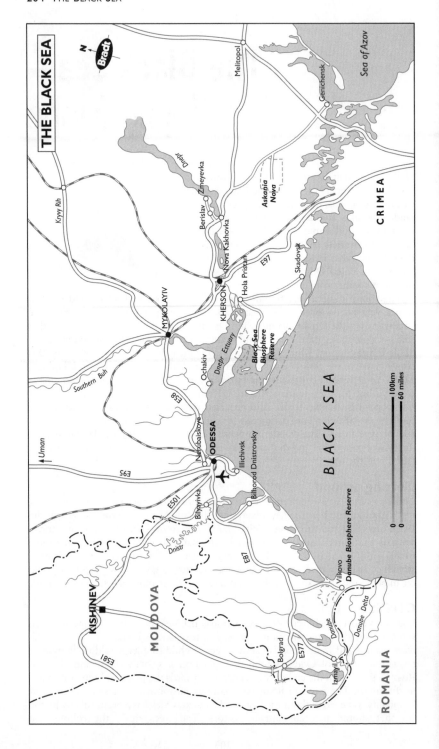

boulevards and the decorated palaces-turned-museums add distinctive French and Italian styles to the present display. As a former Soviet playland, Odessa also comes equipped with all the cheap amusements characteristic of seaside towns: jewellery stands, ponies, street clowns, balloon-sellers and dancing monkeys. Somehow it all fits together, making it Odessa.

The exact origin of Odessa's name is disputed, but most believe this was once the ancient Greek colony of Odessos dating back to the 3rd century when trade with Kievan-Rus' attracted independent merchants to settle here. For centuries, the Crimean Tatars, followed by the Turks, controlled the harbour with their fortress Eni-Dunya, but the Russians finally conquered in 1789 and envisioned a great commercial and naval port. At only 200 years old, Odessa is one of Europe's younger cities, and the neo-classical buildings date back to Russia's gilded age. In 1803, Tsar Alexander I committed the governorship of the city to the Duke de Richelieu who had led the Russians against the Turks at Izmaïl. The Frenchman is now revered as the father of Odessa, and his statue stands at the top of the famed Potemkin stairs, draped in royal Greek robes. Richelieu slashed trade duties and officially dedicated one-fifth of the port's income to 'making the city beautiful', a task in which he was successful. Granted the status of a free port in 1815, Odessa swiftly rose to third place in the Russian Empire after Moscow and St Petersburg. Opportunity and very relaxed laws attracted a mixed crowd of political refugees and entrepreneurs: freed slaves, Christian dissidents, Ukrainian Cossacks, sailors, Marxists, Bulgarians, Greeks, Jews and Albanians. The boom in Ukraine's grain exports transcended any possible ethnic discord and Odessa's many faces helped make the south a region independent from the highly centralised Russian Empire. Odessa's role in the Russian Revolution was not a small one since workers' unions had already been around for nearly 30 years before the famed uprising of 1905, led by the sailors from the battleship *Potemkin*. Odessa was heavily bombed during World War I and suffered immense damage during the civil war. General Denikin's White Army held Odessa the longest before succumbing to the Bolsheviks. The act of defence was repeated in 1941 when the city's inhabitants held out against the Germans for 73 days, after which the region was placed under Romanian occupation. Odessa's dominant Jewish population was decimated.

Odessa's super strong urban solidarity tends to supersede any national allegiance and that has changed little under independent Ukraine. By reputation, 'Odessites' are incorrigible jokesters, smooth talkers, and a little shifty – it is no coincidence that the city celebrates 'Odessa Day' on April 1. People laugh out loud here, and a common sight of two park benches turned to face one another reveals conversation as the city's favourite pastime. With capitalism in their blood, local business is strong, and instead of Soviet names, the ordered boulevards all hark back to Odessa's golden age – hence French Street, Polish Street, Greek Street and Jewish Street.

Getting there and away
By air
Apart from Kiev, Odessa is the most internationally accessible city by air in Ukraine, and therefore a convenient entry point from Europe and North America. **Malev Hungarian** has five flights a week to and from Budapest; tel: 731 2575 (locally), and **Austrian Airlines** has direct weekday connections with Vienna; (airport office tel: 0482 667 051; email: all-ods@aua.com_nospam). Flights to Kiev are frequent and often inexpensive, usually around US$65 for the one-hour flight. For international flights and connections to Kiev, contact **AeroSvit** at the airport (tel: 0482 379 800; email: aew@te.net.ua). **Kiy Avia** (Preobrazhenskaya 15; tel:

0482 252 389; email: Odessa@kiyavia.com) is best for internal flights to almost anywhere in Ukraine. The central airport is a 20-minute taxi ride outside the city (on the Ovidiopolskaya road); getting there should cost no more than US$4.

By rail

A rush of warm sea air is the first thing to meet you after stepping off the train in Odessa, followed by the most earnest and excited crowds in the country. The fervour of movement and sudden sunshine is a grand finale for those who arrive by rail, and the frequent and relatively fast trains make Odessa an easy destination from almost anywhere else in Ukraine (or Russia). The train station sits centrally in the Privokzalnaya Ploshad 2; tel: 0482 224 242. Avoid long lines by booking tickets at the central rail office at Serednofontansky 12A.

There are at least three overnight trains to and from Kiev on any given day, one of which continues on to Russia. Odessa's very own Kiev train is dubbed the 'Black Sea' *(Chornomorets)* which leaves after 21.00 and arrives around 07.00 or 08.00 the following morning; the standard journey takes ten to 12 hours. Other major Odessa trains go to Vinnytsya (7 hours), Dnipropetrovsk (12 hours), Lviv (12 hours), Simferopol (13 hours), Cherkassy (11 hours) and Kharkiv (14 hours). Odessa's train station is also the principle southern junction for international rail journeys: Kishinev (4 hours), Warsaw (24 hours), Minsk (24 hours) and Moscow (25 hours). Getting to the smaller towns in Trans-Dnistr is quicker by bus or car, however the *electrichki* trains connect to all the villages on the way to Izmail. A very slow train also travels to Kherson via Mykolayiv.

By bus

The main bus station is located at Kolontayevska 58; tel: 0482 325 693. A happy chaos makes catching the bus (the right bus) a task, but this is the best way to get to locations within the region, namely the coast, Bilhorod Dnistrovsky, and Kherson; travel to Mykolayiv is US$3 (2½ hours), Kherson is US$5 (4 hours). Tickets are sold for buses and marshrutka alike, but the schedule can be confusing. Slow buses travel to anywhere, including Dnepropetrovsk (14 hours) and Donetsk (16 hours); take the train instead. (Keep in mind that some buses from Odessa to the Carpathians will pass through Moldova and Romania, cancelling your Ukrainian visa.) **Avtoluks** offers fast and rather plush bus services between Odessa and Kiev twice a day (7 hours; via Uman and Kiev Borispol airport); their central office is at Raskydaylovksaya 18; tel: 0482 377 392; their other office sells tickets directly at the bus station. There are also plenty of marshrutka travelling around the Black Sea region that come and go from the front of the train station.

By sea

Being the largest warm seaport of what was the world's largest country meant that at one time a traveller could take a ship to most anywhere in the world from Odessa. It's hard to miss the towering seaport *(morsky vokzal)* off Suvorova at Tamozhnaya Ploshad 1. Customs and immigration are located inside the main building on the pier and anyone arriving by sea (including private yachts) is required to register; however, a new law permits immediate issue of 'express' visas for sea travellers arriving in Odessa and Sevastopol. Passenger ships still come and go from Odessa, but they are few. Turkey is the only year-round destination, with twice weekly trips to Istanbul; one-way US$85; return US$160 (36 hours' sailing). A single ticket to the northern Turkish resort town Samsun is around US$100 (40 hours' sailing). The other regular transit is from Odessa to Haifa, Israel: once a month except in winter from December to February (US$340 one way).

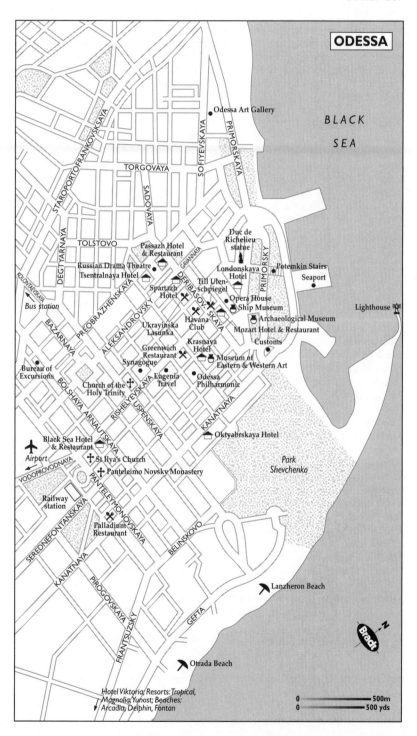

ODESSA

BLACK
SEA

Odessa Art Gallery

PRIMORSKAYA

SOFIYEVSKAYA

TORGOVAYA

SADOVAYA

STAROPORTOFRANKOVSKAYA

DEGTYARNAYA

TOLSTOVO

Passazh Hotel
& Restaurant

Duc de
Richelieu
statue

GAVANNAYA

Londonskaya
Hotel

Potemkin Stairs

Russian Drama Theatre
Tsentralnaya Hotel

PRIMORSKY

Seaport

KOLONTAEVSKAYA

Bus station

PREOBRAZHENSKAYA

Spartazh
Hotel

Till Ulen-
schpiegel

DERIBASOVSKAYA

Opera House
Ship Museum

Lighthouse

ALEKSANDROVSK

Ukrayinska
Lasunka

Havana
Club

Archaeological Museum

BAZARNAYA

Mozart Hotel & Restaurant

Customs

Greenwich
Restaurant

Krasnaya
Hotel

Bureau of
Excursions

Synagogue

Museum of
Eastern & Western Art

BOLSHAYA ARNAUTSKAYA

Church of the
Holy Trinity

RISHELYEVSKAYA

USPENSKAYA

Eugenia
Travel

Odessa
Philharmonic

KANATNAYA

Oktyabrskaya Hotel

Black Sea Hotel
& Restaurant

Airport

St Ilya's Church

VODOPROVODNAYA

Panteleimo Novsky Monastery

Park
Shevchenko

Railway
station

PANTELEYMONOVSKAYA

SEREDNEFONTANSKAYA

Palladium
Restaurant

KANATNAYA

PROGOVSKAYA

FRANTSUZSKY

BELINSKOVO

Lanzheron Beach

GEFTA

Bradt

N

Otrada Beach

Hotel Viktoria; Resorts: Tropical,
Magnolia, Yunost; Beaches:
Arcadia, Delphin, Fontan

0   500m
0   500 yds

Summertime sees a few sporadic links from Odessa to Crimea, namely Sevastopol and Yalta, but foreign cruises seem to dominate the Black Sea routes. The main passenger ship line from Ukraine is UKRferry; Sabansky 4a; tel: 0482 348 296; email: ukf@ukrferry.com; web: www.ukrferry.com. The information booth in the sea terminal station knows the current sailing schedule and also sells tickets; tel: 0482 223 211.

Tour operators

Eugenia Travel Rishelyevskaya 23; tel/fax: 0482 220 554; email: janna@eugen.intes.odessa.ua; web: www.eugeniatravel.com. Southern Ukraine's largest incoming tour operator works out of Odessa and can arrange anything from visas to air tickets to Black Sea cruises. An English guided city tour costs US$15, and a trip to the catacombs is US$20. Eugenia's office is also the best place for general information about Odessa and another office at the seaport handles cruise tickets.

Odessa Bureau of Travel and Excursions; 113 Malaya Arnautskaya; tel: 0482 252 874. Don't be put off by the peeling brown and green signs, for a visit to this corner office is a living relic from Soviet Inturist days. A roomful of smiling grannies can arrange English or Russian tours of the city and its outskirts, including the catacombs.

Ukrayinska Lakoma Deribasovksaya 17; tel: 0482 258 412. Doubled up with a restaurant, this firm does good tours around the city and offers some excursions to regional attractions.

Where to stay

Odessa's accommodation ranks high among Ukrainian hotels, with a rich past of entertaining newcomers to the city by the sea. The following list comprises the standard names. However, like the rest of the country, Odessa's older hotels are all refurbishing themselves towards a more luxurious future – and many intimate new resorts are popping up along the seaside. Odessa picked up on credit cards quickly and any middle or luxury hotel will gladly accept plastic.

Luxury

Mozart Lanzheronovskaya 13; tel: 0482 379 394; email: office@mozart-hotel.com; web: www.mozart-hotel.com. New money and new opportunity have witnessed many attempts at opulence, but few new hotels exude so much class. With a professional staff to match the surroundings, Mozart has become (within months of opening) *the* hotel of Odessa. Located directly across from the Opera House, the complex includes three excellent restaurants, an exquisite conference room, a pool and sauna, internet access, comfortable beds, and a fantastic view. A private electric generator and separate water source leaves the hotel immune to Odessa's problematic services. Standard singles/doubles go for US$145/$185 a night; the four-person family room and the suites with private jacuzzis are US$350.

Londonskaya Primorsky 11; tel: 0482 228 787; fax: 0482 255 370. Built in 1867 and still dreaming of Victorian England, the 'London-ish' hotel is an important architectural monument for Odessa; however, the building's grandeur cannot diffuse the Soviet undertones in style and attitude. The refined restaurant is more liberating. Rooms cost from US$160 to $300/night; the view takes in the busy port of Odessa and the Potemkin stairs.

Krasnaya Pushkinskaya 15; tel: 0482 227 220 email: redlond@londred.com; web: www.londred.com. You can't miss the 'Red' when walking down Puskhkinskaya: the pink and white rococo façade forces passers-by to stretch their neck and stare. Smack bang in the city centre, the Krasnaya offers an all around convenient stay in Odessa. Rooms are large and comfy, and two classes of rooms mean some prices will match a middle-range budget as well. 'Standard rooms' cost US$63–98, while the regular new rooms cost US$126–170. Make sure to specify your preference of shower or bath.

Middle range

Black Sea Hotel Rishelyevskaya 59; tel: 0482 300 904; fax: (0482) 300 906; web: www.bs-hotel.com.ua. A recently remodelled Soviet high-rise, the Black Sea's best attribute is its location near the train station. The least expensive double rooms cost US$40 (a little lower standard); 'reconstructed' rooms cost US$90–120 (with a few real queen-size beds). The staff speak English and an active in-house travel agency does small tours around the city and trips to the beach. Dinner is served in the hotel's Japanese restaurant.

Tsentralnaya Preobrazhenskaya 40; tel: 0482 268 406. Simple and modern inside, 'Central' is a standard night's stay by foreign perceptions with a prime location on Odessa's main drag. Run-of-the-mill rooms cost US$40 (single) and US$60 (double). A lively café attracts an energetic evening crowd downstairs.

Viktoria Genuezka 22; tel: 0482 619 038. Although quite far from anything (except the world's most crowded beach), value-wise the Viktoria is Odessa's nicest mid-range hotel and a quick taxi ride can fix the distance. Singles/doubles cost US$58/85.

Oktyabrskaya Kanatnaya 33; tel: 0482 227 485. Very central, this revolution's namesake is next to Odessa's largest park. This is your typical Soviet hotel, but the hot water runs and the surrounding neighbourhood is one of the city's more enjoyable segments. Rooms are charged per person, on average US$35.

Budget

Finding a cheap place to stay is getting tougher in Odessa, especially if you are a foreigner. Renting a private apartment is one option, or check out the sanatoria which often have good deals.

Passazh; Preobrezhenskaya 34; tel: 0482 224 849. Odessa's best budget hotel was once its grandest. The pink and white exterior may be crumbling, and the staircase and halls are quite shabby, but the rooms are decent and most have hot water with their own toilets. Rooms go for US$5–20, depending on the number of beds and the amount of plumbing. Their poshest of suites is US$30.

Spartazh Deribasovskaya 25; tel: 0482 26 89 24. Now in the midst of renovation, this centrally located hotel used to be the cheapest place to stay, with rooms for as little as US$3. Upon finishing, rooms should still cost little more than US$20, but this city is not known for stable prices. Check it out and don't be afraid to negotiate a little.

Renting apartments

Odessa's innate knack for wheeling and dealing means you can arrange to stay in a private apartment for under US$10/night. As a rule, matronly women around the platforms of the train station will be advertising a '*kvartira*' (apartment) or '*komnata*' (room). Even if you don't speak a lick of Russian, try to negotiate lots before agreeing to go and 'have a look', which is considered close to a 'yes'. Renting a room can be a good option if you want to meet some locals, but if you value your privacy, get the whole apartment and the keys that go with it. Ask about hot water and check the doors to make sure they are secure. Pay in full at the beginning and then pay no more.

Resorts/sanatoria

After a year in the factory, tired proletarians migrated to Odessa's shores for a long break. The tradition of health holidays continues in dozens of sanatoria, with a touch more elegance now. The seaside is mobbed with Russian tourists in summer, but communal joy is part of the fun.

Tropical Krasnye Zori 4/6A; tel: 0482 342 484; email: administrator@tropical.odessa.ua. Advertised as a 'rest centre' by the sea, this brand new resort offers high service with trendy perks, including a high-tech, full-sized bowling alley, a swanky billiard hall and the best private sauna in Odessa. The spacious guarded parking lot attracts visitors who've arrived by car. Only real king-size beds can be found in the rooms. The least expensive rooms go for US$100 a night; suites range from US$150 to US$180. Overlooking the sea, a tastefully decorated restaurant serves delicious Italian cuisine and grilled seafood for around US$12 a plate. A three-minute walk brings you to the beach.

Magnolia Frantsuzky Bulvar 63/65; tel: 0482 687 705; email: magnolia@farlep.net. Flamingo pink and rather joyful, this flowery sanatorium might prove a cheaper alternative to a hotel for long-term visits. Meals, salt-water swimming pools, free massages and complimentary psychotherapy (really) are part of their package deals for the minimum week-long stay. Few rooms have real showers (rather, a hose from the wall) and hot water is sporadic. Rooms cost US$20–50 a night.

Yunost Pionerskaya 32; (0482) 345 000; fax: (0482) 633 377; email: yunost@eurocom.od.ua; web: www.yunost.com.ua. An inspiring communist word like 'Youth' should move anyone towards this high-rise resort on the Black Sea, closer to one of Odessa's cleaner beaches. Rooms range from US$20 to US$80 (suites) a night, with significant discounts for long-term stays (over two weeks). Bedrooms and bathrooms are clean and cosy.

Where to eat

Odessa's restaurants reflect the southern appreciation for good eating and good conversation. Besides hotels and private restaurants, all sorts of little cafés and food stands line Deribasovskaya and some tempting bakeries along Preobrazhenskaya sell fresh pastries.

Ukrayinska Lasunka Deribasovskaya 17; tel: 0482 258 412; web: www.lakomka.com.ua; open 10.00–24.00. If you like theme dining, this very Ukrainian restaurant is decked out in Disney-esque props, suddenly surrounding you with a friendly farm. Besides doing convincingly authentic Ukrainian cuisine, the chef prepares customary Odessa favourites using fresh Black Sea products. Meals begin with complimentary *samogon* (home-brewed vodka), and proud waiters swish back and forth in national dress. A full meal will cost between US$10 and $15 and the restaurant features a full range of Ukrainian, Moldavian, and Georgian wines; credit cards are accepted and there is an English menu. After a meal, consider taking an excursion of the city, since Ukrainskaya Lakomka doubles as a tour agency.

Greenwich Bunina 21; tel: 0482 347 401; web: www.greenwich.com.ua. If after your meal, you're feeling enigmatic and snooty, it might have something to do with the fact that you are sitting in an expensive Russian restaurant trying to be a posh English restaurant posing as an artsy French restaurant. Delicate seafood with complicated sauces dominate the 'art menu'; expect to pay around US$40 per head (a bowl of soup alone costs US$10).

Till Ulenschpiegel Deribasovskaya 12; tel: 0482 429 046; email: till2002@ukr.net. No other corner café embodies the friendly spirit of Odessa better than this Flemish-style tavern. Sophisticated and warm, locals gather round the big copper fireplace for drinks (Russian and Dutch beer) or to enjoy light, intimate meals by the windows. Everything on the menu is made fresh in the kitchen, including homebaked bread and hand-stuffed sausage. Other specialties include fishcakes, omelettes and salads and nothing is priced over US$10.

Kolyba Fontanskaya Doroga 32Б; tel: 0482 348905; email: kolyba@tm.odessa.ua. If you missed the mountains or still crave Ukrainian folklore, Kolyba recreates the mood with all the earnestness of the Carpathians. Slightly contrived but a whole lot of fun, a talented chef cooks up fresh fish, oversized shish kebabs and a variety of salads, all for very low prices. The large sauna can be rented out by the hour (US$15) and if you eat too much, the restaurant/hotel has nine rooms with beds, some with lofts.

Passazh Passazh Shopping Centre, 2nd floor. A good place for rich afternoon coffee and Turkish pastries. Light and savoury meals are also served.

Hotel restaurants

Every upscale Odessa hotel features a restaurant or café, and anyone is welcome to visit for just a meal. The main restaurant at **Mozart** (Lanzheronsvskaya 13) specialises in elegant and diverse meals, and despite all the splendour, prices are comparable to back home (US$15–25 per meal). **Londonsky** (Primorsky 11) is a distinguished setting for lunch and dinner, with an advantageous location for a stop during a walking tour of the city. The cuisine is predominantly Russian and relatively inexpensive. The same company owns and operates the restaurant **Krasny** (Pushkinskaya 15), but offers a rather original menu. Japanese food is served at the **Black Sea** (Rishelievskaya 55).

Late nights

Palladium Italyansky Boulevard 4. The flashiest dinner club in Odessa to date brings a bit of Las Vegas right into the city centre. Colourful shows and overpriced food secure the illusion. Don't say 'mafia' too loudly. Open 17.00–06.00.

Havana Club Deribasovskaya 23; tel: 0482 227 116. Outrageous parties have little to do with socialism, but this funky Cuban café was built in honour of Fidel Castro and dishes out cheesy Russian nightlife with less offensiveness than expected. Food is not the priority, but the kitchen puts together some spicy dishes that resemble Slavic imaginations of the Caribbean. Open 24 hours.

What to see and do

Enjoying Odessa should mean a walk along the long boulevards and bustling seaport. The streets form a slanted grid against the coast, and each is distinct. **Deribasovskaya** is named for the Spaniard De Ribas who actually constructed Odessa's harbour. The street is by far the most lively in Odessa, packed with shops, restaurants and people. Near the corner with **Preobrazhenskaya** is a gateway leading into Odessa's greatest shopping spot, the extravagant 18th-century **Passazh** corridor where a vaulted glass roof shields the designer boutiques and posh cafés (entrance at Deribasovskaya 33). Built to resemble a well-mannered English promenade, **Primorsky Boulevard** stands above the port and descends to the main sea terminal by way of the **Potemkin stairs**. The central building was once the city's government offices and the building at the far end was the palace of the New Russian Governor Vorontsov. The sea terminal below has its exciting moments and also functions as a public gathering place. Odessa's parks are either calm and refreshing or fun and loud; the **Old Market Square** on Aleksandrovsky is most representative. **Park Shevchenko** joins the industrial port to the long coastline of city beaches.

Museums

While each is interesting, Odessa's museums are probably not the city's central highlight as they are often presented. You might want to save them as a break from people-watching or during the rare overcast moment. Because the museums are all rather visual places, non-Russian speakers will still enjoy most of the displays. A small yet diverse art collection occupies a crumbling blue palace, the **Musuem of Eastern and Western Art** (tel: 0482 224 815; open 10.00-16.30, closed Wednesday, entrance 2UAH). Along with a few works by Michelangelo and Rubens, there is a variety of Oriental art on display from Central Asia, Tibet, China and Japan. In the north of the city, Count Pototsky's grandiose palace now houses the **Odessa Art Gallery** (Sofievskaya 5A; open 10.30–17.00, entrance 3UAH), featuring 19th-

THE POTEMKIN STAIRS

Most outsiders will recognise the Potemkin Stairs from Sergei Eisenstein's immortal film, the *Battleship Potemkin*, which recounts one of the more heroic tales from the first Russian Revolution. In June 1905, sailors with the imperial navy mutinied and took control of the most powerful battleship in the Black Sea fleet, the *Potemkin*, named after General Potemkin (pronounced Pa-tyom-kin), Catherine the Great's sly suitor. Already in Odessa the worker's movement had been leading a massive strike for over two weeks, and when the mutinied battleship sailed into the city's harbour, huge crowds gathered near the waterfront. The leader of the rebellion, Valenchuk, had been shot in the struggle, and his body was laid at the foot of the grand Odessa staircase. Thousands came to pay their respects and to support the sailors' uprising. As portrayed in the film, the tsarist troops descended the stairs, firing on the crowds below, while the people fled or jumped into the sea. Around 2,000 people died. Eisenstein's Odessa stairs sequence is praised as the ultimate scene in modern film-making, and despite the intended Bolshevik propaganda, the *Battleship Potemkin* is often considered the greatest film ever made. The actual Potemkin rebellion was a turning point for the revolution since many of Lenin's sceptics had previously believed the military would never show solidarity with the workers' movement. Unrest in the military gave hope to the Bolsheviks.

Usually cities are known for their towers, statues, or buildings, but Odessa is best symbolised by the massive stone descent from Primorsky Boulevard to the pier. Climbing up (or down) the 192 uneven granite steps can be a task, but it is worth seeing both ends, for the stairs were built as an illusion; the lower stairs are much wider than the top, so that the width appears uniform.

century Russian and Ukrainian art, including works by Shevchenko and Aivozovsky. Ukraine's most ancient artefacts are on display at Odessa's **Archaeological Museum** (Lanzherovskaya 4; tel: 0482 226 302; open 10.00–17.00, closed Monday; entrance 3UAH). Officially Ukraine's oldest museum, the collection consists mainly of objects found in nearby Black Sea burial mounds: Scythian gold, Sarmatian swords, Greek amphora, and early Slavic tools from Kievan Rus. The exhibit is relevant except for the Egyptian room, where ill-displayed mummies seem out of place. Next door and much more fitting for Odessa is the **Ship Museum** (Lanzherovskaya 6; tel: 0482 240 509; open 10.00–17.00, closed Thursday, entrance 3UAH). Once upon a time, the palace-like structure was Odessa's famed 'English club' where local Anglophiles and English diplomats gathered for dinners and conversation. During the Soviet era, the bourgeois club became a memorial to Odessa's main industry and the museum has changed little since. If you are a fan of model ships or Russian history, the vivid display will please. Intricate replicas and grand socialist paintings recount the 'natural' evolution from Viking ships to the mighty Black Sea fleet and Soviet merchant ships, all beneath the painted adage that 'Ships are like people, they all die differently'.

Churches

A diverse population brought many different religious buildings to Odessa, but communist activism and Russian history destroyed most and left the few remaining churches in pretty bad condition of which a scant few have recovered.

Your first view of Odessa from the train station takes in the ethereal domes of **Panteleimonovsky Monastery** (Panteleimonsovskaya 66), used as a planetarium during Soviet rule and just recently refurbished. One block east is the small Byzantine structure of **St Ilya's Church** (Pushkinskaya 75). The light green, Greek Orthodox **Church of the Holy Trinity** (Yekaterinskaya 55) is an Odessa architectural monument and the main place for Orthodox festivals and weddings. The main working **synagogue** is at Yevreiskaya 25, only recently returned to the Jewish community after decades of Soviet occupation. A separate book could be written on the Jews of Odessa (as well as the separate communities of Armenians, Albanians, Greeks, etc) A decree by Catherine II encouraged major Jewish settlement of Odessa, and at one time there were 78 synagogues; today there are two. Jewish tradition, art, and business greatly influenced the city, and at its height, the Jewish population made up 70% of the city. Following the violence of the revolution, World War II, and major emigration since independence, Odessa's Jews now number only 30,000 out of the city's one million inhabitants.

Theatre

The symbol of the city, the **Odessa Opera House and Ballet**, was built by Austrian architects in 1887 after the Russian version burned down a decade earlier. Today it is considered one of the world's finest and the Odessa ballet company is famous for rather unconventional performances. The opera is located between Lanzherovskaya and Chaikovskovo; tickets can be purchased at the booth next door, and should never be over US$10; tel: 0482 291 329. The **Russian Drama Theatre** (Grecheskaya 48; tel: 0482 227 250) does all the Russian classics and European favourites, as well as some experimental pieces. The **Odessa Philharmonic** (Rosa Luxembourg 15; tel: 0482 251 536) first housed the busy Odessa stock exchange, but the neo-Gothic brick patterns and Byzantine structure create the look of a mysterious temple. Now home to Odessa's ever-famous philharmonic orchestra, few other evening activities could take precedence to a performance here. Tickets can be ordered by phone or bought at the booth inside the main entrance during the day.

Odessa's beaches

As a rule, the further south you move along the coast, the better the beaches get, 'better' being relative to the murky harbour. Soviet families once made annual pilgrimages to these shores, and the tradition lives on with hundreds of thousands of visitors from all over Russia and Ukraine who come to enjoy the sun. If you haven't noticed, Russians prefer standing when they sunbathe and most beaches are standing room only. The sea is another matter; considering that untreated sewage for over one million people flows gently down these shores (adding new meaning to 'Black Sea'). **Arkadia** and **Otrada** are absolutely filthy, with more rubbish than sand in sight and brown foam swilling through the waves. Arkadia is also the ultimate in post-Soviet beachside glitz, and if you enjoy semi-naked crowds, loud music, and phoney tropical beach clubs, this is the place. Some clubs are private, allowing a bit more space on the beach for a price. Truly, some beaches are cleaner than others, but these also tend to be the most popular. **Delphin** and **Fontan** are relatively safe for swimming and have less garbage than normal, but the beaches are packed full from May to September. The best beach for cheesy amusement is **Lanzheron**, within walking distance of the city centre. The other beaches can be reached by taking the tram along Frantsuzky Boulevard from the train station in the direction of the sanatoria. The trip is long (and hot in summer), so you might consider a taxi.

Outside Odessa
The Odessa catacombs
About 10km north of the city is the back entrance into Odessa's more secretive past. The Odessa catacombs are unlike those in Western Europe, as they are all manmade and relatively new (200 years old). Instead of piling up people's bones, these tunnels were used for all the city's clandestine activities, which have been numerous.

Before Odessa came into being, Russian Cossacks had settled in this area (at the time ruled by Turkey), due to Catherine the Great's policies outlawing Cossackdom in the empire after the Pugachev rebellion in 1773. As the Turkish sultan granted them asylum, the warriors made a pact to no longer fight, hence the village name, Nerubaiskoye ('no-fighting'). Many of these Cossack settlements line the Khadzhibeisky estuary, where easy access to soft limestone permitted the quarrying of unlimited building material. Most of Odessa's palaces are built from this rock. Through trial and error, workers in the late 18th century found that a horse and cart worked best in tunnels between 15–30m deep, and as the city of Odessa rose up, hundreds of level tunnels were cut through the bedrock. An extensive network was left beneath the city, totalling over 2,000km in length. In early years, the Russian gentry found that the constant temperature and humidity were perfect for storing wine, while Odessa's many smugglers found the tunnels to be convenient warehouses for their private business. However the real glory days of the catacombs came to pass during World War II, when Romanian forces invaded Odessa. Unlike the Carpathians, where partisans could hide in forests and mountains, the Odessa resistance took over the catacombs and literally carried out their sabotage work from underground. Throughout Odessa's occupation, the Romanians tried various tactics to empty the catacombs, and there are stories of dogs turning back from the darkness and the ghosts of Romanian soldiers still wandering, lost in the labyrinth. Whatever the case, the catacombs prevented Odessa's 13 partisan bands from ever being discovered.

A trip to the catacombs takes about two hours and is best done by organised tour; all hotels and tour agencies listed in this chapter offer half-day trips that include a trip to the entrance in the village of Nerubaiskoye, the tunnels and the local Partisan museum; entrance costs 6UAH. Group tours usually cost around US$15. If you want to make the trip on your own, there are buses that leave from the train and bus stations to the village, but the schedule changes frequently. A taxi to the catacombs should be around US$10 and the drive takes about 20 minutes. A personal English-speaking guided tour can be arranged by the Odessa Bureau of Excursions and costs around US$15.

Bilhorod-Dnistrovsky – Білгород-Дністровский
The ancient town of Bilhorod rests on the southern shore of the Dnistr estuary, a strategic spot for its entrance into Moldova and Galicia. The Greeks built the city of Tira on this site back in the 6th century BC; however, visitors today come to take in the mighty castle, built in the 15th century to defend Moldova from Turkish invasion. Alas, the Turks prevailed in 1484, and for the next 400 years the town and battlement were known as Akkerman. The Soviets renamed it the 'White City on the Dnistr', harking back to the days of early Kievan-Rus and the Galician kingdom. The castle is open every day from 10.00 to 18.00; entrance costs 5UAH. The structure's perimeter is over a mile in length and the fat walls and bulky towers are open for exploring. Some trains connect with Odessa, but the most convenient option is to sign up for an organised day trip that provides motor transport back and forth from the city. Most hotels and the travel agencies listed all offer excursions to Bilhorod.

The Dnistr and Danube Delta

Southeast from Odessa lies the convergent wetlands of the Dnistr and Danube rivers, a rich natural location that has only just come under international scrutiny. The Dnistr delta is closest to Odessa and provides some amazing natural scenery and plenty of wildlife for viewing. Covering a long territory of marshes, lakes and natural canals, the **Dnistr National Park** is home to over 300 species of birds, including plentiful populations of egrets, cormorants, spoonbills and pelicans, as well as some very rare varieties like the glossy ibis and yellow-crowned night heron. Major campaigns to preserve the delta and expand the park into Moldova look towards outside interest and ecotourism to fund local education about the wetlands.

Alvona is an Odessa-based eco-tourist company specialising in exclusive week-long tourist packages of Odessa and the Dnistr delta for around US$500 per person (although the price drops significantly based on the number of people in the group). The tour centres on the wetlands with boat trips through some of the wildest areas, as well as some interaction with locals in the very remote villages of the delta. Contact Alvona Tour Company, Preobrazhenskaya 40, Offices 101–105; tel: 0482 496 777; email: alvona@tm.odessa.ua; web: www.alvona.com. Seeing the delta is nearly impossible without a boat, but if you want to travel down there on your own, take the bus from the Odessa station to the village of Bilyayivka. Make sure to get off before the border with Moldova and stay well on the Ukrainian side.

The Danube delta is less accessible and less exciting on the Ukrainian side, so that most visitors come up from Romania; however, regular trains and buses from Odessa to Izmail bring you pretty close to these northern wetlands. The **Dunaisky Biosphere Reserve** was established only in 1998 and takes in the best wild spots on the Ukrainian side. Interested travellers should contact the reserve in the village of Vilkovo: Tatarbunarskovo Povstannya 132, #4; tel: 04843 311 95.

MYKOLAYIV – МИКОЛАЇВ

Over half a million people call the city of Mykolayiv (Nikolayev) home, and if you come this way, you'll wonder why. As part of New Russia in 1789, General Potemkin ordered a shipbuilding centre to be constructed at the mouth of the southern Buh River. Since then, skilled labourers have hammered together Russia's navy and commercial fleet, until Ukrainian independence, when this massive port turned to rust overnight. Now Mykolayiv holds the title for Ukraine's hard-drug capital and all the problems that go with it (the syringes littering the street are depressing); the city has also gone down in history as the official entry point of AIDS into Ukraine. But pushing negativity aside, Mykolayiv separates the tourists from the travellers, and if you are into witnessing the harsh reality of Ukraine's economic meltdown, the unemployed masses are plentiful and usually friendly. Ironically, this is where Trotsky attended high school.

Getting there and away

The best part of Mykolayiv is leaving, for the landscape on the way to Kherson or Odessa is truly beautiful, with fields of wheat and gigantic marshes that are noisy with seabirds. If you are travelling between Crimea and Odessa, you'll pass through. The bus station is at Oktyabrskaya 8 (Zhovtnevy 8 in Ukrainian). A bus to Odessa is two-and-a-half hours, Kherson is one-and-a-half hours and the train to either place is twice as long. The quickest way to Odessa or Kherson is by marshrutka or taxi, which can be arranged at either station. The direct overnight train Kiev–Mykolayiv comes and goes once a day (12 hours); the train station is at the end of Pushkinskaya.

Where to stay and eat

If you are convinced you want to stay, you can try the **Hotel Kontinent** (Admirala Makarova 41; tel: 0512 477 520; email: kon@sp.mk.ua). It's a three-star by Ukrainian standards and quite new; singles are US$15, doubles US$20, suites US$50.

KHERSON – ХЕРСОН

Because Kherson is neither Odessa nor Crimea, few Ukrainians or foreigners venture into this temperate south-central region or its capital. What they miss are the vast expanses of Ukraine's true steppe, some unique national parks and a good-natured town that still prizes its agricultural achievements with collective pride. The Dnepr's widest curves cut through the northern part of the region ending in the river's delta just below the city of Kherson, while the scattered sandbanks along the shores of the Black Sea and the Sea of Azov are recent tourist hideaways with lots of empty beaches and animated birdlife.

While Kherson had its own share of Scythian pre-history and Cossack folklore, the actual city came into being by decree of Catherine the Great in 1778, who hoped to use this final point on the Dnepr as both the Black Sea port and the shipbuilding centre for her new fleet. As with all of New Russia, the empress sought to reinstate the ancient Greek ideal, changing the original name from Alexandria to Kherson, believing that this was in the historical Greek colony of Chersonesus Heracleotica. Catherine's suitor, General Grigory Potemkin, is considered founder of the city, who helped with the expansion of a colossal star-shaped fortress, of which now only the gates and arsenal remain. In a way, Kherson feels cheated of its birthright by its rival cities Odessa (which became the major Black Sea port) and Mykolayiv (which took over the shipbuilding industry). Kherson is now the smallest of the three, with 300,000 inhabitants and a predominantly rural focus, which also makes it the most appealing in terms of recreation. Nobody is trying to sell the town itself on merit of aesthetics, but the sight of the broad blue Dnepr does inspire grand thoughts not unlike those of Ukrainian poetry. This love for the land is best exhibited in Kherson's bountiful summer markets and resilient farmers. Kherson-grown fruits and vegetables are famous all over Ukraine, especially the perfectly round and super sweet watermelons ripe with 260 days of sunshine a year.

Kherson's tourist industry is rather highly developed for a town of this size (in eastern Ukraine) and the nearby wetlands and prairies allow for some unconventional possibilities to see some of unconventional Ukraine.

Getting there and away

Kherson is a true crossroads between the north (Kiev), the south (Crimea), and the southwest (Odessa). The train station (tel: 0552 532 008) is at the very northern end of Ushakova. There are two daily trains to Odessa via Mykolayiv, but as the trip takes six hours by rail, it's better to find a marshrutka near the bus station and cut your travel time in half. Two overnight trains come and go from Kiev every night (11 or 13 hours) via Kryvy Rih, while another overnight train travels to and from Simferopol (8 hours). There are also frequent trains to Russia.

Kherson's bus station is located at Novonikolayevskoye Shosse 6; tel: 0552 249 403. Buses travel back and forth from Odessa all day long (4 hours), usually via Mykolayiv (1½ hours). Overnight buses to Simferopol (6 hours) and Sevastopol (8 hours) are uncomfortably hot or cold depending on the season, and if travelling to southern Crimea, take the train. The private bus company Gunsel has a twice daily bus service to and from Kiev (10 hours) via Mykolayiv and Uman; their office is

JOHN HOWARD (1726–90)

A man about which little real fact is known, John Howard is remembered in Ukraine as the generous doctor who contracted typhus from Russians in Kherson while trying to save the town from the disease. Actually, the Englishman was not a doctor of any sort, but a dedicated traveller who added meaning to his wanderlust through philanthropy. After inheriting a small fortune from his father, John Howard chose to spend it on the road, embarking on several European tours, each with a humanist bent. At one time he attempted sailing to Portugal to offer help in the aftermath of an earthquake, but his ship was captured by French privateers and he spent two months in prison before returning to England. Following some research at home, and as a newly appointed sheriff, he launched a campaign of prison reform in England, successfully passing two acts in the House of Commons and then going on to inspect the conditions of foreign jails. His personal investigations led to an interest in the plague and he began travelling incognito so as to witness first-hand the conditions surrounding the disease and quarantine policies. His journey to the Russian empire was an intense ordeal where he crossed Europe overland by carriage to St Petersburg and then continued the 2,000km south to Kherson, where he intended to continue on to Constantinople. Asked to check on a woman dying from the fever, John Howard chose to personally nurse the victim, contracting the disease and dying soon after. The tall obelisk sundial on Ushakova was erected in his memory – his grave is in a village outside the city.

in the bus station (tel: 0552 264 729). Trams, trolleys and marshrutka run up and down Ushakova, and if you stay in the city for more than a day, you will figure out the pattern; however, Kherson is a city conducive to frequent taxi runs – most destinations cost around US$1. Dnepr River cruises will often stop in Kherson for at least one day.

Where to stay

For the time being, there are two decent hotels in Kherson. The **Hotel Fregat** (Ushakova 2; tel: 0552 241 321; email: fregat@ukrincom.net; web: www.hotelfregat.com) is named after the very first frigate of the Russian navy, built in Kherson. As the city's Inturist hotel, the Fregat preserves its Soviet look with cleanliness and disco-like charm; only a few rooms have been remodelled. There are showers only, and hot-water supplies can be dubious, but the brand-new sauna and Turkish bath is large and inviting. A single room costs US$20 and a decent double runs between US$30 and US$40 a night, depending on how 'improved' it is; the very best suites go for US$80. As the highest building in town, and located right next to the Dnepr River, this is the best view of the city. Like all Inturist set-ups, the 'Fregat' is Kherson's main base for all tourist infrastructure, and their second-floor travel agency will prove helpful for English-speaking guides and arranging excursions in the countryside or to any of the nearby nature reserves; email: office@hotelfregat.com.

The **Brigantina Hotel** (Patona 4; tel: 0552 273 551; fax: 0552 270 481) is a classic example of how in Ukraine, less money can sometimes buy you better. The Brigantina is a nicer place to stay than the Fregat, and the regular rooms cost US$20–30, with some budget rooms for under US$5 and luxury suites for only

THE WOMEN OF KHERSON

Do a web search on Kherson and half the sites will advertise the lusty and lonely Slavic women of Kherson oblast. Trans-continental 'dating' has become an exploitative source of income throughout Ukraine, and the exploitation runs both ways. Kherson has a special reputation for its southern damsels, though many disgruntled male travellers have ended their 'romance tour' in some swindle or scam in Kherson. Most of these women find wealthy foreign men a great source of temporary income for themselves and their friends, and lifestyles have changed in Ukraine to the point that few women are actually willing to marry for a visa. Once they've emptied your wallet, they usually disappear to undisclosed locations – even if you did chat online for months beforehand.

US$65. The renovated rooms are well heated in winter and there is continuous hot water for the whole hotel. The sauna and internet access are pluses, while the hotel's location on 'the island' can be a downside. Transport to anywhere in town is by taxi (US$1).

Where to eat

Paradise Suvorova 7/9; tel: 0552 241 023. Located above a health spa and sauna, this lavish restaurant is more down-to-earth than it seems. The English menu is a mixed bag of Ukrainian, Italian, and Chinese food with specialties like chicken cordon bleu and a plethora of fruity desserts – it's all tasty and quite inexpensive (main dishes cost under US$5).

Krynychka Ushakova 42; tel: 0552 240 157. Considered Kherson's finest, this folksy Ukrainian restaurant serves traditional dishes that by this point in your trip might seem a little repetitive; however, quality of food and service are both very high.

Café Favorit corner of Suvorova and Oktyabrskoi Revolutsii; tel: 0552 246 072. Much to its credit, this hidden wine cellar is the only café that serves cold drinks cold, perhaps in all of Ukraine. Diverse and dependable Ukrainian cuisine attracts Kherson's younger crowd for late dinners and early drinks. Service is above average and a large meal will still cost about US$5.

What to do

The city offers no great single attraction, but this is the obvious base from which to visit the region. While you are in town, visit the **Kherson Natural History Museum** (Lenina 9; tel: 0552 241 061; open 10.00–16.00; closed Monday and Tuesday; entrance 3UAH; 12UAH for a guided tour). Besides the typical Soviet exhibits of industry and agriculture, the museum presents a comprehensive and interesting display of all the animals and plants that live in the region, including a special room dedicated to Askania-Nova. Quaint and informative, the **Kherson Art Museum** (Lenina 34; tel: 0552 243 164; open 10.00–16.00, closed Tuesday and Friday, entrance 5UAH) is dedicated to all Ukrainian art, but most specifically the work of Oleksi Shovkunenko, a Kherson native who rose up in the world of socialist realist painting. **St Catherine's Cathedral** remains one of Kherson's few churches, built in classical form and incorporating parts of the original Kherson fortress foundation. (General Potemkin's body was first buried in this churchyard, but later removed by Catherine the Great's resentful son.) If you come to Kherson during the summer, a trip to the outdoor market is imperative if nothing more than to see and smell. Strawberry season (May and June) is best.

NEAR KHERSON
Askania Nova – Асканія Нова

Although wildlife conservation was never a prominent point of Soviet rhetoric, this 100km² of virgin Ukrainian steppe somehow missed mass cultivation and exists today as the only natural steppe landscape left in Europe. Askania Nova was set aside as a nature park over 150 years ago, but it was the son of local German settlers, Frederick Falz-Fein (1863–1920) who dedicated his life to preserving this spot and bringing in the animals that attract so much interest today. Today, the park consists of various zones, some of which remain completely untouched and inaccessible – relics of Ukraine's original steppe ecosystem.

Askania Nova is now the base for a Ukrainian Research Institute that seeks to preserve the dwindling steppelands of Ukraine and maintains a vigorous breeding programme for endangered species, including the strange-looking and very rare Saiga antelope, as well as herds of Turkmeni Kulans and Przewalski horses used to repopulate the species' former habitat in Central Asia and Mongolia. This is the only place in Europe to see a Przewalski horse 'in the wild' – the only remaining undomesticated Eurasian horse breed. The park's birds put on a better show than the mammals, and birders visiting Ukraine should make Askania Nova a priority. Extinct everywhere else in Ukraine, the steppe eagle (*Aguila rapax*) can be regularly spotted in the air and trees, while rarer steppe species include the famed great bustard (*Otis tarda*), Demoiselle crane *(Anthropoides virgo),* and long-legged buzzard (*Buteo rufinus*).

Askania's open zoo follows a slightly 'world communist' mentality, advertising herds of animals from six different continents who share this single territory. Conservation purists may shudder, but watching how the free-roaming American bison distance themselves from the zebras who avoid the Indian zebus running from the South American emus is bizarrely impressive. Also prancing across these plains is the genetically engineered (hence endemic?) Soviet 'steppe deer.'

Askania is usually done as a day trip from Kherson, since travel there and back can be very long, although watching the wild steppe grasses will keep you entertained. As of now, there is no place to stay in or near the park, and there are few amenities like food since most everyone comes on an organised tour. The reserve opens on May 1 and stays open until late October; entrance into the park costs only 6UAH, but a package tour from your hotel will cost a lot more. For additional information, contact the park: Askania Nova, Stepova 3; tel: 05538 612 32; email: bp_ackania-nova@chap.hs.ukrtel.net.

Getting there and away

Askaniya Nova is two-and-a-half hours away from Kherson, on a good day. Otherwise, the trip can take up to four hours. Two buses travel there from Kherson bus station, one in the morning and another in the evening (which will leave you out there stranded). Because Askania features on practically every national itinerary, most package tours will arrange the transportation, and the hotels in Kherson can prove very helpful in facilitating the journey, since this is really Kherson's main attraction.

Kherson's wetlands

Entering the wilder regions of Kherson oblast is still not an easy process, and for the time being, it is wise to use a travel agency for arrangements, limited locally to the Kherson Inturist at Hotel Frigate. Popular day tours usually take in birdwatching spots or include fishing trips with a guide. Independent travellers are able to venture freely in **Hola Pristan** Гола Пристань, the last town on the Dnepr delta and a grand finale to Ukraine's most central artery. Here, the cacophony of sea birds is invigorating and travellers are granted a glimpse of a people whose lives are connected to the river. Not far away is the **Black Sea Biosphere Reserve**, established to protect bird habitats and nesting grounds among the marshes and sea islands of Kherson's southern coast. Much of the reserve is permanently closed to tourists, but there are certain locations where visitors can see rare species in migration, including flamingos, black-winged stilts, and great white pelicans. Contact the Reserve's office in Hola Pristan, Lermontova 1; tel: 05539 264 71. Buses leave Kherson for Hola Pristan every hour and the journey takes about one hour.

Zmeyevka – Змеевка

When Sweden fell to Russia in 1790, the inhabitants of Dago Island in the Baltic Sea made a plea to be spared from serfdom. Catherine the Great granted their request with an empire-building twist: the Swedes would be sent south to settle part of New Russia. Over 1,000 industrious Scandinavians founded the village of Zmeyevka, and today, this display of Swedishness on the banks of the Dnepr attracts many cruise visitors. If travelling from Kherson, the trip is about 120km, best done overland by bus to Berislav and then a taxi to Zmeyevka (around $5). The Hotel Fregat also offers a day trip to the village.

Crimea Крым

Ukrainians believe Crimea is the most exotic place on earth and with good reason. This strange peninsula looks absolutely nothing like the rest of Ukraine. Instead of rolling wheat fields, the landscape is broken into deep canyons and jutting cliffs. Sharp mountains seem to pop up from nowhere and straying from the road the noise of passing cars quickly turns to the roar of falling water. Here the hillsides are covered with a different kind of green and the warm breeze feels unmistakably Mediterranean. Little bays shine a turquoise glow that hints at the tropical and the sea is impassive with small waves that tumble on to the black pebble beaches. The sun shines unclouded year round attracting tourist armies from the north, but the boardwalk crowds are fairly easy to avoid. The region's main appeal is its natural diversity and constant change of scenery. The trekking is unique, mountain bikers are only just discovering the dramatic terrain and underground caverns are spectacular and accessible.

No less exotic is the human element. Behind the neon glitz of the tourist traps are the leftovers of fallen empires that once laid claim to these seaports and mountains: Byzantine cave cities, Greek ruins, Russian palaces, Genoese castles, and Soviet battleships. The oriental mystique attached to the peninsula is half-imagined, but the Crimean Tatars have returned from exile and are asserting a renewed cultural presence. With the wild rock-faces and poetic Turkish names, it is not surprising that so many legends are attached to the Crimea.

CRIMEAN HISTORY

The pre-historic Cimmerians were the most prominent inhabitants of Crimea until the 7th century BC when the Scythians arrived. The Cimmerians retreated into the coastal mountains and were named the Tauri by the ancient Greeks – Crimea was Taurica. The ancient Greek city states built numerous colonies on the Crimean coast, including Chersoneus (Sevastopol), Yevpatoria, and Feodosia. By the 1st century BC, most of these ports were being governed by Rome. Their energy and resources were largely devoted to blocking invasions from the northern steppe. In AD250 the Goth tribes invaded, and a century later the Huns arrived and decimated the local population. Another century later the Alan tribes invaded, but stayed and became allies to the now governing Byzantine Empire. The accepted legend states that the Apostle Andrew landed in Crimea (near Kerch) in the first century and raised the first cross on 'Russian' land. In the 5th century, Saints Cyril and Methodius came from Constantinople to Chersoneus, bringing Christianity and the Cyrillic alphabet to Ukraine. The new religion began to spread among the smaller colonies, and one odd civilisation rose up from converted Alans, Goths, and Greeks. This became the principality of Feodor, whose capital Mangup lasted

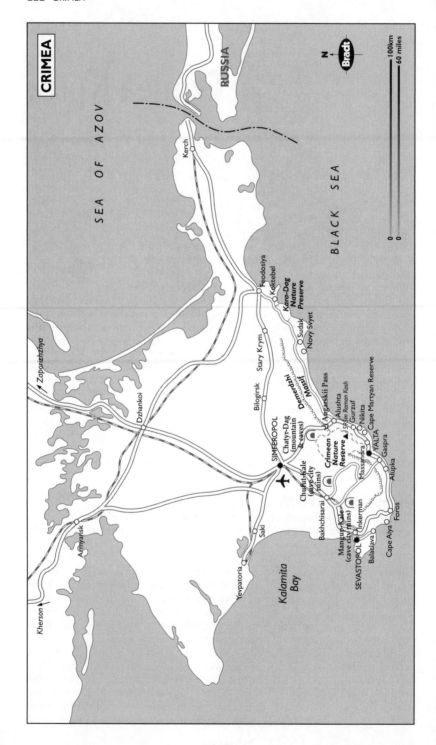

until the Ottoman conquest. Its people were later known as 'Crimean Greeks' who left during the Russian Empire to settle Mariupol on the Sea of Azov.

From the east, the Jewish Khazar Khaganate spread towards Crimea. The Khazars reached Crimea in the 8th century and opened up the region to its first Turkic tribes. The handful of Karaim who live in Crimea today are descendants of the Khazars. Kievan Rus had expanded to the south by the 10th century and Slavic princes ruled over Tmutorokan at the eastern tip of Crimea. Prince Vladimir was baptised at Chersoneus in 988 before returning to Kiev to 'convert' his people. Prince Svyatoslav destroyed the Khazar Khaganate but this opened up Crimea to invasion by the Pechenegs who conquered it in 1050.

The Crimean khanate

Crimea had always been linked to the romanticised Silk Road so attractive to medieval merchants. In return for not supporting the Crusades in the 13th century, Constantinople granted the Genoese a trade monopoly over the Black Sea region (it didn't hurt that they would provide a buffer from northern raids). In fact, there was much competition with the Venetian merchants and the many impressive fortresses built along Crimea's southern coast were not simply a defence against the Mongols but also a visible business presence. The main Genoese port was set up in Kaffa (Feodosia) and for a time they controlled the entire coastline. These merchant towns lasted until the Ottoman invasions of the 15th Century and medieval Italian castles still stand at Sudak and Cembalo (Balaklava).

The Mongol's 1223 hit-and-run attack included a large raid on Crimea. After they conquered Rus' in 1237 the peninsula became a comfy retreat for various tribes (the word for Crimea stems from the Turkish name for the peninsula, *Kyrym*). When the Golden Horde evaporated, new khans struggled for control of the area. The Crimean khanate was established in 1441 by Haci Giray Khan and the capital was built at Bakhchisarai. The Giray dynasty ruled the peninsula for over four hundred years, with some help from abroad: the Ottoman Turks invaded in 1475 and the Crimean khanate was made a tax-paying protectorate. As part of the empire, Crimea was granted its first ever 'autonomous' status, allowing Tatars enough independence to continue their own slave trade. As vigilantes the Ukrainian Cossacks made frequent raids on the Turks.

The Russians and Turks have always been fighting one another, and Crimea is unfortunately located between the two. After the Pereyaslav Agreement, Russian armies moved south in hopes of conquering their enemy's tributary. They were unsuccessful many times over but finally made an entrance in the early 1700s. This rivalry placed the Crimean Tatar's in a difficult position and in 1772 they were forced to choose Russian 'protection'. Catherine the Great signed a treaty granting Crimea independence as a protectorate of Russia, but in 1783 the peninsula was simply annexed to the empire.

The Russian Empire was not kind to the non-Christian Crimean Tatars and most left for Ottoman Turkey. Over a period of 100 years, these mass migrations decreased the Crimean Tatar population to less than a tenth of its original size. Meanwhile, Catherine was giving away Crimean estates to her favourites, as well as inviting Russians, Ukrainians, Bulgarians, Germans, and the Swiss to settle the area. Soon, the deserted Tatar villages were alive again and many Turkish names were preserved for exotic flare. Crimea was suddenly a place of sunshine for the Russian nobility, and many of the neo-classical buildings in Sevastopol and Simferopol are reminiscent of St Petersburg's canal-side palaces. The strategic shape and location of the peninsula also made it a vital military outpost for Russia and the imperial navy soon came south.

The Crimean War

Europeans know Crimea best for the infamous war fought in the years 1854–56. By 1853, international tensions were running high, but the spark that lit the fire was a dispute between Russian Orthodox priests and French Catholic clerics who both laid claim to Christian sites in the Holy Land. Russia and Turkey's centuries-old row was to provoke the first battles, and soon Great Britain and France had sent a joint force to the Black Sea. When the Russians destroyed the Turkish fleet in 1854, the European press went wild and the allies (soon joined by Sardinia) declared war on the tsar. The first fighting took place in Wallachia (Romania) and Bulgaria, and eventually the Russian army was forced into retreat. Fearing a new offensive from the powerful Black Sea fleet, the allies planned a siege on Russia's homeport, Sevastopol. The remembered battles at Alma, Balaklava, and Inkerman all took place around Sevastopol with great losses on both sides, but the port was not taken until 1856. The Treaty of Paris officially ended the war with conditions unfavourable to Russia and Britain and France still hurting. Cemeteries and battlefields have remained in memoriam.

The turbid 20th century

By the turn of the century, Crimea had become the playground of Russia's wealthiest families who built their summer palaces in the small seaside towns. Russian writers and artists also romanticised Crimea as an inspiring location for work and rest. However, these were short-lived days. Things quickly turned chaotic with governments rising and falling faster than the peninsula could be reoccupied. When Nikolai II abdicated in 1917, the Crimean Tatars raced to establish an independent Crimean state. They managed to form a national government but it was abolished one month later by the Bolsheviks. In March 1918, the Soviet Socialist Republic of Tauride was formed only to be abolished one month later by the Germans. The Germans then set up a regional government that lasted until the following allied occupation, but was consequently abolished by the Red Army. The Crimean Socialist Soviet Republic was formed at the beginning of the Russian civil war but went into exile at Kherson while the White Army held the peninsula for a year and a half. Finally, the Red Army gained control in 1920 and the republic was made a part of the Russian Socialist Soviet Republic. In 1921, Crimea was granted the status of an Autonomous Soviet Republic and Lenin's campaign for *korenizatsya* ('making roots') allowed the Crimean Tatars to use their language and enjoy free expression of their culture. This changed at the end of the twenties, when Stalin began targeting the non-Russian nationalities (although Stalin himself was Georgian, not Russian).

The Nazi invasion of Crimea was a separate occupation from the one in Ukraine, and the resistance in Crimea kept Sevastopol free until July 1942. The occupation ended two years later and the Crimean conference at Yalta marked a decisive end to World War II. After liberation, Stalin accused the Crimean Tatars for betraying the Soviet Union and deported them en-masse to work in Uzbekistan. It was a calculated genocide that killed almost half of the deportees within the first year.

Crimea was simply reduced to a Russian oblast (province) until 1954, when the Crimean Autonomous Soviet Socialist Republic was transferred to the Ukrainian SSR in remembrance of the Pereyaslav Agreement between Russia and Ukraine. The sixties and seventies witnessed an improved standard of living in the Soviet Union and Crimea fast became the chosen holiday destination for those who could. Young pioneers were sent to Crimea on holiday camps and a family might be awarded a week in one of the numerous seaside health resorts. Yalta and Alushta burgeoned into major tourist towns, while Sevastopol continued as the USSR's valued warm sea naval port, closed to everyone but military personnel and their families.

In March 1991, Gorbachev held a referendum on preserving the Soviet Union. Around 88% of Crimeans were in favour, the highest in Ukraine and above average for Russia. That same year, Gorbachev was put under house arrest while on holiday in Foros. Suddenly the world focused its attention on this small Crimean town while awaiting the fate of the coup.

When Ukraine gained independence, Crimea was *the* object of dispute with Russia. The area was ethnically Russian and home to the treasured Black Sea fleet. If war were to break out between Ukraine and Russia, it would be a fight for Crimea. The Crimean Tatars were finally allowed to return from exile, but this complicated an already complicated cultural friction. Crimea stayed Ukrainian on the maps, but the peninsula has kept is autonomy and the most Ukrainian thing one can find there is the money. Free enterprise has lessened the political tensions and hoards of Russian and Ukrainian tourists migrate yearly to the sunshine. The tourist pomp is quickly overriding this odd monument to Russian imperial glory, as well as the concerns of the Crimean Tatar refugee population.

The Autonomous Republic of Crimea

Ukraine has allowed Crimea to keep the autonomous status it has known for so long, but the Russian-Ukrainian divide is still a sensitive issue. Crimea's population is 2.5 million and comprises a record 80 ethnic groups, which makes their slogan 'Prosperity in Unity' appropriate. Russian, Crimean Tatar, and Ukrainian are all official languages. There is a Crimean parliament and separate constitution, and they have their own flag – a plain white field with a blue and a red stripe. Otherwise, the word 'autonomous' is still open to interpretation. For travellers, this means occasionally dealing with a whole new, separate bureaucracy. Keep your passport with you at all times, but more importantly, keep in mind that you are in a separate land that's proud to be different.

CRIMEAN PRACTICALITIES
Getting around

Simferopol is the transportation hub for all of Crimea and very difficult to avoid if you are travelling from the mainland. Trains are slightly pointless for travel within the region, since the lines extend north only. Sevastopol to Simferopol is the most obvious rail link while the line from Kerch to Dzhankoi sets a record for the slowest train in Ukraine. Motor transport is the best option. Buses and marshrutka connect all the towns and popular sites. Major routes branch out to Yevpatoria, Sevastopol, Yalta and the southern coast, and eastern Crimea (Kerch, Feodosiya). The coastal road from Alushta up to Sudak and Feodosiya is very beautiful but very mountainous. The direct bus will take many more hours than travelling on the regular routes via Simferopol. A new 'lux' bus travels a constant circle (Simferopol–Alushta–Yalta–Sevastopol) in under four hours, while the world's longest trolley line goes from Simferopol to Alushta and Yalta, stopping at every bus shelter along the way.

If you value elbow room, private taxis can always be negotiated for inter-city travel.

Green Rural Tourism in Crimea

This is the business euphemism for getting out of the city and simply enjoying nature. EU-funded projects have helped catalogue and classify the homes of Crimean villagers who are willing to accept paying guests for short stays. In

THE CRIMEAN TATARS

Crimea has been home to so many different ethnic groups it's hard to keep count; however, the Crimean Tatars actually formed their nation in this peninsula. As isolated descendants of the retreating Golden Horde, the Crimean khanate succeeded in unifying the people under one government. The Ottoman Empire made Crimea a tributary in 1475, but the relationship was quite free and the two worked very much as allies. For three hundred years this was their country and they developed a very individual religious and cultural identity. The population was 98% Crimean Tatar at the time of Russia's occupation. They began to emigrate *en masse* to Turkey when Catherine the Great deported the last khan and began the systematic destruction of every Tatar building and monument. The Tatar nobles who stayed were quickly assimilated into the Russian gentry and the people became a minority in their own country.

When Tsar Nikolai II abdicated, the Crimean Tatars came back to Simferopol in hopes of launching their independence campaign but the Bolsheviks had already taken control over the Russian navy. The Crimean government was quickly forced back into exile. During Lenin's regime Crimea's Tatar and Russian intelligentsia was targeted and sixty thousand were killed in less than six months (another 100,000 died of starvation). A period of calm followed during the *korenizatsiya* movement when Simferopol was symbolically called Ak-Mescid and Tatar schools and theatres were opened. Tatar language was making a comeback (the language has gone from Arab script to Latin and then to Cyrillic in a very short time), but then Stalin executed the leader of Tatar *korenizatsiya* and a new wave of oppression erupted.

Shortly after Crimea was liberated in 1944, Stalin made a declaration that the Crimean Tatar minority had conspired with the Germans and henceforth the minority nation was an enemy to the Soviet people. The entire Crimean Tatar population was deported in less than three days. Most were sent away in railway cars to Central Siberia and Uzbekistan and thousands died in transit; one overloaded ferry was purposefully sunk in the Black Sea and those who could swim were shot. In the Soviet east they were subjected to forced labour under harsh conditions, usually cutting down trees. It is estimated that nearly half of the Crimean population did not survive past the first year.

Despite a later apology from the Soviet government, the Crimean Tatars were only given permission to return to Crimea in 1989 and serious repatriation efforts took place only in 1995. The return of Crimean Tatar refugees into independent Ukraine has been highly problematic. Ukrainians and

theory, the experience offers visitors a chance to see the countryside while encouraging the locals to preserve their natural surroundings. Rooms cost between US$5 and $40 per night. Unfortunately, the programme suffers from a bureaucratic reservation system, but the brave should encourage a good thing and give it a try. Have a look at their website: www.greentour.crimea.ua; or send an email: cr-greentur@narod.ru. The Crimean Mountain Club also functions as an official contact (see *Simferopol tourist information*, pages 231–2).

SIMFEROPOL – СИМФЕРОПОЛЬ

The capital of the Crimean republic is a rather eclectic town of relaxed attitudes and Russian officialdom, but a pleasant place all the same. The city was built for

Russians are both fighting for their own nationalistic stance in Crimea, and many find a renewed Muslim presence unsettling, although movements in favour of repatriation have always been peaceful.

As the minority nation within a minority government (Crimea) in Ukraine, the Crimean Tatars must normally choose to side with the more powerful national government as the lesser of two evils. Unable to get dual Ukrainian citizenship due to their Uzbek passports, Crimean Tatars were forced to live a continued refugee existence in their own country. Most of their homes had been occupied or destroyed, so that now many Crimean Tatars are forced to live in shanty towns outside Crimean towns. But things have definitely improved of late. Ukrainian passports are being issued and there are now Crimean Tatar representatives in the Crimean parliament. Still, attitudes and opportunities are unsettled. The pro-Russian Crimean government publicly considers the Tatars a beneficial tourist attraction but an underlying racism is evident.

At last count, a quarter of a million Crimean Tatars had returned and now make up 12% of Crimea's population. A few million Crimean Tatars still live in Turkey, the United States and throughout the world. Bakhchisarai is still recognised as the Crimean Tatar capital, but the returned refugees live throughout the peninsula with larger concentrations in Yevpatoria, Feodosiya, and Stary Krym. There is a Crimean Tatar Museum in Simferopol but it is empty and without money.

Visiting the Crimean Tatars in Crimea is a unique experience to witness such an ancient culture making its way in the 21st century. Most of the Crimean Tatars you will meet have returned to Crimea only in the last five to ten years. The older populations remember the deportations or can tell you stories of Siberian labour camps and long years of cutting down trees. The younger population recall a very hard life in Uzbekistan and the upheaval of starting all over again in this homeland. As Sunni Muslims, the mosque is a centre for both cultural and religious activity, but most customs are preserved in the home. Three days after a baby is born, there is a naming ceremony, when the parents ritually bathe the child and then whisper the child's name into both ears. On the streets of Bakhchisarai you will also see young children greet their elders by kissing their hands and then pressing them against their forehead as a token of love and respect. Crimean Tatar food is a delicious alternative to Ukrainian fare with its staples of rice pilaf, mutton, dumplings and honey pastries (be sure to try *lagman* and *köbete*). If your interest in the Crimean Tatar situation transcends the souvenir markets and food stalls, check out web: www.iccrimea.org.

passing through, and its reputation relies on the recreational delights that surround it rather than its own sunny streets of busy traffic. To its own merit, Simferopol has something remarkably cosmopolitan about it, even though its 400,000 inhabitants appear by and large Russian. Fragments of Islamic architecture poke out occasionally and the ethnic mix is more than meets the outsider's eye.

Above all, Simferopol is a great place to engage in the gentle Russian pastime of having a stroll. With good weather for most of the year, the town's many parks, footbridges, and boulevards make for an agreeable urban hike. The Salgir River flows through the centre with a lovely side path shaded in bending willows and giant cypress trees. The cobblestone streets of the central quarter (around Ul Pushkina and Gorkovo) make up a pedestrian-only zone lined with newly

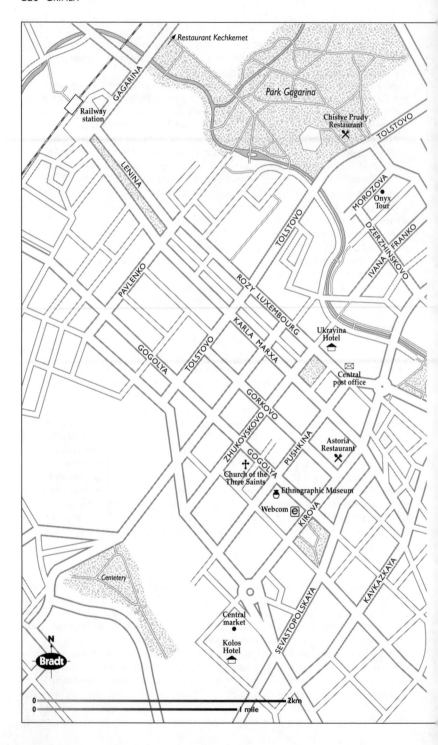

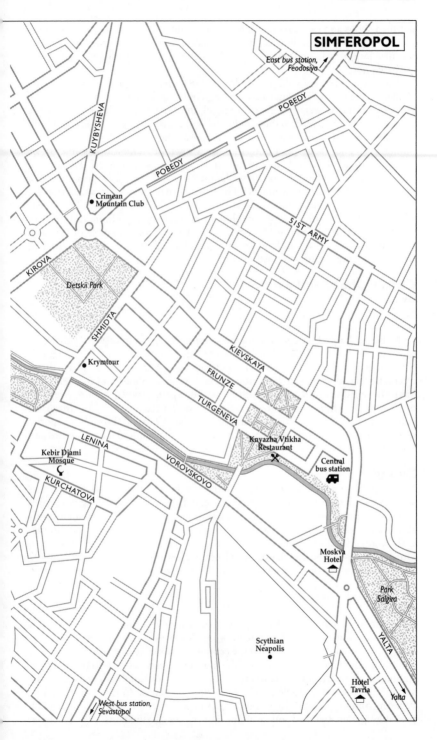

polished shops and cafés. As the transportation hub of Crimea, any trip you plan will most likely put you here for at least a half-day. This is also the best place to organise longer treks and other outdoor activities since so many tour companies are based here.

The city is relatively young, founded in 1784 after Crimea was taken over by Catherine the Great. The ancient sounding Greek name was added to signify the purpose of the newer city to connect all the scattered settlements under a centralised power. Over two thousand years ago, the late Scythian civilistaion built their 'Neapolis' as a fortress and a trading post. The ruins still stand in eastern Simferopol. The Tatars then built their own town of Akmescid (*Ak-mechet*), or 'White Mosque', of which the 16th-century mosque still remains. During the Crimean War, Simferopol stayed well protected and was used primarily as a morgue and a base for the wounded. The Russian civil war also wreaked havoc on the city and its people as this was a stronghold for the White Army. The USSR granted Simferopol its greatest compliment by situating a perfume factory here while the rest of Ukraine was digging coal. A good concentration of die-hard communists are still living large in Simferopol alongside everyone involved in Crimea's booming tourist industry.

Getting there and away
By *air*
Simferopol Central Airport is located on the far northwest side of the city. There are regular flights to both Kiev airports, Kharkiv, Lviv, and Odessa. A trip to Kiev costs about US$50. During the summer season there are additional daily flights to most regional centres of Ukraine. In the city, air tickets can be bought at Sevastopolskaya 22, tel: 0652 272 116. Lufthansa and Turkish Airlines have direct international connections to Simferopol. The Ukrainian ministry of foreign affairs has just opened a consular office in the airport that grants special eight-day permits to Crimea on arrival in lieu of a Ukrainian visa. This applies only to citizens of Canada, EU, USA, Switzerland, and Japan; tel: 0652 295 740. From the airport a taxi is best, but trolleybus #9 goes from the airport to Simferopol city centre and several direct buses leave from the airport to Crimea's coastal cities.

By rail
Simferopol's train station is the site most likely to be on a postcard of the city. The white walls, high arches and square tower blend Turkish architecture with socialist realism in a fitting style for the main gateway of the city. Most routes point towards Russia and pass through Zaporizhzhya, or go west to Odessa. There are at least two daily trains to and from Kiev (16 hours), one to Kharkiv (10 hours), Dnepropetrovsk (9 hours), Donetsk (11 hours), Odessa (12 hours), and Lviv (27 hours). An average coupé ticket to or from Simferopol any city on the mainland to costs US$15.

By bus
There are three main bus stations, Central, East and West, and then a small depot by the train station. The direction of your destination usually determines the station you should depart from, but the central avtovokzal is where most long-haul bus voyages will arrive. Simferopol is the most important destination of the south, so finding a bus to/from any Ukrainian city is not a problem. Finding a seat in the summer is more of a problem. The posh bus companies do run a good service between Simferopol and Kiev, but it is still an overnight journey and you'll probably prefer the bed on a train. For closer destinations (eg: Kherson,

Zaporizhzhya) you can take a quicker day bus. *Zapadnaya* (West Station) is at the end of Sevastopolskaya and has buses to Bakhchisarai and Sevastopol while *Vostochnaya* (East Station) is at 243 Pobedy and has buses for Feodosiya and Kerch. A taxi to either bus station should cost under US$2. Remember that you can get a bus to anywhere from the Central station, and there are plenty of regular marshrutka leaving from the train station (by McDonald's).

Where to stay
Simferopol does not have the same hotel development as the coastal cities of Crimea, but the available hotels do have a very wide variety of rooms. As of yet, none of the following accept credit cards:

Ukrayina Rozy Luxemburg 9; tel: 0652 510 165, fax: (0652) 278 495. This is considered the 'main' hotel of Simferopol and has something for every budget. The remodelled 'lux' rooms are comfortable and clean (US$105 single/$120 double), followed by the regular rooms (circa 1953) with shower (US$15 single/$30 double). Bare singles with a sink are US$5. Ukrayina may be slightly lower quality than the others, but it has the best location for seeing the city, and for getting between bus and train stations.

Moskva Kievskaya 2; tel: 0652 232 113, fax: 0652 237 389. This is the former Inturist hotel, built in the 1970s but newly remodelled in typical post-Soviet glitz. Its best asset is its location next to the Central Bus Station and the Scythian Neapolis. Rooms cost US$50/$90/$150 (single/double/suite). All rooms have private bathrooms with shower or bath and there is a good restaurant. For people with cars, there is a guarded parking lot here.

Tavria Bespalova 21; tel: 0652 233 919. This former Soviet 'tour base' consists of two buildings, one remodelled to a higher standard with middle-range prices, and the other preserved in its original Soviet state. All remodelled rooms have showers. Remodelled singles cost from US$20 to $30, doubles $40 and the suites start at US$70. There are varying degrees of cheaper rooms as well.

Kolos Subkhi 4; tel: 0652 272 384. A basic hotel with basic quality and basic prices.

Where to eat
Kechkemet (Ul Gagarina 22) is one of Simferopol's better restaurants serving (surprise!) traditional Hungarian food for around US$15 a meal. **Chistye Prudy** is at the main entrance to Gagarin Park and serves believable Armenian food. For sophisticated Ukrainian cuisine, try **Knyazha Vtikha** (Turgeneva 35). A full meal costs US$7–10. The **Astoria** (Pr Kirova 32) offers the typical Russian/European fare. There are also plenty of smaller cafés and bars in the pedestrian area that serve food at all hours.

Getting organised
Tourist information
If you have specific needs, or just want somebody else to organise your travel to the rest of Crimea, Simferopol is the right place to start. Here are a few good contacts:

Krymtour Shmidta 9; tel: 0652 250 350; email: info@krymtur.com; web: www.krymtur.com. This joint-venture company is the most established in the area and deals only with incoming tourists to Crimea. They offer a huge variety of package tours and have branch offices in every town.

Crimean Mountain Club Ul Kievskaya 77/4; tel: 0652 249 528; email: afk@crimea.com. This club was founded in 1890 and is the oldest group of its kind in 'Russia.' The office is not easily accessible since they share with Ukraine's local branch of the Green Party but they can be very helpful if you want to head off into the hills.

Onyx Tour Morozova 13; tel: 0652 245 822. Crimea's caves are truly spectacular and worth a visit. Oniks Tour is the private spelunking club that owns access to Mramornaya and Eminé-Bair-Khosar Caves and conducts excursions to other local caverns. Professionals can set up a challenging underground tour, while first-timers can choose an easier group tour that is just as impressive.

Internet
WEBCOM Kirova 22; tel: 0652 255 132; web: www.poluostrov.net. A centrally located computer club open 24 hours (7UAH/hour).

What to see and do
There is no prescribed tick-list for Simferopol: the sights are there to see, but the city is more conducive to walking around and simply hanging out before or after your other Crimean travels. One of the oldest buildings in the city is the **Kebir Djami Mosque** (Kurchatova 4). Built in 1502, this is the exception that outlived both Catherine the Great and the Soviet Union. **The Church of the Three Saints** (Gogolya 16) is a beautiful white church with black cupolas built in 1871. During Soviet times the church was used as the city's archives, but now it belongs to the Moscow Patriarchate (open everyday 07.30–19.00.). Just down the street is the **Ethnographic Museum** (Pushkina 18; tel: 0652 258 712). The permanent exhibit presents 13 of the ethnic groups that have lived in Crimea, and each display was designed and donated by locals.

The **Scythian Neapolis** is an unfinished archaeological dig working to uncover what used to be the capital of late Scythian civilisation. These 'Royal Scythians' were heavily influenced by contact with the Greeks and flourished from the 2nd century BC to the 3rd century AD. The surrounding wall still remains, as well as dozens of half-excavated tombs and large palace ruins. Take the #4 trolleybus to the end of the line or walk from the Hotel Moskva.

Simferopol's parks are its saving grace. A nice walk begins in **Park Gagarina** and criss-crosses the Salgir River through other small parks, ending in **Park Salgira** (which then extends to the reservoir). **Detskii Park** (Children's Park) is a classic example of Soviet family entertainment and contains various amusements aimed at the youngest generation. Lastly, on Sunday afternoons there is a big outdoor book market across from the *vokzal*.

OUTSIDE SIMFEROPOL
Chatyr-Dag – Чатыр-Даг
This long, sloping plateau stands alone and is one of the highest in Crimea (1,527m), inspiring its Tatar name which transcribes as 'Roof Mountain.' The karst landscape is pockmarked but very green and open. On the lower eastern side of the mountain is the **Angarskii Pass** (Ангарский Перевал) which has its own bus stop on the M18 road between Simferopol and Alushta. This seems to be the base from which the popular hiking route goes to Chatyr-Dag (and Demerdzhi) and one of the few locations where it snows enough for winter sports.

Another trail goes from Mramornoye on the road from Simferopol. Like standing on a roof, much of Crimea is visible from the top. Take care – this spot lies right between the rising steppe and the seaside mountain ridge and is prone to very high winds.

The caves of Chatyr-Dag – Пещеры Чатыр-Дага
Chatyr-Dag is more renowned for what lies beneath: all along its lower side are literally hundreds of limestone caves. Two of the largest have been set up for

Above Gorgany Range, Carpathian Mountains (AE)

Below Waves crashing, Black Sea (AE)

Above Maize and *kalina* berries, Galicia (AE)
Right Babushka with herbs, Dikanka, Sloboda (AE)
Below Sunflowers, Sloboda (AE)

regular visitors and are located very close to one another. The caves are maintained by Onyx Tour (see Tourist Information), who can arrange tours and transportation from Simferopol. Otherwise, you can get there on your own by bus/trollyebus to Zarechnoye of Mramornoye or simply hike. Next to Mramornaya there are cabins for hikers (US$4 a night per person/US$25 for the whole house) as well as a café and a Russian *banya*.

Mramornaya – Мраморная

'Marble' cave was only discovered in 1987 and is now one of the most visited caves in all of Europe due to its easy access and remarkable formations. It is a relatively shallow cave at 68m deep, but it is almost 2km long and filled with oozing geological shapes. The fat ochre pillars all seem to be melting and the glossy stalagmites are humorously statuesque, while deeper in the cave, white calcite 'moon milk' is still dripping ghostly forms onto the rocks and cave pools form tiny calcite pearls. The cave took its present shape sixty thousand years ago when a series of subterranean riverbeds collapsed one on top of another, leaving two 'floors'. The destruction created a massive room in the centre, filled with house-size boulders, now jokingly called 'Perestroika Hall.' The air is so cool and so unpolluted that things appear smaller than they actually are. Visits are by guided tour only. The normal one-hour tour costs US$4 and takes in the upper level and all its formations. If you really want to feel like you're spelunking, there is a three-and-a-half hour tour through the lower levels where you'll get to wear a hard hat with a light beam in it. This is a bit more physically demanding but shows some truly incredible untouched spots. A maximum of five people can go to the lower level at one time and costs US$15 per person, including equipment.

Eminé-Ba'ir-Khosar – Эмине-Баир-Хосар

The cave's Tatar name translates as 'the Well of Maiden Eminé' and comes with a genuine Romeo and Juliet legend. Eminé's love was killed by her father's tribe and she began searching the mountains to find his lost soul. When told that he would be waiting in the heart of the earth, she climbed down into the bottom of the cave and found its deepest crevice. Staring into the darkness, she was overcome by grief and threw herself from the edge. The story matches the cave, which opens in a gaping hole and then spirals down to an incredible depth of 120m. The vivid colours and sheer size of this cave make the visit even more exciting than Mramornaya. Eminé is unique for its small crystal flowers, an absinthe-coloured lake and stalagmite forests. The 'hall of idols' really does look like a jade shop and the caramel flows of clay are unusually inviting. There is also a small 'museum' inside the cave where the prehistoric finds of the cave are liberally displayed, including mammoth teeth, sabre-tooth tiger bones and onyx crystals. The tours vary in length and depth – the full tour costs US$4.

YEVPATORIA – ЕВПАТОРИЯ

Miles of natural sand beaches secured this town's fate as a resort. Spread along the northern shore of Kalamita bay, Yevpatoria is still a prime destination for Russian seaside holidaymakers and is packed during the summer. The port has gone through all the reincarnations of a Crimean town, starting with its Greek phase. Kerkinitida was a wealthy trading centre that even issued its own currency at one time. The Scythians seemed to attack this port more than the others and eventually took it over. Trade petered out and the city fell into oblivion for almost a millennium. Then Kievan Rus and the Genoese followed with brief appearances in the region, but only under the Ottoman Turks did the medieval Tatar city Gözlev establish itself as the centre of the Black Sea slave trade. Gözlev was surrounded by a thick 4km-long city wall and boasted 12 mosques. In their ongoing rivalry with the Turks, the Zaporizhzhyan Cossacks frequently raided the port. Later, Catherine the Great built a new Russian city and added the name of an ancient slavic king Yevpator. Here the Russian aristocracy created a spa town along the designs of those they visited in Switzerland and Italy. During the Crimean War, the port was easily taken by the allied forces and occupied for the whole of the conflict. Sanatoria (health resorts) occupied the whole beachfront in Soviet times and the tourist/health industry now reigns supreme, with a special focus on children. Compared to the southern coast, this is still very much a quiet town. The boardwalk and high-rise hotels should not detract from the town's cultural relics: the Dzhuma-Dzhami Mosque, the Karaim Kenassa and the old imperial Russian resorts.

Getting there and away
There is a direct train to Kiev although its schedule tends to change frequently. There are regular trains to Simferopol, as well as buses, which take about two-and-a-half hours. Less frequent buses travel to Feodosiya (4½ hours) and Yalta (4 hours). The train station is at the end of Frunze, while the bus station is just across from the train station on Internatsionalnaya. At one time, frequent ships ferried passengers to Odessa, other Crimean cities and Turkey, but this is a thing of the past.

Where to stay
The many hotels and sanatoria stem from the Soviet era. There are resorts all along the beach, but many require a minimum package of a week or so. The largest hotel in town is **Yevpatoria** (Pobedy 1/64; tel: 06569 515 48) with the full range of prices and some high standards with bathroom and hot water. Prices are US$50 for a single or double room; US$100 for a suite. Similar but less expensive are **Krym** (Revolyutsii 46; tel: 06569 105 49) and **Ukrayina** (Lenina 42/19; 06569 365 04) where rooms are from US$10 to US$50, with suites at US$70.

If you are keen to try out the Soviet version of a spa vacation (complete with Russian concepts of medicine), Yevpatoria will provide an authentic first time. **Planeta** (Kositskovo 29/73; tel: 06569 603 20; email: planetacom@evp.sf.ukrtel.net) is a modern, higher-quality resort with a big swimming pool and several 'lux' rooms. A standard room is US$25, junior suite US$40 and full suite US$60. Right on the beachfront is **Pobeda** (Frunze 4; tel: Kiev 044 220 66 50; email: kurort@i.kiev.ua) which has remained true to the Soviet tradition that founded it. The hotel is intended for families with children.

Where to eat
There are not a lot of places to choose from, especially for a resort town. Hotels **Yevpatoria** and **Ukrayina** both have good in-house restaurants, as well as the resort **Planeta**. **Atlant** (Frunze 20) does some seafood and typical Russian meals, whereas **Armenia** (Demysheva 160) serves its namesake's cuisine. There are also many smaller cafés that serve food. The milk bar **Molochnoye** (Revolyutsii 51) is a fun café that serves milkshakes as well as very basic meals.

What to do and see
Enjoy the beach! Kalamita Bay is one of the calmer spots on the Black Sea (in terms of waves, not people). Most transport goes to Solnyshko beach but a long walk should take you away from the worst crowds. On the main street of Revolyutsii is the **Dzhuma-Dzhami** – a working mosque returned to Crimean Tatar ownership in 1990. The original structure was built in the 16th century by Khodzha Sinan and

it is here that the Crimean Khans were crowned. The minarets and Sufi-inspired design are amazingly well-preserved and the symbol of Yevpatoria today. Not far is the **Tekiye Dervishes Monastery** (14th century) with a similarly distinctive spiritual architecture. The old **Turkish bathhouse** (Krasnoarmeyskaya 50) has remained from the days of the sultan and is open to visitors. Yevpatoria also contains one of the last remaining buildings of the Karaims, the non-Talmudic Crimean Jewish nation. The **Karaim Kenassa** (Matveeva 68) is an assembly of holy buildings and arcades built by the Karaim in the early 19th century.

BAKHCHISARAI – БАХЧИСАРАЙ

Most people stop in Bakhchisarai to meet the Crimean Tatars, which is a worthwhile goal for these parts. This small country town was once the eminent capital of the Crimean khanate and has been the centre of Tatar repatriation for the last decade. Minarets grace the skyline and the crumbling tile-roofed buildings look anything but Slavic. The town is stretched along the canyon bed of the Churyuk-Su River right where the sloping fruit orchards turn into mountains. As you move upstream, the cliffs cut deeper and the mooing of cows echo off the lumpy rocks. Hikers will want to explore the unique countryside dotted with Crimea's most ancient cave cities.

The site was first designated 'Eski-Yurt' by the Golden Horde in the 13th century. In nearby Chufut-Kale, the Crimean khanate was separately established in 1427. After the Ottoman Empire brought the khanate under its rule, the Crimean khan, Abdul Sahel Girai, moved his capital to Bakchisarai ('The Palace in the Garden'). The construction continued for three and a half centuries with new halls and courts added to the palace by the descendant khans. At the height of the Crimean khanate, there were 32 mosques in Bakchisarai – of which most were destroyed during the Russian occupation in 1783. Catherine the Great did spare the palace, supposedly for its romantic appeal. These dry landscapes are still dear to the heart of Orthodoxy and pilgrims still come to worship at these early Christian sites. Today, Bakhchisarai is a resurrected ghost town. Its newest inhabitants have lived most of their life in exile and are slowly rebuilding their city, while the rest of the world has just started to take an interest.

Getting there and away

Bakhchisarai is the main stop between Simferopol and Sevastopol. Taking the hourly bus or a marshrutka is the best option (an hour either way). Eight trains pass through everyday, two of which go on to Kiev, another to Donetsk. There are sometimes direct buses from Yalta (1½ hours). The *vokzal* and bus station are at the end of Ulitsa Rakitskovo. The marshrutka and bus routes leave from this square and go directly to the khan's palace, then up to the end of the main road, turning around at the base of the Assumption Monastery.

Where to stay and eat

This is still a small town with limited choices. **Bakhchisarai** (Simferopolskaya 3; tel: 06554 251 97) has normal rooms for US$10 and up. **Avtomobilist** (Krymskaya 12; tel: 06554 268 72) is a motel for visitors travelling by car and **Elita** (Lenina 110; tel: 06554 474 02) is more glam than élite. These three hotels have OK restaurants. Closer to the Khan's Palace are plenty of food-stands and cafés for the tourist crowds that pass through in summer. The *chebureki* and *baklava* sold on the street are delicious. If you want genuine Crimean Tatar cuisine, go to **K'yavé Khané Gul'fidan**. The restaurant is next to the palace (across the moat) and serves up the real thing.

What to see
The Khan's Palace

Pictures of this building are in every Crimean tourist brochure and its high-domed mosque is *the* symbol for Crimea's oriental image. The lofty minarets and rows of Turkish chimneys clearly stand out from the rough-and-tumble look of the town. Here the Crimean khans once held court and kept a sizeable harem. The original structure follows the combined design of Persian, Turkish, and Italian architects and spontaneous additions since 1551 made the ensemble an elaborate cluster of painted walls and lacy woodwork. The entire complex is a protected historic site that functions as a series of museums but also serves as a community centre and working mosque for the Crimean Tatars.

The palace is unique for a former Soviet museum since you are free to walk around and explore the various buildings and small gardens on your own. A self-guided walking tour gives you a small idea of what life was like for the khanate royalty. On the left of the main entrance is the original 'big' mosque from which the muezzin still calls prayers. It is not open to visitors. The other courtyards and buildings are open although some are just used as storage space for unrelated exhibits. The **Divan Chamber** was the literal seat of government where the khan and Ottoman emissaries discussed government affairs and made plans for war. The **Small Mosque** has remained in its original condition and stands as a monument to the liberalism of the Crimean Tatars – during restoration, frescos were found with scenes of men, animals, and flowers, all considered idolatrous images and shunned in mainstream Islamic design. The **Summer House** was a late addition to the palace and its latest renovation has a strong Soviet disco feel. The **Fountain Yard** is a collection of the fountains that have been moved from other parts of the

THE FOUNTAIN OF TEARS

In the corner of the Fountain Yard of the Khan's Palace stands a small marble fountain with a wistful history. Khan Krim Gerei fell deeply in love with a Polish girl who was added to his harem as a war prize. When he first looked on her face he shouted out 'Dilara Bikech!' meaning 'Beautiful Princess.' The khan became obsessed with her but alas, his love remained unrequited. Unable to cope with harem life, the girl died after one year. The khan was grief-stricken and fell into a deep depression. He built a giant tomb for the girl and it is written that he cried day and night for years afterwards. His courtesans ordered a fountain be made that would 'contain' the khan's endless heartache so that he would begin to address the affairs of state. The fountain was built by the tomb of the girl and later moved by Catherine the Great into the fountain yard. Water is carried from shelf to shelf tumbling out periodically like the overflowing tears of a grief remembered. The Sufi design brings the water to the bottom of the fountain where it trickles into a spiral, the symbol of eternity.

After visiting the palace, the romantic poet Pushkin was inspired by the khan's tragic love story and penned the famous poem *The Bakhchisarai Fountain*. He picked two roses from the garden, and placed them on the top of the fountain (red for love, and yellow for chagrin). The tradition is still followed with freshly cut palace roses. The popularity of the poem kept the palace from being destroyed during the Russian Empire and led to it becoming a museum during the Soviet era. The moral of the story is that if you want to preserve a place, write a poem about it.

REBIRTH OF CRIMEA FOUNDATION (RCF)

Due to Ukraine's already high unemployment and the difficult social conditions of Crimea, returning Crimean Tatar refugees have had little opportunity for work and self-support. The RCF Crimean Tatar co-operative secures international grants and uses them to re-educate the refugees in traditional Crimean Tatar craft to allow them the chance for an income. One of their centres, Marama, conducts short courses for Bakhchisarai women on traditional embroidery. These Crimean Tatar designs and handicrafts are applied to handbags, handkerchiefs and hats, then sold in the marketplace near the Khan's Palace during the long Crimean summer. Men are also taught traditional jewellery-making and beadwork. Buying something from the market is not your average souvenir shopping, but helps to secure a place for the Crimean Tatars in their capital.

The RCF has also opened a House of Crimean Tatar Art in Bakhchisarai, Rechnaya 125. For a small donation, guests visiting this preserved Crimean Tatar home are served a real Crimean meal, enjoy a permanent exhibition, and best of all, interact with Crimean Tatars. For more information or prior contact, email: rcf@tavria.net.

palace, including the famous Fountain of Tears. Elaborate calligraphy over the doorways pays homage to individual khans, bestowing the Islamic blessing to 'Forgive him and his parents'. The **Harem** is in a separate building and is the one house remaining out of the four that belonged to the khan's wives. Apparently, women in the harem were allowed a peek of the outside world from the top of the **Falcon Tower** where the khan's hunting birds were kept. Also in the yard is the khan's cemetery, where 16 former Crimean khans are buried. Through the staterooms on the second floor of the palace there is a museum display of Crimean Tatar artefacts. There are beautiful examples of Islamic calligraphy in illuminated 13th-century Korans and original *sharia* books used in the Crimean khanate. The exhibit also features Crimean Tatar clothes, objects and utensils, as well as old photographs of Crimea and its people before deportation. The palace is open 09.00–16.00, and closed Tuesdays and Wednesdays. Labels are posted in English and Russian. Entrance is 15UAH for foreigners and 4UAH if you can ask for a ticket in Russian. (Photography inside the complex is also charged per frame.)

Somewhat more interesting than the palace itself is the activity around it. Out on the street, or in the main courtyard, the Tatar men in their black astrakhan hats gather to talk and little Tatar *babushki* sell traditional Crimean Tatar food. On Fridays, the place is busy with families coming and going to prayer. If you take the time to stand and watch or else have a chat (Crimean Tatars are notoriously multi-lingual) you'll learn more about this small nation than any museum can show you.

OUTSIDE BAKHCHISARAI
The Holy Assumption Bakhchisarai Monastery

This tiny and very ancient church is built inside a cave so that its small windows appear naturally set into the face of the steep cliffside from which it hangs. Diagonal stairs and open-air tunnels wind up to the single golden dome and the actual chapel with its low ceiling forces a physical manifestation of humility. From this vertical churchyard you can see across the canyon to the cave city of Chufut-Kale. The monastery claims to be the oldest in Crimea, started in the 8th century by Byzantine mystics. They followed the natural contours of the cliff to construct a series of chapels and cells inside the rock. It was closed in 1921, but has now reopened and is home to an order of Russian Orthodox monks (in Soviet days the wide stone steps were used as a backdrop for the film version of *Hamlet*). The monastery is fast becoming an important pilgrimage site, not least for its holy fountain that brings health and blessings to those who drink from it.

Sincere travellers can approach the father of the monastery and receive his blessing to be a guest in the monastery for three days. During this time your food and accommodation are provided for, but be prepared to get up very early, to pray lots and to work hard. The monks spend much of their day rebuilding their monastery by hand.

To get there take the #2 bus or any marshrutka and go to the end of the line, or take a taxi. From the base, the trail curves up around the hillside for 500m. From the monastery it is one kilometre across and up to Chufut-Kale.

Chufut-Kale – Чуфут-Кале

The 'Fortress of the Jews' is a medieval ruin perched high on a plateau, and the most-visited of Crimea's 16 cave cities. The Christianised Alan tribes were the first to use this strategic spot, and their many monasteries earned it the name Kyrk-Or (Forty Fortresses). The nations that passed through Crimea all left populations in this city, including the Armenians and the Karaim Jews who were descendants from the Khazar khaganate. The Crimean khanate built their first capital here in the 15th century and ruled with tolerance, but many of the Greek Christians moved to Mangup. After relocating his capital to Bakhchisarai, the khan decreed that the Karaim Jews could trade freely in the city during the day, but then had to return back to their mountain home by nightfall. The Karaim's predominated in Chufut-Kale for the entire reign of the Crimean khanate.

The city streets are still intact and the ruins make for interesting exploring. The 14th-century Karaim Kenassa is next to the southern entrance and there are countless homes hewn out of the rock. Hiking back down to the canyon bed brings you to the lower caves that run along the hillside. Among the grazing goats are new shrines to the oldest Orthodox saints. St Cyril, founder of the Russian alphabet, visited here in AD862.

Tepe-Kermen – Тепе-Кермен

'Castle on the summit', this cave city is at the top of a mesa-like hill and is surrounded by a much less tampered natural area. The knobbly grottos atop the plateau made a convenient base from which 240 cave structures were built into an impenetrable town. Founded in the 6th century, this is the oldest of Crimea's cave cities and at one time the most populated. The king's palace is still recognisable on the southwest side and the 8th-century cave chapel is a testament to human labour with its altar and pillars carved entirely from the white rock. It is best to hike here from the eastern gate of Chufut-Kale. Follow the top of the ridge south for two miles. The only ascending path goes from the northeast side of the hill. There are no local springs here, so make sure you have some water with you.

Mangup-Kale – Мангуп-Кале

The ancient capital of the Feodor was the largest fortress and city in Crimea for about 500 years. A Turkish traveller writing in the 17th century remarked that Allah had used the rocks to build his own castle long before any people had come here. The twisted white cliffs rise straight up from the thickly forested slopes. The plateau is in the shape of a four-fingered hand with extremely sheer drop-offs on

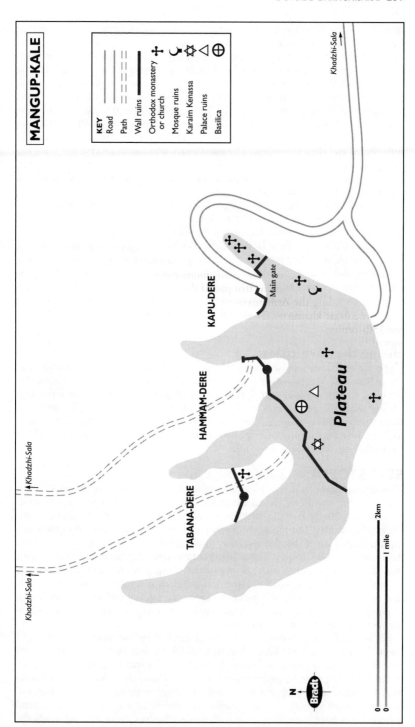

MANGUP-KALE

KEY
Road
Path
Wall ruins
✝ Orthodox monastery or church
☾ Mosque ruins
✡ Karaim Kenassa
△ Palace ruins
⊕ Basilica

KAPU-DERE
Main gate
HAMMAM-DERE
TABANA-DERE
Plateau

Khadzhi-Sala
Khadzhi-Sala
Khadzhi-Sala

N

0 ———— 1 mile
0 ———— 2km

Bract

three sides – an obvious strategic advantage. The fort was ordered built by Justinian I in the 6th century, but it was the independent Crimean Greeks who used this vantage point to establish a long-lasting regime in the southwest of the peninsula. Feodor was a medieval Orthodox Liechtenstein, carrying on its own diplomatic relations with Russia, Romania and Hungary. Its capital was its greatest strength – the Turks persisted in a six-month siege before taking the city in the 15th century, and then only through trickery: the Turkish army began marching away quickly, as if surrendering, leaving sentries hidden by the gates. When the Feodorites opened the gates and charged after the Turks, they found themselves quickly surrounded and their city taken. The ruins today attest to its diverse use until the 1700s when it was deserted. The original Byzantine ramparts, the citadel, Orthodox cave churches, the mosque and the underground dungeons are all still intact and open for exploration.

In recent years, Mangup's challenging surface has become popular with rock climbers and mountain bikers. The ancient mystique has also attracted groups of Russian nonconformists and dabblers in the supernatural. Graffiti is rife.

Mangup is 20km south of Bakhchisarai. Take a bus from the *avtovokzal* most of the way through Krasny Mak to the town of Zalesnoye. On foot, turn left and follow the dirt road to Khadzhi Sala from which three separate trails go up to Mangup. (If you turn right at Zalesnoye, the path will go to Eski-Kermen, yet another cave city.) The first two paths go up through the fingers and are about a 2km hike, while the larger dirt road is less steep but extends 5km. A 4WD taxi costs around US$10.

Hiking the cave cities

If you are in Bakhchisarai and have time to see only one cave city, Chufut-Kale is the closest, but Mangup-Kale is probably more interesting and Tepe-Kermen is the most remote and least visited. A popular walk leaves from Bakhchisarai, through Chufut Kale, Tepe-Kermen, and all the way to Mangup via the town of Kuybyshevo. This is about a 30km hike and can be done in two days or stretched to three. Use a good contour map; you won't get lost, but you'll want to avoid the towns that can distract from the hike.

SEVASTOPOL – СЕВАСТОПОЛЬ

This famous port city is best known for being unknown. Sevastopol was a 'closed city' until the late 1990s, when hyper security around the military was relaxed. Previously, nobody but the Black Sea fleet personnel and their families were allowed in the area, but the years of pampered isolation have worked in the city's favour: this is one of the cleanest cities in the former USSR and the latest trendy destination for Ukrainians. Those who venture here witness an unexpected shift from the humdrum of so many Soviet towns. Orderly white buildings dominate, all built in matching Russian neo-classical grandeur and standing on rows of hills that seem to hover above the water. Squinting across any one of the bays brings visions of an ancient Roman port – the very intention of Catherine the Great when she chose the site to house her navy.

Sevastopol has a personal sense of chic unrivalled by any other 'Russian' city I know. Aesthetics matter here: Bolshaya Morskaya and Nakhimova Boulevard parade some classy shops and small pruned gardens surround the hundreds of monuments to generals, soldiers and citizens. All day, single-file lines of short-haired sailors march back and forth in their ironed uniforms and shiny buckles. Military primness with a smile seems the unwritten city code. The general goodwill may have something to do with the fact that people in this city have jobs.

Outside of the navy, most marine men have been commissioned into international shipping companies and are paid high foreign salaries. A virgin tourist industry has also taken off with only a few unfortunate results – the life-size, fluorescent plastic palm trees and 'dolphinarium' fail to enhance the many natural and historical attractions.

Before Sevastopol, there was Chersoneus – the largest Greek port on the north Black Sea coast and a vital city for Kievan Rus trade. The importance of commerce allowed quick recovery following the Mongol and Ottoman invasions. Russia's interest in this strategic warm-sea port was a major incentive to their taking Crimea from the Turks in 1783. Catherine the Great was delighted with this crossover between her own empire and that of the ancient Greeks and ordered the city built around the ruins. She visited in 1787 with lots of Oriental illusions in her head, claiming the city was straight out of the *Arabian Nights*. Succeeding rulers hoped that the Russian Empire's growing naval power would be launched from this port but in the end their aspirations pulled the Crimean War back to Sevastopol. Under the threat of a conclusive attack by the Anglo-French fleet, Admiral Nakhimov scuttled most of his ships, blocking the entrance to the bay. For 349 days, the Russian army fought on the terrain in and around Sevastopol making the Malakhov mound a household name in Victorian Britain. Once the city fell in August 1855 the Crimean War was over and Sevastopol's identity has been branded ever since. War enthusiasts can visit a number of commemorative museums or walk the overgrown cemeteries and battlefields in Inkerman and Balaclava.

People here are proud of their city in spite of the defeats it has suffered. Stalin granted Sevastopol the title 'hero city' after it held out against the Germans until July 1942. Around here, nobody is spitting on memories of the Soviet Union and this may be the one place in Ukraine you can still hear people address each other as *tovarisch* (comrade). Like all interesting places, Sevastopol is wrapped in controversy. While the rest of Ukraine is trying to convince itself and the world that they are Ukrainian and not Russian, Sevastopol is doing the opposite. The Russian tri-colour is ubiquitous, as is the tsarist St Andrew's cross sewn into the sleeves of black naval uniforms. The popular return to glorifying the Russian monarchy seems a bit more justified in this city once prized by the tsar, but Kiev does not appreciate these displays. When Luzhkov, the outspoken mayor of Moscow, began making claims on Sevastopol, the Ukrainian government moved a chunk of its offices down here. The bureaucrats who transferred were the lucky ones; Sevastopol's coastline and countryside (not to mention climate) make this a very nice place to live.

Getting there and away
By rail
Sevastopol marks the end of the great rail lines connecting the Baltic with the Black Sea, so there are many standard trains to Russia which pass through Kiev or Kharkiv. There are also two direct trains that leave daily for Kiev and one to Donetsk. The frequency of the long-distance trains makes it a good place to begin or end a trip in Crimea. All Sevastopol lines pass through Simferopol, which is between two to three hours away.

By bus
Buses are quickest for getting to other places in Crimea, and a better way to see the magnificent landscapes outside the city. The station is right next to the *vokzal* (tel: 0692 46 16 32). There are buses all day to Bakhchisarai (1 hour) Simferopol (2 hours) and Yalta (2 hours). Two buses go to Foros (1 hour). There is one daily bus

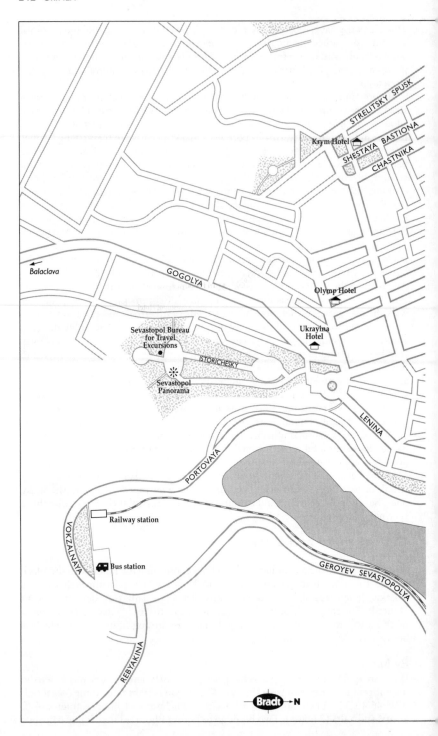

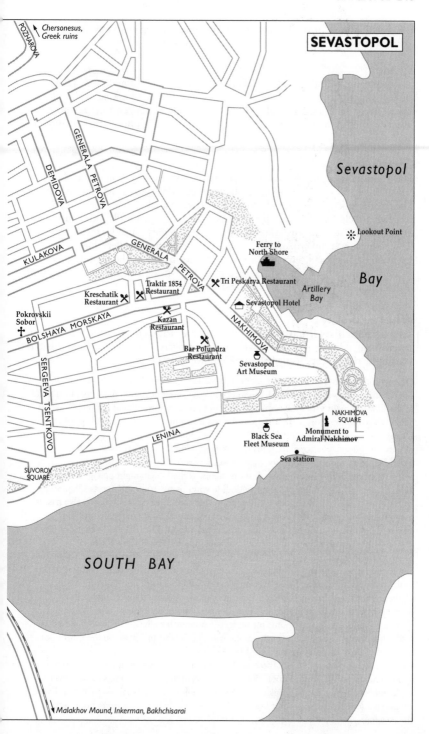

↑ Chersonesus,
Greek ruins

POZHAROVA

SEVASTOPOL

Sevastopol

GENERALA PETROVA

DEMIDOVA

KULAKOVA

GENERALA

PETROVA

✳ Lookout Point

Ferry to
North Shore

Bay

✗ Tri Peskarya Restaurant

*Artillery
Bay*

Kreschatik
Restaurant ✗

✗ Traktir 1854
Restaurant

Pokrovskii
Sobor ✝

BOLSHAYA MORSKAYA

NAKHIMOVA

🏛 Sevastopol Hotel

✗ Kazan
Restaurant

SERGEEVA TSENTKOVO

✗ Bar Polundra
Restaurant

Sevastopol
Art Museum

NAKHIMOVA
SQUARE

Monument to
Admiral Nakhimov

LENINA

Black Sea
Fleet Museum

SUVOROV
SQUARE

Sea station

SOUTH BAY

↓ Malakhov Mound, Inkerman, Bakhchisarai

to Kerch (7 hours) and two to Feodosiya (5 hours). Taking buses any farther seems redundant. Nikolayev is 11 hours by bus; Odessa is 13.

By boat
On occasion summer ferries sail between Odessa, Sevastopol, and Yalta. The service is random and declining, so it becomes a matter of asking at the *Morskoi Vokzal* (Sea Station) Currently, the only regular passenger ship is the *Geroi Sevastopolya* (Nakhimova 5; tel: 0692 540 522) which sails once a week to Istanbul from the main port (US$70 one way/US$140 return).

Getting around
The #9 trolleybus runs between the centre of town to the *vokzal* (the trolley stop is over the walkway on top of the small precipice) and on to the Malakhov mound. The marshrutka run up and down Bolshaya Morskaya, to the *Vokzal* and everywhere else – ask the driver. Taxis are very plentiful and convenient. Anywhere inside the city should cost US$1. Sights outside the city limits (Chersoneus and Inkerman) are US$2 and up. From Artillery bay there is a continuous pedestrian ferry that runs to the north side of the city. The dock is located behind the Hotel Sevastopol and next to the old armoury (Konstantinovskaya Battareya) on the north side.

Where to stay
Keep in mind that for the past 70 years the only visitors to Sevastopol have been government officials and the Nazis. A fast recovery is under way and what is available is rather respectable. All but Hotel Krym take credit cards.

Olymp Kulakova 86; tel: 0692 455 758; fax: 0692 455 736; email: OLYMP@inbox.ru; English-language website: http://olymphotel.com/eng/about.htm. A brand-new plush hotel of the US$100/night variety. Rooms are large and very comfortable and the service lavish. There's a swimming pool and sauna, and the water running from their taps is potable!

Ukrayina Gogolya 2; tel: 0692 542 127; fax: 0692 545 378; email: ukrainehotel@stel.sebastopol.ua. This is a very clean hotel with all renovated rooms, individual bathrooms, 24-hour hot water, and a few real queen-size beds. There are far too many room categories, but the best deal for money is the US$50/night upscale double. The deluxe suite is US$80/night and a single/double without any trimmings costs US$25/$45. Breakfast is included and besides the restaurant there are three cafés. Ukrayina also has its own on-site tour agency that does a good job of organising local excursions and tour guides. They also do pick-ups from the Simferopol airport. The office is in room 214; tel: 0692 540 398; email: ukrainehotel@stel.sebastopol.ua, ATTN: Riviera-Krym.

Sevastopol Nakhimova 8; tel: 0692 591 188; fax: 0692 592 813. After the war, Nakhimova Boulevard lay in ruins and this hotel was the first effort at reconstruction. Today it stands as the most beautiful thing Stalin ever built and would fool most into thinking it was a Catherine the Great original. What it lacks in upmarket quality it makes up for in its location right in the heart of the city. The very best singles/doubles are US$30/$40, but there are a range of cheaper rooms for budget-conscious travellers. The lowest end costs US$6/night with a shared shower down the hall. A full-time masseuse on the third floor gives heavy-duty Russian massages for US$6 an hour.

Krym Shestaya Bastiona 46; tel: 0692 469 000. The requisite Soviet hotel with casino, bar and restaurant on the ground floor. You may be one of the few foreigners to have ever walked through their doors. Singles are US$15, doubles US$17, breakfast included. Every room has a toilet and shower, but hot water comes on only in the morning hours and in the evening.

Where to eat

Finding a good meal is not a problem in Sevastopol. There's plenty of fresh seafood around and a market for good restaurants. As of yet, none of the following accept credit cards.

Kreschatik Bolshaya Morskaya 10; tel: 0692 542 131. Considered the finest restaurant in the city, the décor and the staff's attitudes are slightly pretentious. The menu is mainly fish and seafood and a full meal will cost around US$15 per person. Open until midnight.

Traktir' 1854 Bolshaya Morskaya 8; tel: 0692 544 760. Creative theme-dining honouring the tsarist military and remembering the Crimean War. The Russian army uniforms and thick wooden tables are fitting for Sevastopol and the waiters know their history. The menu is also very original: their specialities include *kurnik* (a Russian chicken pie) and roast duck stuffed with black cherries. English menus are available and a good-size meal will cost US$7.

Tri Peskarya Nakhimova 12; tel: 0692 555 581. This underground portside restaurant is the locals' favourite. They serve tasty salads, clams and mussels and seafood kebabs. They also have 'exotic food' which includes cuttlefish and frog legs. Main dishes are about US$5.

Kazan' Bolshaya Morskaya 3; tel: 0692 544 121. The owner hails from Tatarstan (in central Russia) and serves his national cuisine in a swank Greek setting complete with Doric columns, fake ivy and waiters in dinner jackets. Main dishes are US$8–12.

Bar Polundra Voronina 11; tel: 0692 456 173. This small café embodies a great sense of humour and has to be the most progressive place in Crimea. They serve delicious Italian food in very large portions with hand-drawn placemats, and free English and Russian magazines for lounging. An oversized pizza costs around US$5.

What to see and do

A walk down to the end of Prospekt Nakhimova will give you a good feel of the city and bring you to one of the hearts of naval activity. The 'square' is more of a roundabout encircling the monument to Admiral Nakhimov; the parks and waterfronts all branch out from here. For a good view of the city and bay, climb to the base of the obelisk monument built for the heroic defence of Sevastopol in World War II (on top of point Khrustal'ny). The **Sevastopol Panorama** is on top of the hill at the end of the aptly named History Boulevard. The round monument houses the gigantic 360° painting and life-size model recreating the fated day of the Battle of Sevastopol fought on June 6, 1855. Viewers watch from a central platform meant to be situated on the Malakhov mound with the Russian forces. It really is an impressive display. The museum downstairs shows leftover artefacts from the Crimean War such as cannonballs and uniforms. Entrance is US$2 for foreigners, 70UAH for individual guided tours in English. The booth across from the panorama is the **Sevastopol Bureau for Travel Excursions** (tel: 0692 542 860). If you want an English-speaking guide for the city, or to arrange day trips outside the city (Mangup-Kale, Inkerman, or Balaklava), this is a good place to start. The real **Malakhov mound** is covered with monuments to both the Crimean War and World War II. The original defensive tower has survived along with some cannons and artillery guns. On Bolshaya Morskaya is the uniquely designed old naval church. **Pokrovskii Sobor** was built in 1905 and reopened in 1992. The **Sevastopol Art Museum** (Nakhimova 9; open 10.00–17.00, closed Tuesday) is not particularly famous but has a few real gems: Korovin's *On the Shores of the Black Sea*, Aivozovskii's *Constantinople in Moonlight* and Kasatkin's *The Courtroom Hallway*. Besides the hermitage in St Petersburg, the oldest museum in 'Russia' is the **Black Sea Fleet Museum** (Lenina 11; tel: 0692 542 289; open 10.00–17.00, closed Monday and Tuesday). The collection spans the entire history of the Russian navy, with nice exhibits on the Crimean War and a healthy dose of Soviet propaganda.

The ancient site of **Chersonesus** (Khersones) still stands as the largest Greek ruins in Crimea. Ukraine's first city was founded in 528BC and unoriginally named 'peninsula'. It was independently governed as a democratic city-state until it became a Roman protectorate in the 1st century AD. Later, Byzantium took control of the port and it is here that Prince Vladimir was baptised a Christian. The very spot is shaded by a small gazebo and close by is **St Vladimir Cathedral**, built to commemorate the event in the 19th century. I suggest skipping the very bare museums and walking straight to the ruins by the seaside. These alone make a fascinating exhibit and the grassy streets and old temples cover an extensive space. Beware of open wells and deep holes. The grounds are open every day, 09.00–19.00; US$2 entrance for foreigners. Chersonesus is about ten minutes away by taxi.

The **north side** of Sevastopol is well off the beaten path and a pleasant ferry ride across the bay. The **Brother's Cemetery** (Bratskoye Kladbische) holds the war dead from the Crimean War onwards, as well as some of the Russian sailors who perished in the recent *Kursk* submarine tragedy. Not far away is the shore of Kalamita bay and **Uchkuyevka Beach** is one of the nicer places to swim.

OUTSIDE SEVASTOPOL
Inkerman – Инкерман
This small town lies at the mouth of the Chornaya (Black) River and is best known for its trademark bright white stone used to build Sevastopol and the Livadia Palace in Yalta. Among the cliffs on the road from Simferopol you can't miss the windows and the miniature teal cupolas sticking out from the rock face. St Kliment's Monastery was founded in the 8th century and named for a bishop from Rome who worked in the local rock quarries. Above the two cave churches are the ruins of the 15th-century Feodorite Kalamita fortress.

The Battle of Inkerman was the last Russian offensive before the allied siege of Sevastopol and the greatest land battle of the Crimean War. On the morning of November 5 1854, Russian forces marched to the British barrier but were unable to break through. The battle was incredibly intense but decided by midday: the British army had lost a quarter of its men while the Russians had retreated leaving nearly 12,000 casualties. The actual battle was fought in the now-forested plains west of Sevastopol and the ridges south of the Chornaya River. Most of the area is open for walking if you are keen; the top of St Kliment's ravine is the site of 'Shell Hill' and close to where the barrier once stood.

Balaclava – Балаклава
Yes, the full hood that looks silly but keeps you very warm is named after this picturesque port. In the first winter of the Crimean War, British women read reports that their men were dying by the hundreds of exposure to the cold. They began knitting close-fitting covers that left only the eyes exposed, then sent the packages to 'Balaclava' where the British High Command had sheltered its warships and military. The Royal Navy was over-enthusiastic with the number of ships it harboured here, and in November 1854 a vicious winter storm sunk a good portion of the naval force, including the prized *Black Prince*.

The legendary Battle of Balaclava was fought in the valleys above the entrance to the town. This was a surprise attack by the Russians who took the Turkish cannons and were then charged by the doomed Light Brigade. Aficionados of the Crimean War will recognise the terrain and visitors are frequently finding historical mementos in the dirt. With a few exceptions, the area is open for walking. A small white pinnacle stands as a memorial.

THE CHARGE OF THE LIGHT BRIGADE

Lord Alfred Tennyson's famous poem remembers the tragic events of Balaclava in his famous ballad 'The Charge of the Light Brigade'. On October 25 1854 the Russian forces succeeded in taking the Turkish cannons and it looked as if they would advance and take the port from the British. The 93rd British Highlanders kept a portion of the Russians from entering Balaclava in a defence referred to as the 'thin red line'; however, the causeway heights appeared open to attack. Through blunder or miscommunication Lord Cardigan was commanded to charge the Russian force at the far end of the valley, which can be seen today with its three high sides and its low flat centre. Surrounding the 'Valley of Death' was the combined force of the Russian infantry, artillery, and cavalry; the command to charge was suicidal. The Light Brigade's 'noble six hundred' were precisely 673 cavalrymen who calmly mounted their horses and made the advance. Less than 200 survived the hail of cannons and bullets from all sides and even the debate continues as to why such a nonsensical command was given. In Victorian England the Light Brigade became a legendary example of unwavering obedience to orders but also exposed a major weakness in the British military. The 'Jaws of Death' is now a very peaceful meadow with a few scrubby trees and some low crop fields but it is less hard to imagine the surrounding ridges lined with cannons. The ridge closer to Balaclava is higher if you want to get a better perspective of the battlefield.

The British were not the first to discover the calm inlet hidden behind winding sea cliffs. Homer's Odyssey mentions the hideout of ferocious pirates where sailors were lured to its protected shores before being attacked. Curving sharply from the sea, the back of the cove dips into an underwater cave before opening up into an underground 'harbour', a phenomenon that inspired the spot's Turkish name (*Balaclava* mean's 'Fish Nest') and later brought the Soviets, who built a secret, nuclear submarine repair station inside the cave, completely hidden from prying American satellites. Aside from Balaclava's notorious past, this is a very peaceful town to visit with its deep turquoise water and the open hills. On top of the pyramid-shaped mound is the remaining tower and ruins of the Genoese fortress of Cembalo and a good start for a walk down the coast. Getting to Balaclava is an easy 12km trip by bus or taxi from Sevastopol.

Diving in Balaclava

The underwater sites in this area are one of a kind. You are not likely to see pretty fish, but there are plenty of caves, sunken English warships, Greek ruins and the very James Bond-like underwater submarine factory. **Akvamarin** (Nazukina 5; tel: 0692 530 352) is the local dive shop that offers about 30 different dive sites of varying difficulty and certification courses. They have an extensive English web: www.voliga.ru.

CAPE AIYA – МЫС АЙЯ

This small national park marks the beginning of Crimea's southern coast with a striking change in vegetation and physical terrain. Here is one spot where natural Crimean flora and fauna have remained undisturbed. The many millennium junipers and Crimean strawberry trees scent the air, as do the rare orchid species.

Some of Crimea's endangered animals are also prominent here, including eagles and falcons. Level walking trails cut through to the very beautiful coastline from the village of Goncharnoye, which can be reached by bus or taxi from the Sevastopol–Foros road.

THE SOUTH COAST – ЮЖНЫЙ БЕРЕГ

This narrow strip of land between the Black Sea and the jagged ridge of the Crimean mountain chain has the warmest weather in Ukraine and is consequently mobbed from May to September. The natural attractions are worthy of such attention: the mountain landscapes are simply stunning and there are plenty of miniature beaches hidden between bits of rocky coastline. The 'Russian Riviera' actually does have a Mediterranean climate complete with aromatic shrubs, sunshine and dry air, but any comparisons fall short of describing the very unique world of the Crimean shore. Previous definitions of people, land and nature don't apply on the southern coastline where seemingly separate worlds gather, play and relax.

The biggest cities of Yalta and Alushta are the most active centres for accommodation and transportation as well as a useful starting point for mountain treks. It's hard not to be disappointed by the pseudo-tropical resort culture that seems to permeate. The Russian/Ukrainian nation has been vacationing in this spot for over two hundred years and certain coastal areas are a tad overdeveloped. Bolshaya Yalta (Greater Yalta) is expanding to a continuous holiday-zone between Foros and Gurzuf, but this has not erased the distinct character of the smaller seaside towns within. These little hovels were the Mecca of the Soviet Bohemian movement and there are still tiny patches where travellers sleep on the beach and live off the fish they catch. People seeking a quiet rest by the sea (or mountains) have usually discovered their own secret spot to which they return year after year.

YALTA – ЯЛТА

Yalta is Russia's most popular tourist trap and should be enjoyed as such, for the town holds more of an appeal than its stony urban beaches and imported palms. In the shadow of the overpriced concrete high-rise hotels there are still the fanciful turn-of-the-century beach houses now overgrown with vines and flowers and the solemn glow of the Yalta lighthouse. I used to think that Soviet citizens went crazy about Yalta only because they were not allowed to go anywhere else, in which case the sweeping mountain-view against the open sea *would* be truly spectacular. But now that people have the freedom and money to travel elsewhere, over two million 'locals' still head to Yalta each year. The town's romantic nature still remains. National park completely surrounds the city and many smaller trails branch off from the outskirts. Getting to any spot along the southern half of the coast usually entails passing through Yalta and it can be a good base from which to hike Ai-Petri, the Grand Canyon, and 'Bear Mountain', Aiyu-Dag.

As is told, an ancient Greek ship was lost in a vicious Black Sea storm and the sailors believed they would die drifting endlessly. When they caught a glimpse of Aiyu-Dag's purple outline, they began shouting *'Yalos! Yalos!'* meaning 'Shore!'. The beachside community of castaways grew into the town pronounced *Yalta*, which had a short-lived Genoese and Turkish existence before the Russians built the first stone buildings and the port in the 1830s. Besides the fishing (which still goes on today) Yalta was the place to go for cures from all the nasty diseases common in St Petersburg. Following the late-19th-century fashion of being Russian the gentry began choosing Yalta over the European seaside spas. The last tsar, Nikolai II, built his summer palace here which later brought world fame to

Yalta in 1945 when the allied leaders met in Livadia to finalise post-war plans. Yalta continued to be the favoured retreat of Soviet leaders but swiftly assumed a capitalist role at independence. (Lenin's statue now faces a beachside McDonald's.) A dedicated mafia has really spruced things up and as a result, Yalta is now one of Ukraine's most expensive cities.

Getting there and away

A beaten path leads to Yalta from Simferopol via Alushta, which you will have to follow if you are coming from anywhere on the mainland. There are numerous buses, marshrutka, private taxis and the trolley which leave from Simferopol's train station and go to Yalta's avtovokzal (the trip takes from one to two hours). The trolley takes the longest and is the cheapest. After 15 minutes the novelty wears off and you'll wish you were on a fast minibus. Taxis from Simferopol airport will stake very high prices, but it should cost only around $US50 to get to any hotel on the south coast. If you are driving or want to take one of the less frequent buses, you might want to consider going through Bakhchisarai, which is a smaller and more pot-hole riddled road but very scenic. Long-haul buses also go directly to Yalta from Odessa, Dnepropetrovsk, and Kirovohrad.

Getting around the south coast is very easy. There is an open platform at the Yalta bus station from which various forms of wheeled transport leave all day long to the coastal towns, usually in a circle via Sevastopol or to Alushta. Farther destinations like Feodosia and Kerch run twice daily leaving early in the morning or in the late afternoon. Smaller marshrutka run down to Alupka and Foros or up to Nikita and Gruzuf, stopping anywhere you want along the way. Besides the avtovokzal, the main marshrutka junction is at the square of Pushkina by the movie theatre, 'Spartak'.

Yalta is also a popular cruise-ship destination, but these days Black Sea cruises originate only in Turkey or the Mediterranean. There is still one passenger ship that leaves every Tuesday from Yalta to Istanbul and returns the following Monday. The journey costs US$90 single/US$180 return. Tickets can be purchased at the Morskoy Vokzal (sea station), Roosevelt 5; tel: 0654 323 064.

Where to stay

Yalta is made out of hotels but still provides a relatively small supply when considering the inflated demand. The result is complete overpricing and a lot of difficulty in getting a room during the highest season: most resorts have three to four different prices depending on when you come. July and August are often double the price of January–April. New Year, May–June, and September are in between the two. Renting an apartment can be a very good option in this city (whether or not you are looking, you will be approached upon arrival). Here are just a few of the hotels in the area (all middle- and high-end hotels accept credit cards):

Luxury

Oreanda Lenina 35/2; tel: 0654 390 608; fax: 0654 328 336; email: info@hotel-oreanda.com; web: www.hotel-oreanda.com. Considered the best and definitely the most elegant in Yalta, this century-old hotel is located on the waterfront and furnished to the highest standard. Everything is brand new, the rooms are spacious and well-decorated, and the staff speak English. The main restaurant is classy and in good taste while the nightclub is a little extravagant. Use of the private beach and the elaborate pool complex is included in the price, and many local tours can be arranged in-house. Superior rooms face the sea, standard ones face the mountains, with a 30% price difference betweeen the two. In terms of superior low season/ high season rooms, singles cost US$90/180, doubles US$160/300, and suites are US$280/500 per night.

Paradise Sosnovy Bor 37; tel: 0654 326 051; fax: 0654 336 649. Near Massandra, this is a small but fully refurbished resort with only seven suites. Its individual attention to guests and quiet location are its greatest attributes. High-season rooms are US$80–120.

Middle range

Bristol Roosevelt 10; tel: 0654 271 603; fax 0654 271 609; email: office@hotel-bristol.com. An old 'English'-style hotel close to the port and recently renovated to a very comfortable standard. Rooms cost around US$30 per person.

Palace Chekhova 8; tel: 0654 324 380; fax: 0654 230 492. This is one of Yalta's originals, still functioning in a Victorian *pension* style, with a choice of the number of meals you take at the hotel. A single is US$50, doubles are between US$60–80. The US$85 suites have queen-size beds. All rooms have AC.

Massandra Drazhinskovo 48; tel: 0654 352 591. Built in Massandra Park, this is one of the few hotels whose quality of service is higher than its reasonable prices. Massandra's rooms can go as low as US$15 per person but are about US$30 on average.

Yalta Drazhinskovo 50; tel: 0654 350 150; fax: 0654 353 093. This 16-storey hotel was Inturist's greatest moment: olympic-sized pool, three restaurants, cinema, and live dolphins. With over 1,000 rooms of varying standard, there is wide price range. In summer, the cheapest rooms are US$50/80 single/double and definitely not worth that much. Located about one mile past the port near Massandra.

Vremena Goda Rudanskovo 23; tel: 0654 343 045; fax: 0654 343 288. A small, remodelled hotel in the city centre with pool, sauna, private beach access and a fine restaurant. The least expensive rooms are singles, around US$35 (US$50 in season); doubles are around US$70 and the roomy suites average US$100/night.

Budget

Energetik Pushkinskaya 23; tel: 0654 329 305. Technically, this is a resort but for the sake of price counts as budget accommodation (around US$15 a night); near Primorsky Park.

Krym Moskovskaya 1/6; tel: 0654 271 710. This slightly dingy Soviet building is in a very central location and has the cheapest beds in Yalta. A double with bath is US$16, a single US$8. Rooms with just a sink are US$4 and suites are US$30. Hot water is sporadic, and prices double during the high season.

Niva Kievskaya 44; tel: 0654 324 392. Fairly cheap rooms of the Soviet variety.

Polyana Skazok Kirova 167; tel: 0654 395 219. Although its called Yalta's 'camping' this is really a motel on the outskirts of the city, not far from Uchan-Su. The name means 'Fairytale Glade' which sounds much more mystical than the chainsaw-carved Disney-esque statues covering the grounds. Singles are US$20, doubles US$50 but prices fluctuate. They also have smaller cottages that run for much the same price.

Zarya Kommunarov 7; tel: 044 220 6650 (in Kiev); email: kurort@i.kiev.ua. Little wooden cottages not far from the beach with a central cafeteria. About US$15 a night with breakfast.

Sanatoria/Health Resorts

Resorts line the coast in the hundreds. Here are a couple of established ones that have experience with foreigners:

Sosnova Roscha (Gaspra) Alushtinksoye Shosse; tel: 0654 242 247; fax: 0654 242 301; Right at the base of Ai-Petri. New rooms and new equipment make this quite a plush resort and the health clinic is very modern. About $80/night for two people in season which includes all meals and 'diagnostika'.

Nizhnyaya Oreanda (in the suburb of Oreanda); tel: 0654 312 548, 322 212. This functional-turned-posh resort is the favourite of Ukrainian parliamentarians and was only recently opened up to the foreign proletariat who can pay. Actual prices fluctuate, but they tend to hover around US$100.

Where to eat
A multitude of restaurants all along the south coast cater to every holiday taste and wallet. There are also plenty of all-night food shops and delicatessens open in the cities and along roadsides. **Oreanda** (on the ground floor of the hotel) serves exquisite Ukrainian food and hosts an original Turkish buffet in the evening. Main dishes cost US$10–15. Across from the hotel is the wooden ship **Hispaniola** whose restaurant is not as tacky as it may seem – the food is accurately Greek and the atmosphere dressy but relaxed. Further up the waterfront is **K Walter** (Naberezhnaya/Morskaya 1) which occupies the façade of Yalta's Marino Hotel and offers a very refreshing view of the sea through its two-storey windows. The food is mostly Asian Fusion (Japanese/Vietnamese) but there are some original European dishes too, eg: the noblewoman, a veal fillet with cream, and the pauper's bag, a heavy pile of meat and potatoes. **Stary Platan** (Yekaterinskaya 1) occupies a former wine cellar and sells itself as a restaurant for wine connoisseurs. Owned by the Massandra vineyard, each featured dish is specifically designed as an accompaniment for a particular Massandra wine. Dishes are US$7–10 and there is a separate wine shop at the entrance.

Less dressy establishments are in abundance on the *naberezhnaya*. On the corner by the park is **Vernisazh**, an extensive outdoor café run by a kind Armenian family. Salads, seafood, and shish kebabs is the main fare, as well as traditional Armenian food. Everything on the menu is under US$5 and it's in English. Between *naberezhnaya* and Kirova are quite a few pizza places, as well as **Aishe** (Lenina 9) which serves Crimean Tatar/Uzbekistani food and fantastic *plov*. Farther away from the city is **Tsarskoye Kukhnya** (next to the Livadia Palace) which serves very refined Russian dishes. For extremely inexpensive meals try **Siren**, a homey cafeteria on Roosevelt (near Hotel Bristol) that serves old-fashioned Soviet fare for less than a dollar.

Tourist information
Inturist is at Roosevelt 5 (tel: 0654 327 604; email: intour@yalta.crimea.ua). As the most experienced Inturist veterans still employed, this office has the authority and connections to get most things done for travellers, including visas, transportation, and accommodation. They offer plenty of tours in any language imaginable and also give Russian tutorials to visitors. Located next to the sea station. In the lower level of the Avtovokzal is **Yalta Inform Servis** (Moskovskaya 8; tel: 0654 325 777; email: yalta-inform@ukr.net) who can organise tours and accommodation upon arrival. The **Yalta Bureau of Excursions** (Ekaterinskaya 3) has been around since 1847 and is still a good place to get a guided tour and find out about local attractions. Also, the booths on the *Naberezhnaya* sell tickets for group bus tours to local sites. You don't have to speak Russian to see the palaces and gardens so it can be a good deal if you don't want to hassle with transport. US$5 to $7 is the normal price to pay for any tour. If you are keen to dive, the **Oreanda Dive-Center** (tel: 0654 390 920; email: oreanda-divers@ukr.net) is next to the wooden ship Hispaniola and offers two-tank dives including equipment for US$70. (It looks murky but I've heard some good reports.) They also can make arrangements for mountain-bike rentals.

What to see and do

There are some real attractions in Yalta besides the electronic mayhem on the boardwalk and the standing-room-only beaches. **Primorskii Park** is a calm green spot by the sea with cypress woods, several monuments and some of the older sanatoria. **Aleskandr Nevsky Cathedral** on Sadovaya was built by Alexander III in remembrance of his father, the II. The church has brand new gold domes and displays original mosaics. The **Chekhov House and Museum** (Kirova 112, open 10.00–17.00, closed Monday and Tuesday) was the private 'white dacha' of author and playwright Anton Chekhov who came often to Yalta to work. He wrote a great deal of his short stories here, as well as the plays *The Cherry Orchard* and *Three Sisters*. In Yalta's southern suburbs stands the **Livadia Palace** (open 10.00–17.00 everyday except Wednesday; the #5 marshrutka goes to Livadia from Yalta), built by Tsar Nikolai II as his family's summer residence. The white renaissance mansion was completed in 1911 and is surrounded by a simple but vast garden overlooking the sea. The Romanovs spent only four summers here before their arrests and the small church behind the palace is now a shrine to their memory. The Yalta Conference of February 1945 took place in the largest hall and it is here that Stalin, Churchill and Roosevelt discussed the fate of Germany and adopted the 'Declaration on Liberated Europe'. The American delegation was housed in the Livadia palace, while the British delegation stayed at the Alupka Palace and the Russians at Yusupovsky.

Short walks from Yalta

Yalta's great natural attraction is Europe's highest waterfall. **Uchan-Su** means 'flying water' in Tatar, and the water really does fly from a height of 98m. From the Yalta bus station take the 'taxi-bus' with the sign Водапад (*Vodapad*, 'Waterfall') which stops at the restaurant where the trail begins. Also, the **Botkin Path** leads to the falls from Polyana Skazok. Lightly ascending into the Crimean Game Preserve, this trail is named after Sergei Botkin, the private doctor of Tsar Nikolai II. He made the startling discovery that walking in the outdoors was good for one's health and recommended the tsar's family to take daily strolls 'in nature'. The 8km path is tame with a few rocky inclines, but the tall pines and skittish birdlife do make you feel healthy and it's a good introduction to the Crimean Mountains. The **Tsar's Path** was the trail actually used by the tsar and his family in their daily 'constitutional' to cure their tuberculosis. It begins behind Livadia palace and winds through 6km of mountainside to Gaspra. To take away the bourgeois stigma of the place, it was called the 'Sunny Path' during Soviet days and this is the name still carved on the stone markers. The trail *is* rather sunny and stays level at about 100m above sea level. Besides an occasional stumble across construction sites, the path is lined with forests of twisted trees and the air smells heavily of cypress. There are several lookout points along the way from which there are tremendous views of the sea and Ayu-Dag. Beware of uncovered manholes! Just past the 5km mark there is a turn-off that descends through pine scrub, then hillside vegetable gardens to the **Swallow's Nest** (see Gaspra).

Further walks

Ai-Petri Ай-Петри is the craggy mountain with a row of rock teeth standing high above Alupka. This may be the heart of Yaltinsky Mountain-Forest Reserve but it is also the most visited natural spot in Crimea due to the road and cable car that go right next to the summit. The Taraktash trail from Uchan-Su is slighlty uneventful since it follows the winding road most of the way (though it's great for mountain bikes). For extended walks it is better to cross the 'Yaila' from above the Yalta road

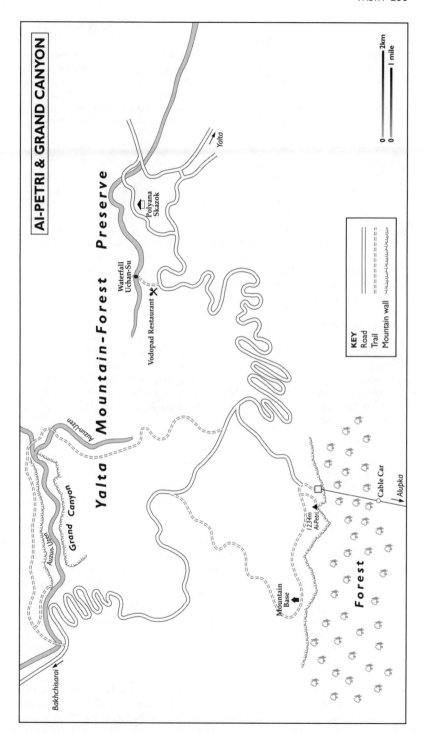

AI-PETRI & GRAND CANYON

Yalta Mountain-Forest Preserve

Polyana Skazok

Yalta

Waterfall Uchan-Su

Vodopad Restaurant

KEY
Road
Trail
Mountain wall

Auzun-Uzen

Grand Canyon

Auzun-Uzen

Bakhchisarai

Mountain Base

1234m Al-Petri

Forest

Cable Car

Alupka

0   2km
0   1 mile

TREKKING IN CRIMEA

Experienced hikers and mountain climbers may be amused by the over-cautious attitude that permeates local minds in regards to exploring Crimea's rocky terrain. Much of this stems from Soviet days when everything was hyper-regulated and 'adventuring' non-existent. These are not difficult mountains. Crimea's tallest peak is Roman Kosh which at 1,545m is a hill by world standards. That said, these mountains are known to be particularly dangerous for two reasons: Firstly, very sporadic weather can turn a sunny sky into thick fog in minutes, and secondly, the unique terrain has one side gradually sloping upwards and then the other side dropping eight hundred metres to the sea. Over 30 people die each year in these mountains, mostly from falling off unexpected drop-offs. In addition, many trails pass through government-regulated reserves and foreigners caught without a guide or a license will have problems. The trails mentioned in this book are free and open, but it is still not a bad idea to have a guide for longer treks, and other journeys should be cleared beforehand.

Gorna Spasatelnaya Sluzhba is the local Mountain Rescue Service based in Yalta (Prigorovskaya 10; tel: 0652 328 715). If you are going out on your own you must (technically) contact them and register yourself. They offer good information and if stopped along the way, this will be the one case where it was better to have asked permission than to seek forgiveness. Going the private route saves the hassle. **Dimas Tour** (Krupskaya 20/1 #28; email: dimasyalta@ukr.net) is a company of knowledgeable young mountain guides who tailor-make longer treks (up to ten days) in Crimea for individuals and groups. They speak English, do equipment rentals (eg: sleeping bags, tents, etc) and have very reasonable rates. A guide for an individual traveller costs US$30 a day, or US$70 for a three-day trek.

and swing back around. There are also two trails through the woods from Alupka, so a long trek may lead from the sea back towards Bakhchisarai via Ai-Petri. The summit is 1,234 m high and the landscape behind the peak is characterised by its strange moon-like rock formations. Deep snow covers the summit from December until late April.

Crimea's **Grand Canyon** is unique in that it was created by tectonic activity rather than simple erosion and therefore looks like a deep crack running through rolling green hillsides. The gorge is between Yalta and Bakhchisarai at about 4km from the village of Sokolinoe and accessed from either end. One trail passes above the north side, another descends into the canyon. It is grand in terms of wonderful trekking and striking scenery but not in size: the deepest cleft is 320m and the length is a little over 3km. The Auzun-Uzen' river trickles or tumbles through these tight walls depending on the season and the small clear pools and waterfalls are inviting swimming spots.

YALTA TO FOROS
Gaspra – Гаспра

The sharp cliffs of **Cape Ai-Todor** mark the confines of this highly romanticised village 7km south of Yalta. St Theodore was the founder of the difficult-to-reach monastery at the top of the cape which fell into ruin during medieval times.

During the 19th century the spot was popular for couples wanting a view and the small wooden dacha hanging to the cliffside was commonly referred to as the 'Swallow's Nest'. The German oil baron Shteingel bought the dacha in 1912 and used the site to build an imitation Gothic mini-castle as a gift to his mistress. It was abandoned two years later due to the war and in 1927 a major earthquake left it in ruins until it was rebuilt in the 1970s. Today the **Swallow's Nest** (Ласточкино Гнездо; *Lastochkino Gnyezdo*) is the over-photographed symbol of good times in Crimea and functions as an 'élite' Italian seafood restaurant. Main dishes cost US$10–20. Perched at the very edge of the stone overhang, the view is remarkable – especially if you are afraid of heights.

Most of the health resorts in Gaspra were once palaces belonging to the Russian aristocracy. Next door, **Koreiz** is the palace of Prince Felix Yusopov who was the wealthiest man in the world during his lifetime. The home at Ai-Todor was just one of five permanent residences and the family owned so much land in Crimea that Felix's father gave his mother a mountain as a birthday present. Yusopov married into the Romanov family through the tsar's niece which made him privy to the Rasputin scandal. He later conspired and killed Rasputin for which he was exiled briefly before the tsar was deposed. The prince escaped arrest during the revolution by hiding out in this Crimean house for nearly three years. He made one foray back to St Petersburg to collect jewels and two Rembrandts which funded his escape and new life in Paris. The palace is a popular stop after Livadia Palace and is next to the cable car to Ai-Petri. All transport to Alupka passes through Gaspra and there is a long path of down and up stairs to the Swallow's Nest from Café Yakhta.

Alupka – Алупка

Tiny Alupka is right underneath the Ai-Petri mountain chain and was chosen by Count Vorontsov as the site for his ostentatious palace mixing English gothic and Indian mogul styles. The vast gardens and fanciful buildings make up the frequently visited **Alupka Palace Museum** (Open 9.00 to 17.00 everyday, entrance US$1). Vorontsov was the governor-general of Russian Crimea in the second half of the 19th century and he spent twenty years (and nine million pieces of silver) building the palace but never actually lived in it. The interior is the best-furnished exhibit in Crimea today, but the tour is tedious; walking through the palace on your own you'll notice 'the blue room' made to look like Wedgwood and the imitation 16th-century English dining hall. Churchill and the British delegation lived in the palace during the Yalta Conference and the palace is still used to host state dinners. The palace exterior is more eye-catching and the gardens make for pleasant walking with palms and flowers. The lower park was designed to blend with the surrounding environment; 'Chaos' is an arranged rock pile that will tempt amateur climbers. The trail leads to a popular but relatively clean beach. Marshrutka #32 and #26 go to Alupka from the Yalta bus station.

Foros – Форос

At the most southern tip of Crimea is the small town of Foros, usually portrayed by the miniature cake-decoration church clinging to a 400m-high precipice. The nobleman Kuznetsov built the Byzantine **Resurrection Church** in thanks for the life of his daughter whose runaway horse stopped just at the edge of the cliff (its common name is the Traveller's Church). Foros is a very peaceful bit of coastline surrounded by thick forest and broken rock walls that are easily accessible for trekking and climbing. Above the pass at Baidarskiye Gate one trail leads to the small peak Eagle's Nest. The eastern trail follows the top of the wall for 15km to

Hell's Staircase (Чёртовая Лестница). There are various degrees of climbing here, the least difficult path is fine for trekking and goes to the plateau from which the old Genoese road once led to Sevastopol. The Foros wall is about 600m and is a challenging climb attempted by experienced climbers only. Foros is the midway point between the two-hour Sevastopol – Yalta route and minibuses run about once an hour.

Where to stay and eat
This is a much less commercialised part of Crimea and so options are minimal. The main resort is **Foros** (tel: 0654 792 244; email: sforos@mail.ylt.crimea.com; web: www.foros.com.ua) consisting of an average Soviet-style high-rise sanatorium and cafeteria.

YALTA TO ALUSHTA
Massandra – Массандра
Yalta has swallowed up its eastern suburb but Massandra still exhibits a very separate sense of place. For the past two hundred years, the town's name has been connected to the wine produced on these hillsides and prevalent 'sampling stations' lure tourists from the roadside. The French chateau-style **Massandra Palace** was originally commissioned by one of the Vorontsov's (the family of the Russian general ruling over Crimea) but the project was abandoned and only taken up by Alexander III a decade later in 1889. A visit inside shows the obsession of the Russian royalty with imitating English and French styles from centuries gone by. Interestingly, sun-shy Stalin made the palace his summer residence. The estate gardens are now the extensive and beautiful **Massandra Park**.

Nikita – Никита
Further along the coast is the very small **Cape Martyan Reserve**, one of the few remaining spots of natural Crimean plant growth, including the elusive juniper mistletoe, as well as a prized spot for birdwatching year round. The **Nikitsky Botanical Gardens** is behind the reserve and contains a mind-blowing collection of twenty-eight thousand plant species, all growing in the park. A Russian botanist founded the gardens in 1812 under imperial orders to establish a place where all plants of the world could be collected, acclimatised and distributed throughout 'Russia'. The park has shifted from its original agricultural goals to new aesthetic heights, with stunning floral displays and incredible tree exhibits of sequoia and cedars of Lebanon. An on-site café serves exotic fruits and nuts that are grown in the gardens. *Marshrutka* #34 goes to the Nikitsky Gardens from Yalta.

Gurzuf – Гурзуф
At one time, all of Crimea used to look like Gurzuf with its little wooden houses, stone dachas and fishing boats. The Genoese left a few ruins here but the Russians like to remember the town as the spot where Pushkin came to holiday. The town still caters to a resort crowd but is less brash than Yalta proper. These are Crimea's best pebble beaches and a few seaside caves make it an interesting place for swimming. Guruzuf is 15km from Yalta and can be reached by most forms of transport going to Alushta.

Where to stay
Staying in Gurzuf can be a better option than staying in Yalta during the summer. **Ai-Danil** (Gurzuf 3; tel: 0654 335 340) is the high-rise sanatorium at the far end of the shore and offers average comfortable rooms and a few of the 'lux' variety.

Pushkino (Naberezhnaya 3; tel: 0654 363 390) is closer to the city and right on the beach. All rooms have bathrooms and run to around US$20 per person.

Aiyu-Dag – Аю-Даг

'Bear Mountain' is the landmark stone hill that can be seen from most of the south coast. Its sides are mainly cliffs and rocky overhangs while its back and summit are covered with thick pine scrub. Many believe the Tatar name *Aiyu* (Bear) is just a mispronunciation of the Greek word '*Ai*' ('Holy'). I think a good look at the mountain settles the argument. The oft-told legend is that a shipwrecked girl was rescued by a family of wild bears who were enchanted with her singing. The captain of a passing ship found her and took her away while the bears were hunting. The bears saw the departing ship on the horizon and quickly knelt at the shore to drink up the Black Sea and bring the girl back. In return, the girl began singing to stop their draining the sea. All the bears stopped, except for the oldest who was deaf and continued to drink the sea. There is a likeness when viewed from Yalta. The trail to Aiyu-Dag's summit begins in the town of **Partenit** (Партенит), backtracks along the cape and then rises directly north to the top.

ALUSHTA

Alushta is Yalta's biggest competition, offering the same seaside amusements with less bawdiness, lower prices and a bit more green. The Alushta beaches are long and not nearly as crowded, running for miles up the coast. The Demerdzhi Mountains and Chatyr-Dag loom in the background and Alushta is a good base from which to hike these as well as Babugan Yaila and Roman Kosh. There are three national parks close by; the largest is the Crimean Nature Preserve and has the best animal life in the peninsula, but as the Ukrainian president's private hunting grounds, it can be visited only with a special permit.

The town seems to have always been on the fringe of Crimea's history: Aluston was the Greek/Byzantine fortress built here in the 6th century which later extended to a chain of forts in the nearby mountains. For a while, the town was the last outpost of the Feodor principality and named Lustia by the Genoese in nearby Sudak. The Russians put Alushta back on the map as the junction of their coastal road from Simferopol but it was only during Soviet times that the site was considered a possible resort and a few sanatoria were built along the shoreline. Now the waterfront is a huge piece of pavement filled with outdoor cafés in the summer and rather empty in the winter.

Getting there and away

Alushta is the halfway point between Simferopol and Yalta so hourly buses pass through, including the nicer private line running between Simferopol and Sevastopol. The bus station is at the north end of the town at Simferopolskaya 1 and the long distance trolleybus station is at Gorkovo 4. A private taxi from Simferopol will cost US$15 and Yalta should be the same. Presently, there are no passenger ships sailing to Alushta.

Where to stay and eat

Health resorts are the mainstay of Alushta's economy and so it is not an easy place to get short-term accommodation (ie: less than a week). During the tourist rush, the best option is renting a private apartment. **Krymskiye Zori** (Oktybr'skaya 5; tel: 06560 303 00; email: zori@alushta.ylt.crimea.com) is brand new and functions both as a hotel and resort. A room costs US$20–30 in the low season and US$60 during late summer. The hotel **Alushta** (Oktyabr'skaya 50; tel: 06560 30552) has rooms for US$20–40 and **Spartak** (Perekopskaya 9; tel/fax: 06560 3 44 33) is small and comfy with US$20 rooms and less. **Morye** (Naberezhnaya 25; tel: 06560 311 35) is a sanatorium with a few high-standard rooms, a good restaurant and beach access.

Beach foodstands and cafés are in abundance. **Vodolei** is not far from the sea station on the waterfront and serves more refined food as well as shish kebabs. **Lesnoi** (tel: 06560 343 60) is a stone cottage in the mountains 5km away from the city on the Alushta–Yalta road with large terraces for outdoor dining. Besides the restaurant they have a few deluxe suites for overnight guests as well as a sauna.

What to do
Besides the sunshine and water there are some very unique landscapes to explore in the area. The **Crimean Nature Preserve** is a guarded 70,000 acre mountain space filled with what remains of Crimean wildlife: mouflon, mountain goats, gazelles, foxes and incredible bird species. It is a very difficult place to visit and the private companies that can arrange a permit usually sell the tour as a hunting trip. Crimea's tallest mountain, **Roman Kosh**, is inside the preserve so mountain climbers will also have to go through a private company to get there. A lot of interested tourists could create a positive demand and (throwing all subversion out the window) I would urge travellers to make a point of speaking out to tour guides and officials about facilitating sightseeing visits and keeping the animals alive. There are many other hiking spots near Alushta: on the Alushta–Simferopol road is Angarskii Pass which is the trekking centre to both **Chatyr-Dag** and **Demerdzhi**. All buses as well as the trolley will stop at Angarskii Pass and a taxi from Alushta costs US$7.

DEMERDZHI – ДЕМЕРДЖИ
The Demerdzhi massif is directly north of Alushta and is much more removed from civilisation than other popular spots in Crimea. The strange rock forms and tall stone fingers make up an alien landscape with interludes of open mountain plains covered with tall grasses and wildflowers. This is one of the highest plateaux in Crimea so the view of the peninsula is striking. Wind erosion has formed the layered cylindrical shapes and a legacy of Soviet directors have attached names and legends to almost every single rock formation. The Tatars also had their names and *Demerdzhi* means 'Smith' after the legend of an evil blacksmith that once lived here. Some truly beautiful sites include the powerful waterfall **Dzhur-Dzhur** and the staggering **Valley of Ghosts**. Most Crimean tour companies offer treks in Demerdzhi, but this the best place on the peninsula for independent hikers. There are plenty of trails so that hikes can be shortened or lengthened to fit your whim; the following is a suggested walk:

Day 1 Angarskii Pass to Polyana Man passing by Pakhkal-Kaya mountain (1,137m). Man's Glade is a good outlook point with established campsites.
Day 2 Continue through the forest passing North Demerdzhi Mountain (1,356m) and then turning east beneath the Yurkiny cliffs. Camp above Dzhurla Waterfall.
Day 3 Climb from the waterfall to the summit of South Demerdzhi (1,239m) then descend into the Valley of Ghosts. Either finish by hiking into the village of Luchistoye or continue towards Dzhur-Dzhur.
Day 4 Visit the waterfall Dzhur-Dzhur (the largest volume of flowing water in Crimea). From here follow the Ulu-Uzen' river 10km to the beach at Solnechnogorskoye.

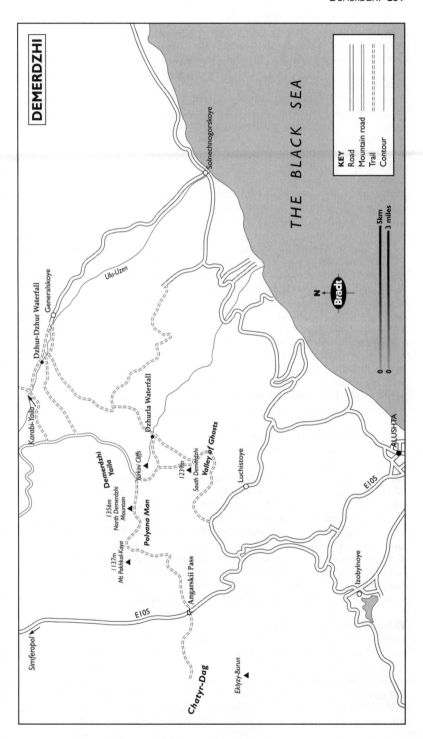

DEMERDZHI

KEY
Road
Mountain road
Trail
Contour

THE BLACK SEA

Solnechnogorskoye

Ulu-Uzen

Dzhur-Dzhur Waterfall
Generalskoye

Karabi-Yaila

Dzhurla Waterfall

Yurkini Cliffs

Demerdzhi Yaila

1356m North Demerdzhi Mountain

1137m Mt Pakhkal-Kaya

1239m
South Demerdzhi
Valley of Ghosts

Polyana Man

Luchistoye

ALUSHTA

E105

Angarskii Pass

E105

Simferopol

Izobylnoye

Chatyr-Dag

Eklyzy-Burun

N

Bradt

0   5km
0   3 miles

A longer trek could continue on to **Karabi-Yaila** which is a much wider plateau to the northeast. The hills are riddled with caves and similar rock formations to Demerdzhi but the trails are much longer and much further from any village.

FEODOSIYA – ФЕОДОСИЯ

As the unofficial capital of Crimea's eastern shore, Feodosiya is nobly different than the built-up southern coast. There is no gaudy post-Soviet investment to detract from the parks or the surrounding landscape, and attitudes are uncomplicated. The city stretches flat across a seaside plain with ultra-wide streets and brightly painted Russian classicist buildings. Children playing on the beach and the resorts advertising mudbaths are unfazed by the never ending action of giant cargo ships and the seaside railway station. Prospekt Lenina (as the main promenade will always be known) is lined with tall silver birch trees for its entire length and old-fashioned lanterns light the city at night so that evening strolls may continue. In short, Feodosiya is a quaint place of redeeming character and unadulterated coastline.

The Greeks claimed Theodossia (*'Given by God'*) in the 6th century BC and turned it into a major centre for grain exports. The Huns destroyed the city in the 4th century and Feodosiya was then ruled by the Khazar kaganate. The Genoese arrived in the 13th century and made Kaffa their capital and it was soon the centre of trade for the Black Sea. The towers of their fortress are still standing in random spots throughout the city. In 1475 the Crimean Tatars conquered the city for the Turks who nicknamed it Little Istanbul. Like Yevpatoria in the west, Feodosiya was vital to the Turkish slave trade and during the 1600s the Zaporizhzhyan Cossacks made repeated attacks on the city to free Ukrainian captives. After occupation, the Russians declared Feodosiya a free trade zone which made it a very cosmopolitan town of merchants. The Armenian artist Aivazovsky was born here and returned to live here even in his fame and wealth. His own investment 'made' the town what it is today and he is honoured in several museums and frequent statues and plaques.

Getting there and away

Even though there are direct trains from Feodosia to mainland Ukraine via Dzhankoi, the train schedule can be quirky. There is a train to Moscow every other day and regular trains to Simferopol and Kerch. If there are no direct trains to Ukraine/Russia on the day you want to leave, going to Simferopol is better than taking the very slow train to Dzhankoi and switching to a train that originated in Simferopol anyway. If you plan in advance and have a return ticket, than you should avoid any hitches. Buses are quicker and the only way to get to Sudak (1 hour) and Koktebel (20 minutes). Kerch is two hours away and there is a 19-hour night bus to Kiev. A marshrutka from Simferopol takes two-and-a-half hours and costs US$4. The bus station is on the north end of town (Engelskaya 28) across from St Catherine's Church. To avoid going to Simferopol, there is a coastal road to Yalta but it becomes a matter of time and energy to keep on the smaller path.

Where to stay and eat

Lidia (Libknekhta 13; tel: 06562 309 01; email: ht_Lidia@poStkafa.crimea.ua) is the poshest place in town and very central. Basic singles and doubles are US$35/$45 while the spruced-up larger rooms range from US$60–90. Their restaurant has a talented chef who does mainly fish dishes but still serves the Russian classics. A full meal should cost under US$15. **Astoria** (Lenina 9; tel: 06562 524 435) is the deteriorated Soviet hotel across from the train station. Their suites are US$25, rooms with a shower and toilet are US$12–16 and just a bed is

I K AIVAZOVSKY (1817–1900)

Ivan (Hovhannes) Konstantinovich Aivazovsky was the son of an Armenian merchant and his wife who had come to Feodosiya from Galicia. As a boy, his charcoal graffiti on the town walls was brought to the attention of the Feodosiya governor who arranged for his education in Simferopol and later at the St Petersburg Academy. In the capital his talent was praised and he was granted sponsorship to travel and paint. In 1845 Aivazovsky was appointed the official artist of the navy which fit his best subjects: shipwrecks, ferocious storms and sea battles. As his style developed, the human elements slowly disappeared and the sea became the prominent focus rather than the background of the painting. His uncanny ability to deal with water, light and air brought him great fame and his ability to produce paintings quickly made him rich. He built his home and studio in Feodosiya and designed a special gallery to enable the townspeople to come and see his work. This kind of generosity sounds big-headed, but there was really no other place in the small town, and the hall became the cultural centre for Eastern Crimea. Aivazovsky left the room in his will 'to the citizens of Feodosiya' and famous pianists are still invited to play here. The Feodosiya Museum displays many of his true masterpieces including Среди Волн ('Among the Waves'), a vast picture of nothing but water and wind which he painted at the age of 82. His Crimean paintings are rightfully displayed with local scenes in Feodosiya, Yalta and Koktebel and the exhibit also shows Aivazovsky's religious phase where he attempted to paint scenes from the Bible. His human figures always appeared crude, so he leaned towards scripture stories that involved water: Moses crossing the Red Sea, Christ walking on water, and the great flood. He was also a true philanthropist, supplying Feodosiya with water, funding the town's museum, starting an art school and lobbying for the modern commercial port and railroad. He is buried in the Armenian church in Feodosiya (on Ulitsa Timiryazeva) with the epitaph 'A man who was born to die left an undying memory'.

US$5. Hot water is sporadic in winter and regulated in summer. A restaurant next door serves the usual Ukrainian. The restaurant **Dacha Stambul** (Lenina 47; tel: 06562 300 82) occupies the ground level of an incredible mansion once owned by the Tatar magnate of Kaffa. Despite the name, there is nothing Tatar on the rather unoriginal, low-priced menu (pork, fish, pilmenny, etc) but it might be worth eating there just to see the building.

What to see

People come to Feodosiya to relax and enjoy the beach and good weather of Crimea. **Dvuyakornaya Bay** south of the city has some clean shoreline and is a beautiful place to walk. North of the city is Golden beach as well as the remains of the **Genoese fortress**. For help with local excursions see the **Krymtur** office at Voikova 46 (tel: 06562 320 31). The main attraction in Feodosiya is the **Aivazovsky Museum** or, more correctly, museums. His picture gallery and house are combined as one building but have two separate entrances and require two separate tickets; both are filled with his paintings. Aivazovsky's genius lay in his ability to paint water and his seascapes have become a standard of technique and emotion in mastering the most difficult natural element. The Feodosiya collection is the largest in the world, a fraction of which is on display. The museum and house are on Galereinaya 2 and the corner of Prospekt Lenina. Each ticket costs 5UAH; open 09.00–20.00; closed Wednesday.

OUTSIDE FEODOSIYA
Koktebel – Коктебель
Around 10km south of Feodosiya is the calm bay and seaside village of Koktebel. The small hills and clean beaches make it a pristine corner that somehow avoided the fate of Soviet development. The Russian symbolist poet MA Voloshin settled in Koktebel in 1899 and started a commune based on his own philosophies of freedom, including naturism. Soon Koktebel became the secret hangout for St Petersburg Bohemians. The secret is out but this is still a very open and relaxed place with most visitors pitching tents on the shore (the nudist beach occupies a kilometre of soft sand to the east of the bay). Koktebel also has a large Crimean Tatar population who fortunately run many of the local restaurants and food stands – this is the right place to sample *lagman* and *köbete*. There are trails from the beach going up and down the coast, into the hills, and on to Kara-Dag.

Kara-Dag – Кара-Даг
The **Kara-Dag Nature Reserve** was established in 1979 in an attempt to preserve some of Crimea's endangered animal species living in this bit of wild landscape. The sharp cliffs are broken remnants of an ancient underwater volcano that erupted over 100 million years ago. The translation of the Tatar name, 'Black Mountain,' refers to its volcanic past. The park surrounds one mountain on the bay of Koktebel and there is an easy walking trail from the town and around the hillside. Foxes, weasels, badgers, jerboas, and rock martens live in the park and common bird species include the kingfisher, Eurasian hoopoe, European roller, the common crossbill, little bittern and European bee-eater.

Sudak – Судак
The Genoese came to 'Surozh' in 1365 and built the monumental square fortress to protect their trade centre at this, the official end of the Silk road to China. The ramparts and some ruins remain draped across the coastal hills and the lower wall is over 2km long. This is Sudak's only real 'site', but it is easy to spend a full day exploring the walls and 14 towers on top of the conical mountain. The city beach is long and sandy and once upon a time the Soviet rose-oil processing plant gave a sweet smell to the air. An equal attraction is the shallow turquoise bay at **Novy Svyet** which is a 7km jaunt down the coast from the fort in Sudak. This very secluded spot is distinct for its ancient junipers and supposedly is the first place to see spring in Crimea. The rocky coastline between Cape Koba-Kaya and Cape Chi-khen is magnificent.

Where to stay and eat
The hotel **Gorizont** (Turisticheskoye Shosse 8; tel: 06566 221 79) is an average standard B&B-style place and not expensive. **Parus** (Naberezhnaya 29; tel: 06566 223 77) is the recently remodelled hotel of the city located near the beach and has a functional restaurant. **Azart Travel Company** (tel: 06566 313 12) are good fixers for this less-travelled bit of Crimea.

KERCH – КЕРЧЬ
This very functional port lies at the easternmost tip of Crimea and represents the end of the line. Russia looms on the other side of the water and the city has become an important crossroads into Asia for round-the-world travellers since crossing the

strait by boat feels more deliberate than driving across the unmarked plains of central Russia. A decade ago special ferries carried trains from one side to the next; now a bridge is planned. Kerch really took a beating in World War II so much of its old Greek charm has been replaced by the elegance of Soviet industry and shipping. Still, the 175,000 inhabitants like to flaunt their unique ancient sights and the coastal area south of the city is pleasant.

The original Greek colony of Panticapaeum was founded in the 6th century BC and within a century had developed into the independent Bosporos kingdom called Karsha. Several ports were built on both sides of the Kerch Strait and inhabited mainly by descendant Cimmerians; some of these are now underwater and make for curious diving today. Legends claim the Apostle Andrew first set foot on Slavic soil near Kerch during the 1st century AD. Around the same time a significant influx of Jews arrived from the Middle East. The area was made a tributary to Kievan Rus but was lost to the Golden Horde. During the Genoese era, 'Cerccio' was used as a trade warehouse, while the Turks realised the strategic importance of the Kerch strait connecting the Sea of Azov to the Black Sea and built Eni-Kale to control the waterways. Russia took Kerch from the Turks more than a decade before the rest of Crimea, but it quickly fell to the wayside and stood almost as a ghost town for one hundred years. Only in the Soviet industrial revolution of the 1920s did the population begin to grow again. Kerch is remembered for its heroic stand against Nazi Germany in World War II: for six months of 1942 a resistant force in the Aszhimushkaisky stone quarries kept the city free. The future was very uncertain for Kerch during the recent Russia-Ukraine tension over Crimea, but now there seems to be some large industrial investment going on and the international border has provided a small boost to the city. Trade and transportation remains the major occupation and you may wonder what brought you here unless you are particularly keen on Greek ruins.

Getting there and away

There is an overnight train from Simferopol but it is only 200km in distance. There is a daily train to and from Kiev (almost 24 hours), Moscow (via Kharkov) and Kherson. A local train goes to the connecting station at Dzhankoi. Transport to the city centre from the Vokzal is frequent. The bus station is at Yeryomenko 30. Buses to Simferopol take five hours and pass through Feodosiya (2 hours away). Also, many of the international bus routes to and from southern Russia stop here before heading to the Ukrainian mainland. Kerch has a ferry to Russia that leaves from Port Krym at the easternmost end of the peninsula (take bus #1 from the bus station). The journey takes 30 minutes and costs US$5. Crossing to Russia requires advance preparation since there is no chance of getting a Russian visa on the spot.

Where to stay and eat

Although Kerch is part of Crimea it has a very eastern Ukraine feel with the hospitality to match. **Zaliv** (Kurortnaya 6a; tel: 06561 345 08) is the higher standard hotel usually recommended to foreigners with average rooms costing US$45–60. **Kerch** (Kirova 11; tel: 06561 211 55) is across from the sea station right in the centre; they also have an office to help with short-term apartment rentals. **Meridian** (Sverdlova 83; tel: 06561 205 56) has US$20/$40 rooms with showers and toilets, as well as a nice restaurant. Cheaper rooms can be found at **Moryak** (Gagarina 3; tel: 06561 572 57). Both in the city centre, **Assol** (Lenina 47) and **Grifon** (Teatral'naya 35) serve Russian café-style food. **Chinzano** (Gorkovo 20) serves decent Italian food and there are many small cafés farther down Lenina.

What to see

From the centre are the long Mitridatskaya steps rising up to the top of **Mitridat Hill**. This is the largest concentration of the most ancient sites in Kerch and was once the acropolis of **Panticapaeum** that included a temple to Apollo. A few pillars are still standing. The other ruins are pieces of the successive kingdoms. At the bottom of the steps in the park is St John the Baptist church, started in the 8th century with its original frescos still intact today; during the Soviet era it was used as a gem museum. The **Melek-Chesmensky Tomb** was the mausoleum of the Bosporan kings and is conveniently located right behind the central bus station. The **Adzhimushkai stone quarries** are to the northeast of the city and there is a museum commemorating the heroic resistance on Ulitsa Skifskaya. Further down the same road is **Tsarsky Kurgan**, a 4th-century tomb also used by the Bosporan kings with a temple-like burial chamber at the end of a long corridor entrance beneath a manmade hill. At the very end of the peninsula near the ferry dock is the Turkish castle of **Eni-Kale**. The fortress was designed by the French in 1703 to give the Turk's an edge over the Russians. It is quite large and provides a good view of the busy channel. Further down the coast are the Greek ruins of **Nimfei** and **Eltigen** as well as plentiful beaches.

The Dnepr Днепр

At 2,286km (1,420 miles), the Dnepr is Europe's third longest river (after the Volga and Danube) and Ukraine's defining waterway. Early Ukrainian civilisation was borne from the Kievan Rus trade routes along the Dnepr and the largest band of Ukrainian Cossacks began their independent governments on the river's largest island. The tourist appeal for the region lies in its historical role and the obvious natural beauty of the Dnepr's banks. Cruising down the river has long been the 'thing to do' when visiting Ukraine, but those who are not travelling by ship may still find they keep crossing the Dnepr in their journey as the river has always marked the cultural and political boundary between east and west. The river's environs (and the entire country) are usually described in terms of right bank/left bank based on a person facing south from Kiev.

The source of the Dnepr (*Dnipro* in Ukrainian) is in southeast Russia and the river flows through Belarus before cutting down the centre of Ukraine. To fulfil Soviet demands for electrical power and industrial prestige, the river was dammed in half a dozen places, forming a series of wide reservoirs that, if nothing else, create some recreational spaces. In summer, boating and swimming are popular and in winter the river freezes solid and ice fishermen congregate on its narrow channels. Despite what you may see or hear, the Dnepr is an extremely polluted river, albeit a very scenic one. A glimpse of industrial cities like Dnepropetrovsk and Zaporizhzhya will assist your imagination in guessing what has gone into the water since the time when the ancient Greek historian Herodotus claimed the Dnepr's water was the cleanest he ever drank. Focus on what's above the surface and appreciate the trees.

Getting around

The most obvious form of transport on the river would be a boat, and a limited public river transport service once connected certain cities (eg: Kiev–Cherkasy); however, these have dwindled in favour of private river cruises. Each river city port features a 'river station' (речной вокзал; *rechnoi vokzal*) that can give you the latest on available routes (in summer only). The main rail line does not follow the river, but crosses to the right bank from Dnepropetrovsk to Kiev, or else sweeps north then west through left-bank Ukraine. If you want to travel by land along the river, motor transport is the best option; the right bank road from Cherkasy to Zaporizhzhya is a picturesque stretch.

CHERKASSY – ЧЕРКАСИ

Built along the widest point of the Dnepr, from Cherkasy you can't always see to the river's other side. Several waterfront parks and a youthful atmosphere make it

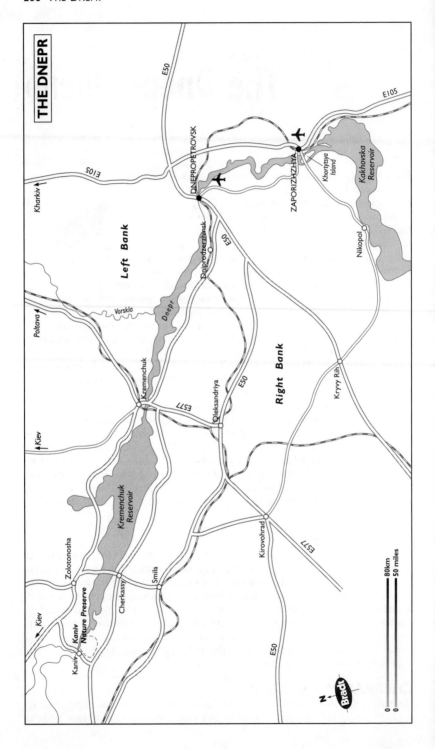

DNEPR CRUISES

Leisurely river cruises up and down the Dnepr were one of the first package deals to be touted to foreigners and are now the most organised trips in the country. The river does not take that long to travel down, but passes lots of interesting places, so itineraries usually hit half the sites on the way down, and the others on the way back. A typical journey will begin in Kiev, make a midway stop in Odessa, Sevastopol or both, and then return to Kiev, lasting around two weeks. The most popular ports of call tend to be Kaniv, Kremnechuk, Dnepropetrovsk, Zaporizhzhya and Kherson. Although some may find the concept of a cruise a little banal, travelling the Dnepr in this way offers a rather comprehensive introduction to the country

The best time to travel down the Dnepr is in May and June, when the willow trees are just turning green, the flowers are still blossoming and the river is not too busy. Every single Ukrainian tour agency will advertise their 'unique' Dnepr cruise when really, they are just ticket dealers, but for now it is the only way to secure a spot. Passage is almost always on the MS Marshal Koshevoy, a vintage East German riverboat circa 1989. When checking prices, make sure you know what is and is not included in the fee, since land excursions are sometimes additionally charged. An all-inclusive 15-day cruise with a 'boat deck' cabin (at the top of the ship) costs around US$1,200 per person, US$900 if sharing the suite. A 10–12 day cruise on the main or lower decks will cost around US$600 per person. Groups of 20 or more can organise significant discounts. Many western travel agencies advertise Dnepr and Black Sea combinations, as do quite a few Russian-based tour operators. All the tour companies listed in *Chapter 4* offer some form of river cruise; SAM has been offering cruises since its inception; in Kiev: Ivan Franka 40B; tel: 044 238 2060; fax: 044 238 6952; email: main@samcomp.kiev.ua; in Dnepropetrovsk: Karla Marksa 59A; tel: 0562 360 404; email: info@samcomp.dp.net.

a pleasant place to come in summer, but few cruises will stop long in Cherkassy, and if they do so, it will probably be for functional reasons. The most famous site is the nearby **Korsun Hill of Eternal Glory**, where a giant iron woman holds a flaming torch in honour of the war dead.

The city was officially founded in the 14th century as a Dnepr River outpost from Kiev. Later, Cherkassy belonged to the string of forts demarcating the end of civilisation and the beginning of the 'wild field'. For a few centuries, the river port was a Cossack stronghold embroiled in constant battles with the Tatars from the south. This was followed by two centuries of Polish rule with the exclusion of Khmelnytsky's liberation war and the peasant uprisings from 1648 to 1654. Russia finally annexed Cherkassy in 1793. Few signs of the old city are left, since both the civil war and World War II were especially destructive. Hitler is said to have flattened the city completely. Today, Cherkassy seems to be the favoured town of foreign students who come here to study Russian. Other visitors come by boat, sailing down from Kiev for the day.

More interesting than the city is the actual region of Cherkassy where there is still the sense of a 'wild field'. Ukraine's greatest heroes – Taras Shevchenko and Bohdan Khmelnytsky – were born in the modest villages still spread across a rather empty plain. Most visitors coming to the region visit the Shevchenko

Museum upriver at **Kaniv**, or the gardens and town of **Uman** in the west (covered in *Chapter 7*).

Getting there and away

People can fly to Cherkassy but considering Kyiv Borispol is about a two-hour drive, it would seem silly. Transit is usually limited to Kiev, Moscow and Crimea. The airport is at Smilyanska 168 and air tickets can be purchased at the office at Ostafia Dashkovicha 30. The train station is at Krupskoyi 1; however, the main lines do not run through here, and the trains that do come through tend to be going north and south. Connections to Kiev are longer than they need to be (over 4 hours). Longer routes service Moscow, Lviv, and Poltava but Cherkassy is always considered a slow connection. You might consider going to Kiev and enjoying your pick of trains. From either Kiev or Cherkassy to the other it is wisest to take the bus. The central bus station in Cherkassy is next to the airport (Smilyankska 162). Nearly all Kiev buses travelling to any Dnepr River cities will stop in Cherkassy, so that everyday there are connections with Kaniv, Kremenchuk, and Dnepropetrovsk, as well as Poltava, Kirovohrad and Uman. Cherkassy is the one city where there is regular river transport to and from Kiev, although the trip can take a leisurely five hours or more. The river station is at the end (or beginning) of Geroyiv Stalingrada; tel: 0472 452 727.

Where to stay and eat

Hotel Dnepr (Frunze 1; tel: 0472 472 360) is located right next to the riverfront. Considered the city's best after renovation in 2001, the hotel is refreshingly clean and well-managed. Rooms cost US$66 for a single, US$100 for a double, breakfast included and credit cards accepted. One block away is the **Rosova** (Frunze 28; tel: 0472 450 321), slightly less expensive (US$50–80) and with a little less

TARAS SHEVCHENKO (1814–61)

No matter where you travel in Ukraine, you are bound to see the portrait of a gentle old man with contemplative brow and drooping moustache – Taras Hryhorovich Shevchenko. In his life, Shevchenko was a poet, a philosopher, a painter and a prisoner; nowadays, he represents the liberation of the Ukrainian nation.

Shevchenko was born a serf in Moryntsy, a village on the right bank of Cherkassy region. Both of his parents died before he was 12, and as an orphan he worked as a shepherd and was trained as a servant. Eventually his master brought the boy to Vilnius and then St Petersburg where he was allowed limited study with a painter. Other artists noticed the boy's sketching and held a lottery to raise enough money (2,500 rubles) to purchase his freedom. Shevchenko was then accepted into the St Petersburg art academy where he won many prizes for his paintings, and also began a compilation of poems that was published in 1840 under the title *Kobzar*. Named after the wandering bards in Ukraine, the book uses artful verse to express both the beauty and hardship of Ukrainian life. The book was a success and is now the most sacred text in Ukrainian aside from the Bible.

The poet's fame and liberation philosophy eventually brought him under the scrutiny of Tsar Nikolai I who ordered his arrest for participation with a clandestine Ukrainian group, the brotherhood of St Cyril and Methodius. He was first imprisoned in Siberia and later assigned a place in the army in Central remodelling; accepts credit cards. Right in the city centre, the **Hotel Cherkassy** (Lazareva 6; tel: 0472 472 728) is the least expensive option with some rooms for around US$20, but overall still a bit rough around the edges. Farther out is **Hotel Ukrayina** (Lesnaya 1; tel: 0472 321 052; email: Ukraine_hotel@mail.ru). Singles are US$20, doubles US$30, suites US$80. Each hotel features its own restaurant, open to all. In terms of restaurants there is traditional Slavic fare at **Stare Misto** (Khreschatyk 200), or never-fail Chinese at **Peking** (Gogolya 413; tel: 0472 470 041). At the bottom end of Shevchenka, right on the Ploschad 700 let, is **Pizza Service** (tel: 0472 434 593), offering 25 different kinds of Italian Pizza.

KANIV – КАНІВ

The poet Taras Shevchenko – Ukraine's ultimate hero – requested that he be buried near this tiny village on a bluff overlooking the Dnepr River. His desire was fulfilled after his death and now visitors stream in from all over the world to see his grave at this very serene location. Kaniv itself was founded as one of the original fortresses marking the line between civilisation and the open 'wild field' and later became an important Cossack stronghold. Before the Russian Revolution and throughout Khruschev's USSR, Shevchenko's grave was a popular site for clandestine meetings of nationalists and intellectuals. The **Taras Shevchenko Literary Museum** is on top of the main hill near his grandiose grave; tel: 04736 223 65; open 09.00–18.00, entrance 5UAH. The poet lived for a while in the smaller restored cottage in the woods behind. Just three miles south of the village is the **Kaniv Nature Preserve**, founded in 1926 to protect natural Ukrainian plant species. The park is open for walking and enjoying some very lovely views of the river. The main office is in the village; tel: 04736 230 47. Kaniv can be reached by car or bus from Kiev (2 hours) or Cherkassy (1 hour), and most Ukrainian tour agencies offer boat excursions to Kaniv as a day trip from Kiev.

Asia. During this decade of exile, the tsar commanded that Shevchenko be prohibited from drawing or writing, but the poet continued both in secret and many of these works are on display in the art museums of Kiev and Kharkiv today. After gaining his freedom, the exhausted Shevchenko lived for only four more years. His death came just seven days before the universal emancipation of the serfs, and his life of captivity became the symbol of oppressed Ukrainians in the Russian Empire. Shevchenko's poems also illustrated the national cause and built a bond between various movements and societies in Ukraine, as well as other parts of the empire and throughout the Ukrainian diaspora.

By the time Ukraine had its first brief taste of independence in 1918, Shevchenko was revered as the country's greatest hero. Ukrainians still quote Shevchenko's reference to Ukraine when he spoke of 'this land of ours that is not ours'. During the Soviet regime, Shevchenko's anti-Russian voice was toned down and the poet was represented as the universal voice of the repressed peasantry; however, since 1991, most nationalists have used his image as a convenient substitute for the former cult worship of Lenin. Every city has at least one statue of the poet and a street named after him, and schoolchildren must memorise long tracts of his poetry. Socialist or nationalist, Shevchenko was a man who truly loved his country. Shevchenko was buried in St Petersburg, but his body was later moved to Kaniv in order to fulfil the desires of his poem *Testament* where he had envisioned his final resting place: a high mound overlooking the surging Dnepr and endless fields of Ukraine.

KREMENCHUK – КРЕМЕНЧУК

Kremenchuk's dam is the cause of the immense Kremenchutsky Reservoir (the big blue spot on the map of Ukraine) and the hydro-electric plant used to provide energy locally and run the giant chemical carbon plant in Soviet days. An atmosphere of heavy industry does not prevent most cruises from stopping here to enjoy the parks and sandy river beaches. The scant tourist amenities are disenchanting – go stay in Dnepropetrovsk instead. If you must remain in town, there are two choices: **Hotel Ontario** (Butyrina 15) costs US$120–200 and is not even close to being worth it (Ukrainians pay the same price, but in *hrivna*). **Dneprovskye** (Khalamenyuka 8; tel: 05366 225 37) has rooms for under US$25 but the experience resembles camping indoors. If you feel lost and confused, ask for direction at the Kremenchuk Bureau of Excursions; Pervomaiskaya 1; tel: 05366 301 77.

Getting there and away

A frequent overnight train runs between Kiev and Kremenchuk (8 hours) but only during the tourist season (June–September and New Year). Another train connects to Kirovograd (3 hours) and Poltava (3 hours), but buses are quicker and more frequent. Private buses (Avtoluks and Gunsel) also travel to and from Kiev (4 hours) and Dnepropetrovsk (2 hours). The bus station is at Vorovskovo 32/6; tel: 05366 205 04. River transport schedules change frequently; ask at the river station on Pervomaiskaya.

DNEPROPETROVSK – ДНІПРОПЕТРОВСЬК

Pronounced exactly as it is spelled, Dnepropetrovsk is Ukraine's third-largest city and the country's mighty industrial fist. For the longest time, nobody ever felt the need to come to Dnepr (for short) unless they were working here, and today most 'tourists' arrive with some vested interest. It is not a city of sights, but a place to see and be. There is a well-organised metropolis and an active population beyond the flagging steel factories and taking in Dnepr's sleek new dynamic seems to be the greatest attraction. As the largest port on the lower Dnepr and the biggest city in the centre of the country, all cruises make at least a one-day stop and some travellers choose Dnepr as an alternative to Kiev for an east-west gateway. The river occupies a more central focus in everyday life and there's a lot less pomp and a lot more party than in the capital.

History

The first permanent settlement was a 9th-century monastery on Monastyrsky Island where the Dnepr flows directly east before turning sharply to the south at the confluence of the Samara River.

In an attempt to counter the independent island fortress of the Zaporizhzhyan Sich downriver, the Poles built their own fortress near this spot named *Kodak*, but the Zaporizhzhyan Cossacks soon took it over. By 1776, the Russian Empire had finally secured the Zaporizhzhyan lands and Catherine the Great looked to build a southern capital that would rule supreme in 'New Russia'. The chosen sight was conveniently near the two former Cossack bases, though spring floods and swampy fields hampered the building of palaces. Eventually, General Potemkin was able to carry out his orders and the city of Yekaterinaslav rose up from the banks of the Dnepr. However, the original plans were never finished and the city was left a fraction of its intended size.

In 1883, a new metal bridge was built through Yekaterinoslav completing a rail connection that could carry coal from Donetsk to the steel mills in Kryvy

Rih. Soon a gigantic steelworks had been built on site and the city joined in Ukraine's rapid, but very localised industrial revolution. A largely imported Russian working-class population made the town a hotbed of revolutionary activity and after the civil war, the city was renamed Dnepropetrovsk in an attempt to cast off tsarist allusions and to honour the first general secretary of the Ukrainian communist party, Petrovsky. Dnepr was a key city in the Soviet Union for its metal works, engineering, and as a leader in the Soviet space programme, and Ukraine's president Leonid Kuchma was raised, educated and made his political career here. Dnepr has made a smooth transition (more or less) from the Soviet steel industry to the world of international business and finance although that success can be attributed to the city's notoriously shady oligarchs. Luckily, the city's élite have chosen to invest their tremendous wealth and power back into the city.

Getting there and away
By air
Dnepropetrovsk International Airport is probably the busiest airport in the country outside of Kiev, situated 13km (8 miles) southeast of the city centre; tel: 0562 650 496. If Dnepr is your final destination, it is easiest to connect with **Austrian Airlines**' daily return flight from Vienna, Dnepropetrovsk Airport; tel: 0562 771209. **Dniproavia** (Naberezhna 37; tel: 0562 441 757) is the locally based airline, with daily flights to Kiev, connections to Volgograd, Yerevan, Istanbul and Tblisi, and a three-times-a-week service to Frankfurt, Germany. **Aerosvit** (airport; tel: 056 777 1986; email: aerosvit@email.dp.ua) has the most convenient daily flights to Kiev.

By rail
Dnepr serves as the primary rail junction between the industrial east, Kiev, and the west, so even if you never plan on staying here, you may have spent a small moment parked in this city while you slept during a long train journey. The daily *Dnipro* train goes to and from Kiev (9 hours) from the city. However, there are constant trains passing through, such as the daily Kiev–Donetsk connection. Other trains from Dnepr to Donetsk (4 hours) are frequent and practically all trains between Russia and Crimea make a stop here as well. Other daily trains connect with Kharkiv (5 hours), Odessa (12 hours) and Lviv (24 hours). The central train station is at Ploscha Petrovskovo at the end of Karla Marksa, and tickets can be bought in most upmarket or former Inturist hotels.

By bus
The Central Bus Station (Kurchatova 6; tel: 056 778 4090) is within one block of the train station. Ukraine's two major private companies both have offices in the main station. **Avtolux** (tel: 056 778 3979) has four daily connections to Kiev (7 hours), as well as two daily buses to Zaporizhzhya (1 hour) and Yalta (9 hours). **Gunsel** (tel: 0562 31 84 60) also has a quick bus three times a week to Kiev (7½ hours) via Kremenchuk and Borispol Airport, as well as one daily bus to Donetsk (4 hours). All other public buses are yours for the picking. The most obvious regional connections are to Zaporizhzhya, Kryvy Rih and Donetsk.

By boat
As in Kiev, there is plenty of boat traffic during the warmer seasons, although most of these are organised cruises that seldom originate in Dnepropetrovsk. Find out at the river station; Gorkovo 1; tel: 0562 498 267.

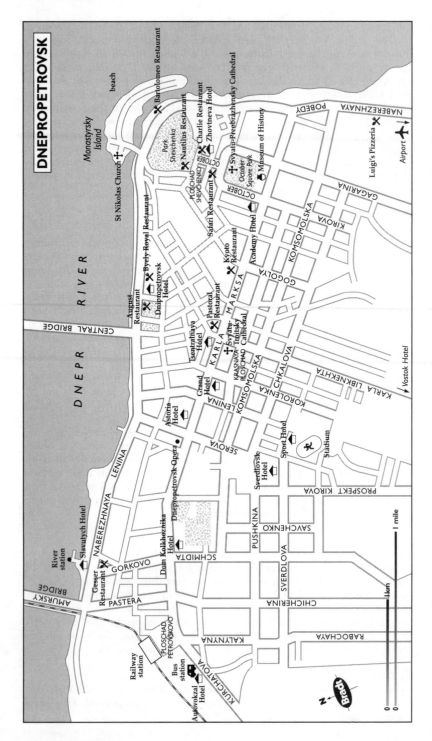

Getting around

Dnepropetrovsk opened its single-line metro in 1996 and then closed a week later due to heavy leaking. The soggy ground of the riverbank was not ideal for tunnelling. However, these days the subway is back up and running and for 60 kopecks you can travel from the train station out to Dnepr's great residential neighbourhoods. Trolleys and trams are still the best way to get around

For a taxi, call: Radio Taxi; tel: 053 (locally), Dnepr Taxi (tel: 0562 333 333), or City Taxi (0562 349 349).

Where to stay

There is big money in Dnepr and those that have it want it to be known. The city has more true luxury hotels than any other in Ukraine. Finding low-priced rooms will be difficult for foreigners, but in Dnepr you tend to get what you pay for, which should be slightly comforting.

Luxury

The following all accept credit cards, willingly.

Grand Hotel Korolenka 2; tel: 0562 341 010; fax: 0562 340 200; email: admin@grand-hotel-ukraine.dp.ua; web: www.grand-hotel-ukraine.dp.ua, http://gorod.dp.ua/hotel/. Ukraine's only five-star hotel outside Kiev is dripping in splendour to the point of being a little bit too much. This is the largest upmarket hotel in the city and already has a national reputation after being open just a few years. The building was the home of a businessman back during the last years of the empire but today the businessmen are back en masse as corporate elitism defines the atmosphere. The swimming pool and fitness club are the city's very best, and keeping in line with the extravagance, the restaurant serves mainly exotic oriental cuisine. The simplest single rooms are US$120, doubles are US$210, and the presidential suite where Kuchma stays is US$750 a night.

Academy Karla Marksa 20; tel: 056 370 0505; fax: 056 370 2931; email: info@academia.dp.ua; web: www.academia.dp.ua. A smaller but very refined option, the Academy has only 20 rooms, all immaculate. Amenities include a decent fitness room, sauna and bar, and the restaurant specialises in Ukrainian and Jewish cuisine. Personal care and a comfortable use of English sets it apart from most. Prices are US$100 for a large single, US$150 for a double, US$200 for suites.

Astoria Karla Marksa 66A; tel: 370 42 70. This very swish hotel stands at the head of Dnepr's main drag (near the Opera House) and caters to a clientele with expensive tastes. The beds are bouncy and the bathrooms spacious. The popular cocktail lounge and swimming pool are also definite highlights. A 'semi-suite' costs US$120 and the super-plush suites are US$190.

Middle range

Dnipropetrovsk Naberezhnaya Lenina 33; tel: 0562 455 327; web: www.hoteldnepropetrovsk.dp.ua. Right on the river and just two blocks down from the main bridge, this 11-storey hotel has a great view of the city, and is usually offered to package tourists as the cheaper alternative to the Grand. On average, rooms are small but generally comfy, costing around US$40 for a single and US$55 for a large double. Each is equipped with shower or bath and there is always hot water. The suites (for US$60) are also not a bad deal. Credit cards accepted.

Zhovtneva Ploschad Shevchenko 4A; tel: 0562 448 803; fax: 0562 722 065. Built in the vaguely historical district of the city next to Park Shevchenko, the 'October' is a rather functional hotel, remodelled in 1999. If you like to walk and be in the centre of the action, this is the place where most outdoor recreation takes place (the island is within walking distance). Expect to pay US$60–70 for an average room; credit cards accepted.

Tsentralnaya Karla Marksa 50; tel: 0562 450 347. As the name implies, the hotel is centrally located on the main street of the city and is a remodelled Soviet high-rise. The prices (singles US$50; double 'suites' US$70) reflect the central location rather than the standard of comfort, but year-round heating/AC is a plus. Accepts credit cards.

Vostok Geroyev Stalingrada 117; tel: 0562 960 703; fax: 0562 960 962 ; email: vostoc@at.com.ua; web: www.vostoc.dp.ua/eng. You can't get farther from the city centre than this, but if you have a car, or think the cab fare is worth the discount, then this is the right place. The building is modern and roomy, with rooms not unlike very nice Soviet apartments. Doubles are US$35 and multi-room suites are $50.

Slavutych Ploscha Desantnikov 1; tel: 0562 331 144 (at the river station). Not very glamorous, but rather fun in a Soviet, space-age kind of way. Rooms are in the US$30–40 range and you get to watch all the boats coming and going.

Budget

Sverdlovsk Sverdlova 6; tel: 0562 428 825. A civilised, Soviet-style hotel with modern facilities, including a travel agent who can issue train and plane tickets, a gym and a flashy disco. The location is not too hot, about four blocks south of Karla Marksa. All rooms are US$25–30.

Sport Schorsa 4; tel: 0562 320 932. Right in front of the city's football stadium, this is where Soviet athletes were housed way back when. Much of the interior has been remodelled, and service is generally good, but the old Soviet protocol pervades in the rooms (small bathrooms, all single beds). Rooms are US$15–25.

Autovokzal Kurchatova 10; tel: 056 778 3965. Proudly displaying its one star, this bus station hotel caters to travellers coming and going, but it is conveniently located near the train station and therefore the rest of the city's transportation routes. For US$10 you can get a room to yourself and a good wash.

Dom Kolkhoznika; Shmidta 3; tel: 056 778 3409. There really should be more hotels out there called 'Home of the Collective Farmers' but as far as I know this is the only one in the world. Originally built as a dormitory for Soviet farmers in the big city, travellers can still get a room here for US$5–10 but bathrooms are shared and the beds a bit creaky.

Renting apartments

Sometimes renting a whole private apartment is a cheaper option for longer stays, and even for just one night. '**Apartments**' is recommended by the city and has a few luxurious options in the very centre; Komsomolskaya 35/1; tel: 0562 321 808; web: www.apartments.dp.ua

Where to eat

Dnepr probably has the highest number of entertainment establishments per capita, and out of these, good food is making its way to the top. **Safari** (Fuchika 12b; tel: 0562 38 98595) sells itself as the ultimate in sophistication but is actually quite laidback in a sports bar/pub kind of way. The menu caters to those who appreciate fine food. Around $30 a head; credit cards accepted. **Berloga** (Demyana Bednovo 11; tel: 0562 374 211) is built to resemble a crude hunting lodge where people can enjoy the simple recipes of old Ukraine. The atmosphere is quite calm and the food is especially tasty. A meal costs around US$15. **Nautilus** (Ploschad Shevchenko 1; tel: 0562 466 576) is in the main park and keeps to their underwater theme with a beautiful aquarium in the middle of the restaurant. Fish and seafood dominate the menu (about US$10 for a main course; US$2 for drinks). **August** (Naberezhnaya Lenina 33; tel: 0562 450 150) has an outdoor terrace right on the Dnepr. Tasty grilled food and live music (that's not annoying) make for pleasant evenings in summer. **Gesser** (Gorkovo 22; tel: 056 778 2756) specialises in beer, but also serves all the food to go with it, including a lot of wild game and hearty Russian meals. Accepts credit cards; US$10 for most dishes. **Kyoto** (Karla Marksa 34b; tel: 056 370 2885) is one of many Japanese restaurants, but perhaps the only one worth mentioning. The US$8 business lunches are popular. **Luigi's Pizzeria** (Naberezhnaya Pobedy 44; tel: 0562 319 329) does Italian pizza as simple or as complicated as you want it; with bar. A meal costs under US$12. If you're just looking for a café, **Pastoral** (Karla Marksa 46; tel: 0562 362 866) serves real Italian coffee, delectable pastries, and soup and sandwiches at lunchtime or a believably Victorian 'English' tea at four.

Some of the nicer restaurants are based in the hotels. The **Astoria** (Karla Marksa 66A; tel: 0562 384 802) advertises a chef that will make anything for anyone, and he actually does, while the **Academy** (Karla Marksa 20; 056 370 0505) sticks to a European menu. Dnepr's highly affluent crowd seems to favour the casino/restaurant combination, the more over the top the better. The menu at **Byely Royal** (Naberezhnaya Lenina 33; tel: 056 744 3501) offers an incredible quantity of Italian and Russian food and the casino goes beyond the normal slot machines and roulette with a colourful show (ahem) and live ring fighting (!). Another popular all-night venue is **Charlie** (Per Oktyabrsky 6; tel: 0562 465 219) where there is a combination French restaurant/sushi bar, billiard hall and casino. And yet **Bartolomeo** (Naberezhnaya Pobedy 9/6; tel: 056 370 1500) takes the cake when it comes to post-Soviet splendour gone completely mad. Dedicated to the concept of the first explorers, the life-size 15th-century ship and surrounding complex is 'not a restaurant, not a club, not a hotel, but a whole world'. Besides the various restaurants, there is a yacht club, Russian bathhouse, tennis courts, children's zoo, casino and a very rowdy nightclub.

What to see and do

Strolling along the riverbank and watching the boats is the number one pastime in Dnepr, and the second is to go out at night. Visitors should try both. In the summer, most activity takes place on **Naberezhnaya Lenina**. **Oktyabrskaya Square** is the other locale for tourist attention (Ploscha Zhovtneva) where a large park and fountain set the stage for the rose and gold **Syato-Preobrazhenskaya Cathedral** which gives a fair idea of what old Yekaterinoslav used to look like. The red, yellow and green **Svyato-Troitsky Cathedral** (Krasnaya Ploschad 7) is probably the most unique building left from the original city. The city **Museum of History** (Karla Marksa 18) is another city architectural monument that is just as impressive as the life-size diorama inside portraying the World War II defence of the Dnepr River. Near the river is **Park Shevchenko** where locals congregate year-round for conversation and dominos, and just across the channel is **Monastyrsky Island** where there was once a monastery but is now the main city beach, as well as **St Nikolas Church**. Dnepr's prominent high street is found at **Prospekt Karla Marksa,** a classical work of socialist city planning. If you can't find it here (shops, post office, food stands, souvenirs), then you won't. Also, the **Dnepropetrovsk Opera** is not the most famous in the country, but what's on offer is usually very entertaining; Karla Marksa 72A; tel: 056 778 4469.

ZAPORIZHZHYA – ЗАПОРІЖЖЯ

Essentially, Zaporizhzhya offers a happy medium between the core identity of Ukrainian tradition and the legacy of Soviet engineering. Tourists like to think of Cossacks when they come to Zaporizhzhya but usually find the city's surface is a blackened shrine to Ukraine's heaviest industry.

These two extremes don't seem to bother present-day Zaporizhians, who are just as proud of the hydro-electric dam as they are the archaeological remnants of Scythians and the most famous of Cossack bands. The name Zaporizhzhya comes from the Ukrainian *za porihy*, meaning 'beyond the rapids'. After passing through the most dangerous part of the journey, early traders sailing from Kiev used to stop on the island of Khortytsya to catch their breath or offer a sacrifice of thanks. Surrounded by rushing water, the large island offered both security and space and new pre-historic sites are still being discovered. The Cossacks came to the island in the 16th century and founded a fortress town and the first universal movement for Ukrainian independence. As an island in the middle of the Dnepr, the Zaporizhian Sich was a neutral milieu left undefined by cultural concepts of the Russian left bank or Polish right bank and today, Zaporizhians use Russian and Ukrainian interchangeably.

In an attempt to wipe the Cossacks off the map, Catherine the Great destroyed the Sich in 1775 and renamed the city Aleksandrovsk and it was known as this until 1921 when the Soviets re-instated its former name. Due to its prime location on the river and within the emerging industrial basin, Zaporizhzhya was allotted the fate of 'metal town' during Stalin's five-year plans. The Dneproges dam was started in 1932 in order to provide hydro-electric power to Zaporizhzhya's many factories. It was the first in Ukraine, took decades to finish, was partially destroyed in World War II and then rebuilt. Today it's an impressive sight to see, especially from the top. During the USSR, the name Zaporizhzhya also equated with the smallest and cutest of Soviet-made cars, the Zaporozhets, manufactured in the city's largest factory. The complex has since been taken over by Korea's Daewoo firm and renamed Avtozaz; you can't miss it coming in from the train station.

Block after city block of square buildings, the steelworks, and hundreds of billowing smokestacks make Zaporizhzhya the prototype of the perfect Soviet city, complete with Prospekt Lenina as the city's singular axis. Frankly, the decades of smoke and residue make this one of Ukraine's dirtiest towns and it was not too long ago that breathing around here was hard on the lungs. The decline in industry has cleared the air to some degree and visitors should still enjoy what is here. All Dnepr cruises will stop in Zaprorizhzhya to see Khortytsya and the Cossack Museum, but you should also make an effort to take in the city's behemoth industrial elements as historical monuments in their own right.

Getting there and away
By air
Zaporizhzhya has its own airport in principle but only offers the rare seasonal flight to Kiev and Crimea in summer. The much larger Dnepropetrovsk Airport is only 45 minutes away by car and this is the better city to fly into. Book tickets at the Zaporizhzhya Hotel office.

By rail
By far the best way to get to Zaporizhzhya is on the train. From Kiev there are three connections per day, taking from ten to 12 hours. The main 'Zap' train leaves around 20.00 and gets to Kiev at 07.30. Locally, practically all Zaporizhian trains come through Dnepropetrovsk (1 hour) as well as all trains between Moscow and Crimea, meaning there are daily connections to Kharkiv (7 hours) and Simferopol (7 hours). Local east–west connections join Krivy Rih (2 hours) and Donetsk (4 hours) daily, as well as Odessa (10 hours) and Lviv (24 hours). At the end of Prospekt Lenina, the Zaporizhzhya train station has only just been remodelled and sports a stunning interior, with a full-sized copy of Repin's 'Zaporizhian Cossacks'

painted on the ceiling. At one end is a comfy climatised waiting room that costs 3UAH to enter.

By bus
The central bus station is at Lenina 22; tel: 0612 642 657. The only reason for taking a bus is to come and go from Dnepropetrovsk (1 hour), the airport, or to get to Donetsk (3 hours). **Avtoluks** bus company goes from Kiev (9 hours) to Yalta (8 hours) and back via Zaporizhzhya twice a day.

By boat
A lot of cruises come in at Port Lenina at Leonova 1A, but the central river station is at Gliserna 1; tel: 0612 641 530. As with all boats on the Dnepr, schedules are highly sporadic, so you usually have to investigate options on site. A typical boat tour circumnavigates Khortytsya Island.

Getting around
Prospekt Lenina runs northwest to southeast and the #12 tram goes all the way to the train station. Taxis are also fairly cheap, tel: 008 or 0612 490 490

Where to stay
Right next to the main city building is the **Hotel Ukrayina** (Lenina 162A; tel: 0612 346 673; fax: 0612 246 105; email: gukr@reis.zp.ua; web: www.ukraine.zp.ua). Once the haunt of Soviet industry bosses, this is now the cleanest establishment in the city and feels the newest. The staff speak some English, the service is professional, the bathrooms are spotless and there is always hot water. Practically all the rooms come with heaters and air-conditioning (a real plus) and the suites have genuine queen-size beds. The best deal (quality for money) is the one room 'lux' suite for US$60; regular doubles are US$32, singles are US$27 and the larger suites are US$75. A classy Finnish sauna and simple restaurant are the main amenities.

Slightly larger and with a lot more whistles and bells is the nearby **Intourist Zaporizhzhya** Lenina 135; tel: 0612 339 554; email: intour@express.net.ua; web: www.intouriStcom.ua. They've kept the 'intourist' name as a marketing ploy and now function as the city's central tourist base with travel agents, business centre and internet and five restaurants. Rooms are divided into three classes: economy, standard and business. The lower-priced rooms (around US$15) are of the Soviet variety, the top two standards have been renovated with new furniture (US$80–100), and nice standard doubles cost around US$40; breakfast is US$4 extra.

The smallest of budgets can find refuge at the slightly dilapidated **Hotel Teatralnaya** (Chekistov 23; tel: 643 652) next to the theatre. Singles/doubles with bath and toilet are $15/$22. The very best suite costs US$40 with bathroom and heating/air-conditioning. A room without any plumbing (but with the use of hallway showers) is US$8 for a single, US$12 for a double. Like most cities in Ukraine, there is little to no hot water in summer.

Where to eat
Choices are still limited in Zaporizhzhya, mainly to the hotels. The **Ukrayina** has a basic menu, in English, with a regional menu (borscht, meat, fish); a full meal would cost around US$7. The **Zaporizhzhya** has five restaurants that differ little. The largest of these is a flashy orange and gold banquet hall serving specialties like 'Cossack pork' and cheese steaks. Expect to pay US$10–12 a meal. Out on the

island there are a few different 'Cossack' restaurants, open only in summer. The best of these is **Cossack Podvira,** a restaurant establishment that sells package deals that generally include transport to and from your hotel or boat, a meal and a Cossack riding show. Call 0612 332 556 for more info, or inquire at the Zaporizhzhya Intourist travel office. **Zaporozka Sich** is another club on the island that serves hearty Ukrainian meals but forces the Cossack theme a bit much; tel: 0612 522 552. Not just a restaurant, **Slobodka** (Gorkovo 115; tel: 0612 642 727) also features a sauna, bar and small convenience store selling handy travel food and drinks. The modern café is popular among young people and serves square meals for under US$7. If you're keen on keeping things humble and real, **Café Azariya** (Angolenko 20) serves basic fare for the poorest of pockets but is clean, smoke-free and spacious. Hot borscht is a menu staple, the rest is Ukrainian cafeteria-style food. A few ethnic restaurants are also on hand. You can have Chinese food at the **Shanghai** (Lenina 234), pretty good pizza at the **Pau Bau Pizzeria** (Tsentralny 4; tel: 0612 490 476) and Guinness at **O'Briens Pub** (Lenina 169; tel: 0612 325 723).

Tourist information
Intourist Zaporizhzhya functions as the leading tour operator in the area, with a convenient walk-in office on the main floor, Lenina 135; tel: 0612 336 127. This is the best place in the city to buy train, plane or bus tickets and arrange cruises, visits to Khortytsa or English-language city tours.

What to see and do
Khortytsya Island
Of the Dnepr's 256 islands, Khortytsya is the largest at 12km long and 2.5km wide. The north end is very rocky, with slanted cliffs up to 30m high, while the south end of the island sinks into river marsh with numerous rivulets and flooded basins. The island's central steppe consists of scattered forests and fields, and the diversity of landscape over such a small space makes the island ideal for exploring on foot. The amount of greenery makes it hard to believe that a city of one million people is just on the other side of the river. The Ukrainian government declared the area a national park in 1993 but a lot of work remains to be done in order to identify and fix up the sights and to facilitate accessibility.

The island is named for the Slavic god of the sun, Khoros, although some believe it comes from the Turkish root *ort* ('the middle'), since it is in the centre of the Dnepr. In spring and summer, things are very green, with lots of dark purple flowers, steppe grass and lovely butterflies. Guides will tell you that there are over 100 archaeological sites on the island, from the Stone Age up to the Cossacks, however few are in plain view or clearly identified except for some vague Cossack ruins and the old burial mounds. Some well-marked trails make walking easier. If you are tempted to wade in the water, beware of *chyortov orekhy* (hell nuts), the spiny seedpod of a Dnepr water plant that grows in shallow water.

The first Zaporizhian Sich (there were actually eight in all) was founded near Khortytsya around 1550 by hetman Dmytro Baida. Today the island of Baida lies in the river's eastern channel, and on its northern end are the remnants of the first 16th-century Cossack fortress, built to ward off Tatar invaders. A wooden stockade was later built on the main island and the ranks of Cossacks increased with a number of runaway serfs, freemen and societal non-conformists who were all granted equal status as part of the Sich. Present day Ukrainians view the Zaporizhian Cossacks as the predecessors to the country's independent government.

THE ZAPORIZHIAN COSSACKS

The Zaporizhian Cossacks were responsible for securing the 'wild field' of south-central Ukraine and ousting the Tatar invaders, and are attributed with many other daring feats of war. Despite the rough and rowdy reputation of the Cossacks, life in the Zaporizhian Sich resembled that of a warrior's monastery. No women were allowed on the island, the violation of which was punishable by death. It is probably true that Cossacks were prone to heavy drinking, but this was only permitted in peacetime. New entrants took vows, underwent a series of tests and rituals and lived by a semi-disciplined code. Legend suggests that one of these rites of passage required a Cossack to single-handedly steer a boat upriver through the Dnepr rapids.

The official mark of the Cossack was his haircut, called the *chub*, shaved bald except for a single ponytail springing from the top of the head. A man had to live as a Cossack for seven years before he was granted the title and allowed to wear the chub. Until that time, regardless of his age, he was referred to as *molodnyk* (youth) and a bowl was placed on his head and the hair trimmed around the edge. Cossack dress was distinct: long baggy trousers were convenient for hiding curved swords and horse-back riding. An oversized coloured sash was used as a belt or for a carrier bag slung over their shoulder. Different colours of sashes held different meaning and were supposed to be at least 3m long and wide 'like the Dnepr'. Tying the sash involved at least two people or else could be hung from a tree and slowly wound it around the waist. The other vital Cossack accessory was his clay pipe. A Ukrainian saying often attributed to the Zaporizhian Sich is *'Lyulky ta zhinky ne pozyhai!'* (a pipe or a wife can never be changed).

At its greatest, the Sich consisted of 20,000 Cossacks of 72 different nationalities. In war, the Cossacks abided by vague military hierarchies, but within the Zaporizhian Sich, the group was highly democratic and each Cossack had an equal voice around the table of the *rada*, a title used now by the Ukrainian parliament. An elected hetman presided and led the Cossacks into battle, but decisions about who to attack and who to join forces with was often made democratically. Land on the island was distributed among the ranks and when they were not preparing for war the Cossacks farmed their plots, hunted and fished, and kept bees for honey.

Of all the various Cossack bands, the Zaporizhian Sich was the largest, most serious, and most annoying to the Russians, Poles and Turks. Catherine the Great offered a 1,000 ruble bounty on the head of any Zaporizhian, and her forces attacked the Sich in 1775, razing it to the ground. The Cossacks scattered, some went to farm the Black Sea coast and others joined new bands, but today it is still the Zaporizhians that are remembered as Ukraine's greatest heroes.

The island's main attraction is the **Zaporizhian Cossack Museum** (open 10.00–17.00, closed Monday; entrance 3UAH, 6UAH with a guide – no English language yet). The iron sculpture at the entrance of the museum shows the sun, oak tree, leaves and arrows; an array of important Cossack imagery, and the actual building is not far from the ruins of the original fortress gate of the Zaporizhian Sich. The museum covers the whole history of the city and the island and visitors should expect to spend at least two hours to see everything in the exhibit. The

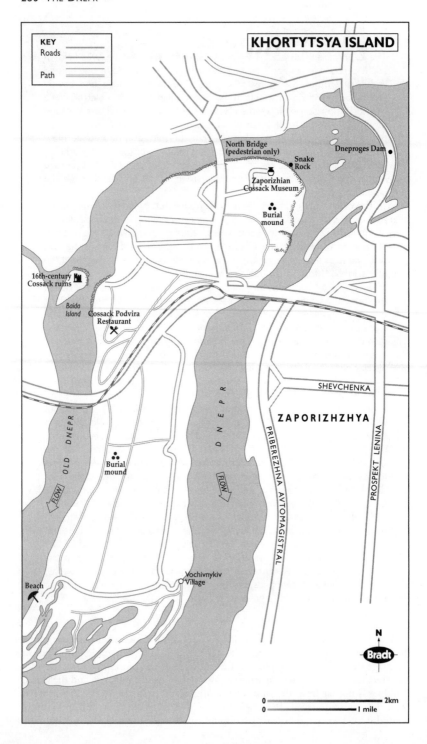

KHORTYTSYA ISLAND

KEY
Roads
Path

North Bridge
(pedestrian only)

Snake
Rock

Dneproges Dam

Zaporizhian
Cossack Museum

Burial
mound

16th-century
Cossack ruins

Baida
Island

Cossack Podvira
Restaurant

SHEVCHENKA

ZAPORIZHZHYA

DNEPR

FLOW

OLD DNEPR

FLOW

Burial
mound

PRIBEREZHNA AVTOMAGISTRAL

PROSPEKT LENINA

Vochivnykiv
Village

Beach

N

Bradt

0   2km
0   1 mile

Above Lichens, Gorgany Range, the Carpathians (AE)

Below left Carpathian deer, Yaremche (AE)

Below right Carpathian woodlands (AE)

Above Ai-Petri Mountain, Crimea (AE)
Below Vorontsov Palace, Alupka, Crimea (AE)
Below right Swallow's Nest, Crimea (AE)

guided tour is pretty informative and interesting, so making prior arrangements for an English translation (in the city) is a good idea.

The exhibit begins with artefacts from the Stone and Bronze Ages and then shows one of the best collections of Scythian objects, mostly found on the island in a current archaeological dig. A variety of daggers, swords, arrowheads and slingshots show the warlike nature of the Scythians, who believed they were the descendants of Hercules by his son Skyf. Several large burial mounds (*kurhany*) can still be seen on the island, from which the jewellery, weapons and armour have been found. To watch over the dead, Scythian 'stone grandmothers' were placed on the mounds, and several of these are on display in the museum and around the island. There are also objects left on the island from the days of Kievan Rus traders, including a 9th-century iron anchor, as well as archaeological finds from the Mongol and Tatar invasions.

A major portion of the museum is dedicated to the life and history of the Zaporizhian Cossacks. Weapons, clothing and a full-sized Cossack ship are just a few of the items on display, along with famous portraits of Khmelnytsky and Ivan Mazepa, surrounded by some of their own belongings.

After the Cossacks left, Khortytsya fell prey to Catherine the Great's ethnic juggling. The empress designated the land for a large group of Swiss Mennonites, whose lives are also represented in the exhibit. The Swiss were known to be peaceful, but they are also to blame for the lack of trees on the island today. Unable to deal with the Ukrainian winter, they burnt all the wood they could find. (One ancient oak spent 6,000 years underwater before popping up to the surface, now on display near the museum entrance.) The Mennonites stayed for more than a century and some of their buildings can still be seen on the lower half of the island. The museum also features several dramatic diorama's including one that portrays the death of Kievan Prince Svyatoslav who was unexpectedly attacked by the Pechenegs, supposedly on Khortytsya. Another display shows the Soviet liberation of Zaporizhzhya in a World War II battle on October 14 1943 (Hitler is rumoured to have come to Zaporizhzhya on four different occasions during the Nazi occupation).

Getting out to Khortytsya involves some manoeuvring since the northern bridge is closed save for pedestrian traffic, and public transportation no longer goes out to the island. The #30 private marshrutka travels out here from Prospekt Lenina and a taxi from the centre to the museum costs US$3. Keep in mind the island is large and fairly sparse, except for a few scattered villages and farms. The best way to walk there is to cross the Dneproges dam on foot, circle around, cross the northern bridge and walk along the northern coast of the island to the museum (about 5km).

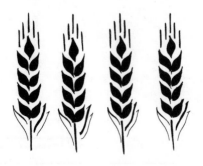

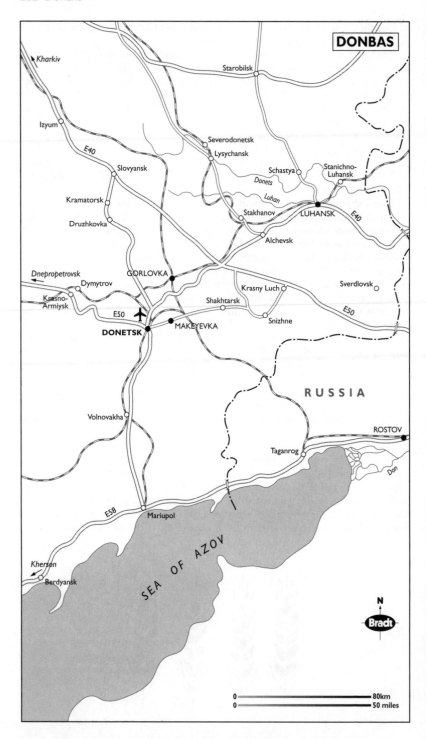

Donbas Донбас

The wholly Russian population and machine-wrought landscape of the Donets River basin contrast sharply with the nostalgic Ukrainian dream of quaint survival on the open steppe. The cluster of mines, factories and cities between Donetsk and Luhansk is home to Ukraine's most obvious proletariat and represents the industrial heart of the country. Only the intrepid few who travel to Ukraine's far east can hope to understand this country's complex spectrum of difference.

Coal (*ugol*) dominates space and time in Donbas. For the past 200 years, millions of lives have been dedicated to extracting load after load of anthracite (for thermal power) and bituminous coal (for coking steel) up from the ground. An inverted earth bares open pits turned to misshapen mountains of black slag, and the strong smell of burning carbon is bound to become a fond souvenir of your visit. Things are not all smokestacks and rust piles though. Sunflowers cover the fields of Donbas in summer, and people still tend to their vegetable patches and goatherds like they do in the rest of the country. Even more comforting to travellers should be the strong confirmation that what you see is what you get. There is no room for tourist show among the stark setting of Ukraine's dirty work, and for every Ukrainian who snubs the east as a polluted coal stove, there is another one that calls it home. Plus, it's touching to visit a place that makes you cough.

History

The Donbas was a largely unsettled area until Russia began its industrial revolution in the 19th century. The nearby metallurgical centres of Kryvy Rih and Zaporizhzhya required tremendous amounts of energy and the carboniferous deposits of the east facilitated a concentration of industry. By the time of Tsar Nikolai II, 99% of the coal used in the empire came from the Donbas. A demand for semi-skilled labour brought a continued influx of ethnic Russians, who formed a strong political block in support of communism and still constitute a major force in Ukraine. Throughout the Soviet Union, the coal miners of Donbas were lauded as national heroes of labour, especially during World War II when they were forced to flood all the mines to prevent any resource benefit to Germany. In 1989, after the turbid years of perestroika, the miners went on strike to demand better living conditions and higher wages, voicing national discontent with the communist government. Political leaders responded positively and without punishment, opening a new era of change, but what followed offered little solace. The first decade of Ukrainian independence has hit the industrial workers hardest as the demand for Soviet production has all but ceased. Strikes in and around Donetsk continued throughout the 1990s as inflation ruined miner's pensions and salaries, and the relaxed state of governance made mines even more dangerous. President Kravchuk settled with the miners by printing so much money that it nearly doubled Ukraine's GDP and exacerbated inflation everywhere else in the country. In 2002, another deadly explosion confirmed once more that Ukraine's mines were grossly outdated and decrepit, but closing the mines is not an option when so many people depend on the meagre but regular monthly income. Donbas looks longingly to the stability of their industry under the former Soviet government and the area is known to take a strong leftist political stance in the *Rada*. Ethnic tensions with the centre and west of the country are also a problem since current policies to make Ukraine more Ukrainian challenge the predominantly Russian population of Donbas. Besides Crimea, Donbas is the only region to have both Russian and Ukrainian listed as official languages, but easterners still feel at odds within their own country and wonder if they are not on the wrong side of the border with Russia.

There's no avoiding Ukraine's most vivid economic and political questions when travelling in Donbas, and while the rest of the country diligently tries to get foreigners to discard all notions of the Soviet-era, around here, hanging on to some of those preconceived ideas will help make sense of what the transition to capitalism really means.

Getting around

Donbas is a concentrated region that was blessed with lots of railways and paved roads for industrial use. Donetsk is the main transportation hub, and getting to Luhansk or Mariupol is a simple case of taking the train or any number of buses. Frequent marshrutka also join all the smaller towns together.

DONETSK – ДОНЕЦЬК

The 'black pearl' of the east is the country's heavy industrial capital and the largest city in Donbas. Before there ever was a city, this area was a large-scale engineering project so that today, coal belts and slag heaps dot the city skyline and most of the round lakes you see are former pit mines filled with water. Coal is such a pervasive element in the life of Donetsk, that their world famous football team is named *Shakhtyor* ('The Miners') and the various monuments feature bulky men with oversized hammers. Because the city's entire economy was linked to large-scale mining, the break up of the Soviet Union was especially devastating. For the past decade, the city's post-industrial reputation has been strongly linked to an unrestrained mafia that has taken the city's welfare into its own hands. Today, amidst the coal dust are the country's newest examples of glass and steel architecture. With such a large base for energy, chemical and metal production, business travellers are the most likely to visit Donetsk; however, the city is also fairly conducive to the curious and wandering.

History

The city of Donetsk was founded in 1869 at the site of an earlier attempt at coal mining. The Welshman John Hughes – an entrepreneur from Merthyr Tydfil – was offered a contract by the Tsar Aleksandr II to start the New Russia Company with the intention to produce smelted iron and eventually steel for railroad construction. Most of the first railway tracks in Russia and Ukraine were hammered out in Donetsk, including those used to build the Trans-Siberian railroad. The town built to house the collection of coal miners and steelworkers was called Yuzovka ('Little Hughes'), after the Welshman and the concentration of so many industrial labourers meant Yuzovka was a Bolshevik stronghold

ALEKSEI GRIGORYEVICH STAKHANOV (1906–77)

When Comrade Stalin let loose a series of five-year plans to industrialise the country in a speedy rush, many Soviet citizens (and party bosses) were secretly sceptical. Still, the party urged people to strive harder and produce more. On August 31 1935, a 29-year-old coal miner by the name of Aleksei Stakhanov extracted 102 tons of coal in just six hours during a work contest held by the local Komsomol (Young Communist League) organisation.

This was ten times that of a miner working in England and 14 times that of fellow Soviet miners. The young man's feat was publicised as a grand achievement of matching self-will with socialism, and soon the excitement of the Stakhanovite movement had taken over the USSR. Every worker was expected to take on superhuman work feats and those who didn't succeed were deemed saboteurs against the regime. The over-achievers were recognised as heroes of labour, a rare individual attention in an otherwise collective society. As for Stakhanov, he was rewarded by Stalin, made a national hero and eventually became the Soviet Union's Minister of Mining Industry. The city of Stakhanov and Stakhanov mine between Donetsk and Luhansk still stand in his honour.

throughout the revolution. Both White and Red armies fought viciously for control over the fuel-rich city during the civil war. After Lenin's death in 1924, 'Yuzovka' was changed to 'Stalino', a name it kept until 1961. The name of a nearby river seemed a safe bet after the legacy of one foreign businessman and a mentally disturbed dictator, so the city has since been called Donetsk. Unemployment and intensive pollution complicate the role of Donetsk within independent Ukraine, but with more than a million inhabitants and the richest mineral deposits of the country, there is hope that eventually the city will be able to function on the world market.

Getting there and away
By air
Donetsk Airport is on the north side of the city on Vzletnaya. Frequent daily flights service Kiev Zhulyany (1½ hours) and there is at least one daily flight to Borispol. Regular flights service Moscow (Domodedovo Airport; 2 hours) and Istanbul (2 hours), and there are connections to Odessa (1 hour) three times a week. If connecting to or from an international flight to Kiev, contact **Ukraine International Airlines**; Airport office; tel: 0622 998 469; fax: 062 335 4464; email: uia@ps.kiev.ua; web: www.ukraine-international.com. For direct domestic and international travel with Donetsk, contact **Donbass Eastern Ukrainian Airlines**, Artyoma 167; tel: 0622 574 422; fax: 0622 588 115; email: ivc@donat.dn.ua; web: www.donbass.aero.

By rail
Donetsk is the leading eastern point of transport for Ukrainian trains, so finding any direct train connection is not difficult. The daily train to and from Kiev, dubbed the 'Little Lump of Coal' leaves Kiev in the evening around 21.00 and gets to Donetsk at 09.00 the next morning, travelling through Dnepropetrovsk (4 hours). There are daily connections with Luhansk (3 hours), Zaporizhzhya (4 hours), Kharkiv (8 hours), Simferopol (11 hours), Odessa (15 hours) and Lviv (28

hours). Frequent Russian trains between Moscow and the south of Russia pass through Donetsk; the first stop across the border is in Rostov-na-Donu (4 hours). Trains coming in and out of Donetsk are required to move very slowly so as not to cause any cave-ins in the mines beneath.

By bus

Buses are quick and convenient around eastern Ukraine, especially for travel between Donetsk and Sloboda or the Dnepr region. The main station is at Ploschad Kommunarov; tel: 0622 664 123. Frequent public buses go to Luhansk (2½ hours) and to Mariupol (2 hours) There are also regular connections to Kharkiv (6 hours) and Dnepropetrovsk (4 hours). For overnight service to the capital, there's **Avtoluks**, Aksakova 21; tel: 0622 667 139; and **Gunsel** (Prospekt Kievsky 10; tel: 062 385 6869) also has a second daytime bus back and forth to Kiev (11 hours) via Poltava (7 hours) and Dnepropetrovsk (4 hours).

Getting around

Thousands of coal mines tunnel beneath the city like an ant farm, which is the reason Donetsk has no metro. Getting around above ground is not terribly difficult since the city was planned by a British businessman and not a team of Soviet planners. Trams and trolleys run on the main boulevards (Artyoma, Universitetskaya, Mira and Kommunarov). For a taxi, call 058 locally, or 0622 530 160.

Where to stay

Even though Donetsk is by no means a tourist town, a number of nice hotels have opened to accommodate foreign businessmen and local high-rollers. Most encouraging is the city's accepted fashion to charge per room rather than per gueSt You might find Donetsk is the place to splurge a little, since you tend to get what you pay for in this town.

Luxury

All accept credit cards.

Donbass Palace Artyoma 80; tel: 062 334 9600; fax: 062 334 9603; email: info@donbasspalace.com. Just opened in 2002, this 5-star hotel on Lenin Square is lavish tribute to the former Stalinist art-deco building that once stood on this corner. The Palace now functions as the unofficial centre for international business conferences and is capable of accommodating large numbers of guests in over a hundred luxury suites. The top 'executive floor' exceeds standards of hospitality found in the rest of the country, including personal butlers and whirlpool baths. The hotel also offers wheelchair-friendly rooms and special services for disabled travellers. Room prices average US$200 a night.

Central Hotel Artyoma 87; tel/fax: 062 332 3332; email: central@ruoil.donbass.com; web: www.central-hotel.com.ua. Modern and flashy, the Central has set a high standard for welcoming business travel to Donetsk. Location is central, attitudes progressive and the staff very efficient. All rooms feature comfortable queen-size beds and shiny en-suite bathrooms. A standard room is US$75, corporate suites are US$110 and lavish junior suites cost US$130.

Legion Ovnatanyana 16A; tel: 062 385 9565; email: hotel@legion.dn.ua; web: www.hotel-legion.dn.ua. More a spa than a hotel, rooms are tactfully simple but elegant. Prices fall into two categories: 'prestige' for US$120 and the larger 'lux' for US$190. All beds are at least queen-size and the bathrooms are warm and spacious. A gourmet restaurant, health club and full-size swimming pool make the Legion a posh daytime hangout for prosperous locals.

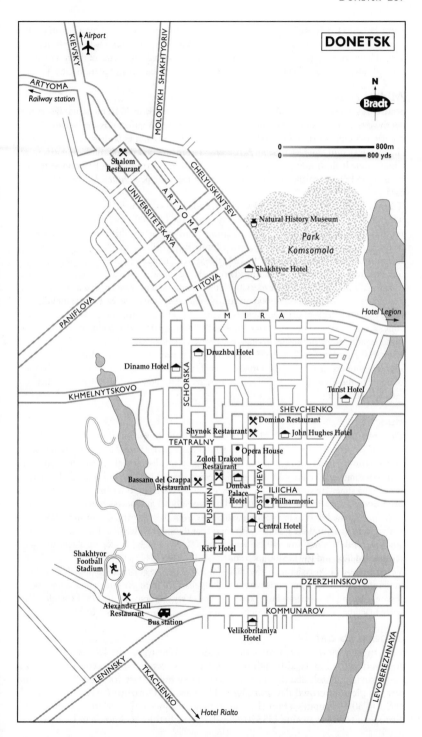

DONETSK

N

Bradt

0 _____ 800m
0 _____ 800 yds

KIEVSKY
↑ Airport

ARTYOMA
← Railway station

MOLODYKH SHAKHTYORIV

CHELYUSKINTSEV

ARTYOMA

UNIVERSITETSKAYA

PANIFLOVA

✕ Shalom Restaurant

Natural History Museum

Park Komsomola

TITOVA

Shakhtyor Hotel

M I R A

Hotel Legion

KHMELNYTSKOVO

SCHORSKA

Dinamo Hotel

Druzhba Hotel

Turist Hotel

SHEVCHENKO

✕ Domino Restaurant

Shynok Restaurant ✕

✕ John Hughes Hotel

TEATRALNY

Opera House

Zoloti Drakon Restaurant

Bassano del Grappa Restaurant ✕

✕

PUSHKINA

Donbas Palace Hotel

POSTYSHEVA

ILIICHA

● Philharmonic

Central Hotel

Kiev Hotel

Shakhtyor Football Stadium

✕ Alexander Hall Restaurant

Bus station

DZERZHINSKOVO

KOMMUNAROV

Velikobritaniya Hotel

LENINSKY

TKACHENKO

↓ Hotel Rialto

LEVOBEREZHNAYA

John Hughes Chelyuskintsev 157; tel/fax: 062 381 0848; web: www.johnhughes.dn.ua. In theory, the hotel is built to look like 19th-century Yuzovka, but ironically looks plush and new. There are a limited number of rooms, but they are well designed and the restaurant serves hearty Germanic food to match the Bavarian décor. Expect to pay from US$70–100.

Middle range

Rialto Tkachenko 145; tel: 062 332 9341. Refurnished nicely in 2001, the Rialto lies in the southwestern corner of the city and is best reached by cab. A quirky classing system of regular and superior standards that are equal in comfort but not in floorspace; generally, singles are US$70, doubles US$90. All bathrooms are new and the plumbing is good; most rooms come with showers, some with bath. An in-house tour agent can take care of ticket booking and the sauna and gym are above average for this type of hotel. Accepts credit cards.

Turist Shevchenko 20; tel: 0622 939 116. The hotel is a 4-star by Ukrainian standards, which means room prices range from US$40 up to the US$100 suite, but a good double room can be had for US$60–70. The advantage of staying here is that it comes with some of the benefits and assistance of the former Inturist.

Dinamo Otechestvennaya 10; tel: 062 342 0385; web: home.skif.net/~ticons. Ikea seems to be the major inspiration for this newly remodelled outfit, also located in the town centre. Quality of stay will meet most expectations for cleanliness and comfort, and a pleasant enough restaurant serves good food on sturdy tables. Dinamo is the best of the middle-range hotels in terms of price and guests' welfare. Standard rooms cost US$45, the junior suites are US$60 and two-room suites cost US$100 (the extra room seems a bit unnecessary). Some unfinished rooms may be available for less.

Kiev Pushkina 4; tel: 0622 920 525. A 3-star by Ukrainian standards, the Kiev is only slightly more expensive than the Druzhba (singles US$35). As there are a limited amount of doubles, the Kiev's a better choice if you are travelling alone. A run-down café is the only special feature.

Budget

Druzhba Universitetskaya 48; tel: 062 337 3331; email: drujba@mail.donbass.com; web: www.internet.dn.ua/hotel_drujba. The hotel follows a Soviet floorplan, so rooms may seem rather narrow, but new carpeting and furniture make it a decent night's stay. Plus, how can you go wrong with a name like 'Friendship'? Singles cost US$25 doubles are US$40 and the US$65 suites are good value for money if you are travelling as a pair.

Shakhtyor Titova 15; tel: 0622 556 614. The largest hotel in Donetsk in terms of number of rooms, situated next to the stadium and across from the city park. Room standards remain very basic, and the doubles with shower and toilet cost US$25. Take away amenities and the price drops all the way down to US$7 a night, or step up a level to remodelled 'lux' and pay US$40 for a suite.

Velikobritaniya Postysheva 20; tel: 0622 920 504. The 'Great Britain' is probably the best option for backpackers since it is within walking distance from the bus station, a few good restaurants, and the mine/stadium complex. The cheapest room are the US$12 singles with shared facilities down the hall; a double with en-suite bathrooms costs US$28.

Where to eat

Like most eastern Ukrainian cities, getting a bite to eat in Donetsk is usually reserved to the hotels, although there are a few exceptions. **Bassano del Grappa** (Grinkevicha 8; tel: 062 381 0858) serves classy Italian fare for US$25 a meal and attracts pleasant crowd day and night. The swanky **Domino** (Artyoma 129A; tel: 062 334 3019) imitates a French chateau in appearance only, serving refined, quasi-European food for around US$30 a head. Probably the best known in Donetsk, the

Alexander Hall (Stadionna 32A; tel: 062 332 2467) is next to the stadium and offers deliberately Russian cuisine in a brilliant post-Soviet setting. **Shynok** (Artyoma 127; tel: 0622 920 282) should also be recommended as Donetsk's answer to the Ukrainian folk restaurant-craze, complete with the décor and a satisfying menu of borscht, varenniki, and a few more adventurous dishes. For yummy Russianised Chinese food, try **Zolotoi Drakon** (Universitetskaya 27A) and for Jewish cuisine, much of which is vegetarian, go to **Shalom** (Artyoma 132; tel: 577 331).

Also, don't be afraid to make a round of the hotel restaurants. **Central** (Artyoma 87; tel: 062 332 3332) is one of the best in the city, with elegant meals for under $15 and a deserved reputation for good wine. The **Donbass Palace** (Artyoma 80; tel: 062 334 9600) features three restaurants: a main floor of international haute-cuisine, an Asian fusion hall (Indian, Japanese and Thai) and a small French-style brasserie. If you're steering clear of restaurant fare, the **central market** is on the corner of Shevchenko and Chelyuskintsev, where everything and anything is sold hot, cold, live or packaged.

What to see and do
People in Donetsk dig coal or do business. If you are not occupied with either, you might still enjoy walking around some of the city's old mining complexes. One of the largest is by the **Shakhtyor** football stadium and restaurant Alexander Hall. The tall hill of mineral refuse is called a *terrakon:* there are dozens like it throughout the city. The **Natural History Museum** (Chelyuskintsev 189A; tel: 0622 553 474; open 10.00–17.00, entrance 3UAH) tells the history of mining and a bit about the regional culture but is mostly a communistic tribute to the glory of labour. The **Opera House** (Artyoma 82; tel: 0622 338 0969) brought culture to the mining masses, as did the **Philharmonic Concert Hall** (Postisheva 117; tel: 0622 338 0018). If you want to really get under the skin of Donetsk, a few local tour agencies arrange interesting mile-deep tours into the coal mines. Try **SAM**, Universitetskaya 36; tel/fax: 062 381 1616; email: samtour@cam.donetsk.ua.

Outside Donestk
Visitors to the Donbas often find they're required to travel to the outskirts for one reason of another. Today these numerous mining towns tend to have large populations but very little activity. Mention **Gorlovka** (Горловка) and you'll often get a facial response of disgust or bewilderment. Famous for its black snow in winter and incredibly high rates of lung cancer for the rest of the year, Ukraine's most austere industrial outpost consists of one single thoroughfare. A new chemical plant has set a precedence for how a little help can do much to revitalise. If you're spending the night, try **Hotel Rodina** (Dmitrova 46; tel: 0624 228 282). Rooms cost US$30 for a single, US$40 for a double, and US$80 for suites. **Makeyevka** (Макеевка) is the largest of the Donetsk suburbs and like the rest of them, began as a smelting plant. Over a hundred marshrutkas shoot back and forth to Makeyevka daily, but a taxi should cost around US$10. For longer stays, there's the **Hotel Victoria** (Terrikonnaya 3; tel: 062 382 9100; fax: 062 382 8926; email: hotelvicktory@skif.net). Singles are $55, doubles $65 and suites $90. Directly south of Donetsk is the main port on the Sea of Azov, **Mariupol** (Маріуполь), named so by the large influx of Greek immigrants who arrived in the 18th century and remain the prominent face of the city today. In the summer, the beaches are packed with sunbathers from all over Donbas, and a limited tradition of seaside nightlife continues year-round despite the unpleasant industrial plant that makes the air taste bad. For a night's accommodation, try **Chaika** (Primorsky 7; tel: 0629

372 186) or **Spartak** (Kharlamyevskaya 13; tel: 0629 334 214). Both have rooms for around US$30, as well as nicer suites for US$70. Mariupol is the rail terminus for a few trains from Kiev, western Ukraine and Russia, always via Donetsk. Buses or marshrutka to Donetsk take under two hours.

LUHANSK – ЛУГАНСЬК

Ukraine's easternmost city marks the final extent of one country and the beginning of the flat Russian steppe across which blows a constant wind. When the air is still, the scent of industry wafts through this 'Wild East' where hardened miners and disenchanted factory workers still linger in a forgotten Russian outpost. But even with the present industrial paralysis, over half a million people call Luhansk home.

The city was founded by order of Catherine the Great who decided to assist her military campaign to expand the Russian empire by building an iron foundry to make cannons and cannonballs. The Empress chose Luhansk for its unending supply of coal, proximity to iron ore and the River Luhan for which it was first named. Since the tsarina's time, the city has officially changed its name four times and finally went from being Voroshilovgrad back to Luhansk in 1990. Few Ukrainian cities preserve the Soviet aesthetic like Luhansk, and visitors will find that the giant row of rusty smokestacks from the Alchevsk metal factory are just as impressive as the Stalin-era monuments to labour and victory. Also, take a good look at **St Nikolas Cathedral** (Mezhdunarodnaya 111), one of the few churches constructed during Stalin's lifetime, in 1950.

Getting there and away
Luhansk is the farthest eastern point in the country and thus the longest train ride to anywhere else, unless you're going to Russia. Most routes must pass through Kharkiv or Donetsk first. There are three daily trains to and from Kiev (18 hours) that usually leave in the early evening and get there the next afternoon, usually via Kharkiv (8 hours) or Poltava (10 hours). A few Russian trains pass through this way, but always tend to go through Donetsk as well, which is a much more accessible rain junction.

The bus station is at Oboronnaya 28. Convenient connections service Donetsk (2½ hours) and local Donbas towns. The private **Avtoluks** bus takes 16 hours to get to Kiev via Izyum and Kharkiv (take the train, pay less and sleep better). Their office is in the main bus station; tel: 0642 542 454.

Where to stay and eat
The highest building in town, the **Hotel Luhansk** (Sovetskaya 76; tel: 0642 510 270) is a Soviet-built 18-storey high-rise remodelled in 1999. Overall, rooms are comfortable and clean, and this is always the most obvious first choice; singles cost US$40, twins (rarely double) are US$50 double, and the two-room suites cost US$80. A tad more modern and a bit more expensive is the **Hotel Druzhba** (Soroki 16A; tel: 0642 535 353). All rooms are heated/air-conditioned and hot water is a sure thing. Singles cost US$50; doubles US$70.

Both hotels have restaurants, and a rather recent venue is **Versailles** (Titova 13; tel: 0642 531 502). French in name and menu, a full meal costs around US$15. Off the main square is the **Café Boulevard** (Kotelnikov 13; tel: 0642 343 320) serving drinks and light meals day and night.

Sloboda Слобода

The city of Kharkiv and surrounding territory is the easiest region to travel to (besides Kiev) and opens up a very different corner of Ukraine. On wheels or on foot, the bounding steppe of eastern Ukraine promises hypnotic landscape viewing, for in Sloboda, the rolling plains really do 'undulate'. In winter, the snow blows into waves and in summer, endless sunflower fields rise and fall with the wind. Alas, the beauty of the east is too often overlooked by tour organisers as an uninteresting expanse of open land that separates a few semi-interesting cities from the rest of the country. This false perception stems from divisive attitudes that figure left-bank Ukraine was too heavily shaped by Soviet industry and collective agriculture to be of any fascination to the outsider.

The term *sloboda* derives from the Russian word for 'freedom', and was often applied to collections of free people in the old Russian Empire, such as monasteries. The Ukrainian name for this region, *Slobozhanschina,* means quite literally, 'Land of the Free' and refers to the fields of Sumy, Kharkiv and Izyum that were simply given to early settlers without charge if they would cultivate the land. Freed Ukrainian serfs and Cossacks were attracted by the offer, as were a large group of Serbians who had fled religious persecution in their own country. Nevertheless, the land deal came with a catch: the Russian government hoped the new settlers would provide a buffer against the constant raids of the Tatars. When Catherine the Great disbanded the Cossack leadership in 1765, this area fell under Russian military protection and governorship, beginning a long legacy of Russian cultural influence. Today, Sloboda falls on the esoteric Russian border – a border that could swing 100 miles in either direction and not make much difference. People here speak both Russian and a highly literary form of Ukrainian and it is no coincidence that so many of Ukraine's greatest writers, thinkers, singers and artists were born here and inspired by the simple and beautiful surroundings.

Getting around
Sloboda features the very best train in the country, the speedy Capital Express that connects Kiev to Kharkiv, but is also convenient for getting between Kharkiv, Poltava and Mirgorod. The train to Sumy is slow, so it is best to take the bus when travelling to and from within the region. Most of Slobozhanschina's more interesting areas are out in the country, and so unless you are in the know about the *elektrichki* trains, it is best to find the right bus or taxi, or else go with an organised tour.

KHARKIV – ХАРКІВ
Ukraine's second largest city dominates the east and easily takes the prize for most aesthetically pleasing industrial metropolis in the country (a title which means little

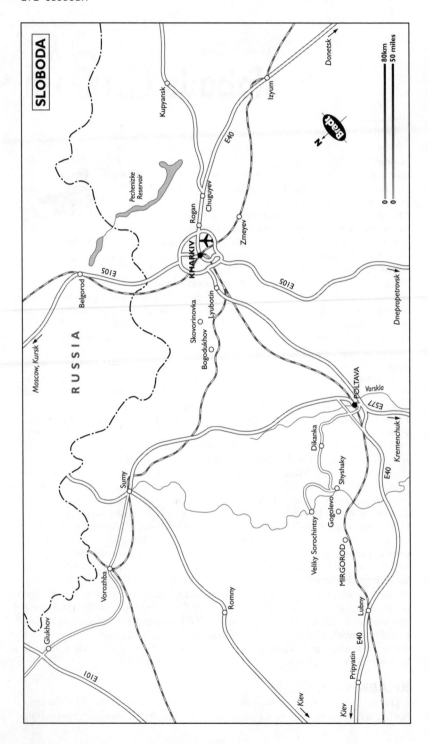

unless you've been to Donetsk or Zaporizhzhya). With over two million people, Kharkiv's beauty lies in its sheer size: the constant motion of humans and its breadth of urban space. Admittedly, few come this way to sightsee, but as a major transportation hub and principally functional city, it is not surprising how many foreign visitors do come and stay here. Less than 20 miles from the Russian border, Kharkiv is also the easiest entry/exit point into that country. About 70% of the city is ethnic Russian and Russian is spoken first and foremost (which is why people say *Kharkov*).

Visiting Kharkiv offers the best introduction to Ukraine's Soviet legacy and the distinct geography that comes with it: the countless war memorials, the hundreds of factories, Stalinist housing, the huge central square and the dominant public sector. The collective achievements of science, industry and art still count for a lot in this city's identity. Locals may not know the Ukrainian national anthem, but they can tell you that the Soviet's nuclear programme began with a fission experiment in Kharkiv. While most of Ukraine has stripped away its emblems of the past, Kharkiv has simply reincorporated them into the present excitement. The city has led the country in its industrial recovery and has the largest student population in Ukraine.

History

Kharkiv is a young city for Ukraine, only founded in 1653 and named after a Cossack leader called Kharkach; or else the city was simply named after the River Kharkiv that flows through it. Either way, the free settlement prospered in the 17th century as a military outpost jointly defended from the Tatars by Ukrainian Cossacks and Russian army regiments. The attraction of free land and strong defence created a steady growth in population and building. Most newcomers came south from Russia and by the mid 18th century, Kharkiv had established itself as an industrial centre, with over a dozen brick factories (as in Chekhov's *Three Sisters*). In 1796 Kharkiv was officially declared the capital of the Russian Empire's Sloboda province, securing the city's primarily Russian existence.

Kharkiv University was founded in 1805 and allowed the region a stable intellectual development unseen in other areas of Ukraine. Fearing that Ukrainian language and culture were about to be swallowed up by the Russian majority, a few academics began to publish literary prose in the Ukrainian language. Known as the 'Kharkiv Romantics', this small group of writers applied the idyllic muse of Russian romanticism to Ukrainian folklore, which later inspired the more politically minded Ukrainian intellectuals of the nationalist movement.

Still, the city was industrialised and governed as a Russian city, receiving a direct railroad link to Moscow in 1869, a whole year before Kiev even had a train station. Competition with Kiev continues to this day, and along with many other firsts, Kharkiv claims the title of Ukraine's first capital. Proximity to urban Russia and a strong industrial base meant Kharkiv lent strong support to the Bolsheviks during the revolution. After Ukraine was thrown into chaos during the civil war, Lenin proclaimed Kharkiv was the rightful capital of the Soviet Republic and thus it stayed during the early years of the USSR. Lenin's 'war communism' witnessed the wrath of the Red Army in pushing forth its ideology in the city, which is why Kharkiv has very few landmark churches today. Sloboda was also one of the first regions in Ukraine to be forcefully collectivised by Stalin, and the tragic famine of 1932–33 hit Kharkiv the hardest. Thousands of starving peasants poured into the city from the countryside, and then thousands more died on the streets. The complete devastation forced the capital back to Kiev in 1934.

World War II brought another wave of destruction, and Kharkiv was battered from both sides. People know of the battle of Kursk and Stalingrad, but drawn-out Kharkiv offensives preceded each. In 1942–43, Kharkiv was captured and lost twice by the Nazis. Hitler's scorched-earth policy left the city in ruins, which is why Sumskaya and Pushkinskaya are two of the only streets with pre-war buildings.

During the latter Soviet period, Kharkiv became an industrial giant for the communist world; in 1967, the one-millionth tractor rolled out of the Kharkiv Tractor Factory, and a tank and aeroplane factory employed tens of thousands. Following independence, the machines all ground to a halt, and a city of two million was suddenly unemployed. Slowly, the many factories have been revamped to make new products and the slicked-back Russian businessman look has been adopted by local techies. (Bill Gates chose Kharkiv as his base from which to launch the Ukrainian version of Windows.) The city still leads the country in education, technology and the military, and most of eastern (Russian-speaking) Ukraine comes to university here or to find jobs. The city's latest historical phenomenon is a sporadic influx of foreigners.

Getting there and away
By air
Kharkov's aviation industry has a long and glorious history, so flying is an easy and often inexpensive option, whether domestic or international. The airport is to the far south of the city off Prospekt Gagarina, tel: (0572) 516 907. A taxi into the city should cost US$3, or take the metro to Gagarina Station and then the airport trolley, or the #119 bus that leaves from the central square by Lenin's statue. **Kiy Avia** (Chervonoshkilna 18; tel: 0572 218 441; email: info@kiyavia.com) flies to the most destinations from Kiev, but connections to Kharkiv are sporadic. **Aerosvit** (tel: 0572 195 370; email: aerosvit@vlink.kharkov.ua; web: www.aerosvit.com) is the nationally respected domestic airline which connects with Donetsk, Lviv, Kiev and Dnepropetrovsk. **Aeromist** (tel: 057 715 3188; email: aeromist@interami.com) is Kharkiv's own airline, which flies twice daily to Kiev and three times a week to Moscow. Fares change, but normally a one-way ticket to Moscow is US$100 and one-way within Ukraine is US$60. For the time being **Austrian Airlines** (office near the airport; Romashkina 1; tel: 0572 148 953) is the only European carrier to fly direct to Kharkiv from Vienna, four times a week. Regular charter routes serviced by Ukrainian companies include Syria, Armenia, Egypt and Turkey. In the city, most hotels have the facilities to book air tickets. The airport hotel (Aeroflotska 16; tel: 0572 516 229) is slightly unnecessary since the city is near and few will make overnight connections, but it is there.

By rail
Besides Kiev, Kharkiv has the most train connections to everywhere else, so rail is usually the best option for travel. The new *Stolychny Ekspress* (Capital Express) has cut the travel time in half between Kiev and Kharkiv. The luxury train does the trip in five hours and goes back and forth twice every day. From Kharkiv, the train normally leaves at 07.00 and 16.30, and from Kiev at 06.30 and 17.30. The train only makes two stops – at Poltava (2 hours) and Mirgorod (3 hours) – and this is the fastest way to get to or from Kharkiv. First-class return tickets cost US$20, second class tickets are about US$15. There are also several overnight trains to and from Kiev, the best is #63/64 that takes about nine hours and leaves around 21.00 or 22.00. Other local trains link Kharkiv with Poltava (3 hours), Sumy (4 hours), Dnepropetrovsk (5 hours), Kremenchuk (6 hours) and Donetsk (7 hours). Longer overnight routes service Luhansk (13 hours), Odessa (15 hours), Kherson (16 hours) and Lviv (20 hours).

Kharkiv is also the major hub for Russian trains, and most connections from Moscow to Crimea, Donbas, and southern Russia will pass here. It is not hard to catch a train to Moscow (14 hours), and there are daily trains to Sverdlovsk and Ufa. Kharkiv's own Trans-Siberian (#53) tends to leave for Vladivostok on even days of the month.

International trains include a frequent Kharkiv–Warsaw connection, rare but direct transits to Berlin and Budapest (normally via Kiev), and a daily train to Minsk (20 hours) in Belarus. Take note that Kharkiv is the border point for all trains going to or coming from Russia, which explains all the uniformed soldiers roaming around and boarding trains. Don't linger too long on your train if you are meant to be getting off here or you will fall under suspicion.

Kharkiv's train station is one of the city's most opulent buildings, located on the main square off Krasnoarmeiskaya and built by the Germans in World War II to use in their eastern push into Russia. Since time began, all foreigners in Kharkiv could only purchase train tickets in the separate *kasa* #1 across the square on Slovyanska. Foreigners are now encouraged to use the special service centre inside the train station, which deals primarily with the first class train to Kiev but still acts as the 'separate' foreigners-only ticket counter. Most Kharkiv hotels will also be able to issue tickets, but they sometimes tack on a hefty fee for the service (up to US$20 extra).

By bus

If travelling to Sumy, Donetsk, Dnepropetrovsk or Poltava, you might consider taking the bus as a quicker option, although the new fast train to Poltava gets there in the same short time with much more comfort. There are currently seven bus stations in Kharkiv; the central and largest station is at Gagarina 22, just south of metro station Prospekt Gagarina. The two private bus companies have their offices here, and both make stops at Borispol Airport, making it a convenient way to travel to or from Kharkiv if you fly into Kiev. The trip to Kiev takes about six hours. Other companies include **Gunsel** (Gagarina 7; tel: 0572 199 719) and **Avtoluks** (Gagarina 22; tel: 0572 215 471).

Buses to smaller villages like Izyum or Bohodukhiv will usually leave from one of the outer stations, but the central station will also have connections or at least know the most up-to-date schedule.

Getting around

Kharkiv's metro is convenient and well-used with some truly beautiful stations (for example, Pushkinskaya has quotes of the poet Pushkin inscribed on the subway walls). There are three metro lines: the red connects Kholodnaya Gora to all the factories in the southeast and the green line goes from the city centre out to residential Saltovka. The blue line has been under construction since the 1980s and finally opened in 1996. One journey costs 50 kopecks.

Otherwise, the city has a developed system of trams and trolleys that branch out from each metro station to make every quarter accessible. If you want a taxi, the same rules apply like everywhere else. Flagging one down will cost about US$2 to US$3 to go anywhere in the city. Private taxis can be ordered from your hotel.

Where to stay

Kharkiv has yet to experience any tourist boom, but while there has been no increase in the number of hotels, what is around has improved a great deal. There is no way to classify Kharkiv's hotels into separate categories as each tends to cover all three ranges.

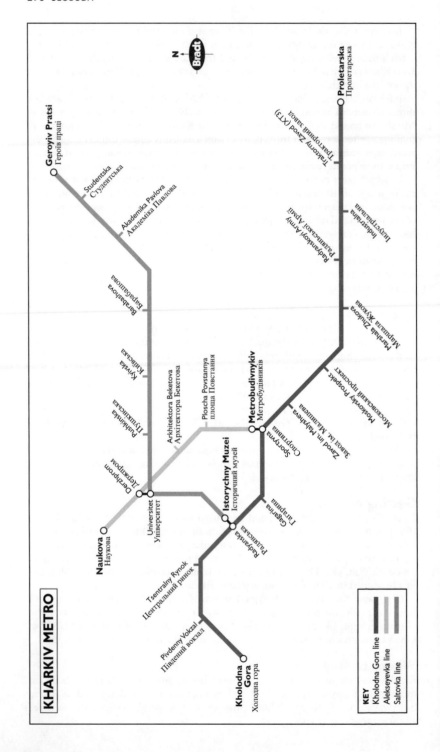

Hotel Kharkiv Ploschad Svobody 7 (metro station Universitet); tel: 0572 456 325; fax: 0572 476 176; email: hotel@kharkov.com; web: www.hotel.kharkov.com. There is no better location than right on the Square of Freedom looking at Lenin. True to Soviet style without even knowing it, the Hotel Kharkiv has done up a separate wing for foreign visitors with recently remodelled and clean 'European' rooms. The separate entrance is around the corner from the main hotel, the receptionist speaks English and rooms can be paid for in credit cards. This is considered the poshest choice in Kharkiv for the time being, although that says more about Kharkiv than the hotel. To its credit, the rooms are large, the service is good and the furniture is Ikea. A single room with a shower is US$40; a double room with a real double bed and bath is US$80. Two-room suites cost US$70 single/ US$120 double and the lavish private apartments are US$200/night. Breakfast is served in the 8th-floor café for an extra 15UAH and the business centre in the lobby has a fast internet connection and small conference room.

If you are looking for budget accommodation, you can get a room in the larger main part of the hotel for much less and enjoy an impressive view out over the square and park. This is a massive shell of a building – a bit dingy, and many rooms are rented for start-up businesses or private parties. A double with toilet and shower is US$30, and if you use the bathroom down the hall it costs US$12. Bare singles are just US$5.

Hotel National Lenina 21 (metro station Naukova); tel: 0572 308 760; fax: 0572 321 023; email: national@national.kharkiv.com; web: www.national.kharkiv.com. Kharkiv's former Inturist hotel kept the city's hospitality industry alive through the lean years and now offers a reliable base for travellers who come to experience the city's regeneration. Various grades of rooms are attached to various prices. A fair single room with facilities costs US$30, a double is US$40. The largest suites (with big beds and two rooms) cost US$80–100 a night; they do accept credit cards. Rooms tend to be cosy and have big bathtubs with 24-hour hot water. When going to your room, take note of the fantastic Soviet-era stained-glass stairwell with depictions of great Socialist landmarks in Eurasia. The National also boasts a tourist agency and translation service that can do city tours and arrange transportation (air, train and bus). The hotel restaurant is typical of most Russian/Ukrainian enterprises and serves the staples; breakfast costs an additional US$4.

Hotel Mir Lenina 27A; tel: 0572 322 330; fax: 0572 322 217. This giant high-rise does not boast the best location, but does offer the best deals in terms of quality versus price, as well as some decent budget rooms. The first two floors make up a commercial centre with a car showroom, the Gold Lion Casino, and beauty salon, but the other 11 floors offer plenty of 'regular' or 'European' rooms. Regular rooms are of the Soviet fashion and cost US$14–20. European rooms are nicely remodelled and cost twice as much. The double with breakfast for US$40 is the best deal, but they also have some 'lux' rooms with genuine king-size beds for US$80 (yes, there is 24-hour hot water and credit cards are accepted). This tends to be the preferred hotel for foreign visitors and group tours. Hotel Mir also features one of the more professional tourist agencies in the city, and they are particularly effective in booking last-minute plane and train tickets throughout Ukraine; main floor; tel 0572 305 574. To get to Mir, take the metro to Naukova and then take any bus, trolley or cab north until you see it.

Hotel Druzhba Gagarina 185; tel: 0572 522 091; fax: 0572 521 064. Just north of the airport in the southern part of the city, Druzhba is Kharkiv's 'motel' aimed at travellers with cars. Rooms are pretty much average, with prices from US$30 for a regular single to US$80 for a suite.

Where to eat

Kharkiv's choice of restaurants is bound to improve over the next few years. Currently, a few dependable establishments have made their name and managed to stay open.

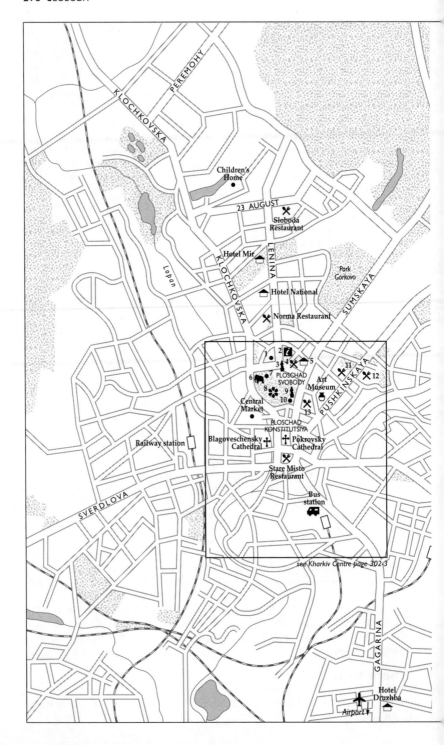

see Kharkiv Centre page 302-3

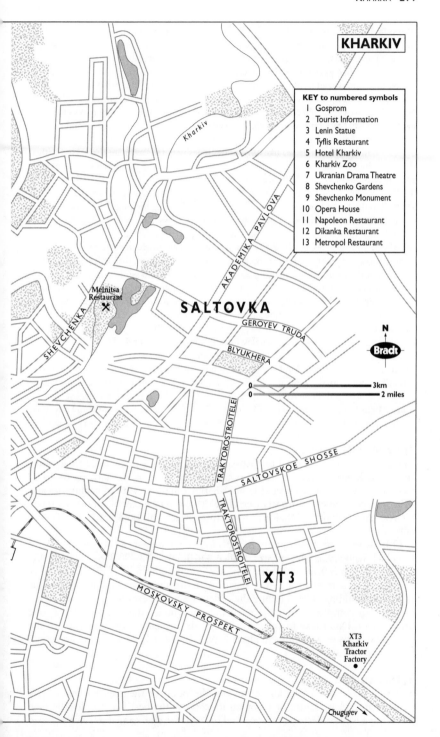

Sloboda 23ᵒᵛᵒ Avgusta 34A; tel: 057 715 50 56. Ukrainian 'restoration' restaurants are all the rage these days, but Sloboda has matched the cliché to fit the country's distinct eastern flavour. This is considered Kharkiv's best restaurant, but the atmosphere is pretty laidback and fun with a live folk band in the evenings. Smoked suckling pig is the house speciality, but be adventurous and try the very authentic *kvas* and *uzvar* (a traditional drink made with dried, smoked fruit). Expect to pay around US$15 for your meal; cash only.

Norma Lenina 11; tel: 0572 175 693. This classy café is made entirely of windows that look out on Kharkiv's busiest sidewalk, yet inside the atmosphere remains cosy and sophisticated. The food is 'high-European' and the overall menu (in English) is quite original. Basic Ukrainian dishes like borscht or crêpes with red caviar are also served with a flare, and this must be the first restaurant in Ukraine to have a smoking and non-smoking section. Main dishes cost US$10 and they do take credit cards.

Tyflis Trinklera 2; tel: 0572 456 296. Kharkiv's most authentic Georgian restaurant is attached to the Hotel Kharkiv and offers a rare peaceful setting for a meal. The food is fantastic, featuring traditional soups, pastries, and spicy stews. Trying the *khachapuri* is a muSt A large meal for two costs around US$20; credit cards accepted.

Metropol Sumskaya 50; tel: 0572 194 040. Swanky and expensive, the Metropol is Kharkiv's latest attempt at gourmet food and service. This is where the city's high-fliers like to dine, but the menu is overrated and a meal costs about US$40 per head.

Napoleon Petrovskovo 37/39; tel: (0572) 477 570. Not quite French, not quite Russian, this centrally located restaurant offers professional service and 'European' cuisine. It is correctly considered one of Kharkiv's nicer places to dine out.

Melnitsa Geroyev Truda, Zhuravlivka park; tel: 0572 686 671. The 'mill' is based on an island in the middle of the River Kharkiv towards the outskirts of the old city. They do delicious Ukrainian and Georgian food. It is an especially nice to eat outdoors in the summer, but can be reached only by car. Most taxi drivers know where it is.

Dikanka Lermontovska 7; tel: 0572 587 558. A small, homey café just off Pushkinskaya. The food is tasty and filling, very inexpensive and served with lots of motherly love.

Stare Misto Kvitky Osnovyankenko 12; tel: 0572 128 095. In the heart of the old city, this small restaurant has a pub-like atmosphere with hearty food and Ukrainian beer on tap.

Tourist assistance

The going rate for a personal English-speaking guide in Kharkiv is US$5 an hour, and most hotels will offer a two-hour walking tour of the city centre. The reception at the newer section of Hotel Kharkiv can direct your tour inquiries and **Mir Service Travel Company** (see Hotel Mir) can take care of almost any travel interest. Along with the National, these three hotels can book travel and theatre tickets.

Otherwise, your best option is the city's own tourist agency at Gosprom; Ploschad Svobody 5, 6th Podyezd, Office #520; tel: 0572 408 238; fax: 0572 452 115; email: gdip2001@rambler.ru. The staff are friendly and helpful, and besides a wealth of local information, they specialise in organising very unique excursions to the surrounding areas. Finding the office is a Soviet experience: go to the big Derzhprom complex. Open the left-hand door under the right-hand concrete bridge (#6). Don't take the elevator; just push through doors until you see the sign. The website www.inform.kharkov.ua can also tell you what is going on, where and when.

What to see

Trying to sightsee in Kharkiv is missing the point of the city. Rather, simply walking around its centre or enjoying its parks is the best way to 'do' the city. **Sumskaya** is the oldest and most central street in the city, named so since the road

SALTOVKA

First-time visitors to Ukraine often criticise the soul-less rows of concrete apartment blocks that make up so many modern Ukrainian cities. But few actually venture into these spaces. Housing in the USSR was all about giving everyone (almost) equal space, and after the utter destruction of World War II, there was some urgency in the task. An easy and quick design was standardised, and today hundreds of millions of people share identical floor plans.

As Kharkiv grew into the major manufacturing centre for the Soviet Union, the fields to the northeast were set aside to house the influx of workers and their families. In the 1970s a new metro line was extended and a grid of boulevards laid out in 15 oversized city blocks to be filled with row upon row of large-scale housing. The classic Soviet *dōm* is constructed of pre-fabricated concrete slabs and comes in small (five floors), medium (nine floors) or large (16 floors). Nearly one thousand of these white buildings make up Saltovka, often called 'Kharkiv's bedroom'. The neighbourhood's design reinforced positive socialist ideals, with majestic street names like Geroyiv Truda ('The Heroes of Labour') and Traktorostroitelei ('The Street of Tractor Builders'), which marked the daily tram commute from Saltovka to the tractor factory.

Today, Saltovka is home to over 600,000 inhabitants, and if you ask any Russian-speaker in the world, they are bound to have a relative living here. Following the throws of marketisation, privatisation and inflation, an individual's apartment became their greatest (and usually only) stable asset. Today in Saltovka there is a great deal of buying, selling and renting going on but for the most part, people have stayed put and decided this is not a bad place to live. Things are quiet, public transportation is good, and there are lots of markets and parks.

Travelling out to Saltovka is beyond the tour guide's tether, but this quintessentially Soviet suburb definitely counts as the real Ukraine. In the evening, looking closely into the hundreds of glowing kitchen windows sitting one atop the other makes it all seem a lot less soul-less. To get there, take the subway to metro stations Studentska or Geroyiv Pratsi and ride the trams or trolleys into the heart of the district. Things to see include the bustling markets near Geroyev Truda and on Traktorostroitelei, the bread factory on Saltovksoe Shosse (the tallest smokestack), and Kharkiv's tallest building, a dizzying 23-storey concrete *dōm* on Prospekt 50 let BLKCM.

leads to Sumy. Despite the destruction of the war, a few examples of Kharkiv's 19th-century architecture remain and today the street is where most of the action is: booksellers, theatres, cafés and clubs.

About midway up the street from the metro station Radyanska is Kharkiv's impressive **Opera House**, a modern and artistic concrete building with excellent shows practically every night. In the park across the street stands the arched **'mirrored fountain'** built as a memorial to World War II. The nearby building on the corner of Sumskaya and Teatralnaya is the former KGB headquarters for Kharkiv and looks like it too.

Further up the street is the main green space for the city, the Shevchenko Gardens, centred around Kharkiv's **Monument to Taras Shevchenko**. Although

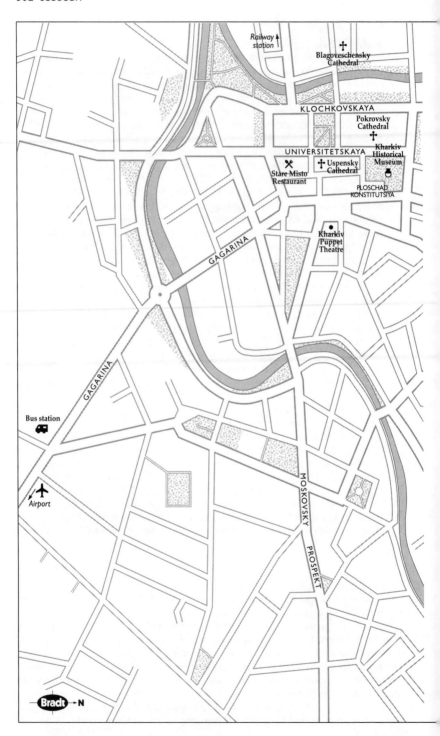

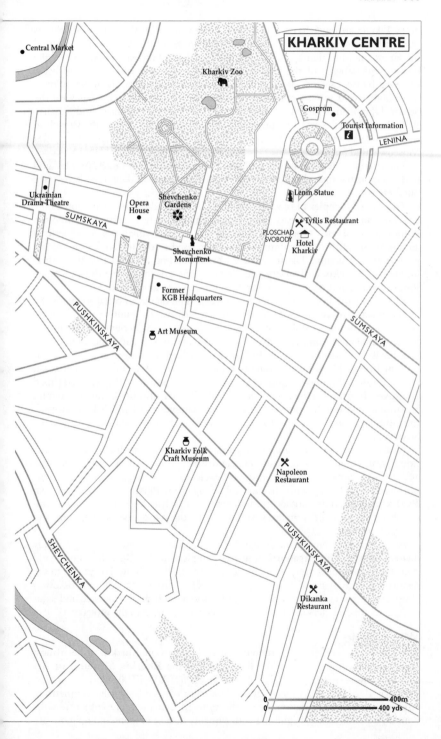

KHARKIV CENTRE

Central Market

Kharkiv Zoo

Gosprom

Tourist Information

LENINA

Ukrainian
Drama Theatre

Opera
House

Shevchenko
Gardens

Lenin Statue

SUMSKAYA

Tyflis Restaurant

PLOSCHAD
SVOBODY

Hotel
Kharkiv

Shevchenko
Monument

Former
KGB Headquarters

SUMSKAYA

PUSHKINSKAYA

Art Museum

Kharkiv Folk
Craft Museum

Napoleon
Restaurant

PUSHKINSKAYA

SHEVCHENKA

Dikanka
Restaurant

0   400m
0   400 yds

every Ukrainian town has a statue dedicated to the poet, the one in Kharkiv is remarkably moving with its 16 human-sized bronze sculptures that spiral around his larger-than-life figure. The memorial is a three-dimensional portrait of the history and struggle of the Ukrainian people, beginning with a peasant baby, followed by the captivity of the Cossack's, and moving on to Ukrainian soldiers from both world wars. Crafted in 1935, the socialist realist style ends with the Soviet Ukrainian triumph of the female academician and male industrialist. Walking through the park (or continuing on Sumskaya) takes you to the **Ploschad Svobody** (Square of Freedom), the largest in the former Soviet Union after Moscow's Red Square.

The open cobblestone space is still the favoured milieu for rallies, parades, and mass demonstrations, directed by the imposing statue of Lenin with his arm outstretched.

The curved complex of blocks and bridges at the head of the square houses the city government and reveals the Soviet Union's early experimentation with reinforced concrete. **Gosprom** (Derzhprom in Ukrainian) is a recognised architectural feat for the country and is often used as the textbook example for post-war construction. The triple-tiered brick building on the left is the central building of **Kharkiv University**, founded in 1805, and named after the local noble Karazin who raised the funds to start the empire's first academy in Ukraine.

Kharkiv's churches are few and far between. The one most often shown is the gold-domed **Uspensky Cathedral** (Universitetskaya 21) built in the late 18th century and turned into an organ recital hall during the Soviet era – it's definitely worth fitting in a concert during your stay. The oldest surviving building in Kharkiv is two blocks north: the **Pokrovsky Cathedral** (Universitetskaya 8) was built in 1689 and is still undergoing restoration to preserve its unique old-Russian style. By far the most unique building in Kharkiv is the candy-striped **Blagoveschensky Cathedral** built in 1901. The fanciful brick exterior mimics Byzantine style and the interior is one of the examples of Kharkiv's light turn-of-the-century design. This was Kharkiv's only church to remain open during the Soviet era.

Nearby is the city's **Tsentralny Rynok** (Central Market) that ranks as a bona fide bazaar, complete with chaos and the distinct aroma of wet cardboard, flesh, and fruit. Shoppers and spectators are welcome, but keep a hand on your purse/wallet and keep with the flow. Walking from Ploscha Konstitutsii down **Pushkinskaya** offers another candid expression of Kharkiv's mood. Along with the shops and student complexes, you'll pass by the synagogue, art museum, and the 'park of youth'.

An impressive, but oft-neglected sight is **X.T.3** (*Khe-te-zey*) – the Kharkiv Tractor Factory. This gargantuan industrial complex supplied the communist world with farm equipment and made Kharkiv's name in the USSR. To get out to the factory, take the metro to Traktorny Zavod (XT3) station and exit on Moskovsky Prospekt. A few examples of Soviet-age tractors are on display outside and signs with human-size letters still offer words of encouragement to the proletariat.

What to do
With so many workers and students, there is plenty in Kharkiv to keep most entertained. Number one on the list should be the **Kharkiv Museum of Art** (Sovnarkomskaya 9/11; tel: 0572 477 575; open 10.00–17.00, closed Tuesday; entrance 4UAH). To get there, either walk from the centre or take the metro to Arkhitektora Beketova station. Few collections in Ukraine represent so fully the country's artistic legacy, beginning with a quality display of icons and religious art.

Most of the paintings are 19th-century Russian impressionist works done by local artists and using local themes like peasants and the Ukrainian steppe. Some highlights include Semiradsky's 'Pirates', Orlovsky's 'Prisoner', Losenko's 'Abel' and Venig's 'Ivan the Terrible and his mother'. The most famous painting in the museum is Ilya Repin's legendary 'Zaporizhzhyan Cossacks writing a letter to the Turkish sultan'. Other works in the exhibit by Repin include his 'Cossack on the steppe' and 'St Nicholas saves three innocents from death'. The **Kharkiv Historical Museum** (Universitetska 10; tel: 0572 228 123; open 10.00–17.00, closed Monday, entrance 3UAH) resembles most Ukrainian history museums with lots of old documents and some traditional clothing and craft from Sloboda.

Although exhibits frequently change, the best place to buy souvenirs is at the **Kharkiv Folk Craft Museum** (Pushkinskaya 62; open 10.00–18.00; entrance 5UAH).

Good theatre can also be expected in Kharkiv. The **Opera and Ballet** (Sumskaya 25) usually features a new show every week. The **Ukrainian Drama Theatre** (Sumskaya 9) does traditional comedies in Ukrainian in one of the city's older theatres. Tickets for either can be purchased on site or from most hotels. Famous among children and adults in Ukraine, the **Kharkiv Puppet Theatre** (Ploschad Konstitutsiya 24; tel: 057 712 7395) puts on amusing performances during the day and in the early evening. The diverse repertoire includes the *Divine Comedy* and the uproarious *12 Chairs*.

For Soviet-style fun and games, head out to **Park Gorkovo** , Kharkiv's outdoor amusement park at the very end of Sumskaya. Trees, war memorials and carnival rides run year-round, as does a child's railroad. Another amusement is the **Kharkiv Zoo** inside the main park; open 8.00 to 20.00; entrance 3UAH. The menagerie is limited, but local animals are well represented: foxes, wolves, wild cats and lots of birds.

Outside Kharkiv

Ukraine's most beloved painter was born and raised just outside of Kharkiv in the small village of Chuguyev (Чугуев). **Ilya Repin** (1844–1930) is best known for his very humanistic version of impressionism, and although he spent much of his life studying and painting in Russia, his work is most often used to illustrate Ukrainian national consciousness. His 'Zaporizhzhyan Cossacks write a letter to the Turkish Sultan' depicts the legendary warriors crowded round a table and composing a scathing rebuff to the sultan's offer to join forces. A little-known fact is that Repin was painting the picture when a Russian noble saw the unfinished product and wanted it himself. As the original work had already been commissioned, Repin hurriedly made a copy and sold it to the nobleman without him knowing it was a copy. Repin was a leading member of the group of Russian artists known as 'the wanderers' and today the majority of his work is on display at the Russian Museum in St Petersburg. Some of his other well-known pieces include the 'Volga Boatmen' and 'Ivan the Terrible and his Son'.

The painter's first home is now a museum of his life, on Nikitinskaya street in the centre of Chuguyev. The village is about 40km from Kharkiv, and a visit to the birthplace and museum is usually offered as a day trip (6 hours) by most hotels or Kharkiv's city tour agency.

Travelling in the opposite direction towards the town of Bogodukhov (Богодухов, *'God of the Spirits'*) there is a turn at Maksimovka (Максимовка) that leads to the minuscule village of Skovorodinovka (Сковородиновка), the final resting place of **Grigory Savvich Skovoroda** (1722–94), Ukrainian philosopher, poet and traveller. Skovoroda was born in Sloboda, studied in Kharkiv, Kiev and Hungary, taught in Pereyaslav and was known as an avid wanderer who criss-crossed Ukraine and much of eastern Europe on foot, telling stories, singing songs and writing poems. He never published a single book in his lifetime but is now revered as a founding father of Ukrainian intellectualism. The epitaph on his grave reads 'The world chased me but could not catch me.' The Skovoroda memorial and museum is built in the home where the philosopher died and reveals Soviet tastes in the portrayal of this life. However, the village offers a good taste of rural Sloboda. Recent focus highlights the philosopher's love of the Ukrainian landscape, and outside the museum is a giant oak tree that supposedly shaded the philosopher in his thought, as well as two ponds where he used to swim. Kharkiv's city agency offers day trips out to Skovorodinovka, but most hotels can arrange the transport as you can get out there only by taxi or marshrutka.

POLTAVA – ПОЛТАВА

This quaint and orderly town represents the country's cultural heartland and is the most visited spot in left bank Ukraine. Poltava's travel appeal is based in the area's longstanding provincial lifestyle and its convenient access from Kiev or Kharkiv – Ukraine's newest train allows visitors from either city to travel quickly and enjoy a more picturesque version of the country.

The city is best remembered for the fateful Battle of Poltava fought in 1709 during the Great Northern War, when Sweden and Russia were vying for control over the Baltic. Swedish King Charles XII planned to march on Moscow through Ukraine and made a first attack at Poltava where a Russian regiment was based near the Vorskla River. The forces of Peter the Great outnumbered the Swedes two to one and the quick defeat was obvious. Peter left a strong military legacy in Poltava and redesigned the city to resemble a miniature St Petersburg, spreading out from a central granite obelisk in honour of the victory. The battlefield is now a park in the north of the city.

For Ukrainians, the Battle of Poltava is a tough piece of history to swallow. The Cossack hetman Ivan Mazepa had long been close allies with Peter, but chose Swedish protection after the tsar grew less conscious of Ukrainian autonomy. A strong retaliation by the tsar divided the Cossack leadership and fizzled all hopes for Ukraine's sovereignty. The Russian Empire was now the major power of northern Europe and would dominate this area for the next 300 years. And yet today Poltava and its environs are known throughout Ukraine as the nostalgic interior, the place where the purest form of Ukrainian language is still spoken freely, unadulterated by foreign (Russian) influence. Hearing the melodious dialect of Poltava is a delight.

All kinds of disputed metaphors are used to compare the function of Ukrainian cities with parts of the body (ie: Kiev is the head), but Poltava has always been linked to Ukraine's soul. Literature fans come this way to see the native land of writers like Gogol, Mirny, Korolenko and Kotlyarevsky – a land of cultural festivals, strong tradition and frequent country markets. Poltavschina has remained Ukraine's great agricultural prize and is known as one of the cleaner spots this side of the Dnepr.

Getting there and away
Riding into Poltava on the train gives the best view of the town with its perched convent and cupolas and rows of tin-roof cottages. If you are arriving from the east, enjoy the curves. This bit of track holds the record for the sharpest turn of any railroad in the world.

Poltava is the main rail stop between Kharkiv and Kiev, meaning train travel to or from anywhere else in the country should be planned through those cities. There are two train stations in Poltava: Pivdenna (Ploscha Slavy 1) and Kyivska (Stepana Kondratenka 12), on the western side of the city. Most inter-regional trains stop at Pivdenna where foreigners must buy their tickets at the *Servisna Kasa*; tel 0532 132 001. The *Capital Express* goes to Kyivska station, passing through Poltava twice daily in both directions to Kharkiv (2 hours) and Kiev (3½ hours). Tickets in either direction cost US$10–15 depending on class of seat.

There are also plenty of slow trains, including the main Kharkiv–Kiev connection that gets to Poltava after midnight, and a direct overnight train to and from Kiev that conveniently arrives in the morning. To and from Kharkiv via Poltava, direct trains service Simferopol (14 hours), Luhansk (12 hours), Odessa (13 hours) and Ivano-Frankivsk (20 hours). The train to Kremenchuk (3 hours) is a popular route, but by bus the journey takes half the time.

Because train options are somewhat limited, taking the bus from Poltava can sometimes be a good idea. The private bus company **Gunsel** has a twice-daily service to Poltava between Kiev (5 hours) and Donetsk (6 hours). Their office is at the main bus station, best reached by taxi of the #7 bus; Velikotyrnovskaya 7; tel: 0532 663 786. **Avtoluks** also has a daily service to Kiev, with an office at the main station; tel: 0532 585 019. There are also regular buses to Kremenchuk (1½ hours), Dnepropetrovsk (4 hours) and Cherkassy (5 hours). Poltava's other bus station is better for local destinations and is located near the city centre; Shevchenka 65a; tel: 0532 396 79.

Tour assistance
If you need some extra help seeing things or getting something done, try **Eurotur** (Gogolya 25A; tel: 0532 501 374; email: evrotour@sedtor.net.ua). The agency has an ecological bent and does a variety of interesting local tours in and around Poltava.

Where to stay
Despite its small size, Poltava is not entirely new to tourism but still lacks a strong hotel base. For now, the 'best' accommodation (in terms of comfort and

'WALRUSES'

If you visit Ukraine in winter, you may be shocked to see people running barefoot through the snow or jumping naked through holes in the ice. They splash around in the water happily and then walk back across the ice with frozen hair and smiles on their faces. These are Ukraine's *morzhei* (the Russian for 'walruses') and they are not madmen, but followers of an old form of Slavic yoga. True walruses bathe outdoors every day of the year, in rivers, lakes or the sea. The ability to withstand 0°C water takes at least six months of daily training, and an average winter swim will only last slightly longer than one minute, the time it takes to get the full 'effect'. (I've seen some old men stay in the water for more than two minutes!) Walruses claim the practice of bathing outdoors in winter strengthens their immune system to the point that they never catch cold in winter. A bather prepares for each frigid dip by doing intense physical exercise beforehand, slowly peeling off layers of clothing, widening a hole in the ice and then jumping in. Walruses normally swim in the early morning, and the best place to see them in Ukraine is on the Vorskla River in Poltava, the Kharkiv River in Kharkiv, all along the Dnepr and in Crimea.

sophistication) is **Gallery** (Frunze 7; tel: 0532 561 697; fax: 0532 563 121; email: slbipol@kot.poltava.ua; web: www.hotel.poltava.ua). Small and élite, this private hotel is connected to a modern art gallery next to the new pedestrian shopping zone of the city centre. Big beds, good plumbing (24-hour hot water), internet access, guarded parking and a new sauna put it a step ahead of the rest of the city. Rooms are charged per person: a double bed with shower is US$50 for one person, US$75 for two. The half-lux with bath and shower are the best deal for US$120. According to the brochure, the luxury suites allow 'your dreams to be embodied in a reality' but cost US$200/night. Credit cards accepted.

Hotel Kiev (Simnaya 2/49; tel: 0532 224 286) is a rather shoddy option, but offers a good location for independent travellers between the city centre and Kievsky train station. They do have a few decent suites with bath that cost around US$45 a night. Otherwise, the Kiev falls in the budget category in terms of price and quality. A normal double with bath costs US$12, and for a bed you pay US$4. Slightly better is **Hotel Turist** (Mira 12; tel: 0532 220 921) near the river. Overall the complex makes a dismal impression, but they do have some remodelled rooms with clean bathrooms. A single is US$15, a good double is US$20 and the best quality option is the US$60 suite. The former Inturist is the **Motel Poltava** (Hrushevskovo 1; tel: 0532 230 024) on the far southern edge of town. The location is terrible but the remodelled rooms are the nicest of the former Soviet variety. Singles are US$30, a new double with shower (24-hour hot water) is US$40, the slightly larger half-lux is US$65. Kiev, Turist and Poltava accept cash payment only.

Where to eat

Restaurants in Poltava are also sparse, but not disappointing. For now everyone in town seems to be carrying on about the ultra-refined **Ivanova Gora** (Soborna Ploshcha 2; tel: 0532 560 003; fax: 0532 563 221; email: iv-hora@poltava.ua; web: www.iv-hora.poltava.ua). Built near the historic site of Belaya Besedka (the owners claim that a strong 'bio-energy' envelops the restaurant), almost every tour bus in Poltava parks here for a meal. The 'luxury' restaurant serves a rather unadventurous national cuisine with the exception of Poltavsky Holushki, a local dumpling soup. But overall the food is tasty and not expensive. A banquet room is now the coveted venue for up-and-coming Ukrainian pop stars. For something more down to earth, try **Obolon** (as in the Ukrainian beer) (Oktyabrskaya 51; tel: 0532 220 988) near the central circle. The menu is classic Ukrainian cuisine and nothing on the menu costs more than US$2. Each hotel also features their own restaurant. **Gallery's** is small but with good food; the hotel Kiev's **Shanghai** serves convincing Chinese food with surprisingly good service; a full meal will cost under US$10.

For sit-down coffee and pastries at teatime, breakfast time or night time, the **Cafe Venetsia** (Venice) (46 Oktyabrskaya; tel: 0532 274 496) comes with strong recommendations by travellers. The very clean, very calm and very sophisticated café sells a huge range of fresh cakes, savoury rolls, and pastries baked fresh in-house every day. Handmade chocolate truffles and rich coffee make it hard to leave.

What to see and do

Much of Poltava's centre is pedestrian-only and there are parks at nearly every other block, so enjoy the walk if you can. The city spreads out from a grand roundabout centred on the tall pinnacle monument commemorating the Battle of Poltava. The circle and surrounding white neo-classical government buildings were built as a direct replica of the Palace Square in St Petersburg. Eight boulevards lead from the circle into various city districts. Most of the action and best shops are on Oktyabrskaya and Lenina.

Poltava has preserved a few examples of whimsical, modern Ukrainian folk architecture. Two very rare structures include the very beautiful red-brick **Old Russian Village Bank** (Oktyabrskaya 39), and the mosaic **Poltava Natural History Museum** (Lenina 2; open 10.00–17.00, closed Wednesday; entrance 3UAH). It is worth visiting the museum just to see its decorative exterior and the very traditional interior with its flower and vine design and wall painting. The full-time exhibit is like most of its kind, telling the story of Poltava through presentations on local nature, industry and agriculture. Religious art, traditional costumes and *pysanky* are also on display, along with a room dedicated solely to Chernobyl and another to old farm equipment.

At the end of Oktyabrskaya is the Soborny Maidan, a park and adjoining square with a cluster of historical monuments. The most ancient remnants of Poltava are at **Belaya Besedka**, the high outcropping facing out over the southwest valley. The white-pillared, Greek-style **Friendship Rotunda** was built in 1953 to celebrate the 300th anniversary of the Pereyaslav union between Ukraine and Russia. On the other side of the street is a monument dedicated to the birth of Poltava, claiming the city is 800 years old (some say 1,100), although a nearby and much older Scythian ruin is marked by the single remaining tower of the **Church of the Assumption** (the rest of the church is now being rebuilt). The cute thatched roof cottage (Soborny Maidan #3; tel: 0532 272 073; open 10.00–18.00, closed Monday; entrance 5UAH) is the restored home of writer **Ivan Kotlyarevsky** (1769–1838) who wrote *Eneida*, a Cossack parody of the *Aeneid* and the very first publication of Ukrainian prose. The exhibit is very hands-on and a simple walk around the old house and garden is interesting, even if you don't read Ukrainian.

For war buffs, military historians, interested folk and Swedes, the **Battle of Poltava History Museum** is on Shvedskaya Mogila (Swedish grave); open 10.00–17.00, entrance 5UAH. Period objects and artefacts, some owned by Peter

GOGOL'S UKRAINE

One of the fathers of Russian literature's golden age was **Nikolai Gogol** (1809–52), born in Sorochintsy (Gogolevo) and schooled in Poltava. Ukrainians like to claim Gogol as their own since he was Ukrainian, took much of his material from Ukrainian folklore, and set his tales in the Poltava countryside. Russians also have a claim on Gogol since he wrote in Russian, lived in St Petersburg, and was a member of the Russian civil service. Either way, the seemingly uneventful hinterland of Poltavschina was the rural home he brought to life in his first series, *Evenings on a Farm Near Dikanka*. The fantastical stories are narrated by the tittering yokel and village beekeeper Rudy Panko who, like Gogol, is a devout Christian and a firm believer in witches, devils, magic and spells. Besides painting a rich picture of Ukrainian farm life, Panko recounts the strange things he's seen and heard.

Travellers can get to **Dikanka** (Диканка) on their own by taking one of five daily buses from Poltava's central station (1 hour). These days Dikanka is a bit of a lonely and deadbeat place, which will make it all the more endearing to true Gogol fans. Villagers are both friendly and suspicious towards outsiders but they keep Gogol's statue surrounded by fresh flowers. Due to collectivisation in the 1930s the fields seem rather vast and dramatic, but the village appears unchanged with lots of squawking geese and children playing outside. The small town museum and single café mark the village centre, and the Troitska Church is that same church from the story *Christmas Eve*.

The most renowned of the Dikanka stories tells about the annual country fair at **Veliky Sorochintsy** (Великий Сорочинй), where a young man makes a secret pact with a gypsy in order to win a maiden's hand. The country fair still continues each year in the late summer with lots of costumed dancers, re-enactments of Gogol's stories and Ukrainian folk singing. Gogol was also christened here in the 18th-century Transfiguration Church. To get to Veliky Sorochintsy take the bus from Mirgorod (1 hour; 5 daily).

Even after his success with the Dikanka stories, Gogol sought recognition as a professor of world history in St Petersburg. His students claimed he knew nothing about history and was therefore a failure, but that his storytelling skills were valued by all. His next published book was titled *Mirgorod* and included the swashbuckling Cossack legend *Taras Bulba*. A bright bronze statue of the writer sits outside the Mirgorod train station, but there is little modern reference in the town today. About 25km east of Mirgorod is Gogol's birthplace, now named **Gogolevo** (Гоголево) in his honour. Getting there by train is tricky, since only the rare *elektrichki* go there, but the village is only 25km away and taxis and buses do make the trip. The Gogol family estate and museum honours the writer.

If you have not read Gogol, travelling in his country will make you want to – his opening lines describe the area so well, demanding from the reader in one: 'Do you know the Ukrainian night?' *Evenings on a Farm Near Dikanka* gives a proper introduction to the superstitious culture of rural Ukraine, but his most classic book is *Dead Souls*. His dramas include *The Government Inspector* which is often performed at the Gogol Drama Theatre in Poltava (Oktyabrskaya 23).

the Great, are on display. A monument to Peter I stands next to the museum; across the street is the remarkable 19th-century **Sampson's Church** (the Russians defeated the Swedes on St Sampson's Day) with the Grave of Russian Brotherhood nearby. If you walk around the battlefield you can see the countless other memorials marking the front line of the Russian regiment, and showing where Peter the Great stood during the battle. To the far north is a monument to Swedish losses during the battle.

Poltava's most revered church is the **Khrestovozdvyzhensky Convent**, a mystical white edifice perched on top of the highest hill in the city. Built in 1699, this is the only baroque cathedral in Ukraine to have kept all seven of its original cupolas. The complex consists of four buildings, including a summer chapel, a smaller winter chapel, the dormitory and a choir school (ringing the small bell is said to bring blessings). A visit allows close encounters with the lives of Orthodox nuns and the singing is divine. Bus #18 goes to the convent from the Central Bus Station on Shevchenko. Otherwise, a taxi costs US$2.

MIRGOROD – МИРГОРОД

Literally, the 'City of Peace', Mirgorod was made famous first by the writer Gogol and then renowned for its therapeutic mineral water, now sold all over Ukraine and apparently good for your intestines. If you look closely at the label on the Mirgorodskaya water bottles you will see the **Church of the Holy Assumption** with its silver turrets: Mirgorod means 'City of Peace' in Ukrainian. The church now stands in the middle of the *kurort,* or resort complex, where countless spas heal everything from stomach aches to radiation sickness. Day visitors can drink of the water freely from the *buvyet* and sit on the lakeside beach, but don't expect much in terms of tourist amenities. Even with Mirgorod's huge resort base, access is usually limited to Ukrainians with doctor's prescriptions. Foreigners seeking treatment should contact the *kurort*, Gogolya 112; tel: 05355 526 04. Otherwise, the only functioning hotel is the **Mirgorod** (Gogolya 102; tel: 05355 527 37). All rooms cost under US$10, there is no hot water and the staff will try to keep you from staying. The only restaurant (besides the café in the town store) is **Grand Pizza** (Gogolya 16; tel: 05355 533 82). Besides pizza (US$2) and real Italian ice cream, this is the only place in Mirgorod where you can use your credit card and a clean bathroom.

Getting there and away

The Mirgorod train station (Zheleznodorozhna 2; tel: 05355 524 73) is on the main line of the *Capital Express* speed train linking Kiev (3½ hours) and Kharkiv (2½ hours). The bus station is directly across from the health resort complex; tel: 05355 522 04. Buses link to the smaller villages of Poltavschina, including V Sorochintsy.

SUMY – СУМИ

Historically a large and important city of the northeast, Sumy does not warrant any particular highlighting today except that it is a pleasantly average town of the Sloboda. Founded in 1655 on the river Psyol, this was the largest of the Cossack fortresses in Sloboda. The town's name comes from the old Slavic word for bags (*suma*) after the first inhabitants found three leather bags of gold stashed in an oak tree – or so peasant legend claims. Originally, Sumy competed with Kharkiv in size and industry and during Ukraine's 19th-century sugar rush, Sumy province was growing most of the sugar beets. Civil war, the great famine and several five-year plans left an especially destructive impression on Sumy. Walking through Sumy today bears witness to the stylistic blend of Russian and Ukrainian influences in Sloboda. In recent years, the city has seen an increase in travellers who come for the summer fairs and international organ festivals.

Getting there and away

Sumy is slightly off the beaten path, so the trains are not always convenient. It is best to travel on one of the six daily trains to and from Kharkiv (4 hours). Kiev (twice daily) is a very tedious seven-hour journey. Other routes from Sumy service Chernihiv (7 hours), Simpferopol (13 hours), Minsk (14 hours) and Moscow (16 hours). The train station is at the end of Prospekt Shevchenko; tel: 0542 284 537. Marshrutka constantly run into the city and usually drop off by the central market. A taxi to any of Sumy's hotels will cost US$1 or less.

Sumy is only two-and-a-half hours from Kharkiv by car or taxi, the going rate is around US$40. The bus station is on the west side of town at Baumana 40 and buses go everywhere. It is probably only worthwhile taking a bus to Kharkiv (3 hours), or to the outlying areas, like Glukhiv (2½ hours).

Where to stay and eat

The city's highest standard is found at the **Hotel Khimik** (Pselskaya 14; tel: 0542 224 500; fax: 0542 220 093). Heating, air-conditioning and a private hot-water source mean comfort, and the rooms are spacious and well furnished. Singles/doubles are US$20/US$25 and come with shower and toilet, and all suites have baths; US$55. Breakfast is included and credit cards are accepted. Khimik's restaurant is a typical Ukrainian/Russian-style endeavour serving inexpensive borscht, varenniki and lots of homemade pork sausage. The oldest and most central accommodation is **Hotel Ukrayina** (Frunze 1; tel: 0542 222 220). Standards are low but not abysmal: a single with shower and toilet is US$16, and doubles come only as suites for US$25. There is 24-hour hot water and the sauna can be rented out in two-hour segments for US$7. The third option is the towering concrete high-rise **Sumy** (Maidan Nezalezhnosti 1; tel: 0542 183 068). Rumour has it that a new management has bought the place and that a bright future lies ahead; however, at present the elevator doesn't work and there is rarely hot water. Singles cost US$6, doubles US$10.

Real home-style Ukrainian cooking is rare for a restaurant, but the **Stary Mlyn** (Pereulok Dachny 9; tel: 0542 223 604) pulls it off very well. Housed in a restored mill converted to look like a Sloboda farmhouse, the owner and antique collector pursues a philosophy of advertising Sumy's identity through good food and a cosy atmosphere. The bar is built into the old woodstove and visitors can choose to eat up inside the mill or out on the terrace near Sumy's 'beach'. For a slight change of atmosphere and menu the management also runs the **Carpathian Kolyba** next door.

What to see and do

Most Sumy citizens will point the way to their former courthouse, now the **Regional Museum** (Kirova 2; tel: 0542 221 441; open 09.00–17.00, closed Monday; entrance 1UAH). What sets the display apart from others is the wide collection of World War II memorabilia, much of it German: propaganda, helmets, guns and uniforms. (Perhaps this is retribution for the heavy looting of city treasures from this museum by the Nazis.) A permanent photography exhibit is also quite outstanding. Folk crafts, an old Sloboda farmhouse and a mini-shrine to Shevchenko complete the museum.

Sumy's three main churches deserve mention. The light blue **Spaso-Preobrazhensky Catherdral Church** (Soborna 31) was built in the 18th century and is very open and light on the inside, with two brassy gold domes. The mint-green **Svyato-Voskresenska Church** (Maidan Nezalezhnosti) was built in 1702 and stands as a rare monument to early Sloboda architecture with its compact Greek-cross floor plan and triple turrets (it was also used a fort). The stately high-domed **Troitsky Cathedral** on top of the 'old hill' is the youngest of the three, built in 1901 in imitation classic and baroque styles. The building has only just been reconsecrated a church after decades as a Soviet 'organ hall'. The handmade Czech organ is world famous and frequent organ festivals are played in this spacious chapel.

A number of very small but very ancient villages are spread throughout the region, all of which can be reached by bus or taxi, but rarely included in group tours. About two-and-a-half hours north of Sumy is the historic town of **Glukhov** which originally belonged to 11th-century Kievan Rus and was later the hetman capital of left-bank Ukraine. It was here that Peter the Great tried and hung an effigy of Ivan Mazepa after his 'betrayal' at Poltava. The event took place in front of the **Church of St Nicholas**, built in 1686.

Appendix

LANGUAGE
Ukrainians speak Ukrainian and Russian, both Slavic languages. In the EU and many post-colonial nations of the world, people speak a *lingua franca* like English or French. For Ukrainians, the 'international language' (until recently) was Russian. Aside from Ukrainian, the older generation all speak Russian because they grew up in the Soviet Union. Many studied and can speak some German. You will find the younger generation speaks a fair amount of English, but not enough for you to get away with not learning some of the local language.

The Cyrillic alphabet scares most people off as you are essentially learning to read all over again. Learn it. Simply knowing the letters will enliven your trip, and speaking the very basics of Russian and Ukrainian ('please', 'thank you', 'excuse me') allows you a better connection with the land and people.

Language politics
A long time ago, Russian and Ukrainian were the same language, similar to Old Church Slavonic. History and geography separated the two groups and allowed enough improvisation and evolution to make them two separate languages around the 12th century. Foreign governance, namely by the Russian and Polish elite, meant that for a time the Ukrainian language survived among the lower, uneducated classes only. Strict suppression of the Ukrainian language in the 17th through to the 19th centuries, and during the Soviet era, became synonymous to Ukraine's lack of independence and today, speaking Ukrainian has come to be an important political symbol of freedom and self-determination. Like all national movements, things can swing too far in the other direction, and Ukraine's many native Russian-speakers have begun to make their own linguistic stance.

Where to speak which
You'll find that certain areas of the country speak only Ukrainian, others speak Russian and some use both interchangeably. The regional chapters imply which language is prominent in the respective areas, but language politics are still in flux. Throughout the country, all signs and announcements are in Ukrainian, with the exception of Crimea and a few cases in the east.

In western Ukraine (Galicia, Volhynia, the Carpathians, Podillya and Polissya) try to speak Ukrainian. In Crimea, Donbas, the Dnepr and Sloboda, speak Russian. In Kiev, you can speak either Russian or Ukrainian; the same goes for the western part of Sloboda (Poltava) and areas of central Ukraine (the Poltava dialect is considered the purist and most melodious form of Ukrainian). Also, keep in mind that urban areas may be Russian-speaking, but the countryside will speak Ukrainian. You will meet some people who are very fussy one way or another, and others who are happy to communicate however they can. Be sensitive and try to use whichever language they do.

The Cyrillic alphabet
The Ukrainian alphabet is not as daunting as it may look. Many letters are the same or use the Greek equivalent. If you think that learning a whole new language is not for you, so be it, but getting the alphabet down is key for finding your way around and enjoying your stay.

A self-proclaimed non-linguist traveller recommends finding a video shop in Ukraine and spending an hour or so reading all the Cyrillic covers of movies you know. That's how he learned to read Ukrainian.

Letters		Ukrainian pronunciation
А	а	'ah' as in almond
Б	б	'b' as in boat
В	в	'v' as in vivacious
Г	г	'h' as in halo
Д	д	'd' as in doctor
Е	е	'eh' as in set
Є		'yeh'
Ж	ж	'zh' as in mirage
З	з	'z' as in zebra
И	и	'y' (short 'i') as in myth
Й	й	closes an 'ee' sound or '?'
І	і	long 'ee'
Ї	ї	'yee' as in old English 'ye'
К	к	'k' as in kitten
Л	л	'l' as in lemon
М	м	'm' as in man
Н	н	'n' as in nice
О	о	'o' as in Oh!
П	п	'p' as in pole
Р	р	'r'; short and rolled
С	с	's' as in sesame
Т	т	't' as in tight
У	у	'oo' as in moon
Ф	ф	'f' as in fruit
Х	х	'kh' (gutteral) as in 'Bach'
Ц	ц	'ts' as in bits
Ч	ч	'ch' as in cheddar
Ш	ш	'sh' as in shop
Щ	ш	'shch' as in fresh cheese
Ю	ю	'yoo' as in you
Я	я	'ya' as in yacht
Ь	ь	soft sign, often transliterated as an apostrophe and used after 'hard' consonants д, з, л, н, с, т, ц. 'Soften' a letter by barely making a 'y' sound (as in yes) right as you stop saying the consonant.

Russian letters

Г	г	'g' as in go
Е	е	'yeh' as in yes
Ё	ё	'yo' as in yo-yo
Э	э	'eh', as in Ukrainian 'e'
И	и	long ee sound
Й	й	closes an 'ee' sound or 'ы'
Ы	ы	'y', like Ukrainian 'и'
Ъ	ъ	hard sign; causes an audible break in the word

Vowels are the main difference between Russian and Ukrainian sounds. Ukrainian vowels (and consonants) are always pronounced as written and tend to sound softer. Russian vowels change from long to short depending on where they fall in a word. Remember the key difference is to say the *'yeh'* found in so many Russian words, and saying the same letter 'E' as *'eh'* in Ukrainian. Always remember that 'Г' is 'H' in Ukrainian and 'G' in Russian. Both languages are much more phonetic than English, so just sound the words out. Stresses are underlined. Test your knowledge of Cyrillic by covering the transliterations and reading down the column.

Basics

	Ukrainian		Russian	
Good morning	Добрий ранок	*dobry ranok*	Доброе утро	*dobre oodra*
Hello (formal)	Добрий день	*dobry dehn*	Здравствуйте	*zdrastvwytye*
Hi (casual)	Привіт	*pryveet*	Привет	*privyet*
Good evening	Добрий вечір	*dobry vecheer*	Добрый вечер	*dobry vyecher*
Good night (farewell)	Надобраніч	*nadobraneech*	Спокойной ночи	*spokoiny nochee*
Goodbye	До повачення	*do pobachennya*	До свидания	*dasvidanya*
Yes	Так	*tak*	Да	*da*
No	Ні	*nee*	Нет	*nyet*
Please	Будь ласка	*bood laska*	Пожалуйста	*pazhawsta*
Thank you	Дякую	*dyakooyoo*	Спасибо	*spaseeba*
You're welcome	Нема за шо	*nehma za scho*	Не за что	*nyeh za shto*
Excuse me	Пробачте	*probachteh*	Извините	*eezvineetye*
What's your name?	Як вас звати	*yak vas zvaty?*	Как вас зовут	*kak vas zavoot?*
My name is …	Мене звати	*mehneh zvaty*	Меня зовут	*menya zavoot*
Nice to meet you	Дуже приємно	*duzhe pry'yemno*	Очень приятно	*ochen preeyatna*
How are you?	Як справн?	*yak spravy?*	Как дела?	*kak dyela?*
Fine, good	Довре	*dobreh*	Хорошо	*kharasho*
Bad	Погано	*pohano*	Плохо	*plokha*
Very	Дуже	*duzhe*	Очень	*ochen*
Attention	Увага	*uvaha*	Внимание	*vnimaniye*
Watch out	Обережно	*oberezhno*	Осторожно	*ostorozhna*
Help!	Допоможіть	*dopomozheet*	Помогите	*pamageetyeh*
I (don't) like . . .	мені (не) подобається (ukr)	*mehnee (neh) podobayetsya*	Мне (не) нравиться (rus)	*mnyeh (nyeh) nryaveetsya*

Questions

Do you speak …?	Ви говорите	*vy hovoryteh*	Вы говорите	*vy gavarityeh*
English-	по-англійськи	*pa anhleesky*	по-английский	*pa angleeskee*
Ukrainian	по-українськи	*pa ukrayeensky*	по-украинский	*pa ukrainskee*
Russian	по-россійськи	*pa rosseesky*	по-русский	*pa rooskee*
German	по-німецьки	*pa neemetsky*	по-немецкий	*pa nyemetskee*
French	по-французьки	*pa frantsoozky*	по-французкий	*pa frantsoozkee*
Do you understand?	Ви разумієте	*vy razoomee'yeteh*	Вы понимаете	*vy paneemahyetyeh*
I do not understand	Я не разумію	*ya ne razoomee'yoo*	Я не понимаю	*ya nye paneemayoo*
Repeat,	Повторите	*povtoryteh*	Повторите	*pahvtareetyeh*
What?	Шо?	*scho*	Что?	*shto*
Who?	Хто?	*khto*	Кто?	*kto*
Why?	Чому?	*chomoo*	Почему?	*pochyemoo*
How?	Як?	*yak*	Как?	*kak*
Where?	Де?	*deh*	Где?	*gdyeh*
on the left	на ліво	*na leevo*	на лева	*na lyeva*
on the right	на права	*na prava*	на права	*na prava*
straight ahead	прямо	*pryamo*	прямо	*pryama*

	Ukrainian		**Russian**	
here	тут	*toot*	здесь	*zdyes*
there	там	*tam*	там	*tam*
far	далеко	*dalehko*	далёко	*dalyeko*
near	блізько	*bleezko*	близко	*bleezka*

Buying

How much?	Скільки	*skeelky*	Сколко	*skoylka*
What is it?	Шо це	*scho tseh*	Что это	*shto ehta*
a lot	багато	*bohata*	много	*mnoga*
a little bit	трошка	*troshka*	чутьчуть	*chootchoot*
(too) little	мало	*mal*	мало	*mala*
How much does this cost?	Скільки це коштує (ukr)	*skeelky tseh koshtooyeh*	Сколько это стоит (rus)	*skolka ehta stoyeet*

Needs

I want …	Я хочу	*ya khochoo*	Я хочу	*ya khachoo*
I need …	мені потрібно	*mehnee potreebno*	мне нужно	*mnyeh noozhna*
I am looking for …	Я шукаю	*ya shukayu*	Я ищу	*ya eeschoo*
May I … ?	можна	*mozhna*	можно	*mozhna*
to sleep	спати	*spahty*	спать	*spaht*
to buy	купити	*koopyty*	купить	*koopeet*
to eat	їсти	*yeesty*	есть	*yehst*
to drink	пити	*pyty*	пить	*peet*

Food and drink

bread	хліб	*khleeb*	хлеб	*khlyeb*
cheese	сир	*syr*	сыр	*syr*
sausage	ковбаса	*kovbassa*	колбаса	*kolbassa*
meat	мясо	*myaso*	мясо	*myasa*
fish	риба	*ryba*	рыба	*ryba*
sweets	цукерки	*tsookerky*	конфеты	*konfyety*
fruit	фрукти	*frookty*	фрукты	*frookty*
vegetables	овочі	*ovochee*	овощи	*ovoschee*
apple	яблуко	*yabluko*	яблоко	*yablako*
cherry	вишні	*vyshnee*	вишня	*veeshnya*
mushrooms	гриби	*hryby*	грибы	*greeby*
potatoes	картопля	*kartoplya*	картошки	*kartoshkee*
water	вода	*voda*	вода	*vada*
milk	молоко	*moloko*	молоко	*malako*
juice	сік	*seek*	сок	*sok*
sugar	цукор	*tsookor*	сахар	*sakhar*
tea	чай	*chai*	чай	*chai*
coffee	кава	*kava*	кофе	*kofye*
beer	пиво	*pyvo*	пиво	*peevo*
vodka	горілка	*horeelka*	водка	*vodka*

Useful words

book	книга	*knyha*	книга	*kneega*
map	мапа	*mappa*	карта	*karta*
money	гроші	*hroshee*	денги	*dyengui*

	Ukrainian		Russian	
ticket	квіток	_kveetok_	билет	_beelyet_
train	поїзд	_poyeezd_	поезд	_poyezd_
bus	автобус	_avtoboos_	автобус	_avtoboos_
stamps	марки	_marky_	марки	_markee_
blanket	ковдри	_kovdry_	одеяло	_odeyalo_
room	кімната	_keemnata_	комната	_komnata_
house	дім	_deem_	дом	_dom_
tree	дерево	_dehrehvo_	дерево	_dyerevo_
mountain	гора	_hora_	гора	_gora_
flower	квіти	_kveety_	цветы	_tsvyety_
wheat	пшениця	_pshehnytsya_	пшеница	_psheneetsya_
sunflower	соняшник	_sonyashneek_	подсолнечник	_pahdsolnyechneek_
rainbow	веселка	_vehsehlka_	радуга	_raduga_

Descriptions

small	малий	_maly_	маленкий	_malyenky_
big	великий	_vehlyky_	большой	_bolshoi_
new	новий	_novy_	новый	_novy_
old	старий	_stary_	старый	_stary_
beautiful	красний	_krasny_	красивый	_kraseevy_
important	важливо	_vazhlyvo_	важно	_vazhno_
cold	холодно	_kholodno_	холодно	_kholodna_
hot	горячий	_horyachy_	горячий	_gahryachee_
delicious	смачно	_smachno_	вкусно	_fgoosna_

Numbers

Ukrainian and Russian numbers are fairly cognitive. If you know 1–10 and the constructions, you can say any number in either language:

0	нуль	_nool_	нуль	_nool_
1	один	_odyn_	один	_ahdeen_
2	два	_dva_	два	_dva_
3	три	_trih_	три	_tree_
4	чотири	_chotyry_	четыре	_chyetyreh_
5	пять	_pyat_	пять	_pyat_
6	шість	_sheest_	шесть	_shehst_
7	сімь	_seem_	семь	_syem_
8	вісім	_veeseem_	восемь	_vosyem_
9	девять	_dehvyat_	девять	_dyevyat_
10	десять	_dehsyat_	десять	_dyesyat_

11 through 19 are formed by adding the suffix 'надцять':

11	одинадцять	_odynatsat_
12	дванадцять	_dvanatsat_

20 through 40 are slightly irregular:

20	двадцять	_dvatsat_
21	двадцять один	_dvatsat odyn_
30	тридцять	_trihtsyat_
40	сорок	_sorok_
50	пятдесять	_peedehsyat_

60	шістдесять	_sheesdehsyat_
70	сімдесять	_seemdehsyat_
80	вісімдесять	_veeseemdehsyat_
90	девятнносто	_devyahnosto_
100	сот	_sto_
124	сто двадцять чотири	_sto dvatsat chotyry_
200	двісті	_dveestee_
300	триста	_trihsta_
400	чотириста	_chotyrystah_
500	пятсот	_pyatsot_
1000	тисяча	_tysyacha_

Days and time

	Ukrainian		**Russian**	
today	сьогодні	_s'yohodni_	сегодня	_syevodnya_
tomorrow	завтра	_zavtra_	завтра	_zavtra_
the day after tomorrow	післязавтра	_peeslyazavtra_	послезавтра	_poslyezavtra_
yesterday	вчора	_fchora_	вчера	_fchyera_
Monday	понеділок	_ponehdeelok_	понедельник	_ponyedyelneek_
Tuesday	вівторок	_veevtorok_	вторник	_vtorneek_
Wednesday	середа	_sehrehdah_	среда	_sryedah_
Thursday	четвер	_chetver_	четверг	_chetvyerg_
Friday	пятниця	_pyatnytsya_	пятница	_pyatneetsa_
Saturday	субота	_soobohta_	суббота	_soobohta_
Sunday	неділя	_nehdeelya_	воскресенье	_voskresenye_
What time is it?	Котра година?	_kotra hodyna_	Который час?	_katory chas_
now	тепер	_tehpehr_	сейчас	_seychas_
hour	година	_hodyna_	час	_chas_
minute	хвилин	_khvylyn_	минута	_meenoota_

Appendix

FURTHER INFORMATION
Books on Ukraine

A comparatively small amount has been written about Ukraine in English, and the volumes that have been written tend to intimidate all but the most dedicated scholars. The bible of Ukrainian history is Orest Subtelny's 700 page *Ukraine, a History* (University of Toronto Press, 1988). Since then, the noted Ukrainian scholar Paul Robert Magosci has also published an excellent (and longer) *History of Ukraine* (University of Washington Press, 1996) which incorporates the present context of independent Ukraine. The most current work on all things Ukrainian is Andrew Wilson's *The Ukrainians: Unexpected Nation* (Yale University Press, 2000). The work is a scholarly look at Ukrainian politics, economy and society, yet the chosen subject matter and writing make a good read. The book I do recommend for all those travelling to Ukraine is Anna Reid's *Borderland* (Weidenfield & Nicolson, 1997). The author worked as a correspondent for the *Economist* during the early years of Ukraine's transition and artfully connects Ukraine's past with its present regions and people.

Very little Ukrainian literature exists in translation, but I would suggest Gogol's *Evenings on a Farm Near Dikanka 1&2*. These dark but comic tales describe Ukrainian folklore like none other. Leonard Kent has edited a *Complete Tales of Nikolai Gogol* (University of Chicago Press, 1985) with *Evenings* ... as well as *Mirgorod*, which includes the famous story of the Cossack hero *Taras Bulba*. Most of Sholom Aleichem's work (translated from Yiddish) takes place in Ukraine and offers poignant insights into the relationships between the Ukrainians and Ukraine's former Jewish community.

For Ukrainian language guides, the most comprehensive is *A Language Guide to Ukraine* (Hippocrene Books, 1994) by Linda Hodges and George Chumak. Lonely Planet also does a pocket-sized *Ukrainian Phrasebook* that can be useful for travellers in Western Ukraine.

A note about websites

I have listed relevant websites in the corresponding regional chapters. Like most of the internet, Ukrainian websites can pop up out of nowhere or else disappear overnight. Your feedback is most welcome for current listed sites, as well as any suggestions of sites that I might have missed.

Bradt Travel Guides

Africa by Road	£13.95	London: In the Footsteps of	
Amazon	£14.95	the Famous	£10.95
Antarctica: A Guide to the Wildlife	£14.95	Madagascar	£13.95
The Arctic: A Guide to Coastal		Madagascar Wildlife: A Visitor's	
Wildlife	£14.95	Guide	£14.95
Azores	£12.95	Malawi	£12.95
Baltic Capitals: Tallinn, Riga,		Maldives	£12.95
Vilnius, Kaliningrad	£11.95	Mali	£13.95
Botswana: Okavango Delta,		Mauritius	£12.95
Chobe, Northern Kalahari	£14.95	Montenegro	£12.95
British Isles: Wildlife of Coastal		Mozambique	£12.95
Waters	£14.95	Namibia	£14.95
Cambodia	£11.95	North Canada: Yukon, Northwest	
Cape Verde Islands	£12.95	Territories, Nunavut	£13.95
Cayman Islands	£12.95	North Cyprus	£11.95
Chile & Argentina: Trekking		North Korea	£13.95
Guide	£12.95	Palestine with Jerusalem	£12.95
China: Yunnan Province	£13.95	Paris – Lille – Brussels: The Bradt	
Croatia	£12.95	Guide to Eurostar Cities	£11.95
East & Southern Africa:		Peru & Bolivia: Trekking Guide	£12.95
Backpacker's Manual	£14.95	River Thames: In the	
Eccentric America	£12.95	Footsteps of the Famous	£10.95
Eccentric Britain	£11.95	Rwanda	£13.95
Eccentric France	£12.95	Seychelles	£12.95
Eccentric London	£12.95	Singapore	£11.95
Ecuador, Peru & Bolivia:		South Africa: The Bradt	
Backpacker's Manual	£13.95	Budget Travel Guide	£11.95
Eritrea	£12.95	Southern African Wildlife	£18.95
Estonia	£12.95	Sri Lanka	£12.95
Ethiopia	£13.95	St Helena, Ascension &	
Falkland Islands	£13.95	Tristan da Cunha	£14.95
Gabon, São Tomé & Príncipe	£13.95	Switzerland: Rai, Road, Lake	£12.95
Galápagos Wildlife	£14.95	Tanzania	£14.95
The Gambia	£12.95	Tasmania	£12.95
Georgia	£13.95	Tibet	£12.95
Ghana	£12.95	Uganda	£11.95
Iran	£12.95	USA by Rail	£12.95
Iraq	£13.95	Venezuela	£14.95
Kabul: Mini Guide	£9.95	Your Child's Health Abroad	£8.95
Latvia	£12.95	Zambia	£12.95
Lithuania	£12.95	Zanzibar	£12.95

CLAIM YOUR HALF-PRICE BRADT GUIDE!

Order Form

To order your half-price copy of a Bradt guide, and to enter our prize draw to win £100 (see overleaf), please fill in the order form below, complete the questionnaire overleaf, and send it to Bradt Travel Guides by post, fax or email. Post and packing is free to UK addresses.

Please send me one copy of the following guide at half the UK retail price

Title   *Retail price   Half price*

Please send the following additional guides at full UK retail price

No	*Title*	*Retail price*	*Total*
...	....	......	......
...	....	......	......
...	....	......	......

Sub total   ......
Post & packing outside UK   ......
(£2 per book Europe; £3 per book rest of world)
Total   ......

Name . . . .

Address . . . .

Tel. . . . .   Email . . . .

☐ I enclose a cheque for £ . . . . made payable to Bradt Travel Guides Ltd

☐ I would like to pay by VISA or MasterCard

  Number . . . .   Expiry date . . . .

☐ Please add my name to your catalogue mailing list.

Send your order on this form, with the completed questionnaire, to:

Bradt Travel Guides/UKR
19 High Street, Chalfont St Peter, Bucks SL9 9QE
Tel: +44 1753 893444 Fax: +44 1753 892333
Email: info@bradt-travelguides.com
www.bradt-travelguides.com

WIN £100 CASH!
READER QUESTIONNAIRE

Win a cash prize of £100 for the first completed questionnaire drawn after May 31 2004.

All respondents may order a Bradt guide at half the UK retail price – please complete the order form overleaf.

(Entries may be posted or faxed to us, or scanned and emailed.)

We are interested in getting feedback from our readers to help us plan future Bradt guides. Please complete this quick questionnaire and return it to us to enter into our draw.

Have you used any other Bradt guides? If so, which titles?. . . . .

. . . .

What other publishers' travel guides do you use regularly? . . . .

. . . .

Where did you buy this guidebook? . . . .

What was the main purpose of your trip to Ukraine (or for what other reason did you read our guide)? eg: holiday/business/charity etc. . . . .

. . . .

What other destinations would you like to see covered by a Bradt guide?

. . . .

Would you like to receive our catalogue/newsletters?

YES / NO (If yes, please complete details on reverse)

If yes – by post or email?. . . . .

Age (circle relevant category) 16–25   26–45   46–60   60+

Male/Female (delete as appropriate)

Home country. . . . .

Please send us any comments about our guide to Ukraine or other Bradt Travel Guides. . . . .

. . . .

. . . .

. . . .

Bradt Travel Guides
19 High Street, Chalfont St Peter, Bucks SL9 9QE, UK
Telephone: +44 1753 893444 Fax: +44 1753 892333
Email: info@bradt-travelguides.com
www.bradt-travelguides.com

Index